D0162852

MONEY AND POLITICS

Money and Politics

European Monetary Unification and the
International Gold Standard
(1865–1873)

LUCA EINAUDI

OXFORD
UNIVERSITY PRESS

OXFORD

UNIVERSITY PRESS

Great Clarendon Street, Oxford OX2 6DP

Oxford University Press is a department of the University of Oxford.
It furthers the University's objective of excellence in research, scholarship,
and education by publishing worldwide in

Oxford New York

Athens Auckland Bangkok Bogotá Buenos Aires Cape Town
Chennai Dar es Salaam Delhi Florence Hong Kong Istanbul Karachi
Kolkata Kuala Lumpur Madrid Melbourne Mexico City Mumbai Nairobi
Paris São Paulo Shanghai Singapore Taipei Tokyo Toronto Warsaw

with associated companies in Berlin Ibadan

Oxford is a registered trade mark of Oxford University Press
in the UK and in certain other countries

Published in the United States
by Oxford University Press Inc., New York

© Luca Einaudi, 2001

The moral rights of the author have been asserted
Database right Oxford University Press (maker)

First published 2001

All rights reserved. No part of this publication may be reproduced,
stored in a retrieval system, or transmitted, in any form or by any means,
without the prior permission in writing of Oxford University Press,
or as expressly permitted by law, or under terms agreed with the appropriate
reprographics rights organization. Enquires concerning reproduction
outside the scope of the above should be sent to the Rights Department,
Oxford University Press, at the address above

You must not circulate this book in any other binding or cover
and you must impose this same condition on any acquirer

British Library Cataloguing in Publication Data
Data available

Library of Congress Cataloging-in-Publication Data
Einaudi, Luca.
Money and politics: European monetary unification and the international gold standard
(1865–1873)/Luca Einaudi.
p.cm.
Includes bibliographical references and index.
1. Latin Monetary Union.   2. Currency question.   3. Monetary
unions–Europe–History–19th century.   4. Gold standard–History.   I. Title.
HG209 .E37 2001   332.4′94′09034–dc21   00-068724
ISBN 0-19-924366-2

1 3 5 7 9 10 8 6 4 2

Typeset by Newgen Imaging Systems (P) Ltd., Chennai, India
Printed in Great Britain
on acid free paper by
T.J. International Ltd.,
Padstow, Cornwall

HG209
.E37
2001

To
Barbara and my parents

SEP O 7 2001

Acknowledgements

In writing this book, I have incurred many personal debts and owe many thanks, in particular to my supervisor, Miss Emma Rothschild, who read carefully my long drafts and encouraged me with constructive criticism and comments.

My special thanks also go to Marc Flandreau with whom I had several long and fruitful discussions, to Marcello de Cecco, who followed with interest my research throughout the years, to Boyd Hilton, Clive Trebilcock, Jonathan Steinberg, Gareth Stedman Jones, Niall Ferguson, Filippo Cesarano, and Jean-Marie Darnis, who discussed my research at some stage and played a role in the development of this work. Questions and suggestions by participants at conferences and seminars in Cambridge, London, Paris, and Rome helped me to focus on many important issues and to simplify technical discussions.

I also wish to thank the staff of the Cambridge University Library for their efficiency, and all those who helped in the various institutions I visited, the British Library, the Coin Department of the British Museum, the Historical Archives and the Library of the Bank of England, the library of the London School of Economics, the Rothschild Archives in London, the Archives of the Monnaie de Paris, the Archives Diplomatiques at the Quai d'Oray, the Archives Historiques, the Cabinet des Médailles and the library of the Banque de France, the Archives Nationales de France, the Bibliothèque Nationale de France, the Conseil d'État, the Historical Archives and the Library 'Paolo Baffi' of the Banca d'Italia, the library of the Ministry of Agriculture in Rome, and the Archivio Storico Diplomatico in Rome.

In the course of this research I have received a great deal of support from Trinity College, Cambridge, which financed my research while it was still at a Ph.D. stage, from the Tutor for advanced students, Chris Morley, and from Hazel Felton who always dealt with great humour all administrative problems. I also thank the staff of the Centre for History and Economics, Cambridge, past and present, for their invaluable and friendly help.

An early version of the second section of Chapter 4 was published by the *Rivista di Storia Economica* in December 1997 under the title 'Monetary Unions and Free Riders: the Case of the Latin Monetary Union (1865–78)'. I gladly acknowledge the permission of the journal to republish such material.

I would like to thank the following for permission to reproduce unpublished material: the Banque de France for the pictures of French 25-franc international proof coins, the bibliothèque et archives du Conseil d'État for the portrait of Felix Esquirou de Parieu, and the British Musem for the pictures of British and European international proof coins.

I also owe a debt of gratitude to all the friends who hosted me for various periods of research in London and in Paris and to my parents for their unfailing support. Special thanks to Barbara Ravelhofer for translating a large number of German texts and for her precious help in reading and editing the whole work.

I thank all who have helped and supported me but of course the responsibility for the opinions expressed and for any mistakes remains mine and do not commit the institutions to which I am connected.

Contents

List of Graphs

List of Tables

List of Abbreviations

ABdF	Archives Historiques de la Banque de France, Paris
ABoE	Archives of the Bank of England, London
AMAE	Archives du Ministère des Affaires Etrangères, Paris
AMdP	Archives de la Monnaie de Paris
AN	Archives Nationales de France, Paris
ASBI	Archivio Storico della Banca d'Italia, Rome
ASD	Archivio Storico Diplomatico, Ministero degli Affari Esteri, Rome
BL	British Library, London
BNF	Bibliothèque Nationale de France, Paris
EMU	European Monetary Union
GPBL	Gladstone Papers, British Library, London
LMU	Latin Monetary Union
SMU	Scandinavian Monetary Union
UL	University Library, Cambridge

Gold coins minted in Europe as prototypes of universal coinage, with dual values in francs and local currency. The British coins were not issued to the public, while the others did circulate. Double florin–5 francs international and ducat–100 pence (United Kingdom, 1868). 8 florin–20 francs and 20 francs–8 forint (Austria–Hungary, 1870–92). 1 carolin–10 francs (Sweden, 1868–72). (© copyright the British Museum)

Proof silver and bronze coins minted in Great Britain in 1867, but not issued to the public, 1 franc–10 pence and 5 centimes–decimal halfpenny (© copyright the British Museum)

Proof gold coins minted in France in 1867, but not issued to the public, 25 francs–5 dollars and 25 francs–10 florins, prototypes of universal coinage (© Collections de la Banque de France)

Introduction

This book analyses a European debate on monetary unification, which took place in the 1860s. The debate was started in the first years of the Latin Monetary Union (LMU) formed by France, Italy, Belgium, and Switzerland in 1865 and later joined by Greece. After the formation of the LMU, and the subsequent French diplomatic offensive in favour of a common monetary system, an intense international discussion began over the creation of a 'universal money', with the 'universal' taken to consist of the 'civilized world', which was understood to mean Europe and the USA. Governments and economists considered monetary unification as being theoretically beneficial, although not necessarily in the form proposed by France. All European governments agreed to participate in an international monetary conference in Paris in 1867, which voted unanimously in favour of universal monetary unification coupled with a gold standard, the LMU-franc system, and decimalization of coinage.

Most of the subsequent literature on the subject assumes that the 1867 conference marked the end of the process. In fact in 1869 several countries had already passed laws to adopt the LMU monetary system and had applied to join the Union (Austria-Hungary, Spain, the Pontifical State, Romania, and Brazil), as Serbia, Bulgaria, Finland, Venezuela, and Colombia would do in the 1870s and 1880s. Sweden introduced the LMU gold coinage in 1868. Luxembourg and San Marino had applied as well. Southern and central Germany saw a substantial agitation by the Chambers of Commerce in favour of the LMU system. The British Chancellor of the Exchequer, Robert Lowe, proposed to the House of Commons that Britain should reform the pound to make it a multiple of the coinage of the LMU, while Portugal, Holland, and Norway indicated that they would follow an eventual British conversion. Monetary union in Europe seemed poised to succeed: the Swiss politician and monetary negotiator Feer-Herzog said in October 1869 that

Whatever the destiny of unification in England and in the United States, the most likely outcome in the near future is that the unification planned in 1867 will soon embrace the whole of Continental Europe, maybe with the exception of Russia and Turkey, since it is not to be expected that, once that France, Italy, Belgium, Switzerland, Spain, Greece, Romania, northern and southern Germany, Austria, Sweden, and Norway have implemented the agreement planned in 1867, Portugal, Denmark, and Holland could remain apart.[1]

The Italian economist Sacerdoti noted in the same year that 'a brief look at the progress accomplished on the question of monetary unification in the last few years

---

[1] Feer-Herzog (1869: 27).

will be sufficient to convince us that its realization can be considered as secured for a near future.'[2]

The French government, however, hesitated to implement all the aspects of the project for unification, even though it was sponsoring it. The political figure chiefly responsible for the plan, the Vice-President of the Council of State, Félix Esquirou de Parieu, drew in 1872 a telling comparison between monetary and military power, pointing out that France had overestimated both its financial and its military capacities:

I protested against these repeated delays. Alas misfortunes did not wait to come. They may be imminent for those nations where such symptoms are widespread. Somehow we were in monetary terms what we were in military terms without knowing it. The government was weak, badly informed and in difficulties. The opposition was not any better and provided the government with no help.[3]

The discussions of 1865–70 about monetary unification, seignorage, and mint practices have been consigned since the 1870s to the dusty shelves containing reports on the endless monetary disputes and controversies that afflicted the nineteenth century. They were largely forgotten by historians and economists alike. Only the debate on the gold standard and bimetallism was remembered, to fall itself into oblivion after 1900. The failed attempt to achieve European Monetary Unification has been judged by its outcome, the demise of the project following the Franco-Prussian War in 1870–1 which reduced the international role of France and weakened the appeal of its policies. But between the Italian monetary unification of 1862 and the German monetary unification of 1871 a larger Continental unification seemed poised to move from the realm of fantasy to real life. Behind a dense screen of technical issues, there was an important political debate about monetary and trade policy, the relations between great powers and the future of Europe.

The interest of this process lies in three main aspects: (1) its relation with the political transformations taking place over the period, (2) the structural changes taking place in international monetary arrangements with the adoption of the gold standard, and (3) the development of a theory of monetary union together with the management of a practical experiment.

As Clapham wrote 'the years from 1866 to 1873, as seen from any public standpoint, by statesman or banker, merchant or industrialist, look like a gigantic hinge on which the history of the later nineteenth century turns.'[4] The year 1865 opened with France at the height of its influence on the Continent, while the USA was emerging from a destructive civil war. Growing tension between Prussia and Austria shook a fragmented German world. By contrast, the situation in 1874 reflected the most dramatic shift in the strength of the nations between the end of the Napoleonic Wars and the First World War. France was defeated and humiliated by Germany in 1870–1 and anti-German notions of revenge replaced practical monetary considerations.

During the same period Europe moved from an international monetary arrangement based on three complementary systems (gold in Great Britain, gold and silver in

---

[2] Sacerdoti (1869: 18).   [3] Parieu (1872: 379–381).   [4] Clapham, (1944: ii. 271).

France, and silver in most of the rest of Europe), to a single system based on the gold standard. In the twentieth century the gold standard has become an icon symbolizing monetary stability. The project of universal money was an important factor both in the establishment of the gold standard and in the creation of its myth.

The history of the LMU provides a case study of monetary union planned and implemented, showing the political and economic implications of such an event. The projected European monetary union revealed the clashes of ideas and of interests activated by an ambitious project and how these could prevent its success. The similarities with the process of European Monetary Unification started in 1991 in Maastricht are at times striking. In 1870 Parieu wanted to create a common European coin called 'Europe' in a 'European Union', governed by a 'European Commission' and a 'European Parliament' (see Chapter 2). The French economist Garnier proposed to form a universal central bank. The arguments used by supporters and opponents of monetary unification were often very similar to today's discussions and could be compared with the practical operations of the Latin Monetary Union.

Existing literature on the economic and financial history of the 1860s does not emphasize this episode of European monetary integration, as distinct from the long-term history of the LMU. Several accounts of the four international monetary conferences taking place between 1867 and 1892 have been published, together with studies on the LMU. All these studies have, however, perceived the process of European monetary union as a sideshow to the more important struggle between the international gold standard and bimetallism. The American monetary historians Russell and Willis published in 1898 and 1901 two influential accounts whose aim was to look at the origins of the quarrel between bimetallists and gold monometallists, which raged in the USA for the last quarter of the nineteenth century.[5] Russell depicted the French project of monetary union of 1865–70 as a sort of Napoleonic hegemonic conspiracy without any real chance of success. Willis adopted a more balanced approach to the French project but did not take it seriously either, ignoring the impact it had on England and judging it from its unsuccessful outcome. Both Russell, Willis, and other scholars who followed them worked without having access to the French and British diplomatic, political, and banking archives.[6] They did not have full knowledge of Parieu's project nor of the intense activity of the French government between 1867 and 1870 and of the results it achieved in many countries. Later authors concentrated on the official and well-known history of the LMU, lasting sixty-two years. They conducted little new research on the early days of the LMU, concentrating on recent developments as Marconcini or Fourtens did.[7] With time all books and articles dealing with international monetary cooperation came to include a standardized history of the LMU, associated to other monetary unions of the period, summarizing and updating existing literature, as Janssen and Garelli did.[8] The Belgian historian Mertens in 1944 provided the best multidisciplinary account of the monetary history of the period, covering most of the printed sources, but again he focused

[5] Russell (1898); Willis (1901).

[6] See e.g. Janssen (1911).

[7] Marconcini (1929); Fourtens (1930).

[8] Garelli (1946).

almost exclusively on the gold standard, apparently with a view to the resumption of metallic standards in Europe after the end of the Second World War.[9]

At the beginning of the 1970s, the study of nineteenth-century monetary unions benefited from the breakdown of the Bretton Woods arrangements and of fixed exchange rates, which opened a new quest for a stable international monetary regime. There was a new interest in past experience and attempts to coordinate financial systems, but the research was often conducted by economists who did not go into archives to try to reconstruct a different story and the same sources were employed again.[10] The classical gold standard (1880–1914) acquired a reputation as a system which achieved international stability without the need for a set of rules imposed by international institutions. The origins of such a system could be identified in the period 1860–80 and were examined as a possible model by Eichengreen, Bordo, Panic, Gallarotti, and others, with conflicting results.[11]

In 1989 the Delors report on monetary union in Europe modified again the research agenda, as historians and economists searched for precedents. Every period of history has its own concerns and questions to ask of the past, related to the main pre-occupation of the time, and the present research is not an exception to this rule. Nevertheless the relationship between monetary union and the gold standard retained its hypnotic effect, distracting many scholars from a more detailed study of the political and economic aspects of the struggle to create a common European currency between 1865 and 1873. Flandreau and Oppers worked to provide new analytical foundations in support of the bimetallist case for the 1860s and 1870s.[12] New work was done on the German monetary unification of 1871, but without perceiving the important influence on it of the European project of monetary unification.[13] The LMU could not shake off its reputation as a relatively uninteresting abortive local union. Many articles on historical monetary unions appeared in the 1990s, including those of De Cecco and Redish, providing a glimpse of the wider process or reconstructing some new episodes, as Flandreau did in his *thèse de maitrise* and several articles.[14] Perlman highlighted the contribution of the editor of the *Economist* Walter Bagehot to the British debate of the time while Hefeker stressed the role of free-traders and protectionists in the rise and decline of monetary unions.[15] One reason for the historical neglect of Parieu's attempt to create a European common currency was perhaps that it was the history of something which did not happen, the history of what might have been but whose traces (theoretical debates, diplomatic exchanges, and banking manoeuvres) were apparently lost after defeat. Since history is usually written by the winners, both the French and the bimetallist point of view have faded from the front of the scene. The supporters of the gold standard won in the 1870s the war started in the 1860s against the supporters of silver. The bimetallists were unable to reverse that outcome in the following decades and finally disbanded at the turn of the century, so that until

[9] Mertens (1944).   [10] Krämer (1970); Vanthoor (1996).

[11] Bordo and Schwartz (1984); Eichengreen and Flandreau (1997); Panic (1992); Gallarotti (1995).

[12] Flandreau (1995b); Oppers (1995: 47–70).   [13] Holtfrerich (1989: 216–40); James (1997).

[14] Flandreau (1989); De Cecco (1992); Redish (1993).

[15] Perlman (1993); Hefeker (1995: 489–537).

recently the view of the supporters of gold was the only one to be heard. Similarly, had the French won the Franco-Prussian War, historiography would have been much more friendly to their views on monetary unification.

This study of the early years of the Latin Monetary Union and of the debates on universal (or European) money seeks to reconstruct all the main national debates in a multilateral European framework, using new or insufficiently explored archival resources. The French have tended to defend their national role, while the English have underestimated the strength of the Continental monetary systems as an alternative to the gold standard. German and Italian scholars have concentrated on the establishment of national financial structures after their political unification and American studies have focused on their rising influence and the 'crime of 1873' (the establishment of the gold standard in the USA and the beginning of the bimetallist controversy there).[16] To the traditional use of official reports and parliamentary debates, the present research has added sources in the archives of the Bank of France, the Bank of England, and the Bank of Italy, the French and Italian diplomatic archives, the archives of the French mint, the papers and correspondence of several heads of government and finance ministers of the time (Napoleon III, Rouher, Gladstone, Lowe, and Minghetti). A surprisingly large body of archival documentation has survived, permitting an almost day-to-day reconstruction of the events of the period, enlivened by the private comments of the protagonists. The French, British, and German national debates have been treated with special attention in this work, but substantial sections have also been concerned with Italy, Greece, the Pontifical State, Belgium, Switzerland, and the Scandinavian countries.

The first chapter provides a general overview of the European situation in 1865. It focuses on the relations between the countries involved in the process of monetary unification in order to reconstruct the political and diplomatic background. As most of the process will be viewed through the Parisian archives, looking from the centre of the movement towards its periphery, France's relations with the rest of Europe will be regarded with special attention. The progress of free trade in the period is also discussed as a prerequisite for monetary integration, together with the activities of various international societies formed in the 1850s and 1860s to facilitate commerce and unify the structure of a common market (transport, information, measures, weights, coinage, and commercial legislation). The diversity of monetary systems existing in Europe before 1870 is then analysed. Some essential definitions of the various metallic standards are established, briefly discussing the viability of bimetallism in comparison to the gold standard. In this research the gold standard is not seen as the necessary outcome of the development of nineteenth-century monetary systems. Nor is it assumed to provide a necessarily more stable price system, even if it does provide steadier exchange rates. Some of the main national monetary systems are discussed individually to follow the interaction between silver standards, gold standards, and double standards (bimetallism). France introduced some partial reforms, in an effort to stabilize and preserve the existing bimetallic arrangement, but these reforms were

---

[16] Flandreau (1995*b*); Roccas (1989); Friedman (1992).

powerless against the flow of international arbitrage on precious metals. France's neighbours (Belgium, Switzerland, and Italy) experienced a similar incapacity to solve alone the problem of a stable monetary circulation. The logical solution appeared to be the formation of a monetary union between these four countries which already shared the franc as a common unit.

The birth of the Latin Monetary Union in 1865 is the subject of the second chapter. The combination of archival resources from the Bank of France, the French Ministry of Foreign Affairs, and the Monnaie de Paris makes it possible to reconstruct the different visions of the role of a monetary union associated with various French institutions. Given the dominant role played by France in the Union, the conflict between French institutions shaped the contradictory elements of the LMU constitution, oscillating between the economic and financial goal of unification and the objective of political and diplomatic gain. Félix Esquirou de Parieu emerges as the real driving force of monetary unification in France and in Europe, from his position as high governmental official, politician, diplomat, and economist. Parieu's views triumphed at the 1867 International Monetary Conference of Paris, which supported international unification following the LMU guidelines, corrected by the introduction of the gold standard and an international coin of 25 francs.

Chapter 3 explores the intellectual debate at the European level. It discusses arguments about the advantages and shortcomings of union and the role of the 'battle of the standards' for the evaluation of the impact of universal money. Further developments of union proposed by various economists are also discussed, together with the economic interests associated with the alignment of opinions.

Chapter 4 reconstructs the early years of the LMU, focusing on the difficult relations between the northern Latin (France, Switzerland, and Belgium) and the southern Latin States (Italy, the Pontifical State, and Greece). The latter had to resort to monetary creation to sustain their unbalanced public finances, with immediate effects on the former's monetary circulation. The transmission mechanism of monetary disturbances was the international metallic arbitrage, facilitated but not determined by the existence of a monetary union. Ultimately the Union proved able to repress real and imaginary abuses only after the central member State (France) adopted a more aggressive and centralized stance. The Pontifical coinage was expelled from the Union in 1870, France assumed direct control over the Greek monetary issue, new issues of silver were progressively neutralized and then discontinued, and membership was denied to all dubious applicants. These repressive measures of control were effective but no expansion or deepening of the union could take place under such constrained form of cooperation.

The French institutional debate was connected to these problems but also had a particular dynamic of its own. On the one hand the Ministry of Foreign Affairs fully supported Parieu's views on monetary unification and the adoption of the gold standard because it perceived international constraints (the request by several countries to agree on a gold coinage). The Quai d'Orsay wished to accommodate French commercial interests with the extension of French political influence. On the other hand the positions and the tactics of the Finance Ministry and of the Bank of France revealed more scepticism. The Finance Ministry progressively turned against a monetary unification it had initially sponsored, when it became clear that unification required the abandoning of bimetallism, and monitoring of an increasing number of countries which did not inspire full confidence. The Bank never expressed any support for monetary utopias and began a long battle for bimetallism and against a unification it considered useless and dangerous. Its British counterpart, the Bank of England, had a similarly conservative approach to monetary reform: 'It is always an evil to make a change in the monetary system of a country.'[17]

The British reaction to Continental proposals of monetary unification is considered in Chapter 5. Some of the traditional supporters of the decimalization of the pound were involved in the earlier initiatives in favour of British participation in an international monetary regime. Representatives of the commercial world and academics supported the adaptation of the pound to an international coin of 25 francs. The prevalent view in political and financial circles was, however, set against any change to the British monetary system, supporting the status of the pound as the key international currency. The latter view dictated British policy until 1869, when Gladstone's new Chancellor of the Exchequer, Robert Lowe, challenged the conventional wisdom. A passionate but confused public debate ensued. The financial world, the Bank of England, and part of the press attacked Lowe, who was accused of debasing the currency and altering the standard of value by cabinet colleagues while Gladstone was 'astonished' by Lowe's proposals. Britain nonetheless came close to an agreement with France on a common currency (but not on a single currency, since national coins would remain, linked by a fixed exchange rate without margins of fluctuation).

The case of Germany is in some respects similar to the British one. The mobilization of the Chambers of Commerce and of some economists in favour of the gold standard and monetary unification permitted substantial hopes that at least some German States would join the LMU. The lack of progress of German national unification between 1866 and 1870 boosted the chances of an international monetary unification, accepted in principle by the German trade parliament (*Zollparlament*). Bismarck's final success in 1870, highlighted the political contradictions of a project of monetary unification which was accompanied neither by a federalist programme nor even simply by friendly relations between governments. The Franco-Prussian War proved to be the final blow to the internationalists, some of whom continued their campaign despite the French defeat and the birth of a nationalist German Reich.

The Epilogue of this study describes the dissolution of the atmosphere favourable to political cooperation and monetary union under French leadership. Parieu's plan was replaced by an international gold standard, more limited in scope but able to survive the strong political tensions which would probably have destroyed a more complete and formal frame of monetary union. The memory of how close Europe had been to the adoption of a common currency from Athens to Stockholm was erased with the defeat of the project.

---

[17] Governor of the Bank G. Lyall and deputy governor B. B. Greene, to the Chancellor of the Exchequer R. Lowe, 19 July 1872 (ABoE, Secretary Letter Book, XVII, 44).

The postscript addresses the issue of contemporary relevance of nineteenth-century monetary history. The technical aspects of money have been altered radically in the twentieth century so that any comparison between the conference of Paris in 1867 and the treaty of Maastricht in 1992 has to be extremely cautious. Some general political issues however appear again today and are addressed with a higher degree of awareness. European monetary union is now openly acknowledged as part of a more complete political and economic integration aimed at removing permanently any source of military conflict between member States.

The Appendix contains biographical notices about the most important individuals referred to in the text, a list of the archival resources with the relevant acronyms, a small glossary of technical terms, and some illustrations.

1

The Political and Monetary Situation in Europe in 1865

1.1. THE POLITICAL SITUATION IN EUROPE IN THE MID-1860s

In 1865 the prestige of the second Empire in Europe had reached its zenith. The French army had not been defeated since 1815 and was considered by most, especially by the French themselves, as the best in the world. Napoleon III regarded himself as the arbitrator of European conflicts and felt he could encourage Prussian ambitions to unite part of Germany one day and support Austrian resistance to such a plan on another occasion. Bismarck travelled across France to pay a respectful visit to Napoleon in Biarritz, and Moltke, who was to besiege and seize Paris, was still an obscure Prussian general. The events of years following 1865, marked by a French defeat in Mexico, by embarrassment over the Prussian victory against Austria in 1866, and by humiliation after the war of 1870–1 against Germany, showed that most of the 'grandeur' of Imperial France was only a delusion. The French army had not kept pace with Prussian military reforms and the inconsistency of Napoleonic policy produced its bitter fruits. But in 1865 contemporary observers could only see the apogee of France, even if the events of the following year began to expose the weaknesses of the French regime and put an end to the *fête impériale*.

In 1852, Louis Napoleon Bonaparte, nephew of Napoleon I, had proclaimed himself Emperor of the French under the name Napoleon III. His European projects included putting an end to the conservative European equilibrium established by the Treaty of Vienna and the promotion of the principle of nationalities, which Napoleon I had fully espoused only in captivity in St Helena.[1] The aspiration to so-called 'natural frontiers' was revived, in the form of France's territorial ambitions: Savoy and Nice to reach the Alps in the south, and Belgium, Luxembourg, and the Rhineland to reach the Rhine,

---

[1] Napoleon I reinterpreted and embellished his political career in the name of democratic nationalism during his last years of exile. He also decided to stress his European beliefs. 'Il [Napoléon] eût voulu, pour toute l'Europe, l'uniformité des monnaies, des poids, des mesures, l'uniformité de la législation. Pourquoi, disait-il, mon Code Napoléon n'eût-il pas servi de base à un code Européen, et mon Université Impériale à une université Européenne? De la sorte nous n'eussions réellement, en Europe, composé qu'une seule et même famille. Chacun, en voyageant, n'eût pas cessé de se trouver chez lui.' E. Las Casas (1823–4), VII, 228.

and be protected from Prussia in the north. Following the principle of nationalities, France helped the Italians in their struggle for national unity and, initially, the Germans as well. At the same time, France also laid down claims to the territories inhabited by French-speaking populations.

After the first decade of authoritarian Empire, Napoleon had progressively liberalized the regime, restoring a limited power to Parliament. In 1865 the government was still strongly in the hands of experienced and trusted ministers of the regime, Eugène Rouher, Jules Baroche, Achille Fould, and Pierre Magne.[2] Those men controlled the economic and the interior policy almost until the end of the Empire and played an important role in shaping French monetary diplomacy. Émile Ollivier distinguished himself in the opposition for his willingness to compromise with Napoleon in exchange for further political liberalization. He would become chief minister in 1870 during the brief season of the liberal Empire when F. E. de Parieu, appointed minister, reached the culminating phase of his influence on the French government.

Foreign affairs had remained the reserved field of the Emperor who changed ministers as often as he changed policy (nine ministers between 1860 and 1870). France had recovered a central position in European politics through the alliance with Great Britain in 1853, in the Crimean War against Russia. The improved relations between the two uncomfortable neighbours survived the British fundamental distrust of the destabilizing intentions of Napoleon III. Queen Victoria called Napoleon the 'universal agitator' and the government resented French expansionist views, particularly over Belgium.[3] Free trade after the Cobden–Chevalier Treaty of 1860 had, however, consolidated peace between the two nations.

France's role in the unification of Italy had been paramount. It had provided most of the fighting force in the 1859 war against Austria. By 1865 Italy was entirely united except for Rome, Venice, and Trieste, thanks to French protection. But Napoleon III had lost a large part of the gratitude due to him by the Italians by attempting to promote the creation of three States, two of them possibly under the sovereignty of a French prince, instead of a united Italy.[4] Napoleon opposed unsuccessfully both the desire of central Italy to join Piedmont in 1859 and later Garibaldi's conquest of southern Italy, until he consented, in exchange for Nice and Savoy. Nevertheless he succeeded in protecting the temporal sovereignty of the Pope over Rome. The Italians wanted Rome as their capital but Napoleon could not abandon the Pope without losing essential Catholic support for his regime in France. In 1849 and 1867 Napoleon sent military expeditions to Rome and French troops remained until the fall of the Empire. The French bayonets and Chassepots defending Rome clouded Franco-Italian relations.

Napoleon was attempting to play a strategy of divide and rule in Germany as well, nurturing competition between Prussia and Austria. France was waiting for the first opportunity to acquire territories in exchange for its arbitrage. Bismarck was reassured in 1865 of the Emperor's benevolent neutrality if a war was to break out with Austria,

---

[2] Plessis (1985a).   [3] Herre (1992: 237).

[4] Probably Prince Napoleon (nicknamed Plon Plon) in central Italy, and an heir of the former king of Naples, Murat (1808–15), in southern Italy.

in exchange for an ambiguously expressed promise of territorial compensations for France if Prussia was enlarged. The year after, Napoleon also encouraged Italy to join Prussia against Austria in order to acquire Venice. The previous negotiations did not prevent the Emperor of the French from offering his neutrality to Austria as well, in exchange for Venice, destined to Italy.[5] Once again, in 1865 the final consequences of the French policy in Germany, oscillating between support and confrontation with Prussia, were not visible. When Austria was unexpectedly crushed by Prussia at Sadowa in 1866, French public opinion was shaken by the emergence of a strong North German Confederation through which Prussia gained control over more than two-thirds of Germany. Bismarck had trapped Napoleon and refused all compensation to France, either in Germany, or in Belgium or Luxembourg. From 1866 to 1870 all Europe was nervously waiting for a direct military confrontation between France and Prussia. The year of foundation of the Latin Monetary Union, 1865, was in some respects the last period of peace before the confrontations that would radically change the map of Europe.

During the second Empire, France had progressed from an economic and financial point of view. Per capita income had grown faster in France between 1853 and 1865 than in the UK, the USA, and the German States. In 1865 France's exports represented 16 per cent of the total volume of international trade (compared to 23 per cent for Great Britain), the highest percentage of the century and possibly the highest in its history.[6] 'French capitalism can be said to have achieved its apogee during the second Empire.'[7] Yet 1865 proved also a turning point as economic growth was slowing down and a slump in production and exports was to follow in the 1870s, reducing France's economic weight in comparison to the other great powers.

Napoleon asserted the duty of the State to promote economic expansion through an interventionist policy. His first goal was the mobilization of capital, transforming hoarded savings into investment through a new banking system. Napoleon had provided state support for the formation of the Crédit Foncier in 1852 and the Crédit Agricole in 1860. The brothers Pereire, close confidants of the Emperor, had launched the Crédit Mobilier in 1852, an investment bank conceived to operate on a large scale. It specialized in the establishment and development of joint-stock companies and in underwriting government loans.[8] Their initiative was followed by the creation of several large commercial banks: the Crédit Industriel et Commercial in 1859, the Crédit Lyonnais in 1863, and the Société Générale in 1864.[9] A new Paris was emerging from the hands of Haussman, prefect of the Seine and engineer of the largest transformation centrally directed of a European city. This new city was a large international financial centre with the ambition of displacing London. 'From the 1850s the nation developed a mania for foreign investment; by 1870 it had dispatched overseas one-third of total savings.'[10] The issue of foreign financial investments is important to understand what was at stake for France in the process of monetary unification.

---

[5] Girard (1986: 376–80).   [6] Levy-Leboyer and Bourguignon (1990: 1–9 and 50).
[7] Palmade (1972: 172).   [8] Landes (1956: 204–22).   [9] Kindleberger (1993: 112–13).
[10] Trebilcock (1981: 176). 'Overseas' must be understood on British terms as 'abroad', as a large part of those capitals went to Italy, Spain, and Russia, who were not 'overseas' from France.

The year 1865 represented a peak in French history, in terms both of foreign policy influence and of financial capacity. It was largely on this basis that France could successfully form a currency area in 1865 with the ultimate goal of achieving a universal coinage for the 'civilized world'.

For Great Britain, 1865 saw Palmerston's death, the end of the mid-Victorian political stability and largely unchallenged liberal governments. The period of reform was opening with Lord Russell's announcement that he would bring forward a new bill to extend the electoral franchise. This also meant governmental instability as the Palmerston, Russell, Derby, Disraeli, and Gladstone administrations succeeded each other between October 1865 and December 1868. Internal problems were given priority between 1865 and 1868, limiting British interventions abroad.

British foreign policy in 1865 attempted to influence European questions by voicing concern without taking action. Derek Beales defined British foreign policy as 'near isolationism.'[11] Diplomacy was not backed by force, both because the balance of power in Europe prevented any threat to the British Isles and because the UK could not match Continental armies on the open field without a large increase in expenditure, prevented by the Gladstonian view of public finances.[12] This policy worked in 1859–60 in favour of Italy but did not help Denmark against Prussia and Austria in 1864. Great Britain was left effectively voiceless in the great reorganization of the European map between 1866 and 1871. Neither the Whig Palmerston nor the Conservative Derby feared a strong Germany: in 1865 Palmerston wrote to the Foreign Secretary Lord Russell:

With a view to the future, it is desirable that Germany in the aggregate should be strong, in order to control these two ambitious and aggressive powers, France and Russia, that press her west and east. As to France we know how restless and aggressive she is, and how ready to break free for Belgium, for the Rhine, for anything she would be likely to get without too great an exertion.[13]

One year later Derby declared to the Lords on the creation of a North German power: 'I cannot see that the existence of such a Power would be to us any injury, any menace, any detriment.'[14]

Napoleon III declared to a British diplomat in 1868: 'You English have chosen to withdraw yourselves from the political arena in Europe, and this abstention of England from active participation in European politics is a great misfortune for Europe, and will later prove to be a great misfortune for herself.'[15] After the formation of a hostile German Empire, the British Foreign Secretary Granville acknowledged the truth of Napoleon's words.

The British economic position was still dominant but was no longer unchallenged. France, Belgium, and parts of Germany were becoming increasingly competitive in the manufacturing sector. The British banking system retained its superiority over the rest

[11] Beales (1969: 279).
[12] Swartz (1985: 22–3). 1859–66 was the longest period spent by Gladstone as Chancellor of the Exchequer.   [13] Bourne (1970: 382).   [14] Ibid. 388.   [15] Gorman (1989: 82).

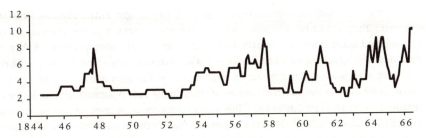

Graph 1.1. *Bank of England discount rate from the Bank Charter Act of 1844 to the Overend–Gurney crisis*

Source: Monthly figures elaborated from Seyd (1874: 94–6).

of the world through a network of merchant banks, discount houses, and joint-stock banks. Britain was directing an increasing share of its growing savings towards foreign investment.[16] 1866–7 marked a short suspension of the sustained growth of income of the period. The financial crisis of 1866 had greatly worried English financial circles. The largest British discount house, Overend & Gurney, went bust, followed by seven banks and by signs of financial panic and economic stagnation. The government had to suspend the Bank Act for the third time in less than twenty years (1847, 1857, 1866), authorizing the Bank of England to issue an additional amount of paper money to supply liquidity to discount houses and banks. The adoption by the Bank of England of a protracted high-interest rate failed to attract gold from Continental Europe and boost its strained reserves, contrary to expectations of central banking practice and theory (Graph 1.1). In 1873, the MP for Glasgow, Anderson, could polemically recall:

[O]ur plan of raising our hire entirely failed during the panic of 1866 to bring us gold from France. During our three months of 10 per cent discount rate, the Bank of France kept their rate at 3.5 and 4 per cent, yet their gold increased till they had actually over £28,000,000 sterling while we, with our prolonged 10 per cent rate, could not get above £12,000,000.[17]

In 1865 Germany was divided in thirty-nine kingdoms, principalities, and free States, all included in the German Confederation, together with the German provinces of the Austrian Empire. Austria held the presidency of the Diet of the Confederation and prevented any attempt to unify Germany. In 1862 Bismarck became Prussia's chancellor and initially embodied conservative resistance to liberal requests. While since 1859 north German liberals subordinated their political preference to their national priority and looked towards Prussia in their aspiration for national unification, a strong opposition to Prussian hegemony prevailed in southern Germany, especially in Bavaria and Württemberg.[18] German princes were in general wary of Bismarck's intentions and 'particularism' was prevalent in the more liberal and Catholic southern States.

---

[16] Edelstein (1994: 175).
[17] Hansard Parliamentary Debates, 3rd series, 215, 25 March 1873, col. 117.
[18] Gorman (1989: 56–7, 77–78).

In the war of 1866, central and southern German States fought and lost against Prussia. Even after the expulsion of Austria from Germany in 1866 and the annexation of Hanover and most north German States by Prussia, these feelings remained. When elections for the parliament of the *Zollverein* (German customs union formed in 1837) were held with universal manhood suffrage in all the German States in 1868, opponents of unification in the southern States of Bavaria, Baden, Württemberg, and Hesse-Darmstadt won 50 seats out of 85.[19] Bismarck's plans were delayed by the opposition of Catholics who opposed the Protestants of the north, of particularists who were jealous of their sovereignty, and democrats and socialists who mistrusted Prussian militarism and conservatism. French foreign policy aimed at preventing the formation of a hostile unified Germany, and weakly defended the autonomy of south German States.

A partial and distorted view of the situation is expressed by some letters received by Napoleon III from various Germans: A. Beckerman from Hanover wrote in 1868 that the King of Hanover in exile in Vienna was grateful for French help and added

It is not France but Prussia which is the true enemy of Germany, the saviour of Germany must be the Emperor Napoleon. I can add that this line has now been adopted not simply by particularists, but also by the whole of German democracy; we will see soon a whole campaign following this direction.[20]

Another German wrote to Napoleon

The simple thought that one day Germany will be Prussified, that Prussian arrogance, lofty rigidity, self-satisfaction, tricks, jokes, stratagems, and artfulness might alter the gentle, honest and modest manners of Germany, fills me and half of the Germans with disgust and horror, as it must affect any German feeling … the other Providence of the people, namely France, will not fail to stop the threat of such a deluge.[21]

Rouher stated his view to the Emperor about the French position towards Prussian expansionism and German unification in 1867 in these terms:

The logic of events condemns us to a policy of wait and see, employed to reinforce the courage of south German governments, to organize militarily, to prepare our alliances; and destined to reconsider further the general situation of Europe, either to consolidate peace, or to engage in a formidable duel with Prussia, or to take resolutely the necessary [territorial] compensations around us.[22]

How far could the southern German States be considered as possible allies of France between 1866 and 1870? From an economic point of view they had their commercial policy tied to a Prussian-dominated *Zollverein*. Their monetary policy was linked to the *Zollverein* just as much through a monetary union, the *Münzverein*. Secret military alliances attached their fate to Prussia from 1866, and Bismarck had deliberately

---

[19] Henderson (1939: 321).

[20] Albert Beckermann of Hanover, Paris, 23 Apr. 1868 (AN, AB XIX, Carton 173, dossier 19, 3).

[21] AN, AB XIX, Carton 176, Mémoire Kahn, Paris, 6 Aug. 1866.

[22] Rouher to Napoleon III, 27 Sept. 1867, in A. Poulet-Malassis (1873: 212).

revealed the secret. Was there any freedom of action left with military, trade, economic, and monetary policy attached to that of Prussia? Rouher's successor at the head of the French government, Emile Ollivier, explained the line of his government in November 1869, acknowledging this fact:

The line of the Main ... has been crossed long ago, at least for what concerns us. Did the alliance treaties not create Germany's military unification and the renewal of the *Zollverein* its economic unity? German unification against us is finished; what still needs to be done, political union, is important only for Prussia, to which it would bring more embarrassment complications than strength. Why should we be interested in preventing the democrats of Württemberg and the ultramontanists of Bavaria from annoying Bismarck in his parliaments, since, when war has broken out, the whole of Germany will be against us?[23]

Independent assessments of the feelings of southern Germany towards the Emperor were not favourable to France. Mistrust of Prussian expansionism could well be coupled with a mistrust of French expansionism. The General Director of the Italian Foreign Ministry indicated in 1867 to the Italian Ambassador in Vienna that the information collected by Italian diplomats in Germany 'differed entirely' from those harboured by the French Ambassador in Vienna, the Duke de Gramont. Gramont had indicated to his Italian colleague 'that the secondary States aspire to shake the Prussian yoke, that the warlike tendencies they have shown recently have to be ascribed to this hope, and that the populations of those States, apparently submissive, are in reality no less impatient than their governments about the Prussian domination.'[24] Unluckily, Gramont maintained his opinions, became France's Foreign Minister in May 1870, and pushed his country towards war and the 'débacle' a few weeks later. Although reluctantly, southern Germany joined forces with Prussia and France was heavily defeated. In the exaltation of victory, amid nationalist pressure, the southern States felt compelled to join Prussia in the German Empire and the King of Bavaria was bribed by Bismarck to offer the Imperial crown to the King of Prussia.[25]

The international position of Italy has already been described in relation to France. In 1865 political unification was incomplete, both because some territories were not yet part of the Kingdom of Italy and because the integration of the various provinces was slow. The new State was weak because it failed to be accepted by many in its southern provinces, leading to a form of peasant insurgent warfare, the *Brigantaggio*. Material unification required expensive infrastructures, new transportation, and a new administration. Perpetual military mobilization and war added charges to an unbalanced budget. Until 1865 Italy borrowed massively in France and only from 1869 did it start to deal more efficiently with its large deficits, achieving a balanced budget only in 1876.

[23] Ollivier (1917: 11–12).
[24] General Director of the Italian Ministry of Foreign Affairs U. Bartolani to the Italian Minister in Vienna De Barral, 18 May 1867. Ministero degli Affari Esteri, *I documenti diplomatici italiani 1861–70*, 1st ser., 13 vols. (Rome: Istituto poligrafico e zecca dello Stato, 1952–90), viii. 654.
[25] Gorman (1989: 13).

The Italian international role of the period was characterized more for its ambitions than for its achievements. The ambition to be recognized as a great power led Italy to build a large modern fleet of cuirassed warships, which was defeated by an older and weaker Austrian fleet in the battle of Lissa in 1866. After 1861, Italian unification was completed thanks to the convergence of interests with Prussia, which defeated first the Austrians and then the French on Italy's account. Nevertheless the Italians remained primarily associated with France until the 1880s, although resentful of French financial influence. Italian political unification was the precondition for its monetary unification, the adoption of a lira derived from the franc, and the creation of an franc-area sufficiently large to make the establishment of the Latin Monetary Union worthwhile.

The Austrian Empire had been seriously shaken by the defeat in Lombardy in 1859. It decided to resist on all sides, attempting to prevent a reduction of its influence in Germany and in Italy. In 1865 Austria refused the offer advanced by the Italian government to sell Venice. The pressure exerted by Bismarck on the *Zollverein* had been met by a compromise involving a common intervention against Denmark for Schleswig-Holstein in 1864. Growing provocation by Prussia broke any hope of compromise. When a Prussian–Italian alliance appeared possible at the beginning of 1866, Austria expected to be able to meet the challenge, with the help of the smaller German States. The defeat at Sadowa-Königsgrätz deprived Austria of any influence in Italy and Germany and accentuated a dramatic turn in Austria's relations with France. Until 1866 France had sided with Italy and Prussia against a dominant Austria, the latter being perceived as the major support of an anti-French *status quo*. Austria had already attempted to conclude an alliance with France before Sadowa, but Napoleon III came to need such an alliance only after Austria had been defeated. The 1866–70 period saw France busy trying to organize a French–Italian–Austrian front, always near to a conclusion but never reaching it.

Defeat forced the Austrians to share power in the Empire with the Hungarians, with the compromise of 1867. The Austro-Hungarian government was in deep financial difficulties and required foreign loans. War expenditures and economic backwardness prevented good public finances. In 1859 Austria had to resort to an inconvertible paper currency; after 1866 its currency union and its commercial treaty with the *Zollverein* was discontinued. In those conditions the Austrian desire to introduce the gold standard was only wishful thinking. The dual empire needed access to the French capital and goods market more than to the French Chassepots and was attracted by the Latin Monetary Union for these reasons.

1.2. UNIFICATION OF THE TOOLS FOR ECONOMIC GROWTH

1.2.1. The Creation of European 'Free Trade' Areas

Various European free-trade zones had been created in the nineteenth century and were progressively united creating a large European market. Low protective duties survived until the late 1870s. The two most important agreements were the German Custom Union (*Zollverein*) established between a large number of German States in

1834 and the Cobden–Chevalier Treaty of 1860 between France and Great Britain, and extended to most other European countries in the following years.

At the beginning of the nineteenth century, trade between German States was made extremely difficult by political fragmentation. Only Prussia, Bavaria, Hanover, Saxony, Baden, and Württemberg had substantial territory. All the others were separated by a few miles and many tariff and custom barriers or transit dues, with all the correlated smuggling problems and expenses in guarding extensive frontiers. In the absence of centralized protection and unified duties, foreign goods that used to enter through the free cities produced substantial losses of income from duties for the bigger States.[26] The circulation of a multiplicity of German, French, and Dutch coins maintained complicated exchange rate conditions, useful exclusively to money changers. The emergence of several customs unions in northern, central, and southern Germany prepared the way to the creation of the *Zollverein* in 1833. The *Zollverein* was a major customs union that covered most of 'Small Germany', thanks to agreements between Prussia, Bavaria, Württemberg, and Saxony. Austria was included only in 1853 and other eligible German States did not immediately participate either. Henderson stresses that the union was not based on a nationalistic appeal to unity, but on trading interests; often States would join only when forced by economic depression and financial distress.[27] The *Zollverein's* coverage of Germany progressed slowly and only in the 1850s did it become almost complete. The *Zollverein* meant no internal tariffs, compensated by a higher external tariff derived from the Prussian model. The income from the external frontier duties was then redistributed to all the participants according to their share of the population of the *Zollverein*.

In the United Kingdom the Anti-Corn Law League and the radical reformers led by Richard Cobden and John Bright had long campaigned for free trade. In 1859 Cobden succeeded in convincing the British Chancellor of the Exchequer W. E. Gladstone that a commercial treaty could be successfully negotiated with France, thanks to the intervention of the French economist Michel Chevalier, Councillor of State and adviser to Napoleon III. Gladstone had been President of the Board of Trade under Peel, when the latter repealed the Corn Laws in 1846 and was favourable to moderate free trade obtained through bilateral negotiations. Cobden believed that if 'the various nations would only agree to allow full commercial intercourse, an era of universal peace would necessarily ensue'.[28] Free trade would greatly benefit consumers by reducing prices. With the authorization of Gladstone, Cobden went to Paris. There, with the help of Chevalier, he convinced Napoleon and his ministers Rouher and Fould (who were to create the Latin Monetary Union six years later) to negotiate a commercial treaty.[29] Apparently Napoleon was finally convinced to sign by his desire to strengthen Anglo-French relations. The French protectionists were a strong political force, inasmuch as that they controlled the legislature. Napoleon could avoid their obstruction only through a international treaty for which he had exclusive power. The Finance Minister, Pierre Magne, was a 'cannon-ball protectionist' and attempted to

---

[26] Henderson (1939: 21–9).   [27] Ibid. 95.   [28] Cunningham (1904: 75).
[29] Morley (1896: 239–70). All details of the negotiations come from Morley.

delay the decision asking for an official enquiry on the subject. Magne used the same tactic against monetary unification and the introduction of the gold standard in France between 1867 and 1870 when he was finance minister. In 1860 Napoleon still controlled the situation and granted only two days for the enquiry, proceeding then to sign the Cobden–Chevalier Treaty against all opposition. The treaty did not abolish tariffs and barriers but reduced them substantially and cancelled all French prohibitions on imports.[30]

The British Prime Minister Robert Peel had expected the repeal of the Corn Laws in 1846 to expand free trade over Europe by the sheer force of the British unilateral example, but the other nations did not reduce their customs duties.[31] The Cobden–Chevalier Treaty was more influential and inspired most European nations to seek the 'most favoured nation' status with France. Most future Latin Monetary Union members concluded a similar arrangement, Belgium in 1862, Italy in 1863, and Switzerland in 1864. The *Zollverein* gained the same status in 1863, Sweden, Norway, Spain, and the Netherlands in 1865, Austria in 1866, and Portugal in 1867.[32] A general reduction of tariffs had therefore been achieved in 1865, increasing international trade. After just a few years of implementation, this network of free trade treaties proved a compelling argument for monetary unification.

1.2.2. *International Associations for Uniform Systems of Weights, Measures, Coinage, or Commercial Legislation*

The growing commercial intercourse of England with the Continent and the international exhibitions of London (1851) and Paris (1855 and 1867) called for an effort towards the rationalization and the internationalization of units of measure in Europe.[33] 'The Great Exhibition of Works of Industry of All Nations', convened on a British initiative in 1851, was the first of a very long series. The exhibition exposed the difficulties in comparing goods measured and priced in a picturesque but anachronistic variety of units of measures and currencies, differing in each country. The adoption of a system of measures based on the metre, the litre, and the gram, the decimalization and the unification of the coinage were all measures endorsed by several special bodies, societies born out of the positivistic mood of time, to push towards scientific and rational homogeneity. The metric system was legalized in the UK in 1862 but did not replace the British units. In the 1850s an important debate took place on the decimalization of the British currency with frequent references to the advantages offered to foreign countries by a decimal system, but few to a common international unit of money.[34]

The London Society for the Encouragement of Art Industry and Commerce invited the British government to exchange communications with other governments in view of a common system of units and coinage. The International Statistical Congress at Brussels debated the subject in 1853, as further Congresses would do in Vienna (1859), in Berlin (1863), and in Florence (1867). Later, the Associations of the Chambers of

---

[30] Rist (1970: 289–90).   [31] Cunningham (1904: 66).   [32] Hefeker (1995: 499).
[33] Russell (1898: 18–21).   [34] Decimal Coinage Commission (1859).

Commerce joined in, especially in Great Britain and the German States, where disparity of units with their neighbours became a greater issue with the increase in trade caused by the Industrial Revolution and the reduction of customs duties. Fewer associations were created in France, Belgium, and Italy, which had already largely adopted grams, metres, the decimal system, and the franc. It was indeed the scientists of these nations (the French J. L. Lagrange and P. S. Laplace, seconded by Italian, Belgian, Swiss, and Dutch scientists) who had conceived together the metre–gram–litre system, on request from the French National Assembly in the last years of the eighteenth century.

An early supporter of international monetary unification, the French engineer A. Léon, wrote that 'Wishing to overcome the obstacles ... some liberally minded individuals from several countries have met following the exhibition of 1855 and have formed, under the presidency of Baron James de Rothschild, an international society with the aim of establishing a general system of measures and currencies common to all civilized nations.'[35] In 1860 the newly formed International Association for Obtaining a Uniform Decimal System in Measures, Weights, and Coins, held its first congress in London.

The International Statistical Congress held in 1863 in Berlin assumed much greater importance. The discussions produced the central element of the scheme for universal monetary unification which would shape discussions for over a decade and gained momentum after the creation in December 1865 of the Latin Monetary Union (LMU).[36] The participants in the Statistical Congress agreed that the equalization of international coins would be a substantial progress. A simplified equation could be obtained with minor modifications in the weight and in the composition of existing coins in the main commercial nations: 1 British pound $= 5$ US dollars $= 25$ French francs.[37] Until 1865 the equalization of the various currencies was widely assumed to be achievable employing as a reference either the franc or the pound or a new scientifically conceived currency. It was the gravitation of a large number of countries and currencies around the franc after the creation of the Latin Monetary Union, together with the enormous issue of French gold coins during the second Empire, which gave the franc its position as the ideal candidate to complete the international set of measures, alongside grams, litres, and metres.

These associations dealt also with the internationalization of commercial law and of bills of exchange. They worked in the same direction as the international postal and telegraphical unions, produced by technical innovation and improvements in transportation. These societies and their congresses played an important role in associating in a single debate economists, politicians, merchants, bankers, and diplomats, thus forming a qualified public opinion for the future. The Association for Promoting an International Code of Commerce promoted lectures in London, Edinburgh, Glasgow, and Birmingham 'to cement peace between all countries, extend commerce, and promote morals and justice'. Its London committee in 1851 included Robert Lowe, future Chancellor of the Exchequer in 1868 and supporter of international monetary unification.[38]

[35] Léon (1862: 9).   [36] Willis (1901).   [37] Jevons (1875: 173).   [38] Levi (1851: 1).

The establishment of free trade in much of Europe increased international trade and created a climate favourable to the simplification of commercial practices. The quest for progress of the nineteenth century also expressed itself with a network of societies for standardization and unification in all fields. Monetary unification was prominent among their objectives but caused a much wider debate because of its technical complexity and its inextricable link with political authority.

1.3. EUROPEAN MONETARY SYSTEMS BEFORE THE LATIN MONETARY UNION

Before the discussion of monetary unification can be undertaken, the extent of the monetary division and fragmentation of Europe must be tackled. The elements of diversity were multiple and various metallic standards existed for coins (gold, silver, or both). Coins were themselves supplemented by a more or less developed banking system supplying paper money. Every nation had different monetary units, often not decimal. Their international value was subject to more or less pronounced fluctuations, depending on the metallic standard followed and on the confidence inspired by its paper currency. This section is divided into two parts. The first part defines and describes the various existing metallic standards. It provides a discussion of the dispute between bimetallism and gold monometallism, which became an essential part of the debate on monetary unification. National monetary systems are analysed in a second part, with special emphasis on the common problems they faced dealing with the fluctuation of the price of gold and silver.

1.3.1. *Bimetallisms, Silver Standards, and Gold Standards before 1865*

Money in Europe in the 1860s largely took the form of coinage, complemented by an issue of banknotes.[39] Inconvertible paper currencies (*cours forcé* in France) were introduced during periods of protracted political, financial, or military crisis. In exchange for loans to the State, the government dispensed the issuing banks from the obligation to convert their banknotes in gold or silver coins at the holders' request. The usual commodity standard was replaced temporarily by paper standard, a *fiat money*, issued with a certain discretion by state banks or by private banks having received the privilege of issue.

Bills of exchange and cheques were also a highly liquid mean of transferring value, but were not recognized as money. For most economists even banknotes were not really money. They were just a '*signe représentatif de la monnaie*' for Michel Chevalier.[40]

---

[39] Coins represented 62% of the circulation of coins plus banknotes in England in 1870, 62% in the German States in 1867, 68% in France in 1870, 78% in Italy in 1866. After the introduction of forced paper currencies the proportion declined to 44% in Italy in 1873 and to 9% in Austria in 1867. For England see F. Capie and A. Webber (1985: 326–9), II, for France see Flandreau (1995a); for Italy see De Mattia (1982: 189 and 198); for the German States and Austria see Hefeker (1995: 515).

[40] Chevalier (1866a: p. vi and 1).

The nature of a national monetary system was thus defined by the composition of the coinage circulating in that particular nation. In all countries the circulation included a certain quantity of coins in gold, silver, and bronze, part of which would have been issued by foreign governments. Foreign coins would outnumber national coins in most small States, as in Switzerland, Belgium, Greece, or in the Balkans.

Of the bronze coins, we need not speak here. Bronze coins had constituted the standard of value in Sweden in the eighteenth century, but they never achieved such a status in any of the European powers in the nineteenth century, where they never provided more than a marginal fraction of the currency.

The standard of value was the unit in which all debts could be legally discharged, without limits in quantity or time. The national metallic standard adopted determined the combination of gold and silver coinage which would be found in the country. Three types of standard existed:

1. 'Single standard' or 'monometallism'. Both the gold standard and the silver standard were monometallic systems. In a country with a monometallic system only one metal could be legally used for payments without any restriction. If gold was such a standard, silver coins were mere tokens, with a limited power to settle debts and with an intrinsic metallic value inferior to its nominal value as money.

2. 'Double standard' or 'bimetallism'. The bimetallist countries recognized an equal role in the payment system to gold and to silver, fixing by law the price of coined gold in terms of coined silver. The official price of gold in terms of silver, fixed at the mint, was set by law and was called the mint ratio. There were as many bimetallisms as there were different gold/silver official mint ratios. In France and in most of its neighbours the relation was 15.5 to 1, it was 16 to 1 in the USA, 15.48 in Spain, and 15.1 in Turkey. Bimetallist countries, and France in particular, served as an intermediary between silver and gold monometallist areas.

3. 'Parallel standards' or 'independent standards'. The definition covered countries that adopted the silver standard but wanted an additional trade coinage in gold for international transactions. Such countries would not fix a bimetallic rate but would let the market price of the two metals determine at what price gold coins should be accepted in private and public transactions. Periodically the market price changes were acknowledged by the publication of official tariffs of exchange between silver and gold coins. Many countries usually defined as having a silver standard had in fact a parallel and independent gold standard as well, with a limited circulation. This was the case especially for the Scandinavians, the Dutch, and the North Germans who had silver currencies but traded heavily with gold monometallic Britain. The quantity of gold thus coined was always limited.

In 1865 the UK and Portugal were on gold standards, France, Italy, and Spain were on bimetallic standards, the German States, Austria, Holland, the Scandinavian countries, and India were on silver standards. For most States the standard was ambiguous. Switzerland and Belgium had made gold circulation illegal but could not keep French gold coins out of their frontiers. Russia and the Ottoman Empire were said to be on a double standard by some authors, on a gold standard or a silver standard by others, because they coined both metals but it was not clear which, if any, had a legal or a practical prevalence. In poorer countries like Greece, the double standard existed only in the text of the monetary law of the country. Almost no gold had been coined and all of it had migrated together with most of the silver coinage as well, drained by trade deficits. National coinage had been replaced by paper and by old, worn-down, and underweight foreign coinage. In 1867 the USA officially had a double standard, but the silver dollar mintage had been practically irrelevant for over twenty-five years and smaller silver coins were debased since 1853, creating a *de facto* gold standard, according to the US delegate at the international conference of Paris in 1867, Ruggles. This was itself superseded by a forced paper currency, the US greenbacks which suffered over 20 per cent of depreciation in comparison to gold, making all discussions on the standard quite ambiguous. Inconvertible banknotes became the real monetary standard of most bimetallic States at some point during the period, as in the USA (1862–79), in Italy (1866–82), in France (1870–8), in Austria (1866–92), in Spain (from 1882), and in Greece (always except between 1869 and 1877), not to speak of Russia and the Ottoman Empire.

It is important though to stress that until the 1860s monetary confusion was not reflected in a general unanimous preference for gold. The 'scramble for gold' had not yet started.[41] Some States had indeed demonetized gold in the 1850s, fearing that it would depreciate because of the excessive supply, and lead to a weaker currency.[42] Between 1850 and 1866 gold was the inflationist form of money. Before 1848 and after 1872 the situation was reversed. In the 1850s the influential French economist Michel Chevalier had insisted on the probable fall of the price of gold deriving from the enormous output of Californian and Australian goldmines. Chevalier highlighted the necessity of adopting silver monometallism in order to prevent inflation. The economic growth of the period and the demand for gold in the French economy proved Chevalier's conclusions to be wrong but his book was a large success.[43] Chevalier's influence was credited with changing Belgian policy in favour of silver and the Portuguese government sent for Chevalier's opinion in 1866, before deciding on its reply to the French proposal to join the bimetallic Latin Monetary Union.[44]

The qualities of the International Gold Standard were widely discussed between 1860 and 1900, between the two world wars, and after the collapse of Bretton Woods in a largely apologetic literature. The system was widely credited with securing stable exchange rates, a set of efficient informal rules for the participants in international trade, and with providing a self-adjusting mechanism. Gold flows would readjust trade imbalances through price changes, provided that convertibility between banknotes and gold was maintained, linking monetary circulation to gold. Some later scholars have disputed the real mechanisms of the gold standard, the merits attributable to it,

---

[41] Gallarotti (1995).

[42] Holland, Belgium, Switzerland, Spain, Naples, and India followed this course of action. Willis (1901: 19).   [43] Chevalier (1859). The book was translated into English by Goschen.

[44] Chevalier (1933: 129).

and the role played by England in the system.[45] Whatever the truth of the various descriptions of the international gold standard for the period 1880–1914, that system did not exist in 1865. High flexibility of prices and wages permitted an easier adjustment to external shocks under the gold standard, but that was typical of the whole nineteenth century independently of which metallic standard was in use.[46] Flexibility depended on the political and social conditions of the period. The coexistence of gold standards with silver standards and double standards prevented any of those systems from working efficiently without the efficient working of the other system. An excessive supply of silver or of gold would be transmitted to every country, independently of the standard it followed. Through multiple arbitrage, England would be affected by large arrivals of silver in Europe, because silver would increase the silver monometallic circulation, but would also partially replace gold in the bimetallic countries, pushing surplus gold towards England.[47] In the same way large arrivals of gold would influence silver monometallist countries as well as bimetallist and gold monometallist.

The system which attracted more criticism at the time was bimetallism. It was said that bimetallism was an unstable regime as it was in fact an alternate standard, shifting continuously from gold monometallism to silver monometallism and vice versa. In order to mint coins of both metals with a fixed weight and fixed relation, States needed to introduce a legal ratio between the two coined metals. The ratio was 15.5 in France and 16 in the USA. As those were commodity-based standards, coined silver had a double nature: money and commercial bullion. If the commercial price of gold bullion in terms of silver bullion (the market ratio) differed from the official price (the mint ratio), then the coins in the metal whose market price was rising over the mint ratio could not be kept in circulation. If, for example, gold was excessively abundant, then its price would fall and the relative price of silver would increase. Once the price of silver had increased over the mint price, silver coins would be collected by bullion dealers and demonetized. They were transformed again into a commodity, either melted into bars or shipped towards a silver monometallic country to be sold at market price. Conversely holders of gold bullion would transport their bars to the mint, obtaining at the legal ratio gold coins whose value was superior to the commercial value of the gold bullion they contained. Free coinage of gold and silver at the mint, together with the freedom to melt, import, and export coins, were essential features of the system. This process of arbitrage was operated by bullion dealers, foreign exchange dealers, and banks. When protracted in time it would introduce in the bimetallist countries a monetary circulation composed exclusively of the depreciated metal. The more often the price oscillated around the mint ratio, the more arbitrage would take place and the more often one metal would replace the other.

---

[45] Bloomfield (1959), stressed how discretionary was monetary policy and how little the rules were respected by central banks. M. De Cecco (1984) showed how the system worked thanks to the British use of Indian commercial surplus with the rest of the world, not through the free movement of gold. He also showed how the Bank of England control of the money market was continuously weakened by the expanding joint-stock banks, until the collapse of the system in 1914, before the beginning of the war. See also Reis (1995) for some recent critical contributions.

[46] Bayoumi, Eichengreen, and Taylor (1996: 11).   [47] Oppers (1945: 52–5).

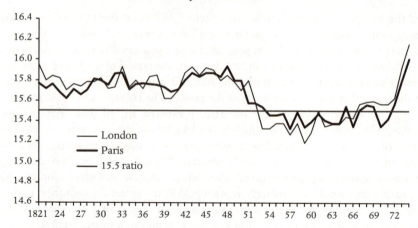

Graph 1.2. *Gold/Silver market ratio between the establishment of the gold standard in the UK (1821) and the restriction of silver coinage in France (1874)*

Source: Series of annual averages from Flandreau (1995b: 340–1).

Opponents of bimetallism have stressed the instability of the ratio, employing graphs similar to Graph 1.2. From the end of the Napoleonic Wars until 1848 the high price of gold (high market ratio) had established in France a substantial silver standard. From 1848 the massive flows of gold from the New World had increased the price of silver (low market ratio) and gold had replaced silver in the French circulation. This was 'Gresham's law': depreciated (bad) money always expels and replaces appreciated (good) money from the monetary circulation. Good money is hoarded or transformed in bullion, while bad money is used in exchanges.

Supporters of bimetallism on the other hand could argue that the market ratio remained quite stable around the 15.5 ratio, from its introduction in 1803 until the structural change of 1872–4.[48] The market ratio in France tended to be closer to 15.5 than in England and never moved very far from it until the 1870s (Graph 1.3).

Bimetallists pointed to the capacity of the mint ratio to stabilize the price of gold and silver, within restricted margins of fluctuation, securing exchange rate stability. The mere fact that a devalued metal could always be brought by its owner to the mint and would be transformed into a legal tender coin at the legal price guaranteed that no one would sell gold or silver for much less than that the mint price.

To permit arbitrage between the two metals, the appreciated metal could not be completely expelled from circulation in favour of the depreciated metal. Friedman

---

[48] In 1872 the German Empire adopted a single currency, based on a gold standard and the Scandinavian countries followed. France suspended silver issue in 1873 to prevent Bismarck from dumping all the demonetized German silver on it. The year later France and its monetary allies restarted a controlled silver issue but the previous events had changed. The price of silver fell further and a self-reinforcing process led to its collapse. This point will be discussed more extensively in Ch. 5. See Mertens (1944) and Flandreau (1995b: 275–86).

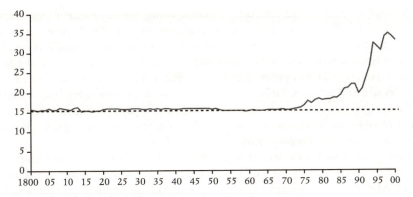

Graph 1.3. *Gold/silver commercial ratio in London, 1800–1900*

Source: Flandreau (1995*b*), yearly averages.

argued that the stability of the ratio was sufficient in itself to prove that point.[49] Others have tried to establish it by calculating the position of the gold–silver points. Gold–silver points were the limits in the margin of fluctuation around the 15.5 ratio within which transaction costs were sufficient to make arbitrage unprofitable. The difficulty in calculating those points did not produce homogeneous results. They were variable according to the period (transportation and insurance costs decreased throughout the century) and according to space (it was more expensive to collect and ship to Paris the coinage from the province of Ardèche than to collect it from the circulation in the capital itself).[50] Flandreau processed the results of the monetary enquiries held in France in 1857 and 1868 to show that silver still circulated in the province in significant quantities even after twenty years of high price of silver.[51] Curiously the best description of how bimetallism permitted the contemporary circulation of gold and silver was given by the monometallist Parieu while presiding over the international monetary conference of 1867:

The result of the variation in value of the two metals, when both are circulating, will be to drive out the more precious metal, in a certain proportion, equivalent in the change in value. Even when the relation is changed, theoretically speaking, monetary circulation is not so much affected as supposed, on account of bank deposits and private savings. There is always a certain quantity of specie in every small place, that only circulates among its inhabitants, and never gets out of a certain circle. Great masses must be operated upon to find a profit in the exchange of metals, and the change of metals takes place slowly by successive movements. For these reasons the general circulation is neither suddenly nor sensibly affected by changes in the relative value of metals, for France has always had much silver in circulation, even when that metal was largely exported.[52]

---

[49] Friedman (1990: 85–104).   [50] Oppers (1945: 61–8) reviews the results obtained.
[51] Flandreau (1995*b*: 70–1).   [52] *International Monetary Conference* (1879: 830).

Bimetallists claimed that bimetallism, compensating the fluctuation in the output of one metal with the other, subjected the price system to smaller fluctuations than a monometallic system in case of an external shock. For example, England was not able to compensate a reduction in the world output of gold with a silver circulation, and therefore required a larger deflation to reduce internal prices than France would in the same situation. The high volatility of the interest rate of the Bank of England, forced to defend its gold reserves, was frequently opposed to the placid stability of the rates of the Bank of France. Between 1844 and 1873 the Bank of England changed its rates 212 times, its French and Prussian homologues 83 and 68 times.[53]

By the mid-1860s France was the largest world holder of coined gold and silver, and its position was central for the world market of bullion. It always minted a quantity of silver substantially higher than England throughout the century, so that England needed the Paris market to purchase the silver it had to send to India but from 1850 France also minted much larger quantities of gold. France was able to intercept the largest share of the great gold wave after 1848 because the bimetallic system offered larger opportunities of arbitrage profit and bullion holders would direct their gold holdings there. Only when France was paralysed by the Prussian invasion and by the payment of the war indemnity between 1870 and 1873 could Britain temporarily overtake it (Graph 1.4 and Table 1.1).

The sheer strength of the French gold and silver market could maintain the stability of bimetallism, even if those figures do not indicate anything about the use of bar metal which was more important in the UK. It is therefore essential to understand how

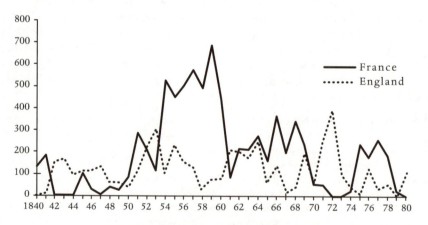

Graph 1.4. *Yearly mintage of gold (million francs)*

Source: Series calculated from Leconte (1995) and Krause *et al.* (1994).

[53] Seyd (1874: 100).

Table 1.1. *Average yearly mintage of gold and silver coins in France and the UK (1840–79) (million francs)*

	Gold		Silver	
	France	UK	France	UK
1840–9	52.7	88.0	90.6	5.1
1850–9	392.3	137.9	31.5	0.3
1860–9	252.7	132.0	20.7	0.0
1870–9	100.6	101.4	41.9	4.3
1840–79	199.6	114.8	46.2	2.4

Source: Calculated from Leconte and Krause. The figures include British gold £1 and £1/2 pieces, British silver crowns and half-crowns, French gold 5-, 10-, 20-, 50-, and 100-franc-coins, French silver 5 francs. Smaller silver coins have been ignored because they represented a smaller share of the issue and because they progressively ceased to be part of the standard of value through the 1860s.

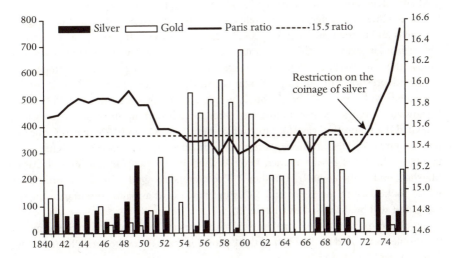

Graph 1.5. *Bimetallism in France: yearly mintage of gold and silver in relation to the interplay between the gold/silver mint ratio and the market ratio*

Source: Flandreau (1995b), for the ratio series, Leconte (1995) and Krause *et al.* for the mintage figures. Yearly figures in million francs. For the construction of the silver series only 5-franc coins have been considered.

the French market worked. Graph 1.5 shows the annual issue of gold and silver coins for the period 1840–75, associating them with the position of the market ratio in comparison to the mint ratio.

The graph shows a certain number of unexpected features. It confirms the influence of the gold/silver market ratio on which metal was minted in larger quantities. Silver prevailed before 1850, gold between 1850 and 1869, and silver succeeded for only a very limited comeback in 1873–4. The graph also presents several exceptions to the rule, as the appreciated metal, which was suppose to disappear, continued to be minted. In 1840–1, 1845, 1851–2, and 1868–9 market price for gold was higher than the mint price, but nevertheless more gold was minted than silver. The quantities of silver brought to the mint when the market price of silver was depreciated appears much lower than the amounts of gold coined when the latter metal was depreciated. The 155 million francs of silver minted in 1873, which so worried contemporaries, do not seem so overwhelming compared to the 6,505 millions of gold minted between 1850 and 1870, an average of 325 millions a year. Gold peaks were higher than silver peaks and silver disappearance from the mint was more complete than gold. There was clearly a bias in favour of gold in French bimetallism and it can help to understand why the 'gold invasion' of 1850 was accepted more readily than the 'silver invasion' of 1873.

The survival at the mint of the metal disappearing from circulation seems to point to the capacity of bimetallism to keep a mixed circulation with variable proportions of gold and silver, confirming some of Flandreau's results.

The qualities and defects of bimetallism remain controversial now as they were in the 1860s and in the following forty years. Bimetallism was destined to a contentious career, from its demise in the 1870s until the end of the century, while gold established itself as the sole standard when it was scarce and prices declined steeply, accompanying a 'great depression'. In the Anglo-Saxon world the defence of bimetallism is usually associated with Irving Fisher,[54] but the pioneer in defence of bimetallism was Wolowski, a Polish patriot naturalized French, who strenuously and successfully defended the theoretical case for bimetallism between 1865 and 1870 in economic and political circles.[55] His intuitions were then formalized by economists of higher reputation, in the 1870s by the French Léon Walras, in the 1880s by the English Alfred Marshall, and in the 1890s by I. Fisher.[56] The bimetallist–gold standard confrontation which took place in the 1860s and 1870s in France is of a major importance for this study and will be discussed in Chapter 3.

Let us turn now to the national impact of the various standards and to the origins of the problems that led to the birth of the Latin Monetary Union between France, Italy, Belgium, and Switzerland in 1865.

1.3.2. National Coinage in Some European Countries until 1865

The French monetary system in use in the 1860s had been introduced during the Consulate, in 1803, by Napoleon Bonaparte. The new *franc germinal* was the final step in a tormented search for monetary stability after the financial collapse of the *ancien régime* and the bankruptcy of the revolutionary *assignats*.[57] The new currency was conceived thanks to the introduction of the new rational and scientific units of weight,

---

[54] Oppers (1945: 52).   [55] Wolowski (1870a).
[56] See Flandreau (1995b) for an extensive study of the formal theory of bimetallism.
[57] G. Thuillier (1993).

the gram, and from the beginning its proponents had great international ambitions for it.[58] The franc germinal had been based on silver by law, but gold coins with a legal value fixed in terms of silver francs were also included in the same text.[59] France therefore had a double standard in practice, but the theory remained disputed.[60] The wording of the law was ambiguous. A large number of official reports and preparatory papers for the new currency had been written between 1790 and 1803 by Mirabeau, Condorcet, Gaudin, and others, on the basis of conflicting opinions. Both the supporters of bimetallism and those of monometallism could claim that the law was confirming their preferences. The practical character of the currency could then adapt to the events of the period. The system combined stability with flexibility and persisted until 1928.[61]

Until 1848 the French currency was mainly a silver currency, when silver was cheap and abundant. The output of silver and gold coinage was decided by market forces since any individual could bring ingots to the mint and have them coined, paying a small fee. From 1848 a steep increase in the world output of gold introduced large quantities of it in France and it gradually came almost entirely to replace silver in the French monetary circulation. The transition seemed to suit the need for larger units and for a more portable form of metallic currency. To facilitate the spread of gold circulation a new gold coin of 5 francs was introduced to replace its silver equivalent, the *écu*, the most important representative of the silver standard. The new coin became an issue between bimetallists and monometallists. It was said that the gold écu was disliked by the peasant and labouring classes for its thinness and light weight (1.6 grams). As the monetary enquiry conducted by the Bank of France in 1868 put it, the gold écu was difficult to handle and easy to lose '*pour les mains calleuses des ouvriers et des cultivateurs*'.[62] The gold écu was also subject to excessive wear and on average it became underweight after only seven years of circulation. After much acrimony and

---

[58] Honoré-Gabriel Riquetti comte de Mirabeau (1749–91), the most powerful speaker of the early years of the French Revolution, described during the debate on monetary reform what he expected from the new currency: 'Attendez de la saine doctrine monétaire un bien d'une plus grande importance, lorsque, unie à la liberté, ce double flambeau éclairera toutes les nations de leur véritable intérêts. Alors elles reconnaîtront la possibilité d'une monnaie universelle et commune, qui ne dépendra ni de la fécondité des mines, ni de l'avarice, ni du caprice de leurs possesseurs; alors la confraternité trop oubliée de l'espèce humaine s'entrelacera par une circulation plus amiable et plus active dans tous les rapports politiques et commerciaux; alors on pourra dire de la doctrine monétaire ce que l'orateur de Rome disait de la loi: 'Elle est une , elle est universelle, elle est la même pour Rome et pour Athènes; il n'y a rien à y ajouter, rien à y retrancher; elle n'a besoin d'aucun commentaire.' Puisions-nous voir cette heureuse époque! Et s'il faut un exemple, que ce soit l'empire des français qui le donne! Mais, pour y parvenir, commençons par simplifier notre régime monétaire' Mirabeau (1825: i. 384).

[59] J. Valance (1996: 144–8). The franc was defined as 5 grams of silver at 900/1000 fineness. The weight of the gold franc was calculated dividing that weight by 15.5. The franc was divided in 10 décimes and 100 centimes, but the décime fell in disuse after 1815.

[60] For the bimetallist view of the origins of the franc germinal see Wolowski (1870a).

[61] For the substitution of the franc Poincaré to the franc germinal see Valance (1996: 262–6).

[62] ABdF, 'question monétaire', IV 'Enquête sur la question monétaire anprès des directeurs des succursales de la Banque de France, 1868':21.

several official enquiries it was discontinued in 1868 in favour of a persistent circulation of silver écus.[63]

More problems appeared in the larger cities when small silver coins became scarce. The arbitragists had initially employed silver écus of five francs for their bullion speculation. When those became rare, smaller silver coins of 2, 1, 0.5, and 0.2 francs, called subsidiary or divisionary coins, started being collected and melted or exported. The reduced margin of profit on small coins made speculation on such items of dubious appeal. Their scarcity depended more on the lack of silver écus and the development of transactions than contemporaries imagined. Scarcity of silver divisionary coins brought difficulties in payment of wages and in the ordinary transactions of daily life. At times public and private institutions had to pay a premium to acquire silver subsidiary coinage.[64] Foreign coins of low fineness, together with light and worn-down coins, remained in France. Heavy coins were separated from the circulation by bullion dealers, to be melted or exported. Two commissions enquired into the matter in 1858 and 1861. The first one proposed to tax exports of silver and actively discourage speculation, but these measure were never implemented because they were 'of little efficacy and contrary to true economic principles'.[65] The second commission proposed to reduce the fineness of all silver divisionary coins in order to reduce their intrinsic value below their market value, cancelling any possibility of profit for arbitragists.[66] The new proposed fineness was 835/1000 instead of the old 900/1000, with a 7.2 per cent profit for the issuer. Since the issue of such coins produced a seignorage profit, the State would resume the monopoly of such issues. The silver écus would retain their full fineness because they were used for international transactions and should remain the unaltered representative of the silver standard. The commission rejected the idea of completing the change and adopting a gold standard, desiring to *'preserve, as much as possible, the simultaneous use of the two metals, each of which is useful in its own way'.*[67]

---

[63] The British Chancellor of the Exchequer Gladstone asked for information about the French gold écu from Chevalier in 1859. Chevalier replied 'Elles sont peu goûtées des comptables qui se plaignent de la difficulté qu'on éprouve à compter des pièces aussi menues et du public qui trouve que cela glisse entre les doigts ... C'est une idée particulière au Ministre actuel des Finances qui, sans tenir compte de la pensée des législateurs[,] veut substituer l'étalon or à l'étalon d'argent.' Magne was that minister but he was a pragmatic bimetallist in the 1860s and 1870s. Gladstone Papers, Correspondence between Gladstone and Michel Chevalier, coll. 44127, fol. 1.

[64] Commission chargée d'éxaminer la question des monnaies divisionnaires d'argent, (1862: 4–5).

[65] Quoted from the French Monetary Commission of 1869 by Willis (1901: 14). The 1858 report is Ministère des Finances, *Rapport de la Commission chargée d'étudier la question monétaire* (Paris, 1858).

[66] The replies of the Receveurs Généraux (regional governmental paymasters) to the query about the destination of the French coins depicts a complex situation, showing how France supplied silver to the whole of Europe. Belgium, Switzerland, and Piedmont imported French coinage for their own depleted silver circulation, in Algeria Arab women used coins as part of their jewellery, Turkey had absorbed the pay of the French army during the Crimean War, Lyon was exporting silver to pay for Chinese silk, Cherbourg was sending silver to England which would use it for trade with India. From the Pyrénées, silver was drained to Spain, the *départments* of the east sent their silver coinage to the German States which paid a 5 to 8% premium on French coins. Ministère des Finances (1867: 26). [67] Ibid. 16.

In the French Senate and *Corps législatif* the defenders of silver held a majority until after the end of the second Empire. Agricultural constituencies were the strongest support of the Empire and they showed a conservative attachment to silver, sealed by traditional hoards of silver écus. Parliament first opposed, then delayed, and finally weakened the reform, proposed by the Commission of 1861 and endorsed by the government. It could not block it because it only had the power to propose amendments to governmental laws and these would have to be accepted by the Council of State before they could become effective. Until 1867 the champion of silver in the Senate was Michel Chevalier. He claimed that export and melting were not the principal reasons for the scarcity of *numéraire*. Such scarcity was in fact due to the development of transactions generated by the increase of population and of income per capita and could be solved by minting an increased amount of small coins.[68] The growth of transactions was certainly an important element but every new issue of silver by the government was immediately withdrawn from circulation by speculators. Other members of Parliament feared that the integrity of the standard was threatened and that the franc was debased. The report of the 1861 Commission was published in 1862 but legislation was approved only in 1864. The government, represented by the Council of State, was unable to resist entirely the pressure of Parliament and only the smallest coins were affected by the reform, leaving untouched the unit of 1 franc and its multiples.[69] This made the reform insufficient as the new issue of small coins could not possibly meet all the needs of divisionary coinage. The Ministry of Finance was then looking for another way of pushing through the change. An international agreement to solve the problem in conjunction with France's neighbours became the best way of imposing the reform on a reluctant Parliament, just as an international treaty had defeated the protectionists in 1860. The premises were laid for the Convention of 23 December 1865 and the birth of the Latin Monetary Union.

The Napoleonic domination over Italy in 1796–1815 had included the introduction of the franc, either as a French franc in the annexed territories of north-western and central Italy, as an Italian lira in north-eastern Italy, or as a Neapolitan lira in southern Italy.[70] Only Piedmont (Kingdom of Sardinia) and Parma retained the French currency after the Treaty of Vienna. The unification of Italy took place in 1859–61 under Piedmontese leadership, and in 1862 Italy unified its monetary system, extending to the

---

[68] Annales du Sénat et du Corps législatif, 'Séances du Sénat Impérial du 13 juin 1861', IV, (1862: 233–6).

[69] The governmental project is: Projet de loi n. 233, Corps Législatif, session 1864, annèxe au procès verbal de la séance du 6 avril 1864, 'Projet de loi relatif à la fabrication de nouvelles pièces d'argent de 2 francs et au dessous, précédé du decret de présentation et de l'exposé des motifs.' The result of the negotiation is: Pièce n. 310, annèxe au procès-verbal de la séance du 28 avril 1864, Rapport fait au nom de la commission avec l'approbation du Conseil d'Etat.

[70] Napoleon I had began the monetary unification of Europe in 1808. The French franc was introduced between 1796 and 1814 in Piedmont, Tuscany, and Rome, all annexed by France, while the Principality of Lucca and Piombino was ruled by Elisa Baciocchi, sister of Napoleon. The Italian lira was introduced in Lombardy, Venetia, Emilia, and the Marche, merged into a Kingdom of Italy, headed by Napoleon I. In the kingdom of Naples, Murat, former marshal of Napoleon, introduced the lira as well but later and with less success. Sardinia and Sicily, defended by the British fleet, retained their old monarchs and currency. Leconte (1995: 143 and 177–83).

new State the Piedmontese coinage. France was the principal commercial partner of the new State and its closest political ally.[71]

Pre-unitary systems were bimetallic in the Kingdom of Sardinia, in Parma, and in the Pontifical State, while the silver standard was established in Lombardo-Veneto, in Tuscany, in Modena, and in the Kingdom of the Two Sicilies. In 1862 the adoption of the Piedmontese lira as the Italian coinage was not in dispute, but the continuation of Piedmontese bimetallism was not unanimously accepted. Italian politicians amused themselves composing Latin verses associating preference for bimetallism with personal duplicity.[72] As in France, the high price of silver was increasing the circulation of gold, whereas silver coins tended to disappear, even if the isolation of many areas, the weakness of the financial system and the scarcity of gold outside major centres tempered substantially the problem. Italy adopted the conclusions of the French Commission of 1861 without hesitation. The écu of 5 lire was preserved at full fineness to be employed for international trade and to represent the silver standard. It would, however, be minted only on request from private individuals and not on state initiative. Divisionary silver coins would keep their previous weight, but their fineness was reduced to the 835/1000 suggested by the French Commission. That reduction would offset increases in the market value of silver over the mint price and small coins would remain available for ordinary payments.

Discussing the new proposed law in 1862, the Italian Finance Minister Pepoli declared that, although he himself preferred a strict gold standard, the choice between bimetallism and monometallism 'is a question that, because of its nature, has to be solved by a mutual agreement between the principal European nations.'[73] Italy was fully aware of its marginal position in the European financial system and followed French leadership, adopting bimetallism and French units of account.

After the approval of the new law in 1862, Italy withdrew 282 different types of coins circulating in its territories.[74] Some of the new Italian coinage crossed the frontier to replace its French equivalents with a higher fineness, thanks to the strong commercial ties of Piedmont with Savoy and the Rhône region.

Switzerland had been traditionally a loose confederation, where every *canton* preserved its monetary sovereignty. Several different systems coexisted until political unification was achieved in 1848, followed by a monetary unification in 1850. The north-east of the Confederation preferred the south German gulden of its German and Austrian commercial partners, while south-western Switzerland pushed to adopt the

---

[71] For the discussion of Italian monetary unification see De Mattia (1959).

[72] In 1873 the Italian Prime Minister Minghetti recalled the joke which circulated in Parliament in 1862 against the bimetallist Minister Agostino Cordova: 'Dupplicis adsertor cur nam fis Cordoba nummi?/ Nil Mirum. Dupplex cor tibi, lingua, fides.' Marco Minghetti to Luigi Luzzati, 3 Aug. 1873, in Minghetti (1978: i, 9–10).   [73] De Cecco (1991: 79).

[74] De Mattia (1959: 13 and 16). The south used ducats, oncie, tarì, grana, and tornesi. The Pontifical State employed zecchini, scudi, baiocchi, and quattrini. Tuscany employed rusponi, fiorini, paoli, and quattrini. The change of governments, revolutions, and several monetary reforms had multiplied the complexity of the various systems.

franc of their Franco-Piedmontese neighbours. As Vanthoor writes, 'the French franc with its status of an international currency won the day.'[75]

Switzerland however decided to opt for silver monometallism and to reserve entirely to the State the right to issue metallic currency. It was a choice in favour of a public and controlled form of money, but such a choice was not enforceable. French silver immediately invaded Switzerland because of the insufficient issue of national coins, constituting up to 80 per cent of the circulation. French gold coins followed soon after, becoming the main form of money despite the efforts of the Swiss government. In 1860 the Swiss law was adapted to the existing situation and French gold received legal tender status.[76] To ensure that the new status of gold did not displace all of the silver divisionary coinage, the authorities reduced the fineness of silver coins of less than 5 francs to 800/1000, a reduction of 11.1 per cent in their intrinsic silver content which would discourage melting down Swiss coins. The measure indeed discouraged melting down but did not keep these coins in Switzerland. They were exported to France and exchanged with their French equivalent with the same nominal value but a higher content in silver. 'Good' French silver was melted and transformed into bullion which commanded a premium, replaced in the French circulation with 'bad' imported Swiss silver. The Swiss unhappily saw their new national currency disappear, replaced again by French gold pieces. Furthermore the Bank of France and the French governmental cashiers refused from April 1864 to accept any Swiss coin, in order to block their circulation in France and defeat speculation.[77] This disturbed frontier trade and made life difficult for travellers between the two countries. The situation was proving to Switzerland that a small country could not determine alone its monetary policy, and had to harmonize it with that of its neighbours.

Belgian monetary history in the nineteenth century is similar to that of Switzerland. Belgium obtained its independence from Holland in 1831 and introduced a new national coinage identical to that of neighbouring France in 1832. Dutch gold continued to circulate according to a fixed tariff. Until 1847 Belgium operated a bimetallic system dominated by silver, without national issues of gold and with a large circulation of French silver and a smaller one of French and Dutch gold.

In 1847, when gold started to flow into France, Belgium decided to issue gold coins. The large flow of gold of declining value pouring from all sources scared the Belgian Parliament, fearful of inflation. The recent coinage law was repealed in 1849 and all gold circulation, national and foreign, was progressively withdrawn from 1850.[78] Belgium attempted thus to establish a silver monometallic system like Switzerland and like Switzerland it failed, for the same reasons. The new Belgian silver with high market value was collected by speculators and replaced with French gold (with lower market value) or with French worn and underweight silver. The profit came from the fact that Belgian coins had a bullion value higher than light silver coins or than new gold coins. As long as different types of money existed, speculation would trade and

---

[75] Vanthoor (1996: 13). [76] Willis (1901: 26–32).
[77] French Minister of Foreign Affairs Drouyn de Lhuys to the French Embassies in Bern, Brussels, and Florence, 1 Feb. 1865 (ABdF, I, 238). [78] Willis (1901: 18–24).

replace the expensive coin with the cheap one, earning the difference between the two. The progressive worsening of the silver coinage disturbed trade and was coupled with the difficulty of dealing with a gold coinage without legal status to settle debts. The reserves of the Bank of Belgium were then subjected to massive requests for any metal made more valuable by the fluctuation of the gold/silver market ratio. The Parliament of Brussels did not take action until 1865, confident in a French action that alone could change the course of monetary events in Belgium.

The United Kingdom had adopted formally a gold standard in 1821, alone in Europe at that time.[79] It was the legal sanction for a situation that had developed through the eighteenth century, after the mint had fixed in 1717 an acquisition price favouring the coinage of gold and discouraging silver.[80] A general consensus was established in England about the superiority of the gold standard. A theatre play of the 1930s mentioned 'through the whole of the period here depicted [the Victorian age] . . . the golden sovereign stood as a symbol of the abounding prosperity over which that other and greater Golden Sovereign [Queen Victoria] presided.'[81]

The units used in Great Britain were pounds, shillings, and pence (£s. d.).[82] While sovereigns (£1) and half-sovereigns (£1/2) were gold coins, with unlimited legal tender, the legal tender was limited to two sovereigns per transaction for silver coins and to one shilling for bronze coins. Silver coins were token coins with a seignorage reducing their intrinsic value under their legal value.[83]

In 1865 the silver circulation was insufficient and composed of coins minted between 1689 and 1865, old and worn, usually under the minimum weight legally tolerated.[84] This situation was also extended on a minor scale to gold coins. No provision for the withdrawal of light coins existed in England until the 1890s. The unfortunate holder of light sovereigns would see them cut into two when chance forced him to make payments to the Bank of England or other public institutions. The coin would become bullion again and he was then forced to bear all expenses of assaying, melting, and coining anew. Obviously everybody avoided carefully having their light sovereigns cut, as the law required, in order not to bear the related costs. The British economist W. S. Jevons calculated that a third of the gold coinage of the UK was under the legal weight in 1868.[85] The difference with France and other bimetallist countries was that the arbitragists' perpetual activity in melting and recoining, kept large coins in circulation for much shorter periods, providing always large new issues.

After the Congress of Vienna Germany was still divided into different States with different monetary systems. Silver was usually the only standard, except in Bremen

---

[79] For the adoption of the gold standard in England see Clapham (1944: ii. 50–76) and Kindleberger (1993: 65). Portugal adopted a gold standard in the 1850s, having a large internal circulation of English gold sovereigns (J. Reis 1996: 170).   [80] Feavearyear (1963: 153–7).

[81] Housman (1937: 11).

[82] The system was duodecimal (divided in 2, 3, 4, 6, 12, or 20 subunits): the pound was divided into 4 crowns, florins, 20 shillings, 60 groats, 240 pennies, and 960 farthings (Decimal Coinage Commission 1859).

[83] Seyd (1868: 290–3).   [84] Josset (1962).   [85] Jevons (1868: 426–64).

which was on a gold standard. Some German States had a limited issue of trade gold coins, like the krone and Frederick d'or in Prussia, the ducat in Bavaria, and the gold thaler in Saxony. Different weight and titles gave different value to coins bearing the same name, such as the thalers of Hanover and Prussia.

The first moves towards a unified currency for Germany took place in the frame-work of the German Free Trade Union (*Zollverein*); but did not concern all the German States. In 1837, the Treaty of Munich fixed a new common value of the currency for the south German States, the 'Süddeutsche Währung'. 24.5 gulden (also called florins) were equal to the common German unit of account, the Cologne mark of fine silver. A north German monetary agreement fixed the Prussian thaler as the reference coin for the area at 14 to 1 to the Cologne mark. In order to facilitate the payment of duties in either Prussian thalers or southern florins, a 4 to 7 exchange rate was fixed between the two currencies at the monetary convention held in Dresden in 1838 by the States adhering to the *Zollverein*. The strategy followed by German negotiators was to establish the parities between regional coins and then fix the parities between the reference coins. The only common coin that was supposed to be minted by all the member States was the '*Vereinsmünze* 2 thalers = 3.5 gulden', a very large silver coin, worth 7.42 francs. But the coin was too big for practical use, and was nicknamed the 'champagne thaler',[86] as it had the same value as a bottle of champagne. Most States minted it very irregularly and it never acquired a large circulation. The strong parti-cularism of the separate German States and their desire to keep all the attributes as well as the substance of independent power, precluded the adoption of a Saxon proposal to create a common coinage called the mark, valued at one-third of the Prussian thaler.[87]

In 1854 the Austrians proposed the establishment of a common gold standard with the German States, in the expectation that the massive discoveries of California and Australia would lead to a depreciation of gold. This depreciation would help Austria to resume convertibility of its banknotes into gold and silver that had been suspended with the 1848 revolutions. The German states however, fearing the weakening of their coinage (silver was expected at that point to appreciate), did not accept.[88]

In 1857 the Austrians obtained the creation of a *Münzverein*, or German–Austrian union of coinage with an exchange rate of 1 north German thaler = 1.5 Austrian florin = 1.75 south German florins.[89] To obtain simple exchange rates, thalers and south German florins had to be reduced by 0.22 per cent and the Austrian florin by 5.22 per cent. The new coins had no legal tender status outside of their geographic area of reference, but a new 1 thaler = 1.75 gulden was minted and given equal legal tender status to the thalers previously minted by member States, giving a dominant position to the Prussian thaler under the name of *Vereinsthaler*. Divisional coins were much more tightly regulated than in the Dresden convention of 1838, with limits established on the amounts that should circulate (the Latin Monetary union was to adopt the same

---

[86] Kindleberger (1963: 121).

[87] Henderson (1939: 138–41) reports the proposal because it was the solution finally adopted in 1871. The balance of power between the different German States was not yet favourable enough to Prussia for that kind of victory.   [88] Holtfrerich (1989: 222–6).

[89] Vanthoor (1996: 28–30).

rules in 1865). The crown was established as the new international gold coin of the union, but fixed parities with silver coins were forbidden (therefore not allowing Gresham's Law to have the effect of driving silver coins out of circulation during periods of falling gold prices) as was the independent coinage of gold coins by member States.

Austria resumed silver convertibility of its banknotes in 1858 but dropped out again during the war with Italy and France in 1859. The return to inconvertibility meant in fact the end of the Austrian participation in the currency agreement. After the defeat in 1866, Austria opted to abandon legally the *Münzverein* in order to pursue a monetary alliance with France, negotiated in the summer of 1867. Prussia had obtained a privileged position for its coinage, which was freely circulating in all Germany. Its banknotes were also spreading, after the creation of the Bank of Prussia.[90] However, the German monetary union was not developing naturally into a single currency, because the south German States defended the prerogatives and the symbols of their independent power. Florins continued to be minted in the south side by side with the thalers. This situation opened some space to the French proposal to create a universal or European coinage, which was intended to solve internal monetary conflicts.

---

[90] According to Tilly, coins represented 86% of the estimated stock of currency in Prussia in 1835 (defined as the sum of coins, government paper money, and banknotes); this proportion had dwindled to 64% in 1855 and 52% in 1865. R. Tilly (1967).

2

The Formation of the Latin Monetary Union and the International Monetary Conference of 1867

The name 'Latin Monetary Union' (LMU), universally attached to the Monetary Convention of 1865, was not attributed by the negotiators of the treaty. According to Parieu it was introduced by the British press (*The Times* and *The Globe*) in 1866 to stress the southern European character of the Union and its possible expansion to countries such as Spain, but not to Great Britain which was part of the Anglo-Saxon world.[1] Ultimately the name LMU became popular because it corresponded to the geographical distribution of its members (France, Italy, Belgium, and Switzerland), and was an equivalent of the German Monetary Union (*Münzverein*) and of the later Scandinavian Monetary Union of 1872. This chapter will briefly reconstruct the formation of the LMU in 1865, describing its main characters. The interpretations of the Union will be discussed by looking at the different aims of the various departments of the French government during the diplomatic negotiations preparing the formation of the LMU. The French Finance Ministry aimed at a limited economic agreement with three neighbours to facilitate trade, while the Ministry of Foreign Affairs had more ambitious views with wider political consequences, embracing the whole of Europe. A larger plan for a European or Universal monetary union was progressively drafted from 1865 onwards, bearing the strong personal mark of Félix Esquirou de Parieu, vice-president of the Council of State and economist with a high reputation. The implementation of these projects required an international mobilization in favour of monetary union and suggested further political developments towards a federal Europe. The International Monetary Conference of Paris in 1867 was the stage where Parieu's plan received unanimous recognition and prepared the way for the adhesion of several countries to the French project of monetary union.

2.1. THE ORIGINS OF THE LATIN MONETARY UNION, FROM AN ANSWER TO GOLD INVASION TO A MODEL FOR INTERNATIONAL GOLD COINAGE

Between 1850 and 1860, France, Belgium, Switzerland, and Piedmont had an unofficial common currency. The individual attempts to protect national divisionary coinage

---

[1] Parieu (1866*b*: 7). For the full content of *The Times* article see Chapter 5, Sect. 1. Despite several attempts it has not been possible to find the original article by *The Globe*.

from the field of application of the laws of bimetallic arbitrage, which implied the disappearance of monetary silver, had progressively broken the homogeneity of coinage between 1860 and 1864. The four countries had kept a full-fineness silver écu, as representative of the silver standard, but divisionary coins had been debased to a lower fineness only in some countries, in different degrees. Therefore coins with an identical nominal value, total weight, and shape, had a different intrinsic value, because of changing proportions of alloy. At the end of 1864, Belgium made some informal and oral enquiries to France about a possible common solution to the problem. The French Finance Minister Achille Fould activated the negotiation in January 1865. Fould recalled to the French Minister of Foreign Affairs the undeniable advantages for trade offered by the 'Communauté monétaire' which had existed informally with Belgium, Switzerland, and Italy. Summarizing all the monetary events of the last years, the disruptive effect of bullion trade and the restriction to foreign coin circulation in France Fould wrote

These restrictive measures create trouble in international relations and their disappearance would be in the interest of all governments. I thought it would be possible to achieve such a result through diplomatic means, regulating in a uniform manner the issue and circulation of subsidiary coins in all countries concerned by way of a special convention.[2]

On 23 December 1865, after a full year of negotiations and a long conference, a Monetary Convention was signed in Paris between France, Italy, Belgium, and Switzerland. The conference of 1865 had worked out a Monetary Union between the four countries, with a single bimetallic coinage, despite the strong Belgian plea in favour of the introduction of the gold standard, weakly supported by Switzerland and Italy but opposed by France.[3] Paper money was not included in the convention. A uniform divisionary coinage with a common reduced fineness was established and was granted reciprocal admission into governmental coffers. The silver écus and the gold coinage remained unchanged in each country, as they were already identical in everything except in name and circulated across national boundaries without real obstacles. Each State remained responsible for its national issue but a new provision was introduced; the free circulation of coins was legalized with a fixed exchange rate of 1 to 1 between French, Belgian, and Swiss francs and Italian lire. All public administrations were given the legal obligation to accept the coins of the four States at par. Individuals would be induced to follow by imitation, but maintained the legal right to refuse foreign coins if they wished.

---

[2] French Finance Minister Fould to the French Minister of Foreign Affairs Drouyn de Lhuys, 19 January 1865, (AMAE, ADC 602–2, fol. 2).

[3] The Belgian delegates deployed all their dialectical skills in the first sitting, with long speeches to demonstrate the common need for a gold standard. Switzerland supported this effort but recognized that its own position depended on the French and Italian decisions. The Italian delegate had received no instructions on the matter and could not express an opinion. A short statement in favour of the gold standard was issued by the Italian delegate at the second sitting, after the arrival of further instructions, but it was more the expression of an academic preference than a national interest put forward (Ministère des Affaires Étrangères, 1865, ABdF, 'La question Monétaire', I, 275 and 307).

The gold coinage and the silver écus (5 francs) had therefore 900/1000 of fineness, while silver subsidiary coinage had a reduced fineness of 835/1000 and a legal price higher than its market value to prevent hoarding and remelting. The mintage of subsidiary coinage was therefore profitable for the states of the LMU, which had reserved to themselves the right of issue, while gold coins and silver écus were minted at the request of private agents, except in Switzerland. The limit to the issue of divisionary coinage was set at 6 francs per inhabitant, together with rules for the return of each others' coinage and the exchange of information. The Belgian delegate Krelinger asked for a centralized issue of the divisionary coinage, distributed by the union according to recognized need, but the Conference declined to accept the proposal.[4] The compromise permitted Switzerland to withdraw its lower fineness silver within thirteen years, at the end of their normal cycle of existence.[5] Italy accepted to reduce its total authorized issue from 150 million to 141 million, 100 million of which had already been minted. France and Belgium undertook to remint their entire divisionary coinage. The monetary system agreed upon at the Conference is described in Table 2.1.

The system thus created exercised a strong power of attraction for medium and small countries, like Austria, Spain, Sweden, Greece, and Romania, for its rational organization, for the quality of the coinage, and for the extent of its circulation. The bimetallic nature of this monetary union could be a worry only for larger or richer

Table 2.1. *Coinage of the Monetary Convention of 23 December 1865 (the Latin Monetary Union)*

	Total standard weight (grams)	Standard fineness (000s)	Pure gold or silver content (grams)	Gold par with the pound (in £s)
Gold				
100 francs	32.2581	900	29.0323	3.9649
50 francs	16.1290	900	14.5161	1.9824
20 francs	6.4516	900	5.8064	0.7930
10 francs	3.2258	900	2.9032	0.3965
5 francs	1.6129	900	1.4516	0.1982
Silver				
5 francs	25.0000	900	22.5000	No gold parity
2 francs	10.0000	835	8.3500	No gold parity
1 franc	5.0000	835	4.1750	No gold parity
50 centimes	2.5000	835	2.0875	No gold parity
20 centimes	1.0000	835	0.8350	No gold parity

Source: Ministère des Affaires Étrangères, 'Conférence monétaire' and various numismatic works.

[4] Ministère des Affaires Étrangères (1865: 275).
[5] The Swiss divisionary coinage had been minted in 1860 and was supposed to be reminted in 1880 anyway, to secure it from excessive wear and tear.

countries who preferred and could afford a gold monometallic coinage. For countries like Austria or Italy the aspiration to adopt a gold standard at that time was only wishful thinking.

2.2. INTERPRETATION OF THE NATURE OF THE LATIN MONETARY UNION

There are two alternative interpretations of the Latin Monetary Union. The traditional view has considered the LMU mainly a monetary extension of the foreign policy of Napoleon III, stressing the French expansionist policy and its hegemonic ambitions.[6] More recently it has been stressed instead that an economic interpretation is more suitable than a political one. The LMU constituted a natural monetary zone, deriving from the extension of free trade and from commercial and financial integration between neighbouring countries.[7] I will argue that the two conflicting interpretations of the nature and objective of the Latin Monetary Union can be combined, taking into account the duality of the French institutional arrangements. Monetary diplomacy in France in the nineteenth century was not the reserved field of any single governmental department. It was a monetary question for which the Finance Ministry was responsible, in which the Bank of France had a prominent interest and role, and the Council of State maintained a sort of right of regard. But international monetary arrangements were also a diplomatic issue where the role of the Ministry of Foreign Affairs could not be questioned. The Ministry of Finance favoured a limited monetary integration but defended with determination the maintenance of bimetallism. The Bank of France took a similar position, but was definitely less keen on monetary unification than the Treasury. Meanwhile the Ministry of Foreign Affairs was extremely interested in monetary unification and the Council of State advised it on the necessary link between unification and the establishment of a gold standard in France. The emphasis placed on the imperialistic aspect of the French policy or on its purely economic and financial logic, depends on the type of source employed by the historian, and its relation to the institution that dominated each specific institutional occasion. The day-to-day working of the LMU bears the imprint of the Finance Ministry, while the international Conferences and Congresses were under the predominant influence of the Quai d'Orsay. I will discuss the articulation of these positions, their nature and development in a subsequent chapter about France. What is important to note now is that these four centres of power determined the oscillating and indecisive policy of France after 1865. The first differences in philosophy will appear in this chapter.

2.2.1. The Political Interpretation of the LMU

It is useful to clarify some of the most misleading interpretations. In 1898 Russell interpreted the process of monetary unification, which he only studied through the international conferences, as a machiavellian plan to dominate Europe by economic

---

[6] Willis (1901).   [7] Flandreau, 'Was the Latin Monetary Union a Franc Zone?', in Reis (1995).

means. The plan was supposedly conceived by Napoleon III himself and reflected the main purpose of the last years of the Empire. It would explain both the French retreat from Mexico in 1866 and the non-intervention in the Austro-Prussian War of the same year.[8] Not a single element in the French archives confirmed this theory. This theory is misleading because Napoleon never got directly involved in the process, as Félix Esquirou de Parieu, the real driving force behind the plan, testified: 'Napoleon III, to whom all decisions were submitted according to the governmental practice of the time, showed some benevolence for the general idea [of monetary unification] without entering into the details of implementation.'[9]

The strong opposition that the plan of European monetary unification encountered in official circles, opposition that delayed any decision until it was too late, would not have been possible had Napoleon been committed to it. The Finance Ministry could not possibly block a major project of Napoleon III. Nevertheless most studies that followed Russell's book echoed this initial preconception down to the recent works by de Oliveira and Droulers.[10]

In January 1865, Fould wanted a treaty restricted to divisionary coins, defining their common fineness and the limits to their issue in each country member of the diplomatic convention, according to the needs of internal transactions. He did not include other forms of money such as bronze coins, silver écus, gold coins, paper money, cheques, or bills of exchange: 'the aim I propose, namely that all subsidiary coins minted in neighbouring countries should be admitted to circulate in France and vice versa'[11] Furthermore he did not show any intention of enlarging this limited arrangement into a European system. Fould defended bimetallism, as international agreements should not modify the French monetary constitution, 'sans rien changer au principe de l'unité monétaire tel qu'il est défini par la loi du 7 germinal an XI'.[12]

Managing the preliminary contacts with Belgium, Switzerland, and Italy, the French Foreign Minister Drouyn de Lhuys extended the purpose of the conference which would create the LMU. Fould was forced to enlarge the scope in his replies to Drouyn in May 1865:

It is evident that there would be undeniable advantages in creating in Europe a large monetary circulation, attached to a single system and identical in its real and nominal value. Such circulation would assimilate those of other countries before long, and we could foresee the time in which, under the influence of a common monetary regime, payments in cash would be protected from the variable conditions of exchange rates.[13]

A conference was summoned in Paris in November 1865. The French delegation was led by Félix Esquirou de Parieu, vice-president of the Council of State, a prolific author on monetary issues and the strongest supporter of the gold standard in France.

---

[8] Russell (1898). The first hundred pages of the book contain countless references to a phantasmagorical centralized direction of the process by Napoleon. [9] Parieu (1871: 148).

[10] Droulers (1990); Oliveira (1991–2). Droulers's book is a numismatic study and de Oliveira's research summarizes the discussion of the time exclusively from a French perspective without analysing the wider implications of the process.

[11] Fould to Drouyn de Lhuys, 19 January 1865 (AMAE, ADC 602–2, fol. 3).

[12] Ibid. fol. 2.   [13] Ibid. fol. 6.

Parieu recalled the 'pan-European' perspective in his speech opening the conference. The delegates 'can limit the field of their discussions to the regime of subsidiary coinage of the four countries, or extend it and consider a larger and more distant perspective, that of a uniform monetary circulation for the whole of Europe'[14] The concept was reiterated as a conclusive remark of the conference by the representative of the Quai d'Orsay, E. Herbet[15], who had been silent until then. Herbet declared that although not formally discussed, the spirit of European monetary unification had permitted the reciprocal concessions offered by the States present at the conference. 'Would it then not be appropriate that, without deviating from its mission, the conference let it be known formally that it wishes to see the monetary union, today restricted to four countries, become the seed of a larger and more prolific union between all civilized states'[16] Parieu greeted Herbet's words, with the support of the Belgian delegate:

Thanks to the solidarity already existing between economic interests, and given the benefits already reaped, every nation increasingly understands the necessity to eliminate one after the other all the obstacles met within international relations. One of the most expensive and disturbing obstacles is the effect of monetary diversity which multiplies the variations of the exchange rate. The idea of a monetary systems unification therefore progresses every day.[17]

The victory of the line defended by Parieu and the Ministry of Foreign Affairs was sealed with the introduction in the Convention of a clause (no. 12) allowing any country to join the Union, provided it had accepted its monetary system and the obligations connected to it. When Fould was informed by Drouyn de Lhuys of the results of the conference, which was hosted by the Quai d'Orsay, he could only ratify this shift in the goals of the Union: 'Just as Your Excellency I believe that the opportunity of joining [the LMU], offered to all countries, will lead in the near future to a new extension of the monetary union sealed by the act of 23 December last, to the great advantage of international relations and the French political influence in the world.'[18] The accent was quite different from improving 'the commercial transactions of the four neighbouring countries' indicated by Fould six months earlier.

The more restrictive wording of the aims of the monetary convention, as written by the Commission des Monnaies, the executive monetary branch of the Finance Ministry, had been eliminated. 'The governments of Belgium, France, Italy, and Switzerland, [were] prompted by a common desire to establish a more complete harmony between their monetary legislation, *particularly for what concerns the necessary precautions against exports of silver subsidiary coins.*'[19] The part of the preamble here italicized was cancelled. The efforts of the Ministry of Foreign Affairs and of Parieu to provide the basis for a European or Universal monetary unification based on the Franc left a serious contradiction in the Union. The States had not formed the Union to

---

[14] Ministère des Affaires Étrangères (1865: 269).

[15] Édouard Herbet was a Councillor of State, Director of the Consulates and commercial affairs at the Ministry of Foreign Affairs.   [16] Ministère des Affaires Étrangères (1865: 351).

[17] Ibid. 352–4.   [18] Fould to Drouyn de Lhuys, 27 Jan. 1866 (AMAE, ADC 603–2, fol. 10).

[19] Avant projet de traité d'union monétaire [manuscript without date, Nov.–Dec. 1865](AMdP, K2-15: 1).

enhance international circulation of national silver coins, they wanted instead to preserve them from being replaced by foreign coins with a lower intrinsic value. When the Convention increased the interchange of coins, every State felt threatened by the flow of foreign coins invading their internal circulation, especially because the movements were more speculative than commercial. Italian and Belgian coins, which entered France and Switzerland after 1865 in large quantities, were to be a source of tension for the remainder of the century.[20]

An exclusively political explanation of the Latin Monetary Union is sustainable only if the policy of the French government could be identified exclusively with the policy of the Foreign Affairs Ministry, which is impossible.

2.2.2. *The Economic Explanation of the Latin Monetary Union*

Flandreau has provided the most complete case for an interpretation of the LMU as a natural completion of the economic integration between neighbouring countries, following a substantial decrease in trade barriers. We have seen in Chapter 1 how the situation of Europe in the 1860s was approaching a 'single market'. Italy, Belgium, and Switzerland were France's most important commercial partners in the 1860s, after the United Kingdom. The intraregional trade in the LMU was around 30 per cent of the total trade of those countries.[21] Even more important seems to have been the role of financial transfers. The French Finance Ministry was ambivalent about a larger European monetary unification but certainly supported an extended franc zone that could challenge the role of London as the main financial centre of the world. The French desire to elevate Paris to that position has been a recurrent dream of the last two centuries, but the dream was never as close to realization as it was in 1865. France was exporting capital at a growing pace at the time. Levy Leboyer's reconstruction of French capital exports shows an increase to 424 millions francs per year in 1850–9, to 763 million francs in 1860–9, reduced to 180 million francs in 1870–9, after the military and financial rout of the Franco-Prussian war.[22] During its peak in the mid-1860s France's capital exports were briefly twice as great as Britain's.

A *mémoire* written by the Finance Ministry in May 1865 for the French chief minister Rouher, during the negotiations to form the LMU, stressed the economic benefits of capital exports but also highlighted the impossibility of separating them from their political implications:

The financial centre of London has held for a long time the monopoly over foreign loans. But when England was lending . . . it was pushed to do so by more considerable advantages than the

---

[20] This does not mean necessarily that other States did not initially share the French desire to expand the Union as far as possible. The Swiss government for example declared 'Nous considérons l'unification des monnaies d'argent des quatre pays non pas seulement comme une condition et un complément nécessaire de la communauté de leur système monétaire, mais comme un premier jalon vers la réalisation d'une monnaie universelle'; Méssage du Conseil Fédéral à la Haute Assemblé Fédérale concernant la convention monétaire entre la Belgique, la France l'Italie et la Suisse (2 Feb. 1866), extracted from the *Feuille Fédérale Suisse*, 24 Feb. 1866. See ABdF, 'Question Monétaire', I, 786.

[21] Flandreau (1994: 74).   [22] Levy Leboyer (1977: 80 and 128).

high interests offered to its capital. On the one side it secured for itself an enormous annual tribute... at the same time it created its worldwide commercial dominance. The nations it financed became clients of its industry and some, such as Portugal, passed entirely under its commercial sovereignty.[23]

But France could not leave such an advantageous position unchallenged and successful efforts were made to update the financial structure. Large credit institutions had been formed during the second Empire (Crédit Foncier, Crédit Mobilier, Crédit Lyonnais, and Société Générale), and important financial operations and international treaties had enlarged French financial capacity and influence. As the French official reported to Rouher:

France now shares together with England the honour of providing capital for the industry of the world and it reaps the profits therefrom. These results already begin to show... Is it thinkable furthermore that the 435 million [francs of government debt], which Italy is partially going to float on the French market, will be exported in coined metal? Nothing would be more inaccurate. The amounts collected in France will be used to pay the balance of supplies of weapons, ammunitions, materials for public works, and we will retain with one hand as suppliers what we will give with the other as lenders.[24]

It would be difficult to find a statement more clear than this about the combined advantages of financial hegemony.

The list of state loans annexed to the *mémoire* and summarized in Table 2.2 showed the high proportion of government debt issued in Paris at the time. The comparative study of discount rates in England and France shows how by the mid-1860s the Parisian market offered a lower and less unstable rate than London, reversing the British advantage of the 1840s and the equilibrated position of the 1850s.

In 1861–5 the Parisian market had lent to governments almost as much as the London market, even if the French government had secured for itself a substantial part of that amount (447 million, approx. 21 per cent of the total), while the British government did not borrow. Under the chancellorship of Gladstone (1859–66) Britain ran a budget surplus and reduced public debt.

When the LMU was planned and the report was prepared, the governments of Italy, Belgium, and Spain, all of them future members of or candidates for the LMU, were preparing to float a total of 635 million francs of public debt on the capital market. The common currency would offer more guarantees of repayment to the lender and grant the borrower easier access to the capital market and better conditions.

A brief examination of the interest rates of the Bank of England and the Bank of France also highlights the improved French position as a favourable market for international lending in 1865 (see Graph 2.1 and Graph 2.2).

[23] 'Des emprunts d'État' 19 May 1865 from the Direction du Mouvement Général des Fonds au Ministère des Finances à Son Excellence M. Rouher, Ministre d'État, Archives nationales AN, Archives privées Rouher, 45AP, carton 20, dossier finances et impôts, 2.

[24] *Des emprunts d'Etat*, AN, Papiers Rouher, 45AP-20, 6–7.

Table 2.2. *Lending to governments (January 1861–June 1865) (amounts effectively paid by the lender in millions of French francs)*

	Loans floated in Paris		Loans floated in London		Total of governmental loans floated in Europe	
	No. of	value issues	No. of	value issues	No. of	value issues
1861	3	664	7	216	12	966
1862	0	0	10	830	11	1019
1863	4	654	9	249	18	1099
1864	4	546	8	419	20	1839
1865 (6 months)	3	242	8	413	12	668
Total	14	2106	42	2127	73	5591

Source: The figures are calculated from the 73 operations described in 'Emprunts d'État. Mémoire du 19 mai 1865 du Ministère des Finances'. The figure for French issues is an upper limit, because three Parisian operations were floated in combination with another market. In total the real French figure must have been some 100–150 million lower.

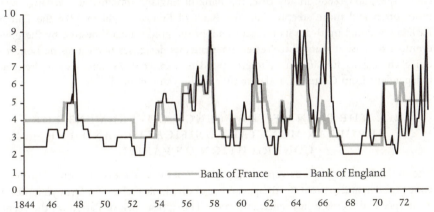

Graph 2.1. *Discount rates in France and England (1844–73) from the English Bank Charter Act to the establishment of limping bimetallism in France*

Source: Seyd (1874).

In the 1840s the cost of borrowing was systematically lower in the UK, except for a short time during the crisis of 1847, which forced a provisional suspension of the British Bank Act. In the 1850s, both the level and the variability of the British discount rate increased. France started to shadow more frequently the British rate, and largely shared the British crisis of 1857. Nevertheless the rate differential was reduced and then cancelled. In the 1860s, after a brief 2.5 per cent rate in England, the French rate became independent from the British rate and, from 1863, lower. The change was so clear that during the 1866 crisis caused by the bankruptcy of the largest English discount house, Overend Gurney of London, the British rate was up to 6.5 per cent

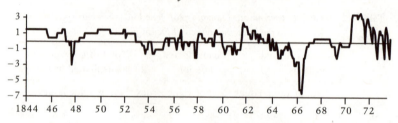

Graph 2.2. *Discount rate differential between England and France*

Source: Seyd (1874).

higher than the French rate. The British tendency towards very low rates in periods of abundant money (2 per cent in 1868), re-established an equilibrium, but only the Franco-Prussian War in 1870 restored the higher convenience of the London market for borrowers. A striking result of the comparison between interest rates is the growing instability, the longer periods of high rates before financial crisis in London (1847, 1857, and 1866). In any case, the Bank of England modified its exchange rate more often and more steeply than the Bank of France.[25] Still in 1874 the Dutch Parliament could motivate its refusal to adopt the gold standard desired by the government because it wanted to 'rester indépendants des crises financières de Londres qui a changé 25 fois le taux d'intérêt pendant l'année 1873' and also to 'remain independent from Germany, today master of the value of gold'.[26]

2.3. THE PLAN OF THE FRENCH GOVERNMENT FOR EUROPEAN MONETARY UNIFICATION AND THE CONTRIBUTION OF PARIEU

The initial French plan was very simple. For Fould it was meant to solve a frontier zone problem and prevent the disappearance of divisionary silver, for Drouyn it meant an unspecified increase in French influence. The appearance of Parieu on the scene provided France with a well-thought-out programme, complemented by a technical knowledge of monetary issues. Parieu was appointed by Fould to be part of the French delegation in July 1865 and was agreed by the Quai d'Orsay to preside over the conference.[27] Although Parieu received his instructions from the Finance Ministry, he quickly forged a special relationship with the Ministry of Foreign Affairs and effectively formed an alliance with it, based on the pursuit of a European Monetary Unification on a gold standard.

[25] The instability of the Bank rate later attracted also the criticism of Professor Foxwell and of the historian of the Bank Andreades. 'These constant and large fluctuations have very injurious effects on trade' (Andreades, 1909: 316).

[26] The French Embassy in Holland to French Foreign Affairs Minister, 7 March 1874 (AMdP, K2–27, 10).

[27] Fould to Drouyn de Lhuys, 5 July 1865 (AMAE, ADC 602–2, fol. 10).

Portrait of the Vice-President of the Council of State, Felix Esquirou de Parieu, by an anonymous colleague
Source: Bibliothèque et archives du Conseil d'Etat.

2.3.1. Who was Parieu?

Given the pivotal role of Parieu in this book and his almost complete absence from the modern historical and economic literature, a short biographical sketch must be provided. Félix Esquirou de Parieu (1815–93) was born in a family of judiciary nobility in Cantal (Auvergne).[28] Parieu became a lawyer and soon entered into competition with another local lawyer, Eugène Rouher, future chief minister of Napoleon III, who would overshadow all his future career, in Parliament, in the Government, and in the Council of State. The French historian Schnerb described in these terms the personal differences between the two men in the 1840s:

Esquirou de Parieu conquers the high esteem of the small world of Riom by different talents [in comparison to Rouher]: a deep knowledge of the law, a versatile dialectic, and distinguished manners. One is all vigour, the other all intellect; Rouher had the tribune's vigour, Parieu was prudent; the latter derived from the aristocracy through his behaviour and spirit, the former remained a man of the people.[29]

After an unsuccessful attempt to enter Parliament as a liberal monarchist, Parieu was elected as a conservative republican in 1848. He rapidly became one of the leading economic and financial specialists of the Assembly, learning English and studying the

---

[28] Vaporeau (1893: 1209–10)   [29] Schnerb (1949: 12).

British income tax. In 1848 Parieu spoke against a proposed constitutional aberration: a President of the Republic wrapped in the immense prestige of universal suffrage but without powers. 'Beware of giving the presidency oak roots and reed foliage.'[30] He opposed the direct popular election of the president, a system which shortly after brought to power the Prince-President Bonaparte. Nevertheless he was called to the government by Louis Napoleon Bonaparte, at the age of 34, together with Fould, Rouher, and Magne. Parieu was Minister of Education between 1849 and 1851, and passed the Loi Falloux, which would favour the influence of the Church in education for several generations. After the *coup d'état* by Bonaparte, he became president of the financial section (1852–5) and then vice-president (1855–70) of the Council of State. The Council of State was the supreme administrative tribunal of the country, but Napoleon III amplified its powers a few days after the *coup d'état*. The Council became responsible for drafting all the regulatory decrees required for the implementation of laws, following the personal indications of the Emperor. The Council contributed to all governmental decisions and dealt with Parliament, with the power to refuse any parliamentary amendment it considered inappropriate. It was the central executive body of the Empire, between the government and Parliament.

Parieu's career stalled after 1855 in his position of vice-president, because his political liberalism differed from the authoritarian policy of the Empire, and his support for Papal rights clashed with Napoleon's policy in Italy. 'At the Council of State M. de Parieu has often been a sort of leader of the opposition, if one can define in such a way a minority which is not excessively deferential and submitted to the influence of the government and the court'.[31] In the late 1850s Parieu led the Catholic and liberal tendency in the Council of State, opposing with Chevalier the repressive measures against political opponents in 1858 and the war in Italy in 1859.[32] He greatly contributed to the Council's policy of diluting a large part of Napoleon's 'utopian' initiatives. A republican MP remarked: 'Whenever a bill bearing the stamp of the Emperor's cabinet reached the great cause list, it was whittled down [by the Council of State], cut, amputated, and arranged in a way that it was doomed to rejection.' Napoleon himself complained that the Council 'always had some legislation to quote against me'.[33] If Napoleon could be considered an authoritarian reformer, then Parieu represented the Council's democratic (or parliamentary) conservatism. In addition to political differences, Parieu's personal struggle against Rouher prevented the return of the former to the cabinet. In 1856 Rouher opposed Parieu's candidacy as Minister of Education. In 1867, presenting the list of prospective interior ministers to Napoleon, Rouher said about Parieu that he 'does not have, to any degree, the qualities of character needed for such a position'.[34] When Rouher finally resigned from the direction of the government in 1869, victim of the new liberal phase of the Empire and the renewed strength of Parliament, a friend reported that 'Parieu is radiant; the fall of Rouher causes him such a joy that he is unable to hide it'.[35]

---

[30] Durif (1868: 19).   [31] Ibid. 47.   [32] Wright (1972: 93–94).   [33] Plessis (1985a: 39).
[34] Poulet-Malassis (1873: 78).   [35] Schnerb (1949: 120 and 261).

Between 1852 and 1865, Parieu could employ his spare time in studying taxation and finance, writing extensively in favour of the income tax and becoming the most skilled proponent of the introduction of the gold standard in France.[36] He was offered the position of Governor of the Bank of France in 1857 and 1863, but refused.[37]

With the progressive liberalization of the regime in the 1860s Parieu could find more space for his campaign in favour of the gold standard. He acquired the undisputed status of the ablest specialist of the French administration on monetary problems, while his internal political marginalization came to an end. Fostering both his good causes and his own political career, Parieu directed all the French monetary commissions of the period 1865–70, the international monetary conferences of 1865 and 1867 and became Minister-President of the Council of State in January 1870, with the first liberal government of the Empire. Even after the fall of the Empire and the loss of his cabinet seat, Parieu was still one of the French delegates at the conferences of the Latin Monetary Union. In 1876, freshly elected to the Senate for the Orleanist party, his passionate speeches in favour of the gold standard were extremely influential. Parieu could afford to impose the policy of the gold party on the powerful bimetallist Finance Minister Léon Say. In a private letter, the senator recalled the minister to the orthodox views of his grandfather, the classical economist Jean Baptiste Say.[38] By the end of the year, silver was proscribed from the French Mints.

In 1865 Parieu was an experienced politician and a skilled economist, with diplomatic capacities and an appropriate knowledge of foreign languages. He was the right man in the right place for monetary diplomacy. He later recalled: 'It was therefore with a satisfaction mixed with some surprise that I saw myself . . . , both as a semi-official publicist and an official representative, in charge of the mission to participate in the development of a plan to bring closer the main monetary systems established in the world.'[39] Parieu displayed a large and unexpected activity in favour of monetary unification, defined 'semi-official apostolate' by Durif, publishing more than thirty long articles on the subject over twenty years, and carrying on a large correspondence, helped by the Ministry of Foreign Affairs. 'It is even possible to declare that, as humanitarian philosopher, he has undertaken for the peace of nations what weapons of precision have done for battles, since a thinker defined monetary unification as "the chassepot of peace."'[40] Parieu was one of the few ministers who resisted the war with Prussia in July 1870.

---

[36] Parieu (1856).

[37] According to Plessis, Parieu wanted to combine the Governorship with the Vice-Presidency of the Council of State (Plessis 1984: 309). For Durif, Parieu refused because he did not want to be neutralized and lose his independence, being directly under the Finance Ministers Rouher, Fould, or Magne (Durif 1868: 45).

[38] 'Arrêter les émissions de bons de monnaie [en argent] et assurer que toute convention monétaire sera désormais soumise au Parlement me parait être le minimum de ce que vous devriez nous garantir sans délai et vous me permettrez d'insister auprès du Ministre des Finances et des Affaires Étrangères mais encore auprès du petit fils de J. B. Say dans ce sens urgent' (Parieu to Finance Minister Léon Say, Paris 15 March 1876, AMdP, Union Latine, Carton (K2–29, 1–2).   [39] Parieu (1868a: 38).

[40] Durif (1868: 63). The Chassepot was a new rifle, recently adopted by the French army and highly considered.

2.3.2. *Parieu's Plan for European Monetary Unification*

Parieu had campaigned since 1858 for the reduction of the fineness of silver coins as a solution for the scarcity of subsidiary coinage. His position had not been accepted by the monetary commission of 1858 but was accepted by that of 1861. The parliamentary opposition in 1864 had led only to a partial implementation of these ideas. Parieu was called to complete this task with an international arrangement, but he elaborated a larger plan, in three articles contributed to the *Journal des économistes* and the *Revue contemporaine* in the eighteen months following the signing of the LMU convention. Parieu advanced the general lines of the policy pursued in the following years:

1. to extend the franc zone as much as possible on the basis of the LMU agreements. The first candidates in his mind were Greece, Spain, and the Pontifical State. Possible nationalistic objections to the adoption of the franc were skilfully anticipated maintaining in each country the national appearance and denomination of the coins. The francs were called lire in Italy, pesetas in Spain, drachme in Greece, or lei in Romania. They were associated, according to the case, to the portraits of King Vittorio Emanuele II or Leopold II, Pope Pius IX or the personification of the Swiss Confederation.

2. to negotiate a simple fixed exchange rate, 'simplified equations', with the other European nations and the USA. Those agreements, similar to those of the German *Münzverein*, should include the United Kingdom, Austria, and the German States.

3. to achieve the first two points through a progressive installation of a gold standard. 'Our 5 francs gold coin, transformed into a *dollar*, and *the écu of the two worlds* would probably be the *coin* of *universal* metallic circulation one day.'[41] In 1865 and 1866 Parieu could still sense the popularity of silver in some countries, like Austria and the German States and was ready to offer a silver parity to these countries. He rapidly realized that with the decline in the price of silver from 1866, gold was becoming the favourite form of money even in the German-speaking countries. Therefore, from the beginning of 1867 he was pushing for an international monetary unification based exclusively on gold[42], but he had in mind something more than the International Gold Standard which would emerge from the ashes of his efforts as a golden phoenix. The persistence of two blocs with different standards would have meant a fluctuating exchange rate between the two blocs. The fluctuation would depend on the variation of the gold/silver market ratio. The fixed exchange rate would resist only if there was a strong bimetallist core holding the gold/silver market ratio fixed at the official rate. Parieu did not believe this to be possible and wanted a single, not a dual monetary

---

[41] Parieu (1865: 14).   [42] Parieu (1867:).

[43] 'Si l'on voulait réaliser en termes précis l'uniformité monétaire sur la base des faits déjà prépondérants dans le monde, on pourrait imaginer que diverses nations contractantes adopteraient pour l'unité d'or commune la pièce d'or de 5 fr., de 10 fr. ou de 20 fr., et, par exemple, notamment la pièce de 10 francs ... qu'on appellerait, je vais le supposer, si l'on espérait y amener l'Europe entière, et sauf la tierce opposition attendue de la part de l'Amérique, ou encore de tout autre nom délibéré d'avance' (Parieu 1867: 350).

area. Furthermore, the persistence of silver standards, gold standards, and double standards cohabiting in a monetary union would only facilitate the operations of international speculation in shifting gold and silver coins from one country to the other. This would deprive governments of their right to keep a chosen metal in circulation and would increase monetary instability.

The Universal coinage would result in fixed exchange rates on a 1-to-1 basis between France and an extended LMU from Athens to Helsinki, with a 2.5-to-1 rate with Austria-Hungary and south Germany, 3.75 to 1 with northern Germany, 5 to 1 with the USA, and 25 to 1 with the UK. The existing gold and silver parities of the various countries with France, compared to the proposed gold parities of the Monetary Union are reconstructed in Table 2.3. The national identity of coins was preserved to facilitate the operation, even if it meant a looser monetary union.

The system was built to rotate around a new common piece, shared by the four major States: the 25-franc gold coin. It was meant to be equalized with a modified British gold sovereign, a modified 5-dollar piece, and a new 10 Austrian florins. To accommodate Prussia, a 15-franc–4 thaler-piece was also conceived. The unit of account could either be 5, 10 or 25 francs, renamed écus, ducats or crowns. Parieu's preference was to use a 10 francs unit, which he would name the 'Europe'.[43] Concerning the competing claim of the pound to become the international money, Parieu conceded that the pound was more ancient and for a long time more abundant than the franc, but he could also point to the much higher issue of francs and lire in Europe; 7 billion francs against 90–5 million pounds (2 billion francs).[44] France would introduce in its own circulation the gold 25-franc-1-sovereign to accommodate England if the latter accepted the equalization, reducing by less than 1 per cent of the weight of the pound. The 25-franc coin became in France the most visible symbol of European monetary unification and was opposed by many because of that.[45]

Due to the lack of common institutions, the French Ministry of Foreign Affairs became in fact the coordinating institution of the Union. It hosted all the conferences, received communications from all the members, summarized the various opinions, dealt with candidates and new members, negotiated the controversial passages, and then despatched circular replies to the whole Union. This preponderance of France was tolerable for medium-small countries, but it was an obstacle for the accession of England, the USA, and Germany. A new and more formal institutional arrangement would have been necessary, had any of those countries entered the Union.

The elements of the plan did not emerge from Parieu's imagination without a context. They were the product of the discussions of statistical and monetary congresses over a decade, and were progressively enriched with new details coming from various international contributions. The theoretical discussion of the advantages of a monetary union are analysed in Chapter 3.

---

[44] Parieu, (1865: 12–13).
[45] The Governor of the Bank of France, Rouland, was particularly clear about it, see Ch IV, sect 2.

Money and Politics

Table 2.3. Current and proposed exchange rates in 1865

Nation/Exchange rate	Exchange rate in 1865		Proposed gold parity of the Monetary Union		
	Gold parity (francs)	Silver parity (francs)	Francs	Dollars	Pounds
France, Italy, Belgium, and Switzerland (franc–lira), Pontif. State (lira)	1.0000	1.0000	1.00	0.20	0.04
Spain (real)	0.2584	0.2629	1.00	0.20	0.04
Greece (drachma)	—	0.9000	1.00	0.20	0.04
Sweden (riksdaler)	Trade coin	1.4167	1.00	0.20	0.04
Norway (speciedaler)	Trade coin	5.6175	1.00	0.20	0.04
Denmark (rigsdaler)	Trade coin	2.8090	1.00	0.20	0.04
Netherlands (gulder)	—	2.1000	1.00	0.20	0.04
Romania (lei)	No national	coinage	1.00	0.20	0.04
Portugal (milreis)	5.5995	Token coinage	1.00	0.20	0.04
Austria (gulden)	Trade coin	2.4693	2.50	0.50	0.10
South German (gulden)	Trade coin	2.1166	2.50	0.50	0.10
North German (thaler)	Trade coin	3.7040	3.75	0.75	0.15
USA (dollar)	5.1824	5.0207	5.00	1.00	0.20
United Kingdom (pound)	25.2218	Token coinage	25.00	5.00	1.00

Source: Parieu's articles and diplomatic correspondence, Leconte (1995) and Krause et al. (1994). Countries on a gold standard have a gold parity with the franc and a token silver coinage. Countries on a silver standard have a silver parity with the franc and often a gold trade token, with no fixed relationship with the rest of national coinage. Bimetallist countries have both silver and gold parity, but the parities correspond in francs only if the legal ratio corresponds to the French 15.5, which was not the case with the USA.

Parieu described the advantages coming from a monetary union based on a gold standard as he saw them:

With the introduction of the gold standard at the appropriate moment, the internal *status quo* is established and secured for us with an abundant and convenient metallic circulation and with the possibility of an agreement with the greatest commercial power of Europe, England, and also with Germany ... [we would also achieve] the gradual destruction in the economic order of one of these frequent barriers which used to divide the nations, and whose fall would facilitate their *mutual moral conquest*, serving as a prelude to the pacific federations of the future.[46]

The name 'Latin Monetary Union', adopted by the British newspapers to stress the alien character of the Union in relation to England, was not accepted by Parieu.

[46] Parieu (1865: 15).

Reading the otherwise witty article of the *Globe*, which passionately asserts the rights of diversity between nations, I came to think that, contrary to those who plan to unite France and Britain through a tunnel under the water, there may be some rare persons among our neighbours who would invent the Channel if it did not exist.[47]

Parieu opted for 'Union Européenne Occidentale', but was willing to modify the name in case of a US application for membership.[48] His reference to the pacific federations of the future was more understandable when he published in 1870 his *Principles of Political Science* in which he called for a 'European Union' in a federalist frame. There would be a 'European Commission' appointed by governments and a 'European Parliament'.[49]

In order to achieve the desirable rapprochement between the institutions of the various nations, why not create a European commission which convenes periodically, initially appointed by the governments and maybe later by the representatives of the people of Europe, a commission which would owe its authority to science, to the fairness of its decisions, and to the openness of its decisional process. It would profit from the example of the eclectic and conciliatory intelligence provided by the experience of the harmonious federal spirit of Germany.[50]

Parieu argued that nations get closer to each other not only when they conclude peace but also when they associate each other with permanent treaties, constituting a sort of enlarged nationality. Theorizing the steps leading to the creation of a union, Parieu expected first a military alliance against a common threat, followed by regular consultations of the allied States, crossed subsidies from a common fund, and then the formation of an institution to arbitrate conflicts. Further on, some financial resources would be permanently allocated to the federation, like the customs tariffs in the *Zollverein*. A common diplomatic representation would appear, followed by a common system of transportation and communication. A city (permanent or rotating) hosting the government would then be attached to the federation. The Union would be cemented by economic and commercial treaties, concerning free trade, maritime transportation, the protection of literary, artistic, and industrial property, the implementation of foreign tribunals' decisions, a common commercial legislation, and finally common currencies, weights, and measures.

The multiplication of such treaties would produce in the long run a sort of general federation of the nations which would consent to it . . . How many sources of concord and mutual affection would not emerge from this coming together? For nations to fight each other, it is necessary that they consider themselves more different than they are these days. The similitude of institutions would help men to recognize the identity of their nature and the fraternity of their races, just as the identity of hats and clothes often highlights the similarity between individuals.[51]

---

[47] Parieu (1866b: 11). The article of *The Globe*, referred to by Parieu, has not been traced.

[48] Ibid. 7.

[49] Parieu (1875b: 336–57). The first edition was published early in 1870, when Parieu was a cabinet minister.

[50] Ibid. 355. Parieu's reference to Germany was written in 1870 before the Franco-Prussian War and was referred to the creation of the *Zollverein* and *Münzverein* by an association of free States. The reference was not to the Bismarckian approach to unification.   [51] Ibid. 347 and 353.

The idea of European federalism already circulated in France in 1848 when Parieu entered Parliament and during the second Empire. In 1849 Victor Hugo had launched the formula of the United States of Europe which he reiterated in 1869.[52] A liberal tradition had built up from the pacifist leanings of Cobden and his combined action for disarmament and free trade.[53] Émile de Girardin, Bastiat, and Michel Chevalier were some of those who expressed some form or another of favour for a European congress for disarmament or even for the United States of Europe.[54] After the Austro-Prussian War in 1866 and renewed tension between France and Prussia, the threat of the return to war on a scale not seen in the Continent since 1815, gave new strength to the idea of a European federation against militarism and imperialism. In France Chevalier had hoped to prevent the Austro-Prussian War with the proposal of a permanent European congress and a sort of international tribunal to defend public law and prevent armed conflicts between European States. He indicated the federal structure of the USA as a model to follow but not without ambiguities.[55] In Dresden the publicist Eduard Loewenthal created in 1867 the League for the European Union. At the same time the 'Congress of the Friends of Peace' met in Geneva under the presidency of Garibaldi and created a left-leaning 'league for peace and liberty' together with a weekly paper called the *United States of Europe*.[56] Even Napoleon III in a speech on 14 February 1867 talked about 'the union of European States in a single confederation', but arguably he did not think of more than a congress of ambassadors and never followed up on this idea.[57] In this situation Parieu's views do not appear to be completely isolated, but they were more articulate than those of his contemporaries and he was apparently the first French minister to express a federalist point of view.

Parieu was a European federalist, but his larger ideas were not part of the plan of the French government. The collaboration between the ministry and the vice-president of the Council of State was therefore not without ambiguities. Parieu was a curious mixture of political realism and utopian aspirations, and he made monetary unification with a gold standard the struggle of his life.

2.4. THE 1867 PARIS INTERNATIONAL MONETARY CONFERENCE AND THE IDENTIFICATION OF UNIFICATION WITH THE GOLD STANDARD

After the ratification of the Monetary Convention by the Parliaments of the four member States in the summer of 1866, the French started a diplomatic offensive. The Ministry of Foreign Affairs on 5 December 1866 sent a circular letter to all its diplomatic agents in the European States, Russia, the Ottoman Empire, and the USA. Each contacted nation was offered either to join the LMU, adopting a coinage on the French

---

[52] Renouvin (1949: 3).   [53] Ibid. 8.   [54] Duroselle (1965: 217–8).
[55] Chevalier (1866b: 758–85). Michel Chevalier had also supported in the 1830s the earlier Sainsimonian and Fourierist view of European federalism.   [56] Renouvin (1949: 11).   [57] Ibid. 22.

model, or to participate in an international monetary conference, in order to discuss new arrangements for monetary unification and 'to facilitate the establishment of a uniform monetary circulation between all civilised states'.[58] Of France's partners in the LMU, Italy offered its help and contacted Portugal and England, supporting the French move. The Swiss government accepted the effort to widen LMU, but no intervention to that effect is documented. The Belgian prime minister Frère Orban was more concerned with a formal introduction of the gold standard and asked France to abandon bimetallism before attempting an otherwise doomed enlargement of the LMU.[59]

The replies were all favourable to an international conference, and all major States announced their participation. Many secondary States accepted the invitation to join the LMU immediately (the Pontifical State, Greece, and Romania), and we shall see in Chapter 4 what happened to these candidates. Two larger powers, Austria and Spain, were favourable and proposed their candidature after the 1867 Conference. The US Secretary of State William H. Seward and the Secretary of the Treasury Hugh McCulloch announced in February 1867 that the USA 'both in its executive and legislative department, had repeatedly manifested its interest in the question of international unification of monetary standards' and was ready to look for an agreement, provided some changes were accepted.[60] Portugal formally declared that it could not join the LMU because the latter had a bimetallic standard and the former a gold standard, but informally stated to the French Ambassador that the final word of the Portuguese was tied to the British decision.[61] The German States were dependent on the Prussian decision as they were all tied to a silver standard by the *Munzverein* treaty until 1878. Bismarck expressed to the French Ambassador Benedetti the regret of Prussia for not being able to reduce the obstacles separating Germany and France from a monetary union. He claimed that his hands were tied by Parliament:

The monetary question is one of those included in the programme of debates of the North German Confederation. To discuss it in advance with a foreign government would mean to predetermine future debates. Once we will know the outcome of such debates, then it will be the appropriate moment to discuss the weakening of the obstacles which still prevent a monetary union between France and the North German Confederation.[62]

The most important reply was the last one to arrive and certainly the most clear-cut refusal. The British Foreign Secretary, the Conservative Lord Stanley, declined the offer to join the Convention, which would require to 'alter very materially the existing monetary system of this country'.[63] Stanley stated that 'Hitherto Parliament and the

---

[58] Ministère des Affaires Etrangères, (1867: 425). The replies to the French offer are published on 426–36.
[59] Frère Orban to the French Minister of Foreign Affairs, Moustier, 23 December 1866, (AMAE, ADC 603–2, fol. 47). Frère Orban was Liberal Finance Minister (1847, 1848–52, 1860–68) and Prime Minister of Belgium (1868–70 and 1878–84), maintaining a consistent stance in favour of the gold standard.
[60] Russell (1898: 39–40).
[61] Moustier to Fould, 16 February 1867 (ABdF, 'La Question Monétaire', I, 543).
[62] Ministère des Affaires Étrangères (1867: 434).
[63] Royal Commission on International Coinage (1868: 159).

public of this country have shown themselves unwilling to sanction any change in the monetary system to which all classes are accustomed, and which has grown up under a long course of legislation.'[64] The British delegates at the international conference would therefore participate in discussing and informing both the other countries about the British experience and the British government about foreign opinions. They would be entitled neither to express an official opinion on behalf of the government nor 'to commit Her Majesty's government, directly or indirectly to any conclusion at which the foreign members of the Conference may arrive'.[65] The reply was in no way surprising and Parieu intended to employ it as an instrument of pressure against a bimetallist French Parliament.[66] The French Consul in Newcastle summarized a few years later the simplistic view of the British reluctance towards European monetary unification. He claimed that the lack of opportunities for profit in the process and a general popular conservatism explained the lack of interest in Britain.[67]

Monetary unification will not be adopted by England for a long time, *if ever it will be*. Those are, according to my opinion, the two main reasons against it, which are not publicly admitted: 1. An Englishman will always think to himself, 'What personal profit can I obtain from this change? In fact, what can I gain if I go through the trouble of campaigning for it and succeed.' Since in this case the answer is negative, his decision will soon be taken and he will say: '*I will not lose my time on this issue*'. (It is the answer given to me by Mr James Hall, whose energy is well known.) 2. For the great mass of the public, a sentiment of vanity and pride (however your Excellency will decide to call it) will keep it out of a movement changing its habits for those of someone else. Concerning the lower classes, one must have lived in this country in order to realize how stubborn it is in refusing regardless of everything whatever causes 'trouble' [in English in the text], and especially what comes from abroad.

The role of London as the main financial centre of the world and the British superiority in manufacturing were of course much more serious reasons for the British refusal to see its coinage adapted to that of France. It would have been difficult to imagine England accepting a position in monetary questions subordinate to its historical enemy. Speculation on such matters always constitutes a dangerous exercise, but one might wonder whether the British refusal might not have suited the French Foreign Ministry, preserving an undisputed French hegemony over what looked like a substantially enlarged Latin Monetary Union. If the goal of monetary unification was financial supremacy over Britain, then the competition between the two countries

---

[64] Ibid. 161.   [65] Ibid. 160–1.

[66] Commenting Frère-Orban's remarks on the gold standard, Parieu had written to the Quai d'Orsay: 'Je ne serais pas surpris qu'en effet des objections à un accord avec nous fussent émises par le gouvernement anglais sur le fondement du double étalon admis par notre législation monétaire. Si l'objection est produite et qu'il fallut la lever pour obtenir avec le gouvernement britannique un concordat monétaire, la situation du gouvernement français pour obtenir cette modification du Corps Législatif serait plus avantageuse qu'au cas où pareille demande seroît formée en dehors de toute perspective d'accord international' Parieu to the French Minister of Foreign Affairs, 12 January 1867 (ADC 600, fol. 16).

[67] French Consulate in Newcastle to the French Minister of Foreign Affairs Lavalette, 14 July 1869 (AMAE, ADC 604-2, fols. 164–65). The French Consul underlined part of the text.

could turn more easily to France's advantage if Britain was not in the European coinage union. From Parieu's point of view, by contrast, the British reluctance was far more serious and precluded monetary unification from achieving anything more than a partial and reversible success within a 'small Europe'.

The International Exhibition of Paris in 1867 became the occasion to bring together all the representatives of the nations contacted.[68] The Imperial government wished the Exhibition to display all the finest products of the French industry and arts, to astonish all the international visitors. Paris was visited during the Exhibition by the Emperors of Austria and Russia, the Kings of Prussia, Bavaria, Belgium, Sweden, Denmark, Greece, Spain, and Portugal, the Prince of Wales, the Sultan of the Sublime Porte, the Khedive of Egypt, and the brothers of the Emperor of Japan.

The most controversial question for the French hosts of the International Monetary Conference remained the standard. The Ministry of Foreign Affairs communicated the various replies to the new Finance Minister Rouher, pleading for the adoption of the principle of the gold standard in view of the International Conference, the first of a series of unsuccessful attempts: 'take soon a decision on the question of the standards, not to force the French delegates at the international conference to decline any discussion on this fundamental point.'[69] Moustier asked for a French commission to deal with the subject and Rouher courteously obliged him a few weeks later appointing a commission headed by Parieu. The Commission included a large number of bimetallists forming a majority hostile to change.[70] A vote taken on 10 April defeated the gold standard by 5 to 3. The members of the Council of State (Parieu and Lavelaye) and former members of it (Chevalier) voted for gold, while the representatives of the Treasury (its General Director and the President of the Commission des Monnaies), of the banks (the Bank of France and Wolowski for the Crédit Foncier), and of the Corps législatif, voted against.

Regardless of the recent deliberation of the French monetary Commission, the International Monetary Conference of Paris, which worked from 17 June to 6 July 1867 is remembered for its unexpected unanimous choice in favour of the gold standard. Indeed the Conference is often considered exclusively as a step towards the defeat of bimetallism and the establishment of the International Gold Standard worldwide, because no further steps towards monetary unification were thought to have been achieved.[71]

How was this deliberation in favour of gold possible, considering that only two out of the twenty countries present had a gold standard? The Conference took place at the Quai d'Orsay. The French delegation was dominated by the Council of State (Parieu and Lavelaye) and the Ministry of Foreign Affairs (Moustier and Herbet), while the

---

[68] The countries were: Austria, Baden, Bavaria, Belgium, Denmark, France, Great Britain, Greece, Italy, Netherlands, Portugal, Prussia, Russia, Spain, Sweden, and Norway, Switzerland, Turkey, USA, and Würtenberg. 'Proceedings of the International Monetary Conference of 1867', in *International Monetary Conference*, 805–6.

[69] Moustier to Rouher, 16 February 1867 (ABdF, 'La Question Monétaire', I, 547–48).

[70] Ministère des Finances (1867).   [71] See e.g. Kindleberger (1993: 68–70).

Treasury had only a representative (Dutilleul).[72] This permitted the French delegation to completely pass under silence the impossibility of convincing the French Parliament, the Finance Ministry, and the Bank of France to accept a gold standard. The Treasury representative intervened just once in the discussions to express and record his regret at the Conference's decision to give legal currency to the coins of the States united in a monetary convention.[73] The French Treasury preferred to declare those coins receivable in the public banks and effectively enforced its preference in the following years. Nevertheless it did not dare to sail against the strong winds of the Conference and declare for bimetallism. Following a suggestion by Moustier, Napoleon III appointed his cousin Prince Napoleon to preside over the second part of the Conference, in order to show his satisfaction for the results achieved by the delegates.[74] Only in the last sitting did Prince Napoleon recognize some difficulties in forcing the gold standard down the throat of French Parliament, adding that the unanimous opinion of the Conference together with already concluded diplomatic arrangements in favour of gold would help to mollify the French Parliament.[75] Indeed, the 1864 refusal by the French Parliament to demonetize divisionary silver had been overturned thanks to the ratification of the LMU Treaty in 1866, but the intangibility of

---

[72] The representative of the Treasury (the bimetallist general director of the ministry) had been appointed only two days before the conference, to replace the president of the Commission des Monnaies, Jules Pelouze, who died shortly before. Parieu had attempted to replace Pelouze with a further Councillor of State presumably a further supporter of the gold standard but Rouher refused. Rouher also declined to dictate a common line to the whole delegation indicating the bimetallist conclusions of previous monetary commissions. 'Quant aux instructions dont vous désirez que les délégués soient préalablement munis, j'ai lieu de penser que les discussions des précédentes Commissions sur des questions de même nature et auxquelles la plupart des commissaires français ont pris part suffiront pour assurer entre eux l'entente et l'unité de vues qui me semblent, comme à Votre Excellence, désirable d'établir.' Rouher to Moustier, 15 June 1867, AMAE, ADC 600 bis–2, fol. 195.

[73] 'Proceedings of the International Monetary Conference of 1867', in *International Monetary Conference*, 866.

[74] The draft of the letter sent by Moustier is still at the Quai d'Orsay: 'Sire, Votre majesté a daigné me faire connaître le haut intérêt qu'Elle porte à la question de l'uniformité monétaire objet des travaux d'une Commission Internationale qui, sur l'initiative du Gouv.t de l'Empereur, est en ce moment réunie au M.tère des Aff.res Etr.eres et dans laquelle tous les États Européens, ainsi que les États-Unis d'Amérique, se trouvent représentés. Déjà la Conférence a discuté divers points importants de ce problème, sous la direction de M. de Parieu, Vice-Président du Conseil d'État, qui a conduit les délibérations avec une compétence et une habileté dont je me plais à rendre témoignage à Votre Majesté. Mais j'ai pensé que l'Empereur ne saurait donner une marque plus éclatante de sa sollicitude pour le succès de la Conférence qu'en confiant la présidence de la Commission internationale à S.A.R.le Mgr. le Prince Napoléon. Si Votre Majesté daignait approuver ce choix, il serait accueilli comme un honneur, par les membres de la Conférence, et ne manquerait pas de faciliter une solution qui viendrait se rattacher si heureusement à l'ensemble des réformes économiques accomplies sous le règne de l'Empereur.' (French Foreign Affairs Minister Moustier to Napoleon III, 21 June 1867, AMAE 600 bis–2, fols. 228–9).

[75] Prince Napoleon argued that 'the adoption of the gold standard, exclusively, would require a modification of the French law, and, of course, the subject would have to be laid before the legislature. The double standard had many staunch advocates in France, who would certainly oppose the withdrawal of silver from circulation. At least it would be very useful for the government to rely on diplomatic arrangements, already concluded, showing that the principle of the single standard is admitted both in theory and in practice by many other states, when the subject is laid before the legislature' ('Proceedings of the International Monetary Conference of 1867', in *International Monetary Conference* 867–8.

the double standard had been confirmed by the *Corps législatif* on that occasion. Part of the French institutional structure tried the same technique again, to eliminate the last representative of the silver standard, the silver écu. This time, however, it attempted to do so without the support of the Finance Ministry. In the short term this strategy did not work, but a few years later the international preference for gold indirectly forced France to drop bimetallism. The conversion of Germany to gold in 1871–3, heavily influenced by the French debate of 1867–70, forced France to suspend the mintage of silver, not to receive enormous amounts of demonetized German silver. The collapse of the price of silver, caused by the French decision, made any resumption of bimetallism impossible in the following years.[76]

The 1867 Conference brought together political and scientific representatives of twenty countries, diplomats, presidents of national banks (Norway, Sweden, Belgium), and Masters of the Mint (England, Bavaria, Belgium, and Switzerland). The conference was effectively presided over by Parieu, although at times he left the Chair to the Foreign Affairs Minister Moustier and in the last part of the Conference to the cousin of the Emperor, Prince Napoleon. The strongest supporters of Parieu's views on monetary unification and gold, during the conference and in the following years, were the Swiss Feer-Herzog, the Austrian de Hock, and the Swedish Wallenberg.[77] The American delegate Ruggles was another outspoken supporter of unification and offered a complete recoinage of the American circulation based on a 5-franc dollar. The operation was facilitated by the absence of coins in the USA, replaced since 1862 because of the Civil War by the greenbacks, an inconvertible and depreciated paper currency. The conditions he posed included the adoption by France of a gold standard and the issue of a 25-franc gold coin, which would suit Britain, Spain, and Austria as well. Thanks to Parieu, Ruggles had personally met Napoleon III before the Conference, to convince him of the importance of the issue. He was gratified with four specimens of the 25-franc–5-dollar gold coin and by the official declaration of Prince Napoleon: 'If France consulted only her individual convenience, she would see no

---

[76] For a more complete description of the unexpected death of French bimetallism, See Flandreau (1995*b*).

[77] Feer-Herzog was a member of the Swiss Federal Council and its main monetary authority. He wrote extensively in favour of the gold standard and monetary unification and attended on behalf of Switzerland the LMU conferences from 1865 to 1878. De Hock was a Austrian privy councillor and member of the upper house. He had just presided in 1867 over an Austrian commission which decided to introduce the gold standard in Austria, and negotiated with Parieu a Franco-Austrian monetary agreement immediately after the conclusion of the International Conference. Oscar Wallenberg was a member of the Swedish diet, director of the Bank of Stockholm and head of the Wallenberg financial empire. The Wallenbergs often served as Sweden's diplomats and Oscar personally convinced the King of Sweden to create a carolin-10-franc gold coin in 1868. Wallenberg represented until the 1880s the pro-French financial interests in Sweden, obtaining the legal circulation of the Swedish carolin in France in 1872, but failing in the same year to convince the Scandinavian Monetary Union to adopt the franc as its currency. Wallenberg was also unsuccessful in 1878 and 1885 in his attempts to obtain legal circulation in France for the Finnish gold coinage, identical to its French counterpart. For Wallenberg's role in the creation of the Scandinavian Monetary Union in 1872 see AMAE, ADC 616–2. For later interventions, see the letter from Wallemberg to the French Finance Minister, 14 September 1885, AMdP, K2 35.

necessity for issuing the new coin; but for the purpose of facilitating the work of unification, she would make the concession requested by the United States.'[78] Ruggles did not however indicate clearly how much the American position depended upon the British decisions. In Washington the equalization of 5 dollars with the pound had been a long-time priority, and several attempts in that direction had failed in the 1850s.[79] Before taking action the USA wanted to wait for England and England did not move, so that the US overtures came to nothing.[80] Ruggles did not have political backing sufficient to support his views, unlike Parieu, Feer Herzog, de Hock, and Wallenberg.

It is not necessary to follow in detail the eight sittings of the International Monetary Conference of 1867, because the result of its debates were the victory of Parieu's plan, with the expected abstention of Great Britain from any practical arrangement and a similar but less clear-cut reaction by Prussia.[81] The principle of monetary unification was accepted by all the delegates. The final recommendations of the Conference were:

1. Monetary unification could not come from the invention of a totally new system, requested by the French economists like Chevalier, Garnier, and Léon, and by the Belgian delegates. Unification should come out of the coordination of existing systems, following the system of the Latin Monetary Union of 1865 (approved unanimously).

2. The adoption of a single gold standard after a provisional bimetallic stage for the countries wishing it (unanimity with the exception of Holland).

3. The adoption of 9/10 as the proportion of fine gold in the coins (unanimous).

---

[78] Report to the Department of State by Samuel Ruggles, 7 Nov. 1867 (Appendix to Royal Commission) (1868: 203). [79] *International Monetary Conference*, 792.

[80] The Chairman of the US Senate Finance Committee, John Sherman, later Secretary to the Treasury under Grant, introduced a bill on January 1868 to equalize the dollar to 5 francs and formalize the introduction of the gold standard. The Bill was never discussed (Russell 1898: 93). Sherman had been providing political cover for Ruggles in Paris in 1867 but was more successful in 1873, sponsoring the adoption of the gold standard in the USA. On 8 Feb. 1870 the US Senate had requested the President to 'invite a correspondence with Great Britain and other Foreign Powers, with a view to promote the adoption by the Legislature of the several powers, of a common unit and standard of an International Gold Coinage.' To oblige the Senate, the Department of State sent a circular to American diplomats posted in Europe. The message however was more focused on Britain than on the LMU and it stated that 'any material change in the unit would render necessary a series of computations, which would occasion an amount of inconvenience to the population of the United States, for which the benefits they would receive from the change would scarcely compensate ... It would appear reasonable that the House as well as the Senate is not disposed to adopt the suggestions of the Paris Conferences without further communication with the British Government' (Printed report of the Department of State, without title, signature nor date, AMAE, ADC 616–1, fols. 13–16).

[81] The Prussian delegate Meinecke declared 'not to be necessary for the success of monetary unification to form a unity identical in weight and denomination, nor to constitute common types; a unity of metallic composition is sufficient, with the conversion of the coins of the union, that may vary in the different States, by simple equation' (*International Monetary Conference*, 845). The representatives of the southern German States then confirmed that they could not adopt a new currency without a common decision of the *Zollverein*.

4. That all gold coins thereafter struck in any of the countries which were parties to the convention should either be of the value of 5 francs or multiples of that sum (the UK and Sweden voted for the 10-franc-ducat, the Germans and Belgium abstained).

5. That the coins previously defined should have legal tender within the States that bound themselves by convention (unanimity with abstention of the UK and most German States).

6. That a gold coin of the value of 25 francs should be struck by those countries which preferred it, and be admitted as an international coin, creating the most visible link between France, England, and the USA (unanimous with the abstention of most German States).

To implement the deliberations of the Conference, France and the other members of the Latin Monetary Union would have had to abandon bimetallism and mint a 25-franc gold coin, the new standard international coin. England would have had to reduce the gold content of its pound by 0.88 per cent to equalize it to the proposed 25-franc gold piece. The dollar would have had to be reduced by 3.8 per cent. All the other States would have had to adapt their coinage to these weights, multiples of the 5-franc gold piece, with 900/1000 fineness. The Conference also requested a constant exchange of information, a common legislation on counterfeit, common controls on issue of depreciated silver, with free circulation of every State's coinage in other States' territory. France was asked to continue its role of central agent and collect the official responses of the States to the proposals of the Conference by 15 February 1868.

The conclusions of the Conference highlighted the success of the campaign pursued by Parieu and the monometallists in favour of gold. It also showed that it was possible to convince many European countries to proceed towards monetary unification even if Britain decided to decline any invitation to join. In order to expand the Union throughout Europe, the French government faced two major challenges: imposing the gold standard in France and convincing the German States.

Economics of Monetary Unification

Before considering the peculiarities of specific national situations, it is important to explore more general intellectual debates to understand what were the common issues in Europe. What was the state of the debate on monetary unions in the 1860s? What were the competing claims of supporters and opponents of unions concerning increased competition, reduced transaction costs, the effects on the metallic standards, and the political advantages of union? How deep should the monetary union be in terms of common currency and common institutions and further political developments, if it succeeded? What were the material interests guiding the alignment of opinions?

The theoretical basis of monetary union had not been fully developed when the deliberation on the formation of the LMU began. Parieu's articles appeared after the creation of the Latin Union in 1865 and became the focus of the European debate, summarizing all previous contributions to the subject and updating the public on further developments and polemics. The idea of monetary union emerged out of various past experiences, often quoted by Parieu and occasionally as part of a vision of a united Europe. There was no theoretical treatise which analysed in a complete and extended fashion the advantages and defects of monetary union, its long-term impact or transitional problems. Many past examples of predatory monetary unions existed. They highlighted how dominant countries had used their political and military hegemony to impose their own coinage on their neighbours, starting with Athens imposing its currency on its allies of the league of Delos in the fifth century BC, and concluding with the Continental system of Napoleon I, based on the franc–lira–peseta in 1808–15. This last system had been put into place in France and its satellites. It covered France, Belgium, Holland, Switzerland, all the States of continental Italy (Kingdom of Italy, Kingdom of Naples, and principality of Lucca, but excluding Sicily and Sardinia) and the Kingdom of Westphalia. Attempts had been made to introduce these units in parts of Spain (Catalonia) and in Baden.[1] Parieu also quoted a letter written by Napoleon I to order the unification of the coinage of all the vassal States of Europe to the French currency.

To the King of Naples   Finkenstein, 6 May 1807

My brother, if you decide to mint new coins, I wish you would follow the same fractional values as those adopted for the French currency and that your coins would bear on one side your

---

[1] Arnold, Küthmann, and Steinhilber (1970: 22 and 362–3).

portrait and on the other the crest of your kingdom. I did the same thing with my kingdom of Italy. Confederate princes do the same thing. This way there will be a monetary identity throughout Europe, a great advantage for trade. No inconvenience would come from adding the value to the text of the coin, such as 'Napoleon of 20 francs'.[2]

These franc–franken–lire–peseta in fact did not circulate widely elsewhere than in France, Belgium, Switzerland, and northern Italy, the area covered by the LMU fifty years after the fall of Napoleon I. Although it constituted the most evident precedent, it was usually passed under silence. According to Parieu, the best example of a more balanced union, based on mutual advantage, was offered by Germany, which was politically divided into a large number of States and therefore had been prone to local or regional monetary conventions for the previous two centuries.[3]

The most complete early discussion of monetary unification presented by Parieu in the debate of 1865–73 was dated 1582 and was written by the master of the mint of Reggio Emilia (Italy), Gaspare Scaruffi.[4] Scaruffi had indicated a series of rules concerning gold and silver coinage which were necessary to guarantee its quality, durability, and therefore its role in facilitating exchanges and not disrupting them as had often been the case with debased coinage. The rules that a 'zecca universale', a universal mint, should follow included the indication on each coin of the common weight, fineness, and unit of value employed.[5] Scaruffi listed twelve advantages coming from monetary unification.[6] The abusive profit of money changers would be cancelled, contracts would always be based on a certain and fixed value without frequent changes in units, weights, and fineness, making it simple for every citizen to understand national and international monetary operations. After Scaruffi only limited and episodical references to monetary union had appeared so that in the 1860s the debate had to be reinvented without reference to great classical economists or political theorists. This explains also why so many authors diverted their attention so swiftly and with so much passion towards the better-known part of the debate, the quarrel between monometallists and bimetallists.

Opponents of monetary unification frequently did not present a strong intellectual challenge to it, acknowledging the self-evident nature of many of its advantages. The Governor and the *régents* of the Bank of France presented the most coherent case

---

[2] Parieu (1871: 148).

[3] The *Münzverein* of 1838 and 1857 had been a continuation of an older but more limited practice. In 1765 for example Mainz, Treviri, the Palatinate, Hesse-Darmstadt, and Frankfurt had already formed a *Münzverein*. Most German coins carried the inscription of convention coin (*Conventions Münze*) or union coin (*Verein Münze*) (Parieu 1867: 322).

[4] Scaruffi (1582). Scaruffi was quoted in Parieu (1867: 332–5).

[5] Scaruffi (1582: 56). The common units were lire-, soldi-, and denari of imperial origin, £.s.d. in Britain, lire in Italy, livre in France.

[6] They included a simplification of the monetary types in circulation, the reduction of forgery and of abusive alterations of weight. A single coinage of guaranteed uniformity would also spare the cost of continuous operations of remintage. Recoinages were carried out to speculate on the higher quality of the coinage issued by some neighbour, melting and replacing it with new coins of lower metallic purity. There were also operations of debasement of local issues for the profit of the Prince, followed by periodical monetary reforms to restore the lost weight and fineness.

against universal coinage, while Wolowski developed a theory in defence of bimetallism. The debate was taking place at a European level even if some countries participated more than others. The French participated more actively, the British interventions were more episodic, and the Italians were absorbed by internal problems (inconvertible paper money and budgetary difficulties). In the German States there was a consensus about the necessity to reform and simplify the monetary system but the main issue was the choice of a new metallic system (gold or bimetallism) followed by the selection of the new monetary unit (mark, franc, dollar, florin, or decagram). The debates were taking places in national and federal Parliaments, in official commissions, in commercial assemblies, in various economic societies as well as in specialized reviews and the general press.[7]

3.1. THE DEBATE OVER THE OPPORTUNITY OF MONETARY UNIFICATION

3.1.1. *Reduction of Transaction Costs*

The first and most popular argument advanced in favour of monetary unification was that it would eliminate or reduce transaction costs. The unhappy fate of travellers and businessmen who would be defrauded of a large part of the value of their money by money changers was often recalled, even in private correspondence. 'In some (very) provincial towns of France you cannot get more than 22 francs for [a sovereign, instead of 25.22 francs]. This is enough to make all tourists toss up their empty purses and shout for Lowe and an international coinage.'[8] The more distant a locality from the capital of the State, the more fraudulent the exchange rate would be. The variability and uncertainty of the exchange rate and commissions were also off-putting. The existence of different types of money, similar but sufficiently different not to be identical, was an international vexation. The French economist Michel Chevalier introduced an argument which proved its enduring popularity. Chevalier wrote that

Already during the *ancien régime*, the diversity of money was disturbing for travellers, a continuous vexation; each time a frontier was passed, there was a loss on the exchange, so much so that whoever had entered Germany or the old Italy with a certain amount of money and had changed it at every new frontier, would have arrived at the other end with nothing left, even if we suppose he had not spent anything for transportation and personal needs.[9]

---

[7] Economists debated at the Société d'économie politique of Paris and that of Berlin, the Political Economy Club of London, the Società di economia politica italiana of Florence, in British, German, French, and Italian associations of chambers of commerce, in various Parliaments of the LMU, of Britain, Germany, and Sweden. The journals and reviews particularly involved in France were *Journal des économistes, Revue contemporaine*, and *Revue des Deux Mondes*, in Britain *The Times* and the *Economist*, in Italy *La Nuova Antologia*.

[8] This amounted to a commission of 12.8% to exchange British currency in French francs (W. G. Humphrey to Lord Overstone, 11 Sep. 1869, in O'Brien 1971: iii. 1185).

[9] Chevalier (1868: 351). The idea of the annihilation of the purchasing power of money after a journey throughout Europe because of the money changers' profit, has been resuscitated in the 1990s and was frequently employed in his speeches in favour of the Euro by the Commissioner for monetary affairs of the EU, Yves Thibault de Silguy (Milesi 1998: 172).

The disappearance of the commission reaped by money changers and bullion brokers would facilitate travel and business and no one would regret it. 'Private relations would be freed from any excessive tax paid to intermediaries,' Parieu wrote.[10] The English economist W. S. Jevons insisted that 'the saving of trouble and loss to travellers [is not] a matter of indifference. As international communication increases, the number of travellers will increase, and we ought to break down, as far as possible, factitious difficulties.'[11] Walter Bagehot, editor of the *Economist*, disagreed:

the difficulty which an Englishman finds in getting francs to pass to France is nothing. So long as countries are large and their inhabitants numerous, no one would wish to derange the many transactions of the millions that stay at home to facilitate a little the few transactions of the hundreds that go abroad. The good to be realized is not equal to the evil to be incurred.[12]

Jevons considered such considerations 'short-sighted.'[13]

The example of the recent Italian monetary unification proved furthermore that the change from the old to the new system of coinage would not cause the disruption many expected, thanks to the use of tables of equivalence distributed to the population. For Sacerdoti, a lawyer from Padua who wrote on the subject and testified in front of one of the French commissions invited by Parieu, fast transition

certainly did not produce confusion in the business world, nor complaints for damages to the rights of those perceiving yearly fixed incomes. The Italian example is of a nature to encourage other countries to embark decisively on radical reforms of money, especially for those countries which are lucky enough to be accustomed, on a much larger scale than us, to international trade and therefore to evaluate in several monies.[14]

Many French publicists insisted on that point: for Victor Bonnet the difficulty encountered by the population when faced by a new type of currency should not be overestimated, 'there is nothing like a well-accepted advantage to triumph over all obstacles.'[15]

Opponents of monetary unification were not impressed by the weight of these arguments and denied that transaction costs would disappear. They pointed to the persistence of banking costs in other forms than money changers' profit, and for that purpose used the statement of the pro-unification Swiss politician, Feer-Herzog. Feer-Herzog had distinguished between international transactions conducted with the use

---

[10] Parieu (1867: 340).   [11] Jevons (1875: 168).   [12] Bagehot (1868a: 1241).
[13] Jevons (1875: 167).   [14] Sacerdoti (1869: 8–9).
[15] Bonnet (1869a). His statement was echoed by Rappet who confirmed that 'les populations se sont habituées promptement aux mesures nouvelles, elle s'y sont familiarisées en peu de temps, comme elles le font toujours avec ce qu'elles ont intérêt à connaître' (Rapet 1869: 44). Rapet feared that monetary unification would force the adoption of new units and therefore changes in prices which in turn would facilitate rounding up of prices and cause inflation. This curious argument has been used repeatedly in the 1990s, including by the Eurosceptic British former Conservative minister John Redwood in 1998.

of coins on the one hand and transactions conducted through the use of bills of exchange (*lettre de change*) or remittance of bullion (*envois de remises métalliques*) on the other.[16] The use of coin would be entirely free from exchange losses after unification, while the use of bills of exchange and remittance of bullion would still be subjected to transaction costs, even if reduced. Feer-Herzog explained that the cost of remittance of bullion or of bills of exchange between two countries would still depend on the balance of trade, on insurance and transportation costs, and on the discount rate of the two countries. Monetary unification had no influence on these three factors and only eliminated the cost of remelting and recoining imported coins, together with money changing.[17] The Governor of the Bank of France, Gustave Rouland, used these remarks to argue about the futility of monetary unification in front of the French monetary commissions.[18] Rouland disputed the international relevance of the use of coins: 'Today, when we travel abroad, we carefully avoid to burden ourselves with gold and silver which would have to be exchanged at the place of arrival. We secure in France bills of exchange or letters of credit on foreign bankers or correspondents who pay them in local currency.'[19] Rouland insisted that by far the largest part of international transactions were conducted by compensation through bills of exchange or by the remittance of bullion. Rouland added an element of credit into all commercial operations and included the interest connected to the offer of credit into the exchange rate, in order to prove that monetary unification could not entirely cancel the cost of exchange and therefore was useless.[20] Rouland omitted to distinguish between bills of exchange at sight, which were payable three days after they were drawn and did not include interest, and bills of credit drawn at three months, date, whose price included interest. Rouland was shifting the argument, suggesting implicitly that the unification of coinage would have been worthwhile only if all international payments became entirely free of cost, something that no supporter of unification had ever claimed.

---

[16] 'Les voyageurs munis de la monnaie universelle n'auront plus à subir les pertes et les ennuis de l'échange' (Feer-Herzog 1869: 4).   [17] Ibid. 4–7.

[18] The French and the Italian languages do not distinguish clearly between currency, money, and coinage. The terms *monnaie* and *moneta* cover all of these and overshadows the difference between a monetary union and a coinage union. Some confusion was made at times between transaction costs on coins and on bills of exchange, both classified as *monnaie internationale* still subjected to the payment of banking fees.   [19] Conseil Supérieur du commerce (1872: i. 50).

[20] Rouland indicated that 'il n'y a que trois façons de payer sa dette à l'étranger, ou par compensation, ou avec du papier ou avec du métal ... Supposons que ce négociant français, à raison des circonstances doive envoyer de l'or à Londres pour se libérer. Comment se procurera-t-il cet or? Il présentera à la Banque de France un bordereau de valeurs que celle-ci escomptera en lui remettant le solde en billets, et il échangera ces billets au guichet de la caisse, pour des napoléons. Mais bien entendu la Banque aura perçu l'escompte, c'est à dire une certaine somme qui représente le loyer du capital, le prix de l'or donné en échange des valeurs du bordereau. Voilà le taux de l'escompte qui apparaît et qui restera toujours comme élément du change, en dépit de l'unification monétaire. Et encore faut-il tenir compte de ce taux dans les deux pays. Prenons maintenant l'hypothèse du paiement en papier. Et bien cette créance, cette traite dont on a besoin sur Londres, il faut l'acheter. Or sur le Money-market, le papier sur l'étranger est plus ou moins cher suivant qu'il est plus ou moins offert et demandé. Et voici encore un élément du change qu'il est impossible d'éviter, quand même toutes les nations auraient une monnaie commune. Reconnaissons donc que la majeure partie des frais du change résiste à l'unification monétaire' (Conseil Supérieur du commerce 1872: 53–4).

Other bankers supported his views, like Alphonse de Waru and Alphonse de Rothschild in France and George Goschen in England.[21] Whereas the majority of the population on the Continent used coins rather than banknotes or bank services, larger business operations had opposite needs, seen from the point of view of the Bank of France, of the Bank of England, or of private bankers. The editor of the *Economist* of London, Walter Bagehot, returned on the subject adding that

[A]n exchange calculation is really the cost of remitting money from one country to another. That cost is substantially the same whether the country from which it is imported has the same currencies or different currencies ... the remitting banks make a charge for selling their drafts, and this is the common exchange calculation in the new shape.... In practical exchange business the rate of interest is to be considered, and the state of credit also. If you buy a bill at three months' date you lose a certain sum in interest, depending on the rate of the day, and you rely on the credit, more or less good of the parties to the bill. These main items of exchange business are in its nature, and no currency change can alter them.[22]

Supporters of unification did not question these facts but attributed to them a different importance and insisted that even a partial reduction of exchange costs would be an important benefit. The British statistician Hendriks acknowledged to the British monetary commission that '[the cost of exchange] could never be entirely removed, it would be unreasonable on the part of the public to expect it because bankers like all other men are entitled to a remuneration for the trouble and risk they undertake; but it should be confined within narrower limits than it is now.'[23] Feer-Herzog stressed that monetary unification would bring the fluctuation of the exchange rate within the gold points, that is within a limited band of fluctuation around the gold parities, determined by insurance and transportation costs. After monetary unification, the fluctuations of the gold parity (the relation between the quantity of pure gold contained in a unit of each others coinage) between France and Britain would be permanently reduced. If the premium to buy a three days' bill on Paris was higher than the price for transportation, a British merchant could simply ship the sum he wished to transfer in gold coins and pay directly insurance, transport, and handling, for a total of less than 1 per cent of the value of the shipment. With a few simple calculations it is possible to quantify the levels of exchange rate variability to which Feer-Herzog referred to: for the period 1832–50, the maximum total variability of the franc–pound rate had been 4.3 per cent, against 2.2 per cent in the period 1850–68, when France had a monetary circulation composed mostly of gold, and against a 1.6–2 per cent variability expected by the Swiss monetary expert with the gold points.[24] In another instance, a British merchant, J. Behrens, declared that he expected the cost of transferring money from France to

---

[21] For Goschen see in Seyd (1868: 684–5). For the French bankers' view see the paragraph below, Ch. 4.

[22] Bagehot (1868a: 1242).   [23] Royal Commission (1868: 15).

[24] Feer-Herzog thought its largest band of fluctuation should be 25.40–25 or 25.45–24.95, while it had been 25.95–24.87 between 1832 and 1850, when silver was predominant in France and 25.50–24.95 when gold was predominant in France (Feer-Herzog 1869: 6). Flandreau (1995b: 102–5) estimates the simple cost of transportation, insurance, and handling to 0.5% until 1854 and 0.3% in the 1860s. Therefore in the 1860s with a par of the exchange at 25.22, the pound should fluctuate between 25.30 and 25.14.

Britain to fall from 3 per cent to 1.5 per cent after unification.[25] The French foreign
exchange specialist Le Touzé declared to the French Commission of 1869–70 that

apart from general elements influencing the evolution of international exchange it is important
to notice that bills payable in cash and drawn on a city within the [Latin] monetary union suffer
from a much less variable loss than those drawn on centres which are not part of the union. The
loss incurred drawing on the States of the Union can vary between 1/8 and 3/4 per cent, while
drawing in francs on Germany can cost from 2 to 3 per cent.[26]

The variability of the Franco-British exchange rate had substantially narrowed after
1850, largely because of the arrival of gold in France. Today these levels of variability
seem very limited, but Feer-Herzog was calling for the smoothest working possible of
the rules of the gold standard in a period when the gold standard existed formally only
in England and Portugal.[27] Furthermore, as noted by the chairman of the British
Chambers of Commerce, S. S. Lloyd, the profit on many commercial transactions was
so low that a 0.75 per cent difference was sufficient to prevent the sale and give a
competitive edge to Belgian or French producers who already enjoyed the benefits of
unification.[28] The Belgian Lavelaye, a well-known and respected economist, defended
the role of coins, recalling that despite the importance of bills of exchange 'the surplus
of imports over exports, resulting from the lack of equilibrium in the balance of trade,
must be paid in money, and, with the increase of the relations between nations and the
immense proportions taken by trade, those surpluses grow as well, varying yearly.'[29]
The Anglo-German bullion dealer Seyd argued that the simplification and transpar-
ency of the new way of expressing transaction costs would anyway encourage trade.[30]
The appendix to this book shows how minimal such improvements were when they
were considered separately from the unification of monetary standards.

There was a widespread dislike for inconvertible paper currencies, which were
depreciated in relation to gold and silver coins, and they were indicated as a source of
renewed fluctuation and difference in the exchanges which threatened the results of
unification.[31] In 1869 inconvertible paper money was depreciated by 18–19 per cent in
Austria-Hungary and by 3–6 per cent in Italy.[32] Nevertheless as the development of

---

[25] Royal Commission (1868: 8).   [26] Conseil Supérieur du commerce (1872: i. 129).

[27] Feer-Herzog replied to Rouland that artificial transaction costs have to be attacked in the same way as
government fight against the cost of transportation of grain in periods of poor harvests, in order to reduce
price fluctuation. 'Pourquoi puisqu'il y a un élément purement artificiel qu'il nous est donné d'abolir,
n'essayerions-nous pas de le détruire, et pourquoi ne ferions nous pas notre possible pour que le change fut
ramené à son expression la plus naturelle, c'est à dire à la simple expression du bilan commercial des places
qui font le commerce entre elles? Arrivée à cette simple expression, le change aura une concurrence tout à
fait naturelle dans le prix du transport et dans le prix de l'assurance des espèces unifiées d'une place à l'autre,
et les plus grands écarts du change entre les deux places ayant une monnaie identique ne pourront jamais
dépasser la somme des frais de transport du métal, de la prime d'assurance et de la différence du taux
d'intérêt' (Feer-Herzog (1870: 11)).   [28] Royal Commission (1868: 1).

[29] Lavelaye (1867: 617).

[30] '[Goschen's argument] is true, but the variations expressed by a percentage would be much simpler and
far more easily understood than the mysterious figures in the present course of exchange' (Seyd 1870: 49).

[31] Le Touzé (1868a: 404–20). See also how the director of the Bank of England Hubbard 'grilled' Jevons
on this in front of the Royal Commission (1868: 98).

[32] Minghetti and Finali (1875: 220); Feer-Herzog (1869: 37).

paper money was not entirely understood, few conceived that it would become the source of unprecedented inflation, exchange rate fluctuation, and monetary diversity in the twentieth century. The Italians Sacerdoti and Rossi had a stronger perception of the problem, being already burdened by a depreciated inconvertible paper money. A Milanese economist, Guglielmo Rossi, pointed to the impossibility of monetary unification with diverging national financial conditions, which would give a different value in each nation to the common currency:

[A]s long as governments will continue to enter into debt higher than the total of their resources and than the metallic currency ... they will naturally feel the need to create monetary surrogates, however those might be called. It will then be even more spontaneous that these non-metallic surrogates of the currency, introduced under the banner of credit and sometimes openly imposed, will be held in high or low confidence according to the confidence inspired by the politician, the financier, the politics or the financial conditions of the State which create it.[33]

3.1.2. Free Trade, Competition, and Price Transparency

A second frequent argument in favour of unification was concerned with the increase in competition to be derived from it. Monetary unification, it was suggested, was a consequence of the increase in competition brought by free-trade treaties from 1860 onwards, but it was also a cause of further increases in competition once 'true prices' appeared. Introducing the LMU to the French Parliament, the French MP Louvet declared that 'monetary unification is the consequence of free trade and the irresistible movement which pushes nations to associate with each other through the strongest solidarity of all, the solidarity of industry and trade, of wealth and well-being.'[34] The existence of different sets of currencies and units of length, weight, and volume throughout Europe made it difficult to compare prices across borders. The price of a fabric was expressed in francs per metre in Paris, in thalers per webe in Hamburg, in carlini per canna in Palermo, and in pounds per yard in London. Most merchants would not be able to know all the necessary conversion rates and make the appropriate calculations to judge whether a business deal was advantageous.[35] As a consequence 'a very great loss is experienced by the general mass of the community in consequence of their compulsory ignorance of the principles upon which [exchange business] depends.'[36] Large trading houses would employ special clerks just for this purpose, and gained a dominant position in international trade, compared to smaller houses.

---

[33] Rossi (1867: 12).

[34] 'Report of M. Louvet to the Corps Législatif on the monetary convention of 1865', *Annales du Sénat et du Corps Législatif*, VIII, 13 June (1866: 11 of the annexe).

[35] An example of the horrific calculations needed, given by a British merchant W. S. Jeffrey, is particularly telling. He was billed in Belgium in an old local unit unknown in the books containing tables of coinage, 'Gulden, solls and deniers. The way we get at it is this: the lengths are all lengths, three-quarters of a yard; the coinage is double one franc less one-eleventh: one gulden is equal to one franc eighty-one centimes; a sol is a twentieth part of a gulden, and a denier a twelfth of a soll. We must bring it into French money first, then calculate it by our table of French money before we can get it into English money' (Royal Commission 1868: 67).   [36] Hendriks in Royal Commission (1868: 14).

The adoption of the metre as a unit of measure by most European countries (with the exception of Britain) in the 1860s and 1870s facilitated matters, but the abolition of complex and variable exchange rates was identified as the only way to understand foreign prices at first glance, improving access to foreign markets and increasing competition. Parieu talked about the establishment of an 'international language of values', improving statistics, and fostering fair competition.[37] Hendriks and Bagehot concurred that most foreigners could not read British prices and were discouraged from buying British goods, because they could not calculate the equivalent in their currency of British currency, weights, and measures.[38] The fact that the British competitive advantage in relation to France, Belgium, and Germany had been eroded in the previous twenty years by the industrialization of the Continent was a further reason not to penalize British manufacturers with an incomprehensible price system. An anonymous English businessman looked forward in a letter to the *Economist* to 'the prospects of obtaining ... a chance of meeting [his] foreign competitors on equal terms in neutral markets' thanks to monetary unification.[39]

The argument was not countered very effectively, and only special interests made an effort against it. Representatives of large export–import houses in Britain played down the complexity of price translation, explaining that calculations were already done professionally but admitted that monetary unification would damage their position facilitating access to international markets by smaller competitors.[40] Governor Rouland disregarded the importance of simplifications in calculations, considering that plenty of books and manuals on coinage and units of measure had been produced for that purpose in recent years.[41] Bagehot noted the reduced impact of improvements in statistics 'ordinary people do not care as yet, and for an indefinite period to come are not likely to care enough about statistical sciences to undergo themselves daily personal annoyance for it. The change of the current coin would bore most men much, and most men care little for philosophy.'[42]

The impossibility of abstaining from a successful monetary union was discussed in Britain as an argument about increased competition. It was developed there because of the particular strength of opponents to monetary unification, while more and more countries in the Continent were associating themselves with the LMU. The idea that

---

[37] Parieu (1866b: 22).

[38] 'On Monetary Unification Advantages', *Economist*, (1866: 1078). See also Bagehot (1868b: 1271).

[39] Behrens (1869: 1075). British businessmen associated with the chambers of commerce and favourable to union repeatedly showed the low esteem they had of the intelligence of those resisting changes in currency. For example J. R. Jeffrey thought that 'at first the conservative feeling, natural to Englishmen, might slightly revolt at it, but as soon as anything like the light of intelligence were to strike upon them they would only be too glad to adopt it' (Royal Commission 1868: 68).

[40] Candy, a merchant in London, had ten French, Italian, and German clerks to follow foreign markets 'Speaking of my own house [an international coin] would be a disadvantage to my interests ... because myself and my clerks ... are able to grapple with any calculation of any monies, no matter what the country might be ... Competition brings many things to a level; it results in an extraordinary diminution of your profits, it affects your interest very much.' In his opinion unification would benefit retail dealers and damage wholesale dealers who were already aware of how to make their calculations and how to conduct their business (Royal Commission 1868: 87).   [41] Conseil Supérieur du commerce (1872: i. 50).

[42] Bagehot (1868a: 1242).

monetary unification was imposed by international events which Britain could not change, whether it liked it or not, was used domestically. The British chambers of commerce distinguished themselves in this exercise, insisting on it very frequently, but the argument was also embraced by Jevons, by Seyd, and later by the Chancellor of the Exchequer Robert Lowe.[43] Abroad Parieu would make use of a similar point enumerating the growing number of European countries acting towards monetary unification and arguing that 'despite the fact that until now England has remained in an isolation cherished by the British tradition, it will be difficult for her to persist longer'.[44] In 1868-69 a substantial number of nations had progressed towards unification and it could be said with some credibility that the process was unstoppable and to stay out of it would damage British business, as was indeed said by the chambers of commerce and by Seyd.[45]

The anticipation that USA, Germany, and especially Prussia would ultimately not join France and the LMU was the main response given against the threat of the ultimate success of monetary unification. Many must have thought that the abstention of Britain itself was sufficient to undermine a European union, thanks to the British influence over Portugal, Holland, northern Germany, and the Scandinavian States. The uncertain outcome of the process was pointed out together with the high costs associated with the transition towards a new currency. Recoinage, repricing, and redenomination were the difficulties and sources of inconvenience and unpopularity indicated by the report of the Royal Commission to counterbalance the arguments advanced by the chambers of commerce.

3.1.3. Political Arguments

The political motives for monetary unification were not discussed as openly and as widely as the economic arguments, but they appear to have played an important part in shaping the convictions of the participants in the debate. The integration of currencies was seen as part of a larger process of economic and political integration guided by economic development and free trade. Parieu conceived the end of war in Europe as its ultimate outcome: 'It is not exclusively the advantage of merchants, statisticians,

---

[43] The British Royal Commission of 1868 noted how 'several of the witnesses state that the competition of foreign manufacturers is now so close that it is of increasing importance to this country that every impediment to the development to our trade should be removed; and that it would be a great detriment to the manufacturing and trading interests of this country, if an arrangement for an international currency to which England was not a party was made by other countries' (Royal Commission 1868: p. vii). See also Seyd (1868: 682); Jevons (1868: 428–9). For Lowe's position see Chapter 5.

[44] Parieu (1868a: 62).

[45] 'We admit that the crisis of 1866 has placed England at a disadvantage, but long before that time France was richer in Gold than we are, and the disproportion between us is now so great, that temporary causes will have little effect either way. One of the reasons why so much bullion is concentrated in Paris, may be due to the fact that the city is now the centre of the large monetary union of France, Belgium, Switzerland, and Italy, and which is about to be joined by Spain, and other States. This should be a hint to us that we must either take our due rank in joining them, or that we must prepare ourselves for a rivalry with so powerful a Confederation' Seyd (1868b) and the Royal Commission (1868: 58).

and travellers which lies behind the great issue of monetary unification: it is a considerable element of material and moral coming together of nations that we have to highlight, to the advantage of ideas of progress and peace, not just in Europe.'[46] The Belgian economist and publicist Emile de Lavelaye shared this approach and supported monetary unification as a further link preventing governments from declaring wars not desired by the people. 'Solving other economic questions with the same approach, the people would come to form this federation of the United States of Europe, ensuring peace and producing an increase of welfare similar to that which the United States are so proud of.'[47] The problem was that the 'Parieu-Lavelaye view' was inconsistent with the French national advantage as conceived by the French Ministry of Foreign Affairs. The government was interested in the development of trade and the extension of the currency union 'to the great advantage of international relations and the French political influence in the world'.[48] For several years both policies were compatible, but when tensions mounted again between France and Prussia in 1870, Parieu's peaceful and federalist views, discussed in Chapter 2, were set aside. It was evident that to create a federation all future members had to trust each other and clearly Napoleon III, Bismarck, Gladstone, the Austrian Beust, the Belgian Frère-Orban, and the Italian Menabrea did not trust each other, conceiving international politics, much as the French did, in terms of strict national advantage. Despite the rhetorical references to great steps in civilization bringing nations closer to each other, the conditions for intense political cooperation between the major European powers did not exist in an era of growing nationalism and uncertain power of elected Parliaments. A monetary union did not prevent war between its members, and indeed the *Münzverein* did not prevent war between Austria and Prussia in 1866.

Most governments chose not to state explicitily their reservations and eventually the British were the only ones to question openly the legitimacy of a French initiative for international money. The Royal Commission appointed by Disraeli in 1868 considered

---

[46] Parieu (1869a: 259). Parieu's position seems to initiate a line of thought, in the French government which was continued in France by Briand in 1929, and then by Monnet and Schumann until Mitterrand. Launching in 1950 the European Community of Coal and Iron (CECA), the French Minister of Foreign Affairs Schumann summarized the position of France as expressed by Aristide Briand in 1930 and Jean Monnet in 1940 (with the proposed Anglo-French Union), as: 'En se faisant depuis plus de vingt ans le champion d'une Europe unie, la France a toujours eu pour objet essentiel de servir la paix. L'Europe n'a pas été faite, nous avons eu la guerre' (Brugmans 1970: 382).

[47] Lavelaye (1867: 622). In a monetary conference 'des concessions réciproques aplaniraient les principales difficultés, les susceptibilités de l'orgueil national s'effaceraient devant l'importance du but à atteindre. Les peuples n'ont aucun intérêt à se battre, et, s'il n'y étaient parfois excites par leurs gouvernants, ils n'en auraient aucune envie. Pour rendre plus forte, plus efficace cette aversion à la guerre, multipliez toutes les relations auxquelles la monnaie sert d'intermédiaire. Que par le libre échange les produits du travail des uns aillent satisfaire les besoins des autres, de façon à augmenter le bien être de celui qui achète, en enrichissant celui qui vend; que le capital accumulé par telle nation serve à féconder l'industrie de telle autre, et alors une lutte à main armée sera presque aussi onéreuse aux vainqueurs qu'aux vaincus. Vous ne pourrez ruiner l'ennemi sans compromettre l'épargne que vous aurez placez sur son territoire, et en frappant un adversaire vous tuerez un débiteur ... Qu'on s'empresse donc d'adopter toutes les réformes qui peuvent fortifier cette entente internationale, en lui donnant pour fondement la communauté des intérêts exprimée par l'union monétaire' (ibid. 636).

[48] Fould to Drouyn de Lhuys, 27 Jan. 1866 (AMAE, ADC 603–2, fol. 10).

the pound to be more suitable than the franc to serve as the common currency and Bagehot suggested the creation of an Anglo-American currency to counterbalance the ambitions of the franc.

The situation was different for smaller or weaker countries, such as Austria-Hungary, Spain, Greece, Romania, Serbia, and the Pontifical States. Joining a monetary union was often a way of connecting themselves to Europe and the most advanced nations, and of importing a better coinage. Smaller States often did not possess an adequate internal monetary circulation. They were plagued by old and clipped tokens, by a multiplicity of foreign and debased units. A substantial part of the attraction of the franc as an international currency was its 'scientific' nature, based on a decimal system and on the use of the gram, invented during the French Revolution as a late product of the age of enlightenment. This new French system of weights and measures showed its capacity for international expansion in the 1860s as the German States and Italy adopted it and Great Britain legalized its use. By adopting the franc and renaming it according to local customs—as lira, peseta, drachma, lei, dinar, or leva—the weakest European States could create a modern and orderly national currency and dispel monetary chaos.[49] Jevons was particularly attracted by this feature of monetary integration, which in the end would have a positive effect on the larger States themselves, because they would receive a more secure coinage in exchange for their exports.[50]

Small and weak States also needed access to the capital markets of London and Paris.[51] They needed both to acquire credibility as borrowers to float successfully a public loan and to acquire the status of an advanced State associated with the richest parts of Europe.[52] Membership of the LMU seemed to provide such credibility. The search for a monetary link with France was not the manifestation of a preference for the Paris bourse, but reflected the opportunity given by France to join the LMU and the absence of any such policy in the UK. Had Britain followed the policy initiated by the French, many more States would have been interested in monetary union. The governments of Portugal and the USA stated this point explictly, but Britain's decision would have also influenced Canada, Holland and Norway.[53]

Monetary union was often part of a larger package of alliances constructed by France to consolidate bilateral relations. Austria turned to France for a monetary union in 1867, when it considered an anti-Prussian alliance. When Italy entered the LMU it

---

[49] Leconte (1995).

[50] 'One benefit of international money which has been insufficiently noticed, is the improvement which its adoption would probably effect in the currencies of minor and half-civilized States. In many parts of the world there is still a mixture of coins of various and uncertain value; and as long as the principal nations coin money on totally different systems, the coins will circulate elsewhere and make confusion ... If all the leading nations combined to issue coins of one uniform series of weight and sizes, these would by degrees form the currencies of the non-coining States, and would effect a reform in the most remote parts of the world' (Jevons 1875: 169).   [51] Flandreau (1994).

[52] Bordo and Rockoff suggested the adoption of a gold standard with full convertibility facilitated access by peripheral countries to capital from the core countries of western Europe (Bordo Rockoff 1996: 389).

[53] The Portugese delegate at the conference of 1867, Count d'Avila, indicated that 'England would have to set the example' (*International Monetary Conference*, 813 and 846). For the US position see printed report of the Department of State, without title, signature nor date (1870) (AMAE, ADC 616–1, fols. 13–16).

still needed French financial and political support to complete its unification. In 1867 the Papal States applied to join the LMU directly to France from which it received protection from Italian territorial ambitions. Greece applied when it needed French support for the Greek uprising in Crete against the Turkish occupants. Romania applied just after it had received French support against Turkey. Turkey did not apply.

In many European countries, the concept of Europe was already associated with progress, wealth, and political freedom, as can be seen from the following speech by the Spanish Finance Minister, Laureano Figuerola, in October 1868. His statement commented on the introduction of the franc in Spain under the name of peseta, after the overthrow of the Bourbon monarchy.

In the new era opened today to our country by the economic reforms which had still been impossible under the fallen regime, we must forget the past by breaking all the ties holding us back to it . . . we must therefore cancel the Lily of the Bourbons from the crest on our coins . . . The advantages coming from stronger links with other European nations speak in favour [of the adoption of the Latin Union's system]. Everything that facilitates trade and relations between nations constitutes an immense benefit, sowing the seeds of wealth, improving the position of citizens and reaffirming civilization and freedom. Adopting the monetary system of the international convention, Spain opens her arms to her sister States of Europe and gives a new and evident proof of its unshakeable resolve to unite with them, to enter in the assembly of free Peoples.[54]

The immediate interest of weak countries was not reassuring for some opponents of monetary unification. The fact that countries with poor public finances were attracted was a valid reason for richer countries to be more careful because the former could use the Union to increase their seignorage profits at the expense of their neighbours, to cover financial difficulties. It was not only the fear of inconvertible paper money issued in large quantities by Italy or Austria, but also the excessive issue of divisionary silver coins by the Pontifical States that could be repeated by any State such as Greece, Romania, or Spain. The president of the French Commission des Monnaies, Dumas, questioned the possibility of checking the dubious quality of issues by a growing number of distant countries. It was possible to control four countries but not forty. It was feared that the circulation of a wide set of foreign money coming from the most diverse places would facilitate forgery and fraudulent alteration of coins.[55] The French

---

[54] Translation of the decree accompanying the new Spanish monetary law, French Embassy in Spain to the French Minister of Foreign Affairs Moustier, 5 Nov. 1868 (AMAE, ADC 604–1 bis, fols. 118–21).

[55] For Dumas, 'le faux-monnayage tendra a devenir plus commun par la diffusion des connaissances scientifiques. Avant de s'engager dans de nouvelles unions monétaires il faut donc obtenir, de tous les États compris dans l'union actuelle, des garanties certaines pour la répression du faux monnayage. En Espagne, par exemple, il parait y avoir sur ce point une tolérance regrettable' (*Procès-verbaux et rapport de la commission monétaire de 1868* (1869: i. 14). For the Bank of France Rouland and De Waru attacked further extensions of the LMU for fear of excessive issue of debased silver, see ibid. i. 15. The Spanish Vasquez Queipo had already said in 1867 that forgery would be made easier by monetary unification, in Vasquez Queipo (1867), quoted in Parieu (1867: 339). For Chevalier 'S'obliger à l'union entre les États, c'est à dire donner le caractère légal à la pièce frappée chez les autres, c'est prendre un engagement très grave: c'est s'engager à considérer comme bien frappée et comme correctement faite la monnaie frappée chez les autres.' For the most important countries that was not a problem, but 'dans les petits états, dans les états nécessiteux, on a eu plus d'une fois l'idée d'introduire dans les monnaies plus d'alliage qu'il ne fallait' (Conseil Supérieur du commerce 1872: i. 37).

Finance Ministers Magne and Buffet complained about the loss of seignorage profits incurred after foreign coins entered massively French circulation, and Parliament proved to be receptive to such remarks. As noted by Jevons, nineteenth-century Parliaments were more conservative in monetary questions than absolutist governments and proved reluctant to endorse major changes.[56] In reply to these criticisms, Parieu, Sacerdoti, and others defended the possibility of insuring a non-problematic enlargement of the Union thanks to continual exchanges of information and documentation. The Austrian monetary negotiator De Hock proposed to expel any State which violated the rules of the Union and Chevalier suggested an international monetary committee with powers to monitor the behaviour of national governments.[57] Nevertheless they were forced to admit that an enlarged monetary union should be limited to gold coins and should exclude silver coins which were more prone to debasement and were favoured by the poorest and most suspicious States.[58] Such a decision was facilitated by the belief in the gold standard shared by most supporters of unification. To be on the safe side, the Paris mint decided quietly to test regularly the silver and gold coins issued by all States which passed or requested a monetary alliance with France.[59]

3.2. THE INTERACTION BETWEEN INTERNATIONAL MONEY AND THE BATTLE OF THE STANDARDS

An overview of the dispute between bimetallists and supporters of the gold standard has been provided in the first chapter. This section will refer to it, exploring more explicitly the relation between the battle of the standards and monetary unification.

Metallic standards created the conditions for natural monetary unions based on the simple correspondence between equal fine weights of silver or of gold. John Stuart Mill wrote in his *Principles of Political Economy* in 1848 that all countries would one day have the same currency and only political obstacles prevented it. Mill added: 'so much of barbarism, however, still remains in the transactions of most civilized nations, that almost all independent countries choose to assert their nationality by having, to their own inconvenience and that of their neighbours, a peculiar currency of their own.'[60] The logic of a common currency based on gold or silver was generally admitted by

---

[56] In 1875 Jevons observed: 'No doubt in times past, kings have been the most notorious false coiners and depreciators of the currency, but there is no danger of the like being done in modern times. The danger lies in quite the opposite direction, that popular governments will not venture upon the most obvious and necessary improvement of the monetary system without obtaining a concurrence of popular opinion in its favour, while the people, influenced by habit, and with little knowledge of the subject, will never be able to agree upon the best scheme'(Jevons 1975: 66). [57] Sacerdoti (1869: 10–12).

[58] 'Nous devons prévoir le cas à l'avenir, non seulement en nous gardant d'étendre outre mesure le territoire de la communauté des monnaies d'appoint, mais en introduisant subsidiaire ment dans la convention de 1865 un correctif pour les éventualités du cours forcé ... [il est conseillable] de renfermer l'oeuvre de l'unification monétaire universelle dans les sages limites de la monnaie d'or ... L'internationalité des monnaies d'appoint en argent... a des raisons d'être là où il existe des rapports de voisinage aussi intimes que ceux qui lient la Belgique à la France, la France à la Suisse, la Suisse à l'Italie, mais ne peut donner lieu qu'à des abus et à des difficultés lorsqu'elle s'étend trop loin' (Feer-Herzog 1869: 38–9).

[59] Tests were conducted in July and Nov. 1868 and in Dec. 1876 (AMdP: K2–16).

[60] Mill (1963–86: iii. 625–6).

economists, but the disagreement about which standard should be used overshadowed other considerations.[61]

Supporters of the gold standard on the Continent were in general also supporters of monetary unification, while bimetallists opposed monetary unification. This sharp divide was due principally to the conclusions of the International Monetary Conference of Paris of 1867 which associated in the strongest terms unification with the adoption of the gold standard and recommended the progressive demonetization of silver in all countries taking part in the process. Supporters of gold almost unanimously endorsed Parieu's project, differing only over details about which monetary unit should be adopted. In the UK the relationship between allegiance to gold and allegiance to monetary union was broken by the status of gold as the undisputed single standard since 1816, making it possible to support gold but not unification. The German banker and politician Ludwig Bamberger was one of the few important supporters of the gold standard on the Continent to oppose monetary unification, considering that an international gold standard was sufficient in itself to foster trade and steady the exchange rate. His view was partially sanctioned by Parieu himself after 1870 when he admitted that with gold and decimalization Germany had adopted two-thirds of the reform he proposed. After the collapse of the project of international money in the early 1870s, Parieu, Courcelle-Seneuil, Frère-Orban, and Soetbeer concentrated their efforts on the introduction and consolidation of the gold standard in their respective countries. This points to the propagandist use of monetary union made in the 1860s in order to advance the cause of gold. After the successful penetration of large quantities of gold in the Continent in the 1850s and 1860s, only a few silver monometallists were left in Europe. After 1865 they rapidly vanished from the scene or converted to another faith.[62]

The bulk of anti-unification bimetallists were practical men, bankers, politicians, and members of the public attached to the *status quo*. Some notable exceptions were the Anglo-German bullion dealer Seyd, the German economists Prince-Smith and Moritz Mohl, and the Franco-Polish economist Wolowski who were pro-unification bimetallists.[63] Wolowski, seconded by the Italian banker Cernuschi, proposed to achieve

---

[61] The bimetallist Wolowski quoted Turgot saying that 'Il n'est pas d'économiste sérieux qui n'ait parlé de l'emploi commun de l'or et de l'argent: le grand Turgot n'a-t-il pas dit que: "l'or et l'argent sont constitués, par la nature des choses, monnaie et monnaie universelle, indépendamment de toute convention et de toute loi"' (Société d'économie politique 1868: 312).

[62] The Dutch Nahuys for example was an early proponent of monetary union based on silver, even before the creation of the LMU but then withdrew from the debate, Nahuys (1865). Chevalier was an ideological convert who abandoned silver for gold in 1867 and thereafter defended gold with all the zeal and intolerance of true converts. In Germany pragmatic conversions tended to transform silver monometallists into bimetallists, in order to preserve the old status of silver but also acknowledge the diffusion of gold. The Prussian government adopted such attitude.

[63] The report of the French Monetary Commission of 1869 acknowledged that its bimetallist minority 'n'a pas contesté en général les avantages qui résulteraient de l'unification monétaire. Elle a seulement soutenu que l'unification était possible avec le double étalon tout aussi bien qu'avec un seul' 'Rapport de la commission sur l'étalon monétaire au ministre des finances' (1869: 105). For Prince-Smith and Mohl defending a bimetallist international money at the German Political Economy society see letter of the French Consulate in Stettin (Prussia) to French Foreign Affairs Minister la Tour d'Auvergne, 21 July 1869 (AMAE, ADC604-2, fols. 180–83). For Seyd see (Seyd 1868: 597–699).

universal money through the introduction of an international bimetallism, or, if such a solution proved impossible, to keep side by side an international gold currency and several internal silver currencies.[64] Such a measure however would leave no international currency in those countries where bimetallism produced a dominant silver circulation, so that the Union would remain a purely theoretical achievement. For Wolowski the survival of bimetallism was clearly much more important than the creation of a single currency. When the quarrel between bimetallists and monometallists exploded as a consequence of the debate on monetary unification Wolowski invented *ex novo* a theory justifying the use of bimetallism.

The French debate was indeed a curious one, opposing two consensus positions which ignored each other until the debate on monetary unification imposed a direct confrontation. Before 1865, the consensus among economists was that the gold standard (or more generally monometallism) was superior to bimetallism because it prevented continuous shifts from one metal to the other according to the fluctuations of market prices.[65] At the same time the consensus among French policy-makers (politicians, bureaucrats, and bankers) was that the existing bimetallic system, for whatever reason, worked satisfactorily and no legislative intervention to modify it was welcomed.[66] Nobody bothered to challenge the opinion of the economists with a serious theory, because it was politically irrelevant. With the debate on international money becoming associated with gold, thanks to the efforts of Parieu, the theory of the gold standard became suddenly of high practical relevance and politically sensitive. Wolowski's defence of the compensatory and stabilizing properties of bimetallism was a case of a theory created to justify a system which was the outcome of a casual series of events but worked despite the objections of theoretical economists.[67] As in the

[64] Louis Wolowski and Giuseppe Cernuschi had been political leaders of the failed national uprisings of 1848, the former in Poland against Russia and the latter in Italy against Austria and then France. Both chose to go into exile in France, where they became prosperous bankers and bimetallist theorists. Wolowski was the first executive director of the Crédit Foncier in 1852–54, and then became professor of political economy at the Conservatoire des Arts et Métiers. For Wolowski monetary unification was compatible with the survival of bimetallism even if the latter was not accepted by other countries. 'On pourrait convenir d'une monnaie internationale en or, qui amènerait partout la solution de tous les engagements, en étant reçue à un taux uniforme dans les caisse publiques. Chaque pays serait libre, pour lui et pour les États qui se rallieraient sous l'empire d'une convention distincte, à consacrer aussi l'argent comme monnaie libératoire à l'intérieur, et l'avantage naturel recueilli par cette combinaison ne tarderait point à la généraliser' (Wolowski 1870a: pp. xxxvii–viii).

[65] Wolowski and Cernuschi's isolation in the economic profession was evident in Société d'économie politique (1867: 430–54). In a later discussion of the same society 'M. Willaumé se plaint que l'on discute trop souvent et trop longtemps la question de l'or et de l'argent; il constate que, ainsi que vient de le dire M. Michel Chevalier, la société est presque unanime sur la question du double étalon, et sur l'opportunité de faire disparaître l'argent comme monnaie principale' (Société d'économie politique 1869: 142–68). The Italian economists under the direction of the liberal minister Marco Minghetti shared in a rather unimaginative way the enthusiasm of their French colleagues for gold and unification (Società di economia politica italiana 1869: 418–27).

[66] Various monetary commissions concluded in favour of the *status quo* in the 1850s and 1860s, thanks to the vote of ministers, MPs, civil servants, and bankers, despite the complaints of the economists Parieu, Garnier, Levasseur, Faucher, and Chevalier. French monetary commissions are discussed in Chapter 4.

[67] S. de Sismondi (1827) defended bimetallism with some of the arguments later developed by Wolowski, but his position remained isolated. See Rastel (1935: 37).

previous decades nobody had seriously debated in a controversial manner bimetallism and gold monometallism, many economists and publicists had adhered without particular reflection to the conventional wisdom favouring gold. When Wolowski questioned this common sense with great ability, he was able to rally 'intuitive' bimetallists and to convince an unexpectedly large audience.[68] His challenge created almost single-handedly the basis for the theoretical controversy which would last until the end of the nineteenth century.[69]

In his classic study on the origins of the gold standard, the Belgian monetary historian Mertens insisted on the weakness of the theoretical arguments advanced to demonstrate the superiority of gold over bimetallism in the 1860s. He stressed both the desire to imitate all the causes of British success and the desire to acquire international prestige.[70] More recently Gallarotti has highlighted again the importance of the ideology of gold and the quest for prestige as important factors in the 'scramble for gold'. The gold standard was associated with 'the admired example of England' and became 'a symbol of sound practice and badge of honour and decency', in Schumpeter's words.[71] For Seyd it was due to 'a sort of anglomania hidden under the appearance of liberalism'.[72] The discussions of 1865–70 provide abundant material to confirm such views. Parieu and Feer-Herzog tried to give a scientific character to trivial arguments

---

[68] Wolowski (1870*a*) is a collection of his interventions on the subject between 1866 and 1870, quoting all the supportive letters he received from academics awoken to the reality of sixty-five years of successful bimetallism in France. They include Jevons, Wirth, Rau, Prince-Smith, Lavelaye, Seyd, Léon Say, Leroy-Beaulieu, Cernuschi, Schmoller, and others. Not all became fervent bimetallists, but all stopped being convinced monometallists. In the 1870s and 1880s Marshall and Walras would follow Wolowski's ideas.

[69] Sometimes, more than an academic controversy, it became a bitter quarrel with personal attacks and insults, justifying the name 'battle of the standards'.

[70] For Mertens 'les milieux commerciaux estimaient que le prestige de l'Allemagne exigeait qu'elle eut une circulation d'or comme sa rivale l'Angleterre, d'autant plus que l'or était considéré comme le métal approprié pour le grand commerce international. Il y eut donc là des motifs d'ambition commerciale et nationale, dont l'influence fut décisive à partir de 1864' (Mertens 1944: 119). Mertens also added that 'Quand nous recherchons les motifs pour lesquels on est porté vers l'étalon or, nous les trouvons principalement dans des considérations de relations commerciales et de prestige international. Il fallait à l'Allemagne une circulation d'or pour son commerce international. Si de plus certains milieux préconisaient l'étalon-or proprement dit, c'est parce que, dans le cadre du mouvement d'internationalisme monétaire de 1867, on considérait l'or comme le seul métal étalon digne d'un grand État.' Mertens argued that the only rational-technical argument in favour of gold is that the weight of gold favours the development of banknotes, permitting a dangerous and abusive development of such instrument of payment. 'On préférait l'or pour de nombreux motifs, mais ceux d'ordre scientifique ne tenaient pas une place importante dans les discussions allemandes, pas plus qu'à la Conférence internationale de Paris de 1867' (ibid. 122–3). Mertens generally thought that the establishment of the gold standard in Britain was due to an involuntary historical evolution, not fully understood nor guided by the contemporaries, which was followed by a theory justifying it. The desire to imitate Britain and achieve its status led the popularity of gold in Europe afterwards, but again economic facts guided the action of men and official decisions followed .

[71] Quoted in Gallarotti (1995: 143).

[72] In 1870 Ernest Seyd warned the French monetary commission on this subject: 'permettez moi aussi de dire que je remarque en France une tendance curieuse, que je signalerais dans un certain sens, comme une espèce d'anglomanie, sous les dehors du libéralisme. Honneur à l'Angleterre, à son peuple: vous feriez bien de les consulter sous bien des rapports; mais il n'est pas nécessaire de copier tout' (Conseil Supérieur du commerce 1872: i. 395).

such as the higher 'portability' of gold compared to silver.[73] Parieu repeatedly used a form of metallic positivism in order to identity high levels of economic development with the exclusive use of gold.[74] The idea of a gold standard providing 'rules of the game' was absent from the debate and the effects of gold on financial integration, on the stability of prices and interest rates were disputed.[75] Monometallists accused bimetallism of inflationary bias, because the cheapest of the two metals would always prevail in the metallic circulation thanks to Gresham's law. They claimed that an international gold standard would stabilize the exchange rate sufficiently to make monetary union effective.[76] Bimetallists replied that gold monometallism would cause deflation and damage debtors because of the increase in the real burden of repayment. They insisted that bimetallism reduced price fluctuations to a minimum because the fluctuations in the price of one metal were restrained by the existence of a minimum legal price in term of the other metal (the French mint price of 15.5 to 1), providing *de facto* a limited band of fluctuation for the price of both metals and therefore for the exchange rate as well.[77] The disadvantage of a limited fluctuation of the exchange was more than compensated by a less unstable internal price level.[78]

In some cases the adoption of a universal gold standard and monetary unification were accused of facilitating and extending the international transmission of cyclical monetary and commercial crisis. The instability of the British interest rate was usually blamed for its disruptive effects. The Spanish Vasquez Queipo, Dutch politicians, and the directors of the Bank of Prussia advanced this argument. Sacerdoti and Parieu replied that national economies were already interdependent because of the

---

[73] According to Parieu 'L'or parait devoir être l'étalon prédominant à cause de sa commodité et de sa résistance supérieure', but also because of its 'portabilité' (Parieu 1867: 351). For Feer-Herzog, 'L'or est le numéraire le plus commode, parce que, sous un moindre poids et sous un plus petit volume, il représente des valeur considérables ... Cette même qualité s'oppose à l'exubérance du papier monnaie' (Feer-Herzog 1869: 48). To pay 200 francs one could either use silver coins weighting one kilogram or gold coins weighting 64.5 grams.

[74] Concluding the 1867 International Monetary Conference of Paris, Parieu recalled 'l'étude des lois qui mettent les métaux monétaires en rapport avec la richesse des sociétés ... Aucune invasion de la barbarie ne parait devoir faire rétrograder jamais le cours de ce mouvement successif qui a remplacé en Europe, dans une grande partie de la circulation monétaire, durant le cours des derniers siècles, le fer et le cuivre par l'argent et ce dernier par l'or.' The proceedings of the conference are in Royal Commission (1868: 188). He later reiterated his view, 'il semble d'après l'histoire, et en écartant telle ou telle transition, que l'or a tendu a prédominer dans les sociétés les plus riches, comme le métal qui permet avec un moindre poids de réaliser une circulation plus commode et plus prompte' (Parieu 1868a: 65).

[75] These terms and these issues appeared in the current form after the First World War and the Cunliffe Report of 1919.

[76] See Parieu and the commission on the reduction of exchange rate variability brought by the gold standard in Franco-German trade as compared to discount on silver in 'Rapport de la commission sur l'étalon monétaire de 1868–9' (1869: 113).

[77] The demonetization of silver needed to establish a legal gold standard would cause a depreciation of silver, causing the appreciation of gold in terms of both silver bullion and consumer goods. Demonetizing silver meant that the quantity of monetary metal would be reduced brutally causing a fall in prices given a more or less stable quantity of goods purchasable. The bimetallist were not monetarists because they did not claim that the fall of price would be identical to the reduction in the quantity of money. Instead they thought that money had real effects on the economy, they welcomed a moderate inflation expecting positive redistribute effects.   [78] See the Appendix for more detail.

internationalization of exchanges. International transmission of financial crisis already existed and differences in monetary systems did not isolate anyone. Monetary unification instead could eliminate speculation between different national currencies, easing financial crises.[79] The attempt to recreate financial barriers between countries would have been a return to a form of mercantilism the demise of which had helped so much the growth of international trade and monetary agreements, reducing the fear of gold and silver drains.[80]

3.3. HOW FAR INTO A MONETARY UNION?

Apart from debating whether the advantages of unification made it worthwhile and which metallic standard was more suitable, economists and politicians discussed how far the arrangements should integrate the various national monetary systems. As we have seen the LMU was limited to gold and silver coins, excluding bronze coins and banknotes. It did not introduce a single unit of account and each State remained responsible for its national coinage, linked by a fixed 1-to-1 exchange rate. National sovereignty was restricted only by a limit on the issue of overvalued divisionary silver coins, and by the obligation to respect common standards of mintage and to exchange information between partners. As the national banks were private, governments had to convince them to abide by the rules of the union but could not order them to do so.[81] In times of intense international speculation in currencies the Bank of France could oppose governmental policy and at one point or another it refused Swiss, Italian, and Belgian coins. No political-administrative institution was formed to manage the union, neither a central bank to run the currency nor a network of national banks officially cooperating with one another. No penalties had been devised for member States overissuing the common currency or suspending the convertibility of their paper currency in gold and silver. The International Monetary Conference had endorsed the methods followed by the LMU, proposing only limited changes. These would include the attribution of official legal tender status to international coins and the withdrawal from the Union of all large silver coins. Furthermore, the Austrian delegate de Hock had proposed to insert an expulsion clause against the States violating the provisions of the monetary convention. In fact the participation in a monetary union of countries whose currencies were not linked by a 1-to-1 exchange

---

[79] For Sacerdoti monetary union 'quando avverrà, permettendo alle specie metalliche di accorrere più agevolmente ove maggiore ne sarà il bisogno, eliminerà gran parte delle speculazioni basate sulla diversità del tipo monetario, le quali presentemente concorrono ad aggravare le crisi' (Sacerdoti 1869: 10). For Vasquez Queipo monetary unification had as a possible effect 'la solidarité des crises monétaires qui en résulterait'. Parieu replied 'la solidarité des crises monétaires se produit malgré la diversité des tarifs monétaires, sans examiner si cette solidarité n'adoucit pas les crises elles mêmes' (Parieu 1867: 339). For a more complete discussion on the national banks see the chapter about France and about Germany.

[80] 'I pregiudizi dei mercantilisti vedevano nell'uniformità del sistema monetario uno sdrucciolo pendio alla uscita dei metalli preziosi dallo stato, senza por mente che essa avrebbe fatto invece l'ufficio di un ponte tra le varie nazioni, atto ad agevolare l'entrata al pari dell'uscita della moneta, secondo i bisogni del momento' (Sacerdoti 1869: 6).   [81] Plessis (1984).

rate made the lack of a common unit of account more relevant. It was indifferent whether one counted in francs or lire, because the two currencies had the same value, but once the pound or the florin were introduced in the Union, with a 25-to-1, and a 2.5-to-1 exchange rate, the need for calculations reappeared.

The incompleteness of the proposals elaborated at the Conference of 1867 had been noticed by many. The lack of a single unit of account and of circulation and the undefined character of the divisionary coins proposed for Britain and Germany had been used in Britain by the Royal Commission on International Coinage to judge the whole scheme unsound. Elsewhere incompleteness encouraged further elaboration with respect to institutions and common currency. The French economist Michel Chevalier rightly pointed to the major weakness of the international scheme for monetary unification, namely that the French character of the proposed international coinage would awake national vanities and create an obstacle to its acceptance.[82] For the most ardent internationalists it was necessary to pass from a common coinage (various equivalent national coins) to a single coinage (a supranational coin circulating in all the States of the union) and to a single currency (supranational coins and banknotes).[83] Parieu wished to identify a common unit in francs used by all participants (5- or 10-gold franc pieces) and then introduce it in all the countries of the Union with a common name, the 'Europe'.[84] The project was shared by others, under different names, like the 'écu of the Union' proposed by Joseph Garnier, chief editor of the *Journal des économistes* of Paris, or the 'ducat' suggested by the master of the London Mint, Graham.[85] Other proposals included the grandiose 'cosmos' (Marbeau), the traditional Italian 'zecchino' (Cesare Cantù), or more modestly the 'unité' (Courcelle Seneuil).[86] Differences in denomination however depended also on which national currency was intended as the pivot of the Union, most frequently the French franc but also the pound advocated by the British commission, the US dollar or the German crown preferred by a few German economists.[87] The most bitter opponents of the adoption of the franc were a group of French economists, led by Chevalier and Léon, defined as 'metric fanatics' by Parieu and 'decimal puritans' by Feer-Herzog.[88] They refused all existing units because they did not correspond to a round weight in

---

[82] Chevalier (1868: 180).

[83] Lavelaye explained 'It would be convenient to create new coins for monetary union. Those new coins would bear on one side the symbol of the issuing State, representing the indestructible principle of nationality; the other would indicate the fixed exchange rate at which the coin would circulate everywhere and would represent the fraternal unity of the human race. Only gold coins would be essential for monetary unification. For silver coinage each State would be free to adopt the French-LMU system, accepting the relative limitations and guarantees' (Lavelaye 1867: 634).   [84] Parieu (1867: 350).

[85] For Garnier see Feer-Herzog (1870: 12). For Graham's proposal see his 'Report on the proceedings of the International Monetary Conference', in Royal Commission (1868). Graham prepared at the mint a complete system of coins in gold silver and bronze with dual values and the label 'international'. It would start with the bronze 'half farthing-1 centime', continuing with the 'decimal penny of five farthing-10 centimes', with the gold 'double florin-5 francs international' and the gold 'ducat-10 francs-100 pence'.

[86] Marbeau (1866); Cantù (1867); Courceille-Seneuil (1868: 76–81).

[87] In support of monetary unification centred on the pound see Slater (1868). For the gold dollar Augspurg (1868). In favour of the German gold crown Mosle (1870).   [88] Feer-Herzog (1870: 27).

grams and proposed a ten gram gold piece, the 'decagram'.[89] No State supported such a view because the introduction of a decagram would have imposed a very difficult exchange rate with all national currencies and required a complete recoinage of all existing monetary stocks, while the franc already existed in large quantities and circulated extensively throughout the Continent. A few British and German economists endorsed this 'natural system of currency' but in fact had different units in mind.[90] The struggle between different monetary nationalisms prompted Parieu to invite the supporters of unification to unite and not to sell the skin of the bear before it was dead. The battle of the unit accompanied on a smaller scale the battle of the standards, confirming the tendency of the French economics profession of the period to get lost in endless controversies.[91]

Chevalier also proposed to create an international committee responsible for the control of the correct issue of international coins, guaranteeing the respect of the agreed weights, fineness, and limits to issue by each member of the Union.[92] The transformation of this international commission into an international central bank would have been a further step which required the introduction of international banknotes. Most economists did not take this further step because they did not believe that banknotes were money but just a representative sign of it.[93] They thought that only coins with an intrinsic precious content qualified as money. Some of them even

---

[89] Léon (1867); Chevalier (1868: 178–210); Stoney (1871).

[90] The problem of the decagram was that 10 grams of gold seemed to have a different weight in France, Germany, and England. In Germany, following the Prussian crown, the coin was understood to be composed of 10 grams of pure gold with an added 10% alloy, for a total weight of 11.1111 grams. In France, Chevalier and Léon meant 10 grams of gold at 900/1000, as for any other French coin, therefore 9 grams of pure gold and 1 of alloy. The British supporter of the decagram, Farr, had in mind a 22 carats decagram (916.7/1000 of gold as in the pound), that he reduced to 915.31/1000, explaining that in reality the pound was slightly debased. Farr's decagram (called 'Victoria') would therefore contain 9.1531 grams of gold, but would have the simple exchange rate of 1 to 1.25 to the pound (Farr 1870). It is evident that no advantage whatsoever could come from decagrams varying between 9, 9.1531 and 10 grams of fine gold and no unification was achieved by that means. The decagram seemed to sacrifice convenience for the sake of the purity of the principle but was designed according to national customs and convenience, neither entirely faithful to principles nor to expediency, therefore discarded by most as both unpractical and not scientific.

[91] Chevalier adopted a particularly arrogant tone, with personal attacks. He wrote that Parieu's plan lacked a rational base and his proposal could not stand the test of a serious discussion (Chevalier 1868: 180 and 210). Parieu replied 'il est facile à des théoriciens de cabinet, habitués à être rigide dans les raisonnements, et peu efficaces dans la pratique, de se cantonner dans des dogmes absolus, aux exigences desquels personne ne se rend, et que souvent, le temps aidant, il finissent par délaisser eux mêmes' (Parieu 1869a: 254). Chevalier snubbed Wolowski and declared there was nothing to discuss; bimetallism was a mistake for ignorant people and his theory was 'absurde' and 'grotesque'. Wolowski replied by accusing Chevalier of 'dogmatisme hautain' (Société d'économie politique 1869: 142–3 and 145). John Stuart Mill had a poor opinion of 'the general vagueness and looseness of thought of French economists', with a few exceptions. 'I think both Reybaud and Michel Chevalier unfavourable specimens of French economists as to close thinking' (Mill to J. E. Cairnes, Avignon, 16 Nov. 1869, in Mill 1863–86: xvii. 164–5).

[92] Chevalier (1868: 184).

[93] See Cernuschi (1866). Wolowski (1870b: 281–90); Chevalier (1871: 5–18). In order to judge the unanimity of the economic profession on the subject see the two debates at the Société d'économie politique after the declaration of inconvertibility in France on 13 Aug. 1870 (Société d'économie politique (1870: 441–50); Société d'économie politique (1871: 470–87).

claimed that banknotes were forged money.[94] The fear of the impact of inconvertible paper money was also considered a reason to exclude it from any Union.[95] British economists recognized more readily the essential monetary role of banknotes because they had not been through the traumatic experience of the assignats of the French Revolution and because the more advanced banking system in the United Kingdom had already marginalized the use of coins.[96] Nevertheless the situation of the British debate on unification did not permit the advance of proposals which would go even further towards integration than the French official plan. Considering the growing role of banknotes, deposits, and cheques in the European economy, it is clear that to exclude them meant to reduce progressively the relevance of any monetary union based exclusively on the coinage. The LMU continued to operate for sixty years on those bases but, with coins progressively displaced by paper money, the Union had a declining impact on the circulation of member States. Politicians discovered the problem of unregulated banknotes later on, after Italy and Greece issued massive quantities of inconvertible paper money, unregulated by the Union. Only Joseph Garnier proposed to create a 'Universal bank' formed by the national banks, in charge of the issue and control of the banknotes of the Union. The scheme was based on a

universal bank or international syndicate formed by the official or national banks of the main trading nations. National banks would preserve their complete independence and separate organization as before, but would create together an international banknote. This syndicate, composed of directors appointed by the national banks concerned, would be responsible for the issue and control of the banknotes. It would not need a numerous work force and would transfer every four years from one capital to another, to guarantee the independence of the syndicate from local influences on one hand and to provide its members with practical knowledge of the various great financial centres on the other.

The plan employs the term 'Écu of the Union' to indicate the international currency (weight 1.6129 gr, gold 9/10th fine, value of 5 francs) and is accompanied by a very telling proof

[94] For a defence of the banknote from these attacks see Courcelle-Seneuil (1866: 342–9).

[95] 'Ce qui cause l'agiotage sur les changes ce n'est pas tant la dissemblance entre les diverses monnaies existantes que le régime du papier monnaie, qu'il ait cours forcé ou non. Entre deux États chez lesquels la circulation métallique est bien établie et où les billets de banque ne subissent aucune dépréciation, comme entre la France et l'Angleterre, par exemple, le cours du change y est généralement très régulier, et, quand il varie, c'est par suite de causes tout à fait étrangères à la différence dans le système monétaire. Avec l'Italie, au contraire le change subit des fluctuations très sensibles du jour au lendemain, et le prix des pièces de 20 francs s'y règle souvent à un taux arbitraire, au préjudice du commerce extérieur et au détriment des particuliers qui voyagent dans la péninsule' Le Touzé (1868a: 404–20, esp. 406).

[96] For Jevons 'All such attempts at definition seem to me to involve the logical blunder of supposing that we may, by settling the meaning of a single word [money], avoid the complex differences and various conditions of many things' (Jevons 1875: 248). Jevons thought that usage would settle the meaning of the term and no nominalistic discussion was necessary. He quoted the transactions for 1864 of Sir John Lubbock's Bank in London, to show that 94.1% of it was in cheques and bills, 5.3% in banknotes, and 0.4% in coin. The Manchester and Salford Bank in 1872 used 68% of cheques and bills, 27% of banknotes, and 5% of coins (coin plus notes were 32% of total turnover against 42% in 1864 and 53% in 1859). The use of the various types of money varying according to the region, the period, the wealth of the population and the type of trade (ibid. 285–6).

Money and Politics

representing a banknote of 20 Écus of the Union. On the front a drawing represents the universal bank, always identical in what concerns languages and denominations: the centre contains a crest bearing the name of the countries where the banknote enjoys legal circulation; on the sides the value corresponding to 20 Écus is indicated, payable in gold by the national banks, that is 100 francs by the Bank of France, 4 pounds by the Bank of England, 20 dollars by the National Banks of America, 40 florins by the Bank of Austria.[97]

Garnier's proposal was favourably reviewed by Parieu and by Feer-Herzog, but was too much ahead of the debate at the time to be accepted by the governments. No supranational institution was formed to manage the Union and the French Ministry of Foreign Affairs remained in fact the coordinating institution of the Union, while the Bank of France served reluctantly as the ultimate central bank of the LMU.[98] The idea that monetary union should be followed by political coordination in a European federation was advocated exclusively by Parieu. The opinion that 'political unification must take place before monetary union' was expressed by the former Belgian Finance Minister Janssen only in 1928, after the LMU was disbanded.[99]

3.4. GAINERS AND LOSERS FROM MONETARY UNIFICATION

Reviewing a series of monetary unions of the nineteenth century, the economic historian Hefeker poses clearly the question:

[E]conomic policy is determined by the influence of gainers and losers of a particular policy, the objectives of the policy-makers themselves, and the institutional setting in which economic policy takes place. Nations' behaviour is generally shaped by domestic interest groups

---

[97] 'Les billets répartis de cette manière par le syndicat ou la banque universelle entre les banques nationales seront des certificats-or assurés de la manière suivante. Sur le revers de ces banknotes, chaque banque nationale imprimera dans sa langue, et avec des dénominations propres, l'engagement de payer l'équivalent de 20 écus de l'Union. Ainsi par exemple les billets français auront un revers plus ou moins semblable à la face des billets de 100 francs de la Banque de France. De cette manière ces notes feront out à la fois le service national et international; et comme elles sont imprimées dans deux localités, la face par la banque universelle et le revers par la banque nationale, elles offrent double garantie contre les falsifications. On conviendra d'un coefficient pour déterminer l'émission qui devra être allouée à chaque pays, et on organisera, avec le moins de frais possible, le mode d'après lequel les banques échangeront entre elles leurs billets respectifs. Comme garantie chaque banque versera à son gouvernement le montant de son émission en or. En échange les gouvernements remettront aux banques leurs obligations, portant un intérêt uniforme. Le total de ces obligations forme la garantie réciproque et universelle. Rien n'empêche si l'association se compose de 10 nations que la réserve de chaque banque ne soit composée des bons de chacune des dix nation proportionnellement à la répartitions du total des notes émises par la banque universelle.

'Je répète ce plan -added Feer-Herzog—non pas pour en discuter la valeur, mais pour montrer par un exemple de plus la largeur des horizons qui s'ouvriront à la suite de l'unification monétaire' (Feer-Herzog 1870: 12–14).

[98] By the beginning of the 1880s the Bank had fully accepted its role and acted as compensation centre of the metallic species of the LMU, serving gold to its partners in exchange for silver through the intermediary of its banknotes (Luzzati 1883: 524–45).

[99] Fourtens (1930: 139). Janssen was also a former central banker and an historian of the LMU, See Janssen (1911).

advocating a certain external policy, while politicians as optimizing agents attempt to achieve their own goals under the restricting need for interest groups' support. Given that international actions are influenced by national interest groups, the question is what interests are behind monetary integration and what makes it survive or fail?[100]

Hefeker's answer is that trade integration was the most important factor. The groups which benefit from free trade supported monetary integration, and their weakening by protectionism in the 1870s undermined the movement towards monetary integration. Furthermore, States competed in the issue of money as a source of income (seignorage) and accepted the loss of seignorage only in exchange for compensation. Nevertheless external shocks could render compensation insufficient for States desperate for cash. Therefore Hefeker considered a single regulatory authority was necessary to enforce a credible coordination mechanism to prevent the dissolution of cooperation as soon as difficulties appeared.

His conclusions are confirmed in this research, but the picture can be enriched by a more detailed study of the conflicting interests shaping this particular historical episode. The objectives and the actions of policy-makers are analysed according to the various national situations in the following chapters together with the influence of specific institutional settings. The remainder of this chapter only discusses briefly some manifestations of interest groups common to all of Europe.

The industrial and commercial support for unification was evident in most of Europe. The associations of chambers of commerce were particularly interested in Germany and Great Britain but also in France and Italy. As seen earlier in this chapter, this attitude was due to free trade and the intensification of competition caused by the spreading of industrialization. The benefits to be derived from integration were not entirely homogeneous within this group. Small merchant houses and retailers could not afford to pay specialists in international exchange for every country they wished to trade with, and were forced either to use the services of an intermediary to export their goods or to abandon several foreign markets. With a single currency the entrance cost in foreign markets would be reduced and small producers would be able to compete with larger companies. The latter, fully equipped with specialized clerks, would, by contrast, lose an element of their dominant position. Generally speaking merchants attempted to reduce their costs limiting bank fees through monetary unification. Bankers obviously resisted such attempts.

The influence of the bankers' opposition has been already hinted at and will be a recurrent theme. National banks and private bankers formed the most active centre of resistance to monetary harmonization throughout Europe. The Bank of France, the Bank of England, the Bank of Prussia, and the Bank of the Netherlands all declared against any change to the monetary *status quo*, refusing to disrupt their longstanding practices. The smooth working of existing arrangements and the possible instability caused by a unified financial system in Europe were advanced to justify their resistance. In the 1860s all these national banks were private, despite the fact that their governors were appointed by the governments (with the exception of the Bank of

---

[100] Hefeker (1995).

England whose governor was appointed by private shareholders). Despite their special links with the State they did not conceive of themselves as central banks serving the interests of the public in priority.[101] They feared unknown effects of change, including the interference of foreign banks with their area of influence but also the erosion of their profit margins caused by the abolition of arbitrage between different currencies and different monetary metals. The abolition of the money changers' gain, so often invoked by the chambers of commerce, would hit national banks, private bankers, and commercial banks as well. After unification the banks could expect to see more pressures exerted by commercial customers to reduce the cost of all banking transactions.

De Cecco highlighted for the 1880s and 1890s the coalition formed in America, Austria-Hungary, and Russia between great landowners, small farmers, peasants, and debtors in favour of the reintroduction of a silver standard (and bimetallism). The strong depreciation of silver meant a devaluation of the foreign value of silver currencies, facilitating exports of agricultural products, while internally the real burden of debts was reduced by inflation.[102] This argument however cannot be extended backwards to the 1860s because the substantial stability of the price of gold and silver did not have any marked effect on prices and the value of debts. Despite Wolowski's warnings, such effects were not yet perceivable and could not solicit the creation of a powerful coalition of interests, so that agricultural interests did not feature in the debate in a conspicuous way. The French diplomats thought they had identified the political leanings associated with the metallic preferences in the discussions of the German Handelstag of 1865. 'L'extrême droite voulait le maintien de l'étalon d'argent; l'extrême gauche préconisait l'étalon d'or; le centre enfin penchait vers le double étalon.'[103] By extreme Right one must understand the Junker conservatives, linked to Prussian agricultural interests. The extreme Left were liberals and progressives, defenders of industrial and trading interests. This schematic division is appealing but explains very little. Liberals tended to be internationalists and attracted by gold, while conservatives defended the *status quo* (gold in England, silver or bimetallism on the Continent) within segmented national systems. However, the political alignments were much more articulate and personal circumstances prevailed over hypothetical party affiliations. In France the bimetallist Wolowski was politically to the left of the

---

[101] For Goodhart 'when the first Central Banks were founded in Europe, there was, however, little, or no, consideration, or attention, given to the possibility of these banks playing a supervisory role in relation to other banks. Instead, the initial impetus was much more basic, generally relating to the advantages that governments felt that they could obtain from the support of such a bank, whether a state bank, as in the case of the Prussia State Bank, or a private bank, e.g. the Bank of England.' These early private banks conducted commercial operations in competition with other private banks, slowly evolving to the non-competitive non profit-maximizing role of a proper central bank. Goodhart (1988: 4). Gallarotti added that 'the modern conceptualization of central banking was foreign to the standard operation of most central banks even up until the eve of World War I.' (Gallarotti 1984: 114). Bagehot quarrelled with the directors of the Bank of England over the public duties of the institution in 1866–73 (Clapham 1994: 283–9).

[102] De Cecco (1984: 49–51).

[103] French Embassy in Prussia to French Foreign Affairs Minister Moustier, 12 Nov. 1866 (AMAE, ADC 603–2, fol. 18).

gold monometallists Parieu and Chevalier.[104] In Germany the National Liberal Bamberger, who represented the centre of the Reichstag, was for gold but against international unification while his opponent from the Progressive Party, Moritz Mohl, was internationalist and bimetallist. The presence of liberal bankers like the Rothschilds in the conservative/anti-unification camp blurred the distinction further.

In the 1860s the French peasantry was said to be attached to the customary use of silver coins and especially to the 5-franc écus, the favoured instrument for saving in the form of hoards.[105] Tiny gold coins, difficult to handle and easy to lose, were said to be intensely disliked. Such preference for silver was expressed through local politicians, state cashiers, bankers, and bimetallist economists, but was compatible with compromise solutions permitting the adoption of a gold standard and monetary unification.[106] It was also to respond to such concerns that the French Monetary Commission of 1870 had voted for 'limping (or crippled) bimetallism', a form of gold monometallism which preserved the existing stock of silver money but prohibited new mintage of silver. That system was adopted by the LMU in the 1870s and survived until the union was disbanded in 1926.

Forecasting that a European currency based on gold would cause a fall in prices, bimetallist economists introduced the question of the debtors' interests. With prices going down, the real value of debts would increase. *Rentiers* would benefit from it but they represented the least dynamic class of society. Debtors would be penalized, including companies which contracted debts to invest and expand, the indebted States (such as Italy that had to invest to create the structures of a new unified nation, build a railway system, pacify the south, and pay for the wars against Austria), and the taxpayers who would have to pay more taxes to face the debt burden.[107] Wolowski was particularly adamant that the interest of debtors had to be protected over that of creditors.[108] The Belgian Lavelaye supported a universal money in gold in 1867 because he still perceived gold as the inflationist metal which reduced the real weight of debts: 'Any depreciation of the currency benefits those who live out of their current work and damages those who live on the income from past work. In the sixteenth

---

[104] After the fall of the second Empire Wolowski became an MP for the republican centre-left while Parieu became a senator for the monarchist centre-right.

[105] Wolowski insisted that 'en fait la pièce de cinq francs en or n'est pas acceptée surtout dans le campagnes; la pièce de cinq francs en argent continue d'y être préférée' (Société d'économie politique 1868: 313).

[106] For the French senator Dumas 'En France au contraire ce sont les classe moyennes qui possèdent l'argenterie ... Peut-on dissimuler que la démonétisation de l'argent pourrait avoir un effet politique facheux et qui serait exploité dans toutes les classes? Les classes riches et moyennes ne perdraient-elles pas sur leur argenterie; la population des campagnes ne regretterait-elle pas la pièce de 5 francs d'argent; dans les villes comme dans les campagnes, n'y aurait-il pas froissement d'intérêts?' (*Procès-verbaux et rapport de la commission monétaire de 1868*, (1869: i. 63). A more complete discussion of the attitudes attributed to French peasants is in the second part of Ch. 4.   [107] See Lavelaye in Frère-Orban (1874: 279–309).

[108] Discussing the effect of the demonetization of silver, Wolowski anticipated an increase in the price of gold, that is a fall in the prices of goods. Deflation would affect 'la dette publique, qui est la dette de tous les citoyens, et qu'on viendrait augmenter, en rehaussant la valeur de la monnaie légale; il s'agit de tous les débiteurs par hypothèques et autres, sur lesquels on pèserait ainsi et dont on augmenterait les charges déjà lourdes, pour faire un riche cadeau aux rentiers et aux capitalistes' (Wolowski 1870a: 39).

century the abundance of precious metal has contributed to the rise of the bourgeoisie, in the nineteenth century the abundance of gold will contribute to the emancipation of the working classes.'[109] The gold monometallists defended the rights of creditors not to see their capital abusively reduced by inflation. Once again since no major exchange or price fluctuations took place during the 1860s the conflict of interests between debtors and creditors forecasted by Wolowski and Lavelaye did not take place and had no influence at the time, despite its great relevance for the following decades.

---

[109] Lavelaye (1867: 633). It is clear that Lavelaye was favourable to the gold standard because gold was, at that moment, available in large quantities and the small inflation it had produced in the last fifteen years (a total of 15% in England, according to Jevons and of 10% in Hamburg according to Soetbeer) had a positive effect. In the 1870s Lavelaye became one of the most qualified supporters of bimetallism, because gold had become the scarce and deflationary metal. 'La limitation de la circulation monétaire, à l'or seul aurait au contraire pour conséquence le renchérissement de ce premier moyen d'échange, la diminution des salaires et des prix et l'augmentations des dettes, notamment des dettes publiques, parce qu'il faudrait payer le capital et les intérêts avec une monnaie plus rare et plus chère. Le maintien du double étalon monétaire est donc une mesure démocratique, car l'abaissement de la valeur de l'argent doit contribuer nécessairement à l'amélioration du sort des classes laborieuses' in Frère-Orban (1874: 20–1). Chevalier was the specular opposite of Lavelaye and supported whatever was the most stable form of currency, the most deflationary in fact, silver in the 1850s and then gold from 1867 onwards.

Managing a Difficult Union:
France and the LMU

4.1. THE DEVELOPMENT OF THE LATIN MONETARY UNION

After the formal ratification in the first half of 1866 of the Convention creating the Latin Monetary Union (LMU), the French Ministry of Foreign Affairs launched a campaign aimed at convincing European and North American countries to consider joining the LMU. Many States were favourably disposed to the proposal, but in the end the only formal addition to the LMU was Greece. This chapter examines the reasons why the LMU lost its chances of further enlargement and development even before the Franco-Prussian War crushed the political equilibrium on which the Union was based. The economic weakness of the Italian, Greek, and Papal governments, combined with the speculative behaviour of their private agents, produced a stream of formal or substantial violations, followed by acrimonious debates and tensions within the Union. The three governments adopted inconvertible paper currencies in various periods expanding forms of monetary issue not formally regulated by the convention, in order to supplement an insufficient fiscal income with seignorage and to support weak banking systems. Italy and Greece were still in a pre-industrialization phase with moderate economic growth while they were burdened by the weight of military expenditure in their pursuit of national unification and the creation of a modern State. To release pressure they temporarily replaced commodity standards with paper standards. Having already lost its richest territories in 1859–60, the Pontifical government was in an exceptional and desperate situation, attempting to resist annexation by the new Kingdom of Italy, without reducing proportionally the cost of the Pontifical government in Rome.

This led the 'northern Latins', especially France and Switzerland, to harden conditions for new members and then to refuse any new monetary agreement not based on gold. Between 1866 and 1870, the extravagantly high production of silver subsidiary coinage by the Papal government and the introduction of an inconvertible paper currency in the Kingdom of Italy, violated either the letter or the spirit of the monetary convention.[1] France and Switzerland were the primary destination of Italian and Pontifical coins, disturbing their monetary circulation. The drive towards the creation of a

---

[1] The LMU convention had created a silver subsidiary coinage of reduced fineness, whose legal price was higher than its market value to prevent hoarding and remelting. The mintage of subsidiary coinage was therefore profitable for the State, which had reserved to itself the right to issue it, while gold coins and silver écus were usually minted at the request of private agents.

universal or a European coinage started with an effort to preserve silver divisionary coinage, and then turned into an attempt to unify exclusively gold coinage. The more limited aim of *monetary unification* (all countries having identical coinage with the same weight and units), replaced *monetary union* (legal obligation to accept the coinage of foreign countries having adopted the same standards and units) and finally evolved towards the international gold standard. A more precise definition and distinction between union and unification is impossible in this context because these two terms have been employed as synonymous by most participants in the nineteenth-century debate.

The moderate fluctuation in the price of silver that took place in the period was just a further opportunity for private agents to arbitrate between different forms of money whose legal price was different from its market price. 15.5 grams of coined silver were equal to 1 gram of coined gold in the mints of the bimetallic LMU, while the market price of precious metal in whatever form—coins, bars or jewellery—was free, although fluctuating around the mint purchase price of 15.5 to 1. The arbitrage-speculation, carried out by banks, financial institutions, bullion dealers, and merchants was present at every moment of the missed expansion of the LMU.

4.1.1. *Italy's Inconvertible Paper Money*

While the parliaments of the four LMU countries were ratifying the Treaty, at the beginning of 1866, Italy was building up its military potential for war against Austria for the possession of the Venetian region. The effect of the rearmament and of war was to deepen the budget deficit, which reached in 1866 the record level of 740 million lire (approximately 11 per cent of GDP), with state income covering only 44 per cent of the expenditure.[2] The stock of debt had been growing since the creation of the Kingdom of Italy in 1861. Expenditure for the creation of unified infrastructures and railways, and for the perpetuation of an armed peace, had maintained a deficit fluctuating ordinarily between 4 and 7 per cent of GDP. In 1865 the debt had reached 4800 million (70 per cent of GDP), mainly held in French hands. At that point further Italian attempts to finance the deficit through international borrowing were discouraged by French and British lenders who wanted Italy to live within its means and not to risk wrecking its finances, endangering the reimbursement of the loans previously contracted.[3] The repatriation of large parts of the Italian debt, held by French nationals worried about the situation, accelerated the collapse of the price of the Italian State bonds (*rente*) in Paris and deprived Italy of large parts of its metallic currency. Italian coinage emigrated to pay the *rente* and the trade deficit (256 million or 3.7 per cent of GDP in 1866), leaving the Italian banks and the public with insufficient currency, just ahead of a war, and with a government unable to meet its obligations.[4] The Finance Minister, Antonio

---

[2] Frattiani and Spinelli (1984).   [3] De Cecco (1991: 31–2).

[4] However, the Italians made a good deal as well, buying back at a discounted price their own debt. The Italian economist Messedaglia 'Questo debito [estero] che al momento dell'introduzione del corso forzoso l'estero ci chiamò a liquidare e a chiudere, e noi dovemmo versargli per questo capo qualche centinaio di milioni, ricomperando in parte a ribasso i nostri stessi titoli commerciali. E altrettanto facemmo della nostra rendita pubblica, offertaci all'estero a prezzo disfatto, come si usa dire; e fù uno dei pochi casi in cui ci è

Scialoja, imposed on the *Banca Nazionale nel Regno* a loan of 250 million at 1.5 per cent interest to the government in exchange for the forced circulation of its banknotes, freed from the obligation to be convertible into gold or silver: it was the introduction of the *corso forzoso* (inconvertible paper currency) so intensely disliked by its contemporaries. Inconvertible paper money was subject to depreciation of its value in relation to coins, depending on confidence in the government, on the quantity of paper money issued, and on general macroeconomic conditions in the issuing country. The various Italian governments of the period tried to return to full convertibility of banknotes in gold and silver and many proposals were drafted, but as long as the budget deficit was so large the necessity to monetize part of the deficit prevented a resumption of specie payments.[5] Forced circulation was finally abolished in 1882 but was *de facto* resumed again between 1892 and 1900.

The LMU treaty, giving free circulation to divisionary silver coinage at 835/1000 fineness, had instantly transformed Italy into the major supplier of such coinage for France, Switzerland, and Belgium, until these States could mint and distribute their own coinage of this type. In addition to subsidiary coins, the full fineness silver and gold coins disappeared from the Italian circulation, thanks to the agio that emerged against the inconvertible paper money.

The French Minister of State, Eugène Rouher, was informed by a special report, produced from the French administration by R. Moser, on the consequences of Italian inconvertibility for the working of the recently ratified Monetary Convention.[6] Moser thought that the renegotiation of the Convention, limiting its validity to frontier zones, was the only way to 'preserve Italy from the spoliation of its subsidiary coinage through speculation and to preserve neighbouring countries from an overflow of those same coins'. Inconvertible paper money

produces a suspension of the metallic standard. Gold coins, silver 5-franc pieces, and silver subsidiary coins temporarily lose their character as money; they become goods with different prices, expressed in terms of discount on their nominal value, daily variable … Gold coins and 5-franc silver écus will stabilize with a discount not too different from the exchange rate with France … The difference of discount will create a speculation to export silver subsidiary coins out of Italy; in case of ratification of the monetary convention of Paris, opening to these coins a market in France, Switzerland, and Belgium.[7]

The combined effect of the reduction of fineness of the silver divisionary coinage and of the inconvertibility of paper money was to create three types of money, each with a different market value:

1. gold coins, silver 5-franc coins (full 900/1000 fineness), and French banknotes, freely convertible in gold: these constituted a currency whose market value was identical to its legal value both in France and in Italy until 1870.

riuscito veramente un buon affare. In tal modo, senza che fosse bisogno d'altro, la circolazione sarebbesi scaricata rapidamente di centinaia di milioni di danaro sonante, e la carta sopravvenne a prenderne il posto' (Società di economia politica italiana 1868: 816–17).

[5] Minghetti and Finali (1875).

[6] 'Note adressée à son Excellence le Ministre d'État par Rod. Moser (Monbélliard (Doubs)) le 10 juin 1866' archives privées Rouher (AN, 45 AP, carton 20, dossier 2).

[7] 'Note Moser' (AN, A. Rouher, 45 AP 20–2, 3–6).

2. silver divisionary coinage: a currency whose market value as bullion was inferior to its legal value because of its reduced fineness of 835/1000, but whose legal value was guaranteed both in France and Italy because of the LMU. In Italy this currency was appreciated in comparison to inconvertible paper money and depreciated in comparison to full fineness coins. In France it was accepted at face value for up to 50 francs per transaction.

3. the Italian inconvertible banknotes were a currency whose market value was substantially inferior to its legal value. Italian banknotes were not circulating at par in France because they were not included in the LMU convention. This form of currency suffered the highest depreciation.

Later a fourth category appeared, not foreseen by Moser: the 5-franc silver coin with full fineness whose market value as bullion became lower than its legal value as coin because of the collapse of the price of silver after 1873.

Immediately after the suspension of convertibility speculators grabbed the opportunity to realize substantial arbitrage profits, seeing that the same good (divisionary coins) had different prices in different places. The Italian silver divisionary coinage was acquired at a discount in Italy and imported into France where it was exchanged at its nominal value thanks to the Monetary Union. The depreciated Italian inconvertible banknotes served as an intermediary to transform French currency into Italian divisionary coinage. After deducting the cost of transportation of the species, of handling and insurance, the profit margin resulted from the difference between the rate of depreciation of Italian paper money to full-fineness coins and the rate of depreciation of Italian divisionary coinage to full-fineness coins. Moser expected costs to be lower than 2 per cent of the value of exported coins and the net profit to be 1.75 per cent. The operation was repeated several times, substantial profit emerged, and all the Italian coins would end up in France.

Moser had described the speculative mechanism which contributed to transporting to France the vast majority of the Italian coinage.[8] He concluded that *'the monetary convention of Paris goes beyond what prudence allows in international circulation. It must not be ratified.'* [9] The Monetary Convention was ratified anyway but Moser's observations were taken into account by the French government.

Today's historians unanimously consider the *corso forzoso* as an element of modernization of the Italian payment system. It increased the use of banknotes, restricted the role of metallic currency to international transactions, and permitted a banking expansion.[10] In 1866 the metallic circulation represented 78 per cent of Italian monetary circulation (M1 = coinage + banknotes) against 68 per cent in France (in 1870).[11] In 1873, after seven years of forced paper circulation, it was reduced to only 45 per cent.[12] Moreover, the premium in banknotes to obtain gold,

---

[8] Willis (1901: 68–70).   [9] 'Note Moser' (AN, A. Rouher, 45 AP 20–2, 9, underlined in the MS).
[10] Toniolo (1988: 102–5) echoed by Romanelli (1979: 80) or Sabbatucci and Vidotto (1994: ii. 268); Kindleberger (1993: 141).   [11] Flandreau (1995a: 271).
[12] The reduction of the role of coinage in the Italian economy was confirmed when, even five years after the resumption of specie payments, in 1887, that figure was at 41 per cent. If the LMU

which fluctuated between 3 per cent and 20 per cent between 1866 and 1882, meant an effective devaluation of the currency, compensating the extremely low protective tariff adopted in 1863, while the Italian economy was still in a pre-take-over phase.[13]

The evaluation of the *corso forzoso* cannot be the same if seen from the point of view of monetary integration. The situation showed how monetary integration was difficult in the presence of diverging economic and financial conditions. Devaluation became the solution for a situation of excessive constraint. The conditions of the Italian economy in 1866 were abnormal. The country was burdened by an armed peace, by the creation of national infrastructures, and by a large budget and trade deficit. It was an unfortunate moment to enter into a monetary union under fixed exchange rates with France. The Italian government monetized a part of its deficit, receiving several loans from the *Banca Nazionale* in exchange for the authorization to issue more banknotes not backed by gold or silver, sometimes receiving directly the new issue of divisionary banknotes, sometimes discounting at the Bank unsold state bonds.[14]

If the LMU agreement was to be considered exclusively an agreement to homogenize divisionary coinage between neighbours, then the *corso forzoso* was not a major matter of concern, because that homogeneity was preserved. If, on the contrary, the LMU was an agreement for the achievement of a wider monetary union, implying identical currency as well as coinage, and therefore stable exchange rates, then the *corso forzoso*, permitting the immediate devaluation of the currency of one of the members of the Union, was destroying the results just achieved. The unifying effort was annihilated thanks to the incompleteness of the Convention which did not include banknotes, a form of money not accepted as such by the majority of the French economists of the time.

From the introduction of the *corso forzoso* onwards (summer 1866) the Italian government would adhere to the French initiatives towards monetary unification without an active role. In 1869 the Swiss government asked Italy to take the lead in convincing France to adopt the gold standard for monetary unification.

I would consider it very appropriate for the three countries mentioned before [Italy, Belgium, and Switzerland] to act together to convince the French government to take this last step. It would mean to convey in a limited conference the delegates of the government which signed the Act of 1865, in order to introduce in the Convention an amendment for the adoption of the single gold standard.

Convention had contributed to contain the growth of metallic currency, banknote circulation had flourished even if at the cost of a 33 per cent increase of prices between 1861 and 1873 (De Mattia 1959: 189 and 198).

[13] The beginning of 'modern economic growth' and industrialization came only in the late 1890s. For the levels of depreciation of the lira see Minghetti and Finali (1875: 220).

[14] From 1874 the government would also perceive a 1 per cent tax on inconvertible paper money (Fabbri 1893). The Italian circulation of paper increase from 141 million lire in April 1866 to 496 million in December 1866, 942 million in December 1870 and 1454 million in 1874 (Willis 1901: 68).

I have already consulted Mr Frère-Orban on this subject and I have checked that the Belgian government would support such an initiative. Mr Artom[15] should have already written to M. Menabrea[16] about this. Italy should take the initiative towards Switzerland and Belgium.[17]

The reply to a similar request advanced in 1873 to Marco Minghetti, then Prime Minister and Finance Minister, is typical of the Italian approach to the problem: 'I perfectly agree and if a conference was held with our participation, I would not abstain from supporting this idea [of gold standard]. But, being under a forced paper currency regime, under which gold and silver have become a myth, although they still have some influence on our circulation, I do not think we can take any initiative.'[18]

A major shortcoming of the Monetary Convention of 23 December 1865 was that, while limiting the issue of silver divisionary coinage to 6 francs for each inhabitant, it did not limit any other form of monetary creation such as paper money, full-fineness silver, and bronze coinage. In increasing the issue of paper money, Italy was respecting the letter of the Convention, because the quantity of divisionary *coinage* was not superior to 6 francs per inhabitant, but was not respecting its spirit, because the introduction of banknotes of 2, 1, 0.5, and 0.20 lire increased the quantity of divisionary *currency*. The Monetary Convention had defined money only as a set of coins, ignoring paper money and respecting the French monetary theories which considered that real money had to have an intrinsic metallic value. From 1867 the French, the Swiss and the Belgian governments repeatedly pressed the Italians and the Greek to enlarge the definition of the forms of money to be included in the total limit of 6 francs per inhabitant.[19] After several years of pressure full-fineness silver mintage was limited from 1874 and suspended in 1878, while subsidiary paper money was considered together with subsidiary silver coinage from 1878. From 1885 inconvertibility of banknotes became a formal violation of the LMU Convention.[20] Italy resisted any modification to the Convention which would have reduced its capacity of issuing money as long as it could. 'The special conditions under which Italy is placed, still subjected to a forced paper currency, imposed on us the duty to resist any proposal aimed at reducing the instruments of metallic circulation,' as said by Italian members of Parliament.[21]

---

[15] Isacco Artom was an Italian diplomat, a former secretary of Cavour, resident minister in Paris and then in Karlsruhe and in Vienna. He was the main Italian representative at the Monetary Conferences of Paris in 1865 and 1867.

[16] L. F. Menabrea was the Italian Prime Minister and Minister of Foreign Affairs from October 1867 to December 1869.

[17] Le chef du Département des Finances Suisses, J. J. Challet-Venel au Ministre de Suisse à Florence, G. B. Pioda, 19 March 1869, in Commission Nationale pour la publication de Documents Diplomatiques Suisses (1879–92: ii. 268–9).

[18] Marco Minghetti to Luigi Luzzati, 7 Aug. 1873, in Minghetti (1978: i, 16).

[19] In 1869 the Swiss government expressed to France its unhappiness at the situation and about growing criticisms of the LMU convention in Switzerland. 'On est ainsi amené à conclure que toute union monétaire est impossible, si chaque État de l'Union se réserve d'établir le cours forcé des billets suivant ses convenances. En d'autres termes la convention de 1865 aurait du prévoir le cas et prohiber toute mesure de ce genre. Elle renferme à ce point de vue une lacune qu'il importe de combler' (French General-Consulate in Switzerland to French Minister for Foreign Affairs La Valette, 10 March 1869, ADC 604-2, fols. 33–4).

[20] Garelli (1946: 100).   [21] Camera dei deputati (1874: 2).

A brief list of the controversies of the late 1860s shows the difficulties of monetary diplomacy in a Monetary Union whose rules have not been properly laid down and accepted explicitly and in full by all its members.

In 1867 Italy increased unilaterally its silver divisionary contingent from 141 to 156 million, because of the increase in population due to the annexation of the region of Venice.[22] The French Minister of Foreign Affairs accepted in principle the Italian declaration but

> The Minister of Finance, however, whom I considered my duty to consult, informed me that the new Italian subsidiary coins already circulate in France in very large quantities and that they have already produced on certain issues some problems because of their accumulation, which might force the use of the means authorized by art. 8 of the Convention of 1865. An excessively rapid increase in the issue of such coins would, in the opinion of Mr Rouher, contribute to increasing such problems.[23]

Rouher threatened to return to Italy its excessive divisionary silver coinage. Italy reached its new ceiling in less than a year but offered to take back the surplus of Italian divisionary coinage circulating in France, exchanging it according to the rules of the Union.[24] Rouher immediately shipped back to Italy some divisionary coinage but was forced to suspend the operation because the Italian Treasury operated very slowly and ultimately, because of its difficult financial situation, had problems in finding either gold or commercial paper over Paris to reimburse France.[25] In fact, the repatriation of Italian divisionary coinage was completely useless. As long as the Italian exchange rate

[22] The Italian ambassador Nigra communicated to the French government that 'Mon Gouvernement me charge d'annoncer cette décision au Gouvernement Impérial, ne doutant pas qu'il voudra donner son adhésion ainsi que les autres puissances signataires de la Convention Monétaire du 23 Décembre 1865' (Italian Ambassador in Paris, Nigra, to the French Minister of Foreign Affairs, Moustier, 17 February 1867, AMAE, ADC 601, Part de l'Italie (1867), fol. 1).

[23] Moustier to Nigra, Paris, 19 March 1867 (AMAE, ADC 601, Part de l'Italie (1867), fol. 2).

[24] 'Le gouvernement du Roi [d'Italie] est tout disposé à procéder à l'échange des pièces divisionnaires d'argent précitées, dès que le gouvernement Français en fera la demande.' Italy asked for advanced warnings in order to collect the necessary amounts of gold for the exchange (Italian Minister in Paris Nigra to the French Minister of Foreign Affairs, 8 Apr. 1867, AMAE, ADC 600, fol. 121). Moustier asked to send 2.2 millions of Italian coins accumulated in Marseilles by the Bank of France (French Finance Minister Rouher to French Minister of Foreign Affairs Moustier, 24 Apr. 1867, AMAE, ADC 600, fol. 153). For further procedural delays see French Minister in Italy Malaret to French Minister of Foreign Affairs Moustier, 14 July 1867 (AMAE, ADC 600 bis-3, fol. 54).

[25] The new Finance Minister, Magne, pressed again by the Bank of France, took up the desperate fight to return to Italy its divisionary coinage. 'Il existe actuellement dans les succursales de la Banque une quantité considérable d'anciennes monnaies divisionnaires d'argent italiennes, sans parler de 6 à 7 millions de pièces neuves appartenant à la même nationalité. À différentes reprises et tout récemment encore la Banque de France s'est plaint de la gène qu'occasionnait à ses succursales l'accumulation dans leurs caisses, des monnaie étrangères et elle a demandé à mon administration de prendre des mesures pour les faire cesser.' In August 1867 a first million has been sent back to Italy, further operations had been suspended for the 'embarras financier du Trésor italien', but now Magne wanted to repeat the operation with half a million at a time (French Finance Minister Magne to French Minister of Foreign Affairs, 15 June 1868, AMAE, ADC 604–1, fol. 148).

remained unfavourable to Italy because of inconvertibility, repatriated Italian coins would migrate again to France.[26]

Italy refused requests to withdraw its divisionary paper money, that is, paper money of 2, 1, 0.5, and 0.2 francs. When Switzerland and France asked it directly, in connection with the application for membership by the Republic of San Marino, sponsored by the Italian government, Italy interrupted the correspondence on the question. In January 1869 Italy had transmitted the request of the Republic of San Marino. The Swiss government replied refusing to accept the proposal because it would be a new uncontrolled source of monetary issue. It then turned against Italy, with a frankness so unusual for the diplomatic practices of the time that thus revealed its exasperation on the subject:

The Federal Council objects that Italy has added to the total amount of its regular issues at 835 / 1000 further 81 millions of paper money in 2-franc notes and 6 million in 1-franc notes. The Council understands this as an unfair interpretation of the spirit if not of the letter of the Convention of 1865 and in any case it attributes the cause of the problems weighing on the other members of the Union to the invasion of Italian subsidiary coinage, driven out of their country of origin by the 2-franc and 1-franc banknotes.[27]

Magne gladly supported the Swiss request that Italy should withdraw its 87 million of divisionary paper money, as 'such breach of the equilibrium is the evident cause of the problems faced by the French Treasury, which force us to limit the issue of our 0.835 coins well below the limit fixed by the Convention (165 million against 239).'[28] Nevertheless Magne had previously acknowledged that the problems due to the circulation of Italian coins was over emphasized.[29]

The Italian government struggled against its own financial difficulties which prevented the abolition of the *corso forzoso*. The budget needed to be sufficiently improved to enable the government to pay back the loan received from the Banca Nazionale in

---

[26] Belgian Finance Minister Janssen later wrote: 'les liquidations des monnaies divisionnaires présentent une grande utilité, parce qu'elles sont destinées à prévenir l'accumulation des monnaies divisionnaires dans un pays où l'activité des transactions les aurait attirées. Toutefois remarquons dès à présent que c'est là un remède inefficace à l'égard des pays à change déprécié. On aurait beau procéder à ces liquidations et rapatrier dans le pays d'origine les monnaies divisionnaires, celles-ci ne tarderont pas à franchir de nouveau la frontière et à se répandre sur le territoire des États contractants. Le fait s'est vérifié ultérieurement à l'égard de l'Italie et de la Grèce, si bien que ces pays ont été forcés de nationaliser leur monnaies divisionnaires' (Janssen 1911: 194).

[27] French Finance Minister Magne to French Minister of Foreign Affairs la Valette, 26 Apr. 1869 (AMAE, ADC 602–6, fol. 21).   [28] Magne to la Valette, 26 Apr. 1869 (AMAE, ADC 602–6, fol. 22).

[29] Magne replied to the Swiss worries that 'En fait, il n'apparaît pas que, dans les transactions journalières, le public établisse des distinctions entre les monnaies nationales et le monnaies étrangères; s'il en était autrement, avec l'immense quantité de monnaie étrangères et particulièrement de monnaies italiennes jetées dans la circulation de la France, les difficultés seraient incessantes et elles sont au contraire fort rares. Il est arrivé cependant à plusieurs reprises que la Banque et le Trésor lui-même aient eu à se prévaloir des restrictions légales imposées à la circulation de monnaies d'appoint, mais ces faits accidentels avaient pour objet, non pas de faire obstacle à la circulation de telle ou telle monnaie en raison de son origine, mais de la défendre contre la surabondance des pièces divisionnaires en général ou même de s'opposer à des spéculations abusives' (Magne to La Valette, 4 Feb. 1869, AMAE, ADC 604–2, fols. 24–25).

exchange for the authorization to issue inconvertible paper money. Furthermore, most of the divisionary paper money was issued in Italy for speculative purposes by local banks, local government, associations or merchants, needing small denomination forms of money and attempting to profit from the confusion.

In January 1868, the French Finance Minister, Magne, worried about information on a large issue of Italian bronze coins (20 million francs), indicated that they would combine with the inconvertible paper money to push Italian silver subsidiary coinage into France, 'already congested'.[30] Magne elaborated on the duties associated with membership of a monetary union:

> Despite the fact that the Convention of 23 December 1865 concerns exclusively gold and silver coins and that each State has maintained complete freedom for what concerns the issue of copper coins, it is nevertheless established that monetary union implies generally as a consequence a reciprocal and effective control between the various States linked by the Convention.[31]

The French considered new bronze issues as the cause of new migrations of silver, Italians considered it a consequence of it and wished to prevent its migration. The Italian Treasury complained to the Italian Foreign Affairs Ministry in March 1868 about the departure of Italian bronze coinage towards France, facilitated by the fact that the French officials in Savoy accepted them in violation of the Convention.[32] Economic forces were stronger than the will of both governments.

In order to quantify the effect of these disputed measures, I have calculated the amount of monetary instruments of less than 5 francs issued by LMU members, between 1861 and 1870 and between 1861 and 1878. Gold coins and large banknotes are not taken into account. It is not an estimate of the monetary instruments available inside the five nations in 1870 and 1878, but of their monetary issue, part of which did not circulate anymore, being exported or melted down. Table 4.1 shows that Italy had issued at the end of 1870 a much larger quantity of divisionary money (defined as bronze coins plus silver divisionary coins plus banknotes of less than 5 francs) than its monetary allies (12.2 francs of divisionary money per inhabitant, compared to 6.1 for Belgium, 4.9 for France, 3.6 for Switzerland, and 2.4 for Greece). If the silver 5 francs were added and included into the definition of subsidiary form of money however, Belgium would become the largest issuer and Italy would be in a situation comparable to that of France.

In the initial period (1865–73) moral suasion had no effect within the Monetary Union. No country which was already a member could be forced to change its practices and accept restrictive modifications of the initial treaty because unanimity was indispensable. Instead new members or aspiring members could ultimately be

---

[30] At the moment of its political and economic unification Italy had coined 36 millions of francs in bronze in 1861–63. With the introduction of the Corso forzoso, Italy tried to replace some of the divisionary coins that had migrated with a new issue of 38 millions of bronze in 1866–7. It was a one-off operation, no bronze coinage was issued in Italy for the following twenty-five years.

[31] Magne asked Moustier to address to Italy 'des représentations officieuses à ce sujet' (French Finance Minister Magne to French Minister of Foreign Affairs Moustier, 14 Jan. 1868, AMAE, ADC 604–1, fol. 23).

[32] Italian Finance Minister Cambray Digny to Italian Minister of Foreign Affairs Menabrea, 31 March 1868 (ASD Moscati VI–646).

Table 4.1. *Issue of small denomination forms of money in the LMU, francs per capita*
(total issue from 1861 onwards)

	Bronze coinage		Silver subsidiary coinage		Silver écus		Paper money (fewer than 5 francs)	
	1870	1878	1870	1878	1870	1878	1870	1878
France	0.30	0.38	4.58	5.69	6.55	15.66	0.00	0.00
Italy	2.85	2.62	6.00	5.55	2.22	12.17	3.35	3.99
Belgium	0.06	0.16	6.00	5.82	32.34	64.55	0.00	0.00
Switzerland	0.04	0.30	3.57	4.33	0.00	2.70	0.00	0.00
Greece	2.00	2.51	0.40	5.14	0.00	8.86	0.00	0.00
Average	1.19	1.22	5.06	5.58	6.49	17.18	1.10	1.44

Source: Coinage issue are calculated from Leconte (1995). Population figures are those implicitly used for the attribution of LMU quotas in 1865 and 1878. The paper money figures are those quoted in the diplomatic correspondence discussed below.

disciplined introducing tougher rules. From 1873 things would change. When the possibility of achieving universal or at least European monetary unification became clearly unrealistic, the central nation changed its behaviour and, flexing its muscles, enforced discipline on the other partners. In 1878 the French government was ready to break the Union if Italy had not accepted the complete and permanent suspension of silver mintage. France also disciplined its partners with the requests for redemption in gold of their depreciated silver coinage held by France. The improved economic conditions and the prospect of the abolition of the *corso forzoso* helped Italy to concede in 1878 to the Union the redemption of its own divisionary coinage held abroad, the withdrawal of divisionary paper money, and the suspension of the mintage of silver écus.[33] But as long as a larger unification was possible and France could not use a 'big stick policy', few of the French requests were successful and they usually remained secret, creating an evident frustration both in the population and in the policy-makers.

It is not surprising therefore that some publicists attributed the increase in prices of goods in France to the estimated 100 million of Italian coins in France, shouting 'might God free us from Italian coins', as if it were a plague.[34] A few years later they would have also shouted 'God free us from the Pontifical coins!'

4.1.2. *The Speculation of the Pontifical State*

The monetary speculation of the Pontifical States was an important cause of the declining popularity of the LMU in 1870, but was overlooked by most historians and

[33] Willis (1901: 187).

[34] Cottet, 'Désastreuse influence de la crise financière de l'Italie sur la circulation des monnaies en France', *Journal des villes et des campagnes*, 17 May 1867, 1 in AmdP, K2–22.

economists.[35] Contemporaries frequently referred to that case in the official debates of 1869–70, but named the Pontifical State as little as possible, for fear of arousing a huge political outcry. The financial situation of the Pontifical State replicated that of the Kingdom of Italy on a smaller scale considering its limited population (500,000 inhabitants) but on a much larger scale considering per capita budget deficit. The existence of the Pontifical government itself was under the constant threat of Italian patriots wishing to unite Rome to the rest of Italy. The Pontifical government was therefore financially desperate and willing to breach openly the letter of the LMU Convention in order to obtain seignorage income and keep afloat a little longer.

The French zeal in admitting the Papal States to the LMU depended on Napoleon's need to secure Catholic political support against the rising liberal, monarchist, and republican opposition in Parliament and in the country during the last years of the Empire.[36] The French Ministry of Foreign Affairs was ready to go to great lengths to please the Pope, initially supported by the Finance Ministry.

The Papal government monitored carefully every sign of evolution in Franco-Italian relations, on which the survival of its temporal power depended. Its desperate economic situation made it extremely open to any financial opportunity arising.[37] The first request for information to Paris, followed by an immediate decision to conform to the conclusions of the Monetary Convention, came in December 1865, even before the end of the Conference forming the Latin Monetary Union.[38] In June 1866 the Papal State introduced a new coinage of pontifical lire replacing the old scudi and baiocchi. The new coins carried the effigy of the Pope but respected the LMU system except for the introduction of two further divisionary coins of 2.5 lire and 25 centesimi which corresponded to old Roman coins.[39]

The Pontifical Secretary of State, Cardinal Antonelli, announced to France on 4 February 1867 that Rome was joining the Union, misinterpreting article 12 of the LMU Convention, which encouraged new accessions.[40] The simple declaration of accession, after the introduction of the coinage of the LMU, was not sufficient, since the agreement of the founding members was necessary. France reacted positively, demanding however some guarantees concerning the exactitude of the Pontifical coins' production and rigorous respect for the limit of 6 francs of divisionary coinage

[35] The two exceptions are Crocella (1983), based on the Vatican Archives, and Flandreau (1995c), based on the archives of the Quai d'Orsay.

[36] The Swiss Feer-Herzog lamented that 'la France, par un motif qui parait politique, reçoit ces monnaies dans ses caisses publiques et possède d'ailleurs aussi longtemps qu'elle entretient des troupes à Civitavecchia un moyen facile de s'en défaire' (Feer-Herzog 1869: 32). Between 1860 and 1870 French troops were the only safeguard left for the Pope against the annexation of Rome by the Kingdom of Italy.

[37] In 1866, for an expenditure of 65.9 millions of francs, the Pontifical budget exhibited a deficit of 33.4 millions (Felisini 1990: 82).

[38] The *Nonce Apostolique* to French Minister of Foreign Affairs Drouyn de Lhuys, 13 Dec. 1865, 1. French Embassy in Rome to Drouyn de Lhuys, 19 Dec. 1865 (ABdF, 'La Question Monétaire', II, 2).

[39] The French Embassy in Rome to Drouyn de Lhuys, 18 June 1866 (ABdF, 'La Question Monétaire',II, 2). The Pontifical States had effectively a bimetallic standard. In 1862 the circulation withdrawn by the Kingdom of Italy in some former Pontifical territories was composed of gold for 30 per cent and of silver for 70 per cent.

[40] The Pontifical Secretary of State Cardinal Antonelli to French Ambassador in Rome, 4 Feb. 1867 (ABdF, 'La Question Monétaire', II).

per inhabitant. The Belgians approved the French position, but the Italian government refused to admit the 2.5-lira and the 25-centesimi coins and refused to give its consent, imitated by the Swiss government.[41]

Long negotiations began at once, but the problem was that the almost inexhaustible French goodwill in favour of the Pope had already created an explosive situation: *Le Moniteur* had published 12 February 1867 the Pontifical declaration as if it had been formally accepted and the Pontifical coins had acquired legal tender in France. On the basis of that note, the Bank of France started to accept the new Pontifical coinage, on a temporary basis, even without formal notification from the Finance Ministry.[42] Several later attempts of the Bank to reject Pontifical coins met requests of tolerance issued by the Finance Ministry, which ordered all public cashiers to accept Pontifical coins.[43] With the resulting public confidence, Pontifical coins were spreading throughout France, especially in the south. The Pontifical coins entered France following the Imperial troops on leave from Rome but were also shipped for speculative purposes, together with Italian coinage.[44] The Swiss, mystified by the note of the *Moniteur*, began accepting Pontifical coins as well.[45]

In the meantime French diplomats negotiated between the Pontifical government requests and the Italian passive resistance, until all obstacles appeared to be removed and all laws and decrees harmonized with those of the LMU. The Pontifical reactions were always extremely slow. Cardinal Antonelli was reluctant to grant concessions and give up minimal differences in monetary legislation, the primary goal of international circulation having already been reached, thanks to French tolerance.[46] Antonelli was buying time until all the members of the LMU had accepted the position of the Papal State. Monetary reform and the circulation of the Pontifical coins in France had re-established an exchange rate close to the par and calmed the financial crisis in Rome (Graph 4.1).

Finally, France sent a formal note of approval on 2 March 1868, followed by the other members, including Italy on 17 July. The French Foreign Ministry invited Cardinal Antonelli to exchange a formal declaration to become officially the fifth member of the LMU.[47] After two months and a half of silence, the Pontifical reply came as a *coup de théatre*. Antonelli declared his intention to refuse the limit to the coinage of divisionary coins, after three years of negotiations and without any previous warning on his part on the subject. Instead of the 3 to 4.2 million of francs

[41] French note on the replies to the Pontifical declaration (ABdF, 'La Question Monétaire', II, 12–14).   [42] Ibid. II, 17.
[43] Letter from the office supervising the branches of the Bank of France to the branch of Lyon, 7 Dec. 1867, 23. Letter from the Toulon branch to the office supervising branches, 21 Dec. 1867 (ABdF, 'La Question Monétaire'. II, 24).
[44] The Toulon chamber of commerce to the French Finance Minister Magne, 28 Jan. 1868 (ABdF, 'La Question Monétaire', II, 25).   [45] Feer-Herzog (1869: 29).
[46] Cardinal Antonelli to French Minister of Foreign Affairs Moustier, 27 Sep. 1867, 19–21. French Minister of Foreign Affairs to the French Embassy in Rome, 6 Feb. 1868, 27–30. Memoir by Cardinal Antonelli to the French Embassy in Rome, 18 Feb. 1868 (ABdF, 'La Question Monétaire', II, 31).
[47] Moustier to the Pontifical Government, 29 Sep. 1868 (ABdF, 'La Question Monétaire', II, 44).

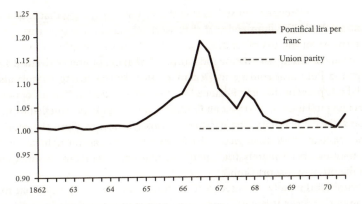

Graph 4.1. *Exchange rate between the Pontifical lira and the French franc, in Rome*
Source: Elaboration from quarterly averages in Pinchera (1957b).

corresponding to the LMU quota, 26 million had already been minted and more would come to complete the recoinage of old coins. This was justified by the need to rescue the Banca Romana, which was close to bankruptcy, and to feed the Roman population after the loss of the richer parts of the State to Italy, while the Italian inconvertible paper money was draining Pontifical coinage. 'The Holy Father asks therefore an exemption from the articles 6, 7, 8, 9 of the convention, at least until 31 December 1877.'[48]

The French were deeply shocked by this completely unexpected revelation. The Finance Ministry took a decided stand against these excesses,[49] while the Quay d'Orsay spent an extra year trying to find a solution. But it was too late and the Pontifical faith in French benevolence had stretched things too far. Magne defined the limitation on mintage as 'the fundamental clause of any Convention', and the right to return emigrated coinage to the issuer as the 'indispensable corollary'.

These two clauses are the safeguard and the guarantee necessary for the contracting parties, and while they are insufficient to prevent unpleasant consequences when one of the parties leaves ordinary monetary conditions through the adoption of inconvertible paper money, at least they limit damages and prevent them from spreading indefinitely. Even if the results of the Convention of 1865 are not those we would have wished for, concerning subsidiary coinage, to abandon the only guarantees offered by the Convention would risk making them even more unfavourable.[50]

[48] Summary of the letter by Cardinal Antonelli to Moustier, 12 Dec. 1868 (ABdF, 'La Question Monétaire', II, 45–46).

[49] Giving his consent to the Papal accession in March 1868, Magne, who had received complaints about the accumulation of Papal coins in France, had requested to be informed about the amounts of Pontifical coins already minted. (French Finance Minister Magne to the French Minister of Foreign Affairs Moustier, 27 March 1868 AMAE, ADC 601–3, Accession des États Romains, fol. 107).

[50] French Finance Minister Magne to French Minister of Foreign Affairs La Valette, 18 Jan. 1869 (AMAE, ADC 601–3, Accession des États Romains, fol. 162).

In May 1869 Switzerland refused all Pontifical coins, calculating that total Pontifical issue had reached 35 million and that they were introduced for speculative purposes on the territory of the Confederation.[51] The Swiss also accused the Quai d'Orsay of negligence and ambiguity in the negotiations.[52] The Bank of France decided again not to accept the Pontifical coinage in December 1869.[53] The strong complaints of the public did not prevent the new Finance Minister Buffet, tired of Roman opportunism, from deciding in January 1870 that all Pontifical coins should be expelled from French circulation. On 17 February, the *trésoriers payeurs généraux* received the order to suspend the 'circulation de tolerance'. The Pontifical coins had no right to circulate in France, they had been merely tolerated, assuming that formal membership of LMU would take place in a short time.

A political crisis rapidly mounted. The Catholic press, relayed by Catholic members of Parliament, accused the new French government of anticlerical plots, defended the rights of the Pope, and the perfectly good quality of his coinage. Rumours were spreading that the Papal coinage was debased and did not respect the legal weight and fineness, being up to 12 per cent under the official weight. A stormy session of the French Parliament on 25 February centred on what could be done and who should bear the costs of the disastrous withdrawal of the Pontifical coins from the French public. The Member of Parliament Vendre quoted the *Journal de Nice* 'The whole trade of the south is agitated after the refusal of silver Pontifical coins. This troublesome measure has taken the proportions of a catastrophe in Nice'.[54] The Finance Minister, Buffet, declared that in an orderly state of things silver divisionary coinage could be minted in limited quantities, proportional to the needs of circulation and used for a small part of the payments. 'Without these two conditions, the mintage of silver subsidiary coins with a lower fineness would be equivalent to forgery.' The Finance Minister of France was accusing the Pope of debasing the coinage! Buffet announced also that the Pontifical coins, tested by the mint of Paris, had revealed a fineness of 0.83176, instead of the declared 0.835, inferior to the limit of tolerance accepted by the LMU.[55] It was not possible to force the Papal government to buy back its own coinage, because it had not exchanged any declaration and was not bound by the LMU rules. Buffet added that France was invaded by 30 million francs of Pontifical divisionary coinage and by 80 million Italian coins, exported thanks to the *cours forcé*. Therefore the French Mint, which had the right to coin 239 million francs of divisionary coins, to which was associated a profit of 7.3 per cent, as the real value of its silver content was

---

[51] ABdF, 'La Question Monétaire', II, 56–9.   [52] Feer-Herzog (1869: 29).

[53] Note pour la succursale de Lyon de la part du Bureau des succursales (ABdF, 'La Question Monétaire', II, 67). The istructions were to reject all pontifical coins, not to favour speculation as 'quelques uns de vos banquiers après s'être chargés, moyennant commission, de les répandre sur votre place, refusent de les reprendre en paiement.'

[54] Procès Verbal du débat sur la monnaie pontificale au Corps législatif, 25 Feb. 1870 (ABdF, 'La Question Monétaire', II, 97).

[55] The nonconformity of the Papal coins to the the finenesse requirements of the LMU was known in Paris since July 1868, but had been kept secret. (AMdP, K2. 16, 'Le vérificateur en chef des essais communique au Président de la Commission des Monnaies et Médailles le résultat des essais sur les monnaies pontificales: ... moyenne 831.74').

lower than its legal value, could not go beyond a total coinage of 170 million, in order not to obstruct the monetary circulation. 'Such restriction on our issue has had the effect of depriving the Treasury of the legitimate profit it could and should have drawn from the difference between the real and the nominal value of subsidiary coinage'.[56] Since some Catholic Members of Parliament insisted on the free circulation of Papal coins, Parieu, Minister Presiding over the Council of State since January, had to intervene. He was forced to stress the national character of money. Parieu was discovering with the abuses of the Papal government the difficulties of monitoring the economic policy of monetary allies. At the end of the debate, Buffet confirmed that the question was decided and the State could accept Pontifical coins only as bullion, with a 9 per cent discount.

The small holders of Pontifical coins panicked: the money changers were asking a 10 to 20 per cent premium to accept the disgraced Pontifical coins in the first few days, the State offered 9 per cent. Soon the major banks (Comptoir d'Escompte and Crédit Foncier) stepped in, offering a reduced 5 per cent discount. The private banks could accumulate large amounts of coins, ship them to Italy, and reintroduce them in the Papal States at par. Once the transportation costs were deducted, a substantial profit emerged. The French State could not do such an operation, nor could it remelt the Pontifical coins and introduce them in the circulation as French coins because of the excessive circulation. If they had to be taken as bullion, their real value was 8.1 per cent under their legal value, with the additional cost of collection, transportation, and recoinage.[57] The Catholic press started a campaign, calling for a boycott of the other LMU coins.[58] A part of the French clergy attempted to exchange at par the Pontifical coins to prevent the discredit of the Papacy. So did the Papal consul in Lyon until he was forced to suspend the operation by the excess of demand and by reprimands from Rome. Many newspapers wanted the government to accept the Pontifical coinage at par and use it to pay the French troops in Rome, but the Defence Minister refused to pay his troops with debased coinage.

The reports of the French clergy warned Rome that the continuation of the Papal fraud would annihilate the flow of pious gifts of money to the Holy Seat, the *Obolo di San Pietro* (Peter's pence). When Antonelli realized this threat against the most important source of income of the Pontifical State, he immediately offered to redeem all the coinage at par accepting the cost of withdrawal.[59] The French Finance Minister rebuffed the Pontifical authorities and declined sharply any further intervention. 'It is quite regrettable that such a proposal has been produced so late, since it could have prevented the crisis and it is now impossible to accept it.[60] The *Journal des économistes* was ironic: 'Pontifical coins have been in the news lately, even more so than the

---

[56] Procès Verbal du débat sur la monnaie pontificale au Corps Législatif, 25 Feb. 1870 (ABdF, 'La Question Monétaire', II, 99).

[57] The Paris mint charged a mintage fee of 0.21 per cent on gold and 0.75 per cent on silver (Seyd 1868).

[58] *La Patrie*: 25 and 27 Feb. 1870, 2 March; *l'Univers*: 1 : 1, 6, 7, 10, and 13 March 1870; *L'Union*: 27 Feb. and 15 March (ABdF, 'La Question Monétaire', II, 93–119).

[59] The Apostolical Nounce Chigi to the French Minister of Foreign Affairs, Daru, 17 March 1870 (ABdF, 'La Question Monétaire', II, 135). See also Crocella (1983: 90).

[60] The French Finance Minister Buffet to the Apostolical Nounce Chigi, 25 March 1870 (ABdF, 'La Question Monétaire', II, 138–9).

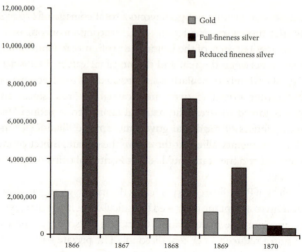

Graph 4.2. *Yearly production of new Pontifical lire*

Source: Elaboration on Mint figures in Varesi (1984: 254–8).

Syllabus and the dogma of infallibility [of the Pope] ... The Pontifical Treasury has gained two or three million and the trick has worked. Cardinal Antonelli is certainly more clever than delicate.'[61]

The Pontifical mint had issued more than 8.5 million lire of reduced fineness silver in the second half of 1866 before the formal application to join the Union.[62] This amounted already to more than double the maximum amount accepted by the LMU. Therefore, while presenting a formal request of accession and claiming to respect the LMU rules, the Papal government had already breached those rules, knew about it, and lied about it. Not only did it deceive the French negotiators about past events but it increased further the production of reduced fineness coinage to 11 million in 1867 (Graph 4.2). While negotiating with the French authorities, 20 million more were added to the circulation, for a total of 30.8 million of reduced fineness silver coins. The Pontifical State, with a population between 500,000 and 700,000, had coined as much as Belgium which had a population of 5 million. Furthermore the new monetary law introducing the franc had been approved on 18 June 1866, but on 4 October 1866 the Pontifical State had decided the forced circulation of the paper money of the Bank of the Pontifical State, with a 15 per cent agio on gold and 10 per cent on silver during the first three months of 1867.[63] From the beginning of the issue of new Pontifical lire, the internal circulation of the State was in paper money. All new coins would be exported immediately and coined exclusively to delay the economical collapse of the State.[64] Crocella summarized the Pontifical behaviour stating that 'the whole negotiation

---

[61] 'Chronique économique', *Journal des économistes* , 3rd ser, 19, Sep. (1870), 501.

[62] The figures on pontifical coinage are calculated from Varesi (1984: 254–8).

[63] Pinchera (1957).   [64] Crocella (1983: 76).

appears not as a way of beginning economic reform but as another attempt, entirely orchestrated by Cardinal Antonelli, to delay the economic collapse of the State.'[65]

The political and monetary crisis had created a unanimous opposition to any further unification on the basis of silver divisionary coinage in France. No more expansion of the Latin Monetary Union took place after those events. As the weakest States of southern Europe could afford almost exclusively silver coinage or banknotes, the survival of the programme of monetary unification had to depend exclusively on the adoption of a gold standard. Magne, several times Finance Minister during the Empire (1855–60, 1867–70, 1870) and the third Republic (1873–5), described his attitude in May 1870 towards monetary agreements with the following words:

Concerning our relations with abroad, proceed rather by good relations than by contracts of union. Surveillance of contracts of union is very difficult. Experience has proved it. Such difficulty increases according to the number and the distance of the members. Good relations would have the same consequences [of union], but it would have the advantage of leaving to each country exclusive responsibility for the defects of its issue, for the discredit and the losses which could ensue from it. It is through its regularity and through the confidence it inspires, rather than because of a contract, that the currency of a country must acquire the right to circulate in another State.[66]

The Papal State's attempt to act as a 'free rider' was heavily punished, but it had discredited the idea of monetary unification. The Papal State was occupied and annexed by Italy on 20 September 1870, just sixteen days after the fall of Napoleon III, defeated and captured at Sedan. The ironic conclusion of the story is that in September 1871, when the payment of the indemnity to Prussia had dramatically reduced the circulation of divisionary coinage in France, the Bank of France reintroduced in circulation, at their nominal value, 1.9 million in Pontifical coins, accumulated at the request of the Treasury to ease the crisis in February 1870.[67] The Bank guaranteed the quality of those coins to the public and their circulation continued for more than a decade after the end of the crisis. As late as 1893, France and Switzerland returned to Italy 5 million of Pontifical coins.

4.1.3. Greek Accession to the LMU

Greece ended up bearing the consequences of the Italian and the Papal monetary policies. Its admission in the LMU was conditioned on the total control by France of its monetary circulation: all Greek coins would be minted in Paris under the supervision of the French Imperial authorities, they would be shipped and delivered to Greece under French control and Greece could not issue any banknote of 5 francs or less without being expelled from the Union. The strongest country of the Union needed to take upon itself all the monetary powers to be sure that the Union would not work against it. France would import monetary disorder and problems if it decided to

---

[65] Ibid.   [66] Letter by Magne to Parieu, in Conseil Supérieur du commerce (1872: ii. 306).

[67] ABdF, 'La Question Monétaire', II. See the note published by the Bank of France in the *Journal Officiel* 1 Nov. 1871, 157.

unite with a country it could neither trust nor control. The difficulties linked to the financial problems of the States and to the participation of insufficiently monitored private interests in the process of monetary creation, multiplied the possibilities of abuses and betrayals of the spirit of the Union, destroying any residual desire to enlarge Monetary Union.

In April 1867 Greece introduced the LMU coinage with a new monetary law and asked to join the LMU in May.[68] The Greek government also requested authorization to use the Paris mint since it could not afford a national mint. The manufacturing of Greek coins would take place 'under the control of officials of the imperial government', 'sous le contrôle des fonctionnaires du gouvernement impérial', as a guarantee of the quality of the coinage.

Willis thought 'it is hard to see why the admission of Greece to the Latin Union should have been desired or allowed by that body ... Economically unsound, convulsed by political struggles and financially rotten, her condition was pitiable. Struggling with a burden of debt, Greece was also endeavouring to maintain in circulation a large amount of inconvertible paper.'[69] Feer-Herzog also protested on behalf of Switzerland, expecting to see difficulties and violations 'therefore we regret that Greece has been admitted to the small circle of the Convention of 1865'.[70] In 1867 France wanted the largest possible number of countries to join the Union, independently of their economic conditions, in order to get as close as possible to a universal or at least European common coinage. The French policy of diplomatic and military support to the enlargement of the Kingdom of Greece, in Crete and towards Macedonia, implied some form of economic support as well.[71]

The Greek request for accession was accepted without problems as the new monetary law followed precisely the LMU rules and the new drachmae were identical to francs and lire. The French thought they had secured the key to an unproblematic Greek membership, since they controlled directly its coinage:

My predecessor already had the honour to inform Your Excellency that the consent of the Finance Ministry to the Greek membership of the Union was largely motivated by M. Delyannis's declaration in his letter of 2/14 May 1867 that Greek coins would be minted in Paris ... The guarantees of proper production of the coinage offered by this clause having heavily influenced the decisions of the contracting parties, it is important to include it formally in the act of accession ... My department considers such a modification as absolutely necessary.[72]

---

[68] The Greek Minister in Paris to the French Finance Minister Rouher, 10 Apr. 1867 and 2 May 1867 (ABdF, 'La Question Monétaire', I, 818 and 824).

[69] Willis (1901: 81).   [70] Feer-Herzog (1869: 40).

[71] Some influence must have been exercised by the philohellenic movement, by the French artistic and archaeological interests that led to the creation of the French School of Athens and the policy of acquisitions of the Louvre, in competition with the British Museum. The French excavation of Delphi started in 1860 and the Victory of Samotrace was bought in 1863. Many of the discoveries arrived in Paris through French diplomats Etienne and Etienne (1992). Traces of classical reminiscences could also be found in Parieu, who said, quoting Mirabeau, that universal money would be as the law was for antique orators: 'elle est une, elle est universelle; elle est la même pour Rome et pour Athènes', Parieu (1869b: 392).

[72] French Finance Minister Magne to French Minister of Foreign Affairs Moustier, 27 Nov. 1867 (AMdP, K2.21, fols. 1–2).

Greece accepted and on 4 December 1868, *Le Moniteur* announced officially the Greek accession from 1 January 1869. The French Finance Minister, Magne, authorized the beginning of the production of Greek subsidiary coins on 7 November 1868. The President of the *Commission des Monnaies*, Dumas, indicated that work was starting on 19 December, but asked for guarantees that 'It is important that all of these coins are introduced in the circulation of *the same country* issuing them, consequently Your Excellency will no doubt consider it appropriate to demand immediately from the Hellenic government formal guarantees securing the export of the coins in question to Greece.'[73] Shortly afterwards, on 19 January 1869, Magne ordered the suspension of the coinage and of the delivery because on 18 January he had discovered that very day 'that the new Greek coins are introduced into circulation directly in Paris'.[74]

Was Greece flagrantly violating the agreements just concluded with France? The combined evidence of the various archives show that Greece had not deliberately attempted the abusive introduction of Greek coins in France. The difficulties derived from the lack of experience of the Greek government in such international dealings, combined with the need to cover sudden military expenditures with new seignorage income. The Greek government had suspended the convertibility of banknotes, believing that such a move was perfectly legitimate, since banknotes were not even mentioned in the LMU Convention and formally inconvertible paper currency was not prohibited. In order too join the LMU, Greece had to create an entirely new coinage, replacing its old circulation of national and foreign coins with new LMU franc–drachma, equal to 1.047 old drachmae, a change that none of the four founding members needed to go through. Lacking an established financial expertise and in order to minimize the cost of the monetary reform, the Greek government had contracted the whole operation to the Parisian firm Erlanger et Cie. Erlanger would have to buy silver on the market, have it minted in Paris, transported in Greece, and distributed to the Greek banks at its own cost and risk, finding its profit in the difference between the cost of silver, mintage, and transportation and the legal price of coined silver.[75] When Greece introduced the *cours forcé* of banknotes at the end of 1868, unable to finance the cost of rearmament due to the Greek uprising in Crete against the Turks, excessive issue of paper money immediately caused its depreciation.[76] Erlanger realized that the profit expected from the operation had vanished. Instead of carrying on a contract paid in paper money, he decided to leave the operation to another French bank, the Maison de Banque Dreyfus et Scheyer, selling Greek coins in Paris at a price lower than their nominal face value. The French government did not entirely grasp the details of the operation at once, even if the Quai d'Orsay attributed the responsibility for the events to the bankers. The reactions were misled, amplified, and protracted by the alarmed

---

[73] President of the Commision des Monnaies Dumas to Magne, 16 Dec. 1868 (AMdP, K2.21, fols. 2).

[74] Magne to French Minister of Foreign Affairs La Valette, 18 Jan. 1869 and 26 Jan. 1869 (AMAE, ADC 601, Accession de la Grèce (1), fol. 130 and 128).

[75] The reply of Erlanger to a late enquiry from the Quay d'Orsay is reported in French Minister of Foreign Affairs to French Minister in Switzerland, 27 Nov. 1869 (AMAE, ADC 601, Accession de la Grèce (2), fol. 34).   [76] S. Lazaretou (1995: 30–31).

communication by the Belgian government that the operation was carried out directly by the Greek government, that Dreyfus and Scheyer had already sold a million in Greek coins, and that this further violation would threaten the existence of the whole Monetary Union.[77] The French Foreign Minister commented on the margin of the Belgian dispatch: 'These observations are absolutely right and teach us a lesson for the future. As for the present we can only take precautions so that further issues will take place regularly.' The Greek received authorization to resume the mintage after draconian precautions had been taken.

Here are the measures adopted and since then strictly followed: coins are enclosed in boxes sealed with the seal of the Monetary Administration of France and of the Greek Legation in Paris, and then transported either to Athens or to some other place in the Kingdom where some French Consular Agents are in residence; two Commissars are in charge of attending the arrival of the boxes, to check their authenticity and integrity and to write a report on the operation, which is finally transmitted to our monetary administration.[78]

The misinformed French Consul in the Cyclades Islands added new worries, insinuating that the new coins were re-exported to France by Greek merchants as soon as they had reached Athens, to the disappointment of both the Greek population and the French government.[79] A new controversy arose and the permission to mint was withdrawn again. The reality was that only 574,520 drachmae had been minted in 1868 and no more until 1874 (dated 1873),[80] but the Greek government had received only 60,000, none of which had been distributed to the public and could have been re-exported to France.[81] Erlanger had received and dispersed in Paris half a million francs and was the only person responsible for the crisis. The Greek government committed the grave mistake of sticking to its dishonest agent, Scheyer, and asking Erlanger to resume the mintage, while the latter looked for all possible excuses not to fulfil his contract. In 1874, under French pressure, the Greek government replaced Erlanger, assuming direct responsibility for the production of its coinage. Transportation and distribution had already been taken over in 1870 by the National Bank of Greece.

Further negotiations about the implementation of the Greek membership were much more demanding once Greece had acquired a shaky reputation. Furthermore, at the end of 1869, France, Belgium, and Switzerland were completely aware of the weaknesses of the Monetary Convention, thanks to the Italian and Papal examples.

---

[77] Belgian Minister in Paris to French Minister of Foreign Affairs La Valette, 1 Feb. 1869 (AMAE, ADC 601, Accession de la Grèce (1), fol. 132).

[78] French Minister of Foreign Affairs La Tour d'Auvergne to French Chargé d'Affaires in Brussels Siméon, 25 Oct. 1869 (AMAE, ADC 601, Accession de la Grèce (2), fols. 6–7).

[79] French Consulate in Syra (Greece) to French Minister of Foreign Affairs La Tour d'Auvergne, 9 Sept. 1869 (AMAE, ADC 601, Accession de la Grèce (1), fol. 198).

[80] Mint records reported by Leconte (1995: 230–1).

[81] The sum of 60,000 fr is advanced by the Greek Finance Minister and confirmed by the existence of only one report of arrival of coins in Greece, sent by the French representatives in Greece, in the archives of the Quay d'Orsay, for 60,000 fr. (French Legation of Tirame in Greece to French Minister of Foreign Affairs La Valette, Athens, 10 March 1869, AMAE, ADC 601, Accession de la Grèce (1), fol. 157).

Images of piles of Italian and Pontifical coins and banknotes must always have been present in the diplomats' and civil servants' minds.

Greece attempted to calculate its population generously, in order to be able to mint a higher amount of divisionary coins, as the Convention was limiting it to 6 francs per inhabitant expected to be resident in each country at the end of the Convention in 1878. Greece asked to mint immediately the total contingent available for the whole duration of the agreement, 9 million drachmae. The LMU member States had no objections to this figure, except Switzerland, but were concerned about further guarantees.[82] The Belgian government requested to be reassured about the final destination of the Greek contingent of coins. Handling the operation directly, the French government was able to reassure its partners that no distribution of Greek coins would take place out of Greece. The Swiss wanted to be sure that Greece would introduce the new coinage replacing the old one, not adding it to the existing stock and leaving room for speculation and reimportation into the rest of the Union, as was happening in the Papal States. Already infuriated by the Italian inconvertible paper money, Switzerland was attempting in fact to extend the definition of divisionary coinage to the small banknotes of 2, 1, and 0.5 francs, to include them in the total limit of divisionary coinage allocated by the Union to each member. The aim was to prevent a new flow of small paper money, increasing the means of payment which would create more room to export the surplus silver circulation to the other member States of the LMU.

The Greek protested violently against the Swiss lack of confidence and discriminatory treatment. The Greek government had never authorized any banknote under 10 drachme, nor ever intended to do so, regulating strictly all the issues of banknotes. Anyway, why should Switzerland impose a limit which was not written in the Convention and which no other State had to respect (the implicit reference was to Italy). 'I do not consider it fair to impose on us an obligation not included in the present Convention, an exception on our account which is not justified by anything.'[83] It was impossible for Greece to introduce the new coinage without receiving it first, and only the insignificant amount of 60,000 francs had been received from France, as the French government knew perfectly well, nor was it possible to withdraw the old coinage from the circulation in shorter terms than those fixed by the Convention. The Swiss government finally accepted the Greek issue, on condition that the Greek assurances about small denomination banknotes would be annexed to the diplomatic documents, becoming a formal commitment. Furthermore new guarantees were added for the transportation to Greece of the coinage minted in Paris, preventing any immediate use in the rest of the LMU. The French Ministry of Finance requested an executive agreement, permitting France and its monetary allies to return to Greece its divisionary coinage, ex art. 8 of the Monetary Convention, containing a real guarantee

---

[82] French Minister of Foreign Affairs, la Tour d'Auvergne to Chargé d'Affaires of Greece in Paris Phocian Rogue, 1 Nov. 1869 (ABdF, 'La Question Monétaire', I, 846–8).
[83] Greek Minister of Finances to Greek Chargé d'Affaires in Paris, Athens, 15 Nov. 1869 (ABdF, 'La Question Monétaire', I, 849–56).

that payment in silver écus or in gold would take place on request. Buffet was pessimistic. Due to the *cours forcé* and lack of good coinage in Greece 'we must not expect much from this agreement which will remain a dead letter for a long time at least; I believe we will find ourselves in relation to Greece in the same situation as with Italy, entitled to use art. 8 but unable to use it.[84]

In a desperate attempt to solve the deadlock, the Greek Prime Minister and former Ambassador to Paris, Delyannis, took direct responsibility for the question. Delyannis announced that he would reply to the French, Swiss, and Belgian concerns about paper money launching a governmental loan to abolish the *cours forcé*. He would also use the foreign currency reserves of the Greek banks, which would be compensated, to secure gold or silver écus to pay any amount of Greek subsidiary coins returned by other members of the Union.[85] The French asked to see a signature under a formal document. The final agreement between France, Belgium, Switzerland, and Greece was signed on 4 August 1870, four days before the fall of the Ollivier government and thirty-one days before the fall of Napoleon III. Magne, returned to the Ministry of Finance, authorized on 20 August 1870 the mintage of 9 million Greek silver subsidiary coins.[86]

Such draconian conditions, imposed by foreign governments, could be accepted only by a weak and almost desperate country and showed that the desire to enlarge the Union further south was essentially exhausted already before the Franco-Prussian war. The Franco-Prussian war, the ensuing French *cours forcé*, the siege of Paris, and the payment of the indemnity to Germany, followed by the recoinage for resumption of specie payments in 1873, delayed the effective mintage of Greek coins until 1874. The whole contingent of subsidiary silver coins was speedily minted and sent to Greece in a few months between 1874 and 1875.

In 1874 Greece was not invited to the conference of the LMU which limited the issue of silver écus, because it did not mint any, but the Greek government asked to be invited for the following year, planning to start the coinage in question. While its delegate was absent for urgent business in Belgium during the 1875 conference, a tentative contingent of 5 million in écus was allotted to Greece by the other States. The following year Greece adopted the Italian technique of negotiation, asking for a contingent of 50 million, meaning 25 and accepting 12 (3.6 of ordinary contingent, plus 8.4 of extraordinary contingent). Afterwards Greece did not renew its requests, but just after the completion of the mintage of its contingent by the Paris mint in 1877, it resumed the *cours forcé*, preparing the recurrent war with the Ottoman Empire. Greece however respected its pledge not to issue banknotes of a value equivalent to that of its subsidiary coins.[87] Except for a few months in 1885, inconvertibility lasted

---

[84] French Finance Minister Buffet to French Minister of Foreign Affairs Daru, 10 Jan. 1870 (AMAE, ADC 601–2, fol. 62).

[85] Greek Légation in Paris, Phocian Roque to French Minister of Foreign Affairs Daru, 28 Feb. 1870 and 12 March 1870 (AMAE, ADC 601, Accession de la Grèce (2), 72).

[86] French Finance Minister Magne to French Minister of Foreign Affairs Gramont', 18 May and 20 August 1870 (AMAE, ADC 601 2, fol. 82 and 130).

[87] *Journal des Débats*, 18 Nov. 1878, (AMdP, K2 20).

Table 4.2. *Location in the member countries of the LMU of their respective subsidiary coinage in 1893 (million francs)*

	France	Italy	Belgium	Switzerland	Greece	Not in the LMU	Contingent allocated in 1885	Amount minted end 1893
French coins	182	18	15	5	0	31.9	264.0	251.9
Italian coins	85	63	7	25	0	22.4	202.4	202.4
Belgian coins	18	1	17	1	0	3.8	40.8	40.8
Swiss coins	10	1	0	9	0	2.0	25.0	22.0
Greek coins	5	2	1	0	1	1.8	15.0	10.8
Total	300	85	40	40	1	61.9	547.2	527.9

Source: Chambre des Députés, séssion de 1894, 656, Rapport de la Commission du Budget sur la frappe des monnaies divisionnaires d'argent, AMdP, K3 43.

until 1910. Greece even defaulted on its foreign debt in 1893 and was never fully integrated in the financial mechanisms of the LMU.[88]

When an estimate of the circulation of the divisionary coinage in the LMU was produced in 1893 (Table 4.2), it appeared that 68.8 per cent of the Italian subsidiary coinage had left the country and formed 62.5 per cent of the Swiss subsidiary circulation, 28.3 per cent of the French, and 17.5 per cent of the Belgian circulation. It also appeared that 90 per cent of the new Greek coinage had left the country and that it did not constitute a substantial part of the circulation of the other countries only because of the limited amount existing of Greek coins (the 45 per cent of the Greek coinage exported in France constituted only 1.7 per cent of the French circulation).[89]

Greek coins did not become a problem comparable to their Italian or Pontifical equivalents. Nevertheless the amounts issued were insufficient for Greece and the advantage of the latter country in joining under these conditions was dubious, having to keep an additional foreign circulation to satisfy the internal needs of subsidiary coinage (86 per cent of its circulation in 1873).

4.1.4. *Enforcement of the rules in the LMU*

On the whole the Latin Monetary Union succeeded noticeably well in disciplining the mintage of silver by its members, avoiding the feared inflationistic effects. Two waves of silver mintage were stopped.

The first wave was the mintage of reduced fineness silver (subsidiary coins) in the mid-1860s (Graph 4.3). It was started to save the limited silver circulation from complete depletion during the phase of high silver prices that was driving all silver

---

[88] Lazaretou (1995: 33).

[89] Chambre des Députés, *Rapport de la Commission du Budget sur la frappe des monnaies divisionnaires d'argent*, séssion de 1894, no. 656 (AMdP, K3 43).

Money and Politics

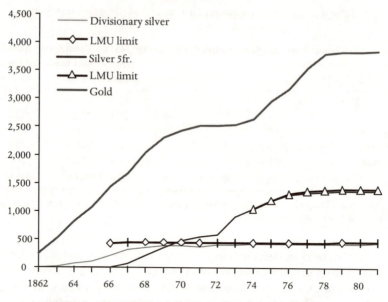

Graph 4.3. *Cumulated issue of the Latin Monetary Union since 1862*

Source: Elaboration on Mint figures in Leconte, (1995). Figures are million francs and include French, Italian, Belgian, Swiss, and Greek issues.

coins to the melting pot. The perceived threat of excessive issue was controlled with a rigid limit to issue, introduced when the Convention was signed, proportionally to the population of each member State. The 7.3 per cent seignorage attached to the issue of silver subsidiary was the irresistible temptation that needed to be contained, as we have seen in detail, by five means:

1. Securing the respect of the limits to issue by the original members through the mutual exchange of information about each others' annual output of coins.[90]

2. Attributing to the stronger government (France) an absolute control over the issue of coins of new weak members (Greece).

3. Threatening to return divisionary coinage to the issuer (Italy and Greece) in exchange for gold, thus imposing on members with an undisciplined fiscal policy a financial loss.

4. Expelling the free-riders from the Union (the Pontifical State).

5. Refusing membership to States which did not guarantee the required conditions (Spain, Austria-Hungary, Romania, and San Marino).

The difficult and gradual construction of these rules meant that after five years of union, the repressive no. 3 and no. 5 became the predominant policies for monetary stability.

---

[90] See Art. 11 of the Convention of 23 Dec. 1865 forming the LMU. This article was drafted and added by the President of the French Commission des Monnaies, Pelouze (Oliveira 1992: 124).

The Romanian application in 1867 was discouraged because of the scarce guarantees for the respect of the qualitative standards and of the quantitative limits of the Union.[91] The preliminary agreement with Austria-Hungary arranged by Parieu and de Hock in 1867 was kept suspended and never ratified, because France refused the adoption of a gold standard and did not wish a monetary union with another country under *cours forcé*. San Marino was flatly refused in 1869. The candidature of Luxembourg was not successful either.[92] Spain's application was kept pending from 1869 onwards until it was withdrawn. The official motivation was the French refusal to introduce the 25-franc coin requested by Spain.[93] Given the fact it was the French government who had promoted the 25-franc international coin scheme, the excuse seemed rather weak. The Colombian application in 1871 could not be accepted, 'il nous sera impossible de l'accueillir, alors même que nous obtiendrions, contre les dangers de cette accession, des garanties complètes, analogues à celles que nous avons exigées de la Grèce.'[94]

This policy was maintained thereafter, refusing the accession to the Union or the legal circulation in France to the coinage of Serbia (requested in 1874, 1879, and in 1880), Venezuela (1879), Bulgaria (1880), and Finland (1881 and 1885). In the 1870s and 1880s France granted selectively access to its internal circulation to LMU-type gold coins of Sweden (1872), Austria-Hungary (1874, but denying to it the full membership in the Union), Russia (1887), and Spain (1891). These decisions depended initially on the French attempt to counter the financial influence of the German Empire in Scandinavia and Austria, but neither prevented the creation of an independent Scandinavian Monetary Union at the end of 1872, nor the progressive shifting of Austria-Hungary towards Germany. Later on, the French position of an international lender, which received interest coupons payable in gold, dictated the benevolence towards Russian and Spanish gold. After the disappointments of the 1860s and in a period of increased nationalism, there was no more possibility for an enlargement of the Monetary Union. The LMU itself, after 1878, survived only to avoid the cost of dissolution and potential new problems from neighbours recovering their freedom to issue devalued silver coins.[95]

Graph 4.4 suggests that the end of the first wave of silver mintage was anticipated by at least two years, thanks to the non-admission of Spain, Romania, and other possible candidates, which minted subsidiary coinage of reduced fineness in the 1870s. The graph represents the yearly issue of silver divisionary coinage of LMU members and of

[91] The French expected Romania to issue only bronze coins initially. They did not show any enthusiasm from the beginning (French Minister of Foreign Affairs to French Finance Minister, 16 Feb. 1867 ABdF, La Question Monétaire, I, fols. 548–9).

[92] Luxemburg announced in 1869 its intention to join the LMU and to have its coinage minted in Paris. French Deputy Consul in the Grand Duchy of Luxembourg to French Minister of Foreign Affairs La Valette, 23 May 1869 (AMAE, ADC 604–2, fol. 51).

[93] Spanish Embassy in France to French Minister of Foreign Affairs la Tour d'Auvergne, 9 Oct. 1869 (AMAE, ADC 602–3, fol. 2).

[94] French Minister of Foreign Affairs Rémusat to French Finance Minister Poyer Quertier, 14 Sep. 1871 (AMAE, ADC 602–1, fol. 7).

[95] Darnis (1994).

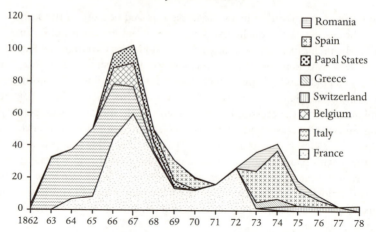

Graph 4.4 *Distribution of the yearly issue of silver divisionary coinage between members and candidates to the LMU (million francs)*

Source: Elaboration on Mint figures in Leconte (1995).

some candidates. The LMU itself reached a peak of issue of 91 million francs of divisionary coinage in 1867 but would have known a second peak of 40 million in 1874 had Spain and Romania been included in the LMU.

The second wave of silver mintage, stopped by the introduction of new LMU limits to issue in the 1870s, was the mintage of silver écus of 5 francs, the last vestige of the silver standard (Graph 4.5). The 5-franc écus were not regulated before 1873–4 because their full fineness (900/1000) did not guarantee any profit to an agent wishing to coin bullion, as long as the market price of silver was not lower than its legal price. The threat of excessive issue was due to the depreciation of silver, which had slowly started in 1866, had accelerated in 1871, but had become really substantial only in 1873 when the German Empire moved to the gold standard and the French and Belgian governments decided to limit the coinage of silver. Until 1873 individuals could freely carry silver to the Mints of the members of the LMU and to have it coined. Coined silver had then a legal price in coined gold (15.5 to 1), higher than the market price for bullion silver.

The limits to issue were decided every year in January at a Conference of the LMU, and the contingents allotted to each country were progressively reduced to zero between 1874 and 1878 (Table 4.3). The second wave was easier to check because the profit from coinage was not initially reserved to the governments but to the individuals bringing silver bars to the mint. In 1874–5, while undertaking to curb speculative issue of silver écus, Italy, Belgium, and Switzerland 'nationalized' the profits, reserving to the government the right to provide the mint with silver bullion.[96] France delayed that operation for some time and the mint, under pressure from

---

[96] Redish (1993: 80).

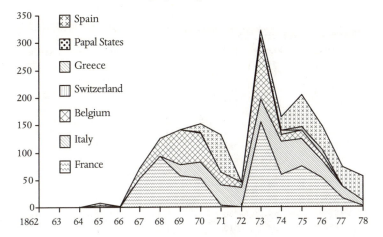

Graph 4.5 *Distribution of the yearly issue of silver écus between members and candidates to the LMU (million francs)*

Source: Elaboration on Mint figures in Leconte (1995).

holders of silver who tried to grasp an easy and secure profit, delivered notes promising coinage for the following year (*bons de monnaie*), before the LMU conference had met to decide new quotas. A forceful speech in the French Senate by Parieu helped to stop this practice in 1876 and contributed to the French Parliament's decision to defeat the defence of bimetallism by the Ministry of Finance and vote in August for the banishment of silver from the French mints.[97] In Italy the *Banca Nazionale nel Regno d'Italia* centralized the withdrawn silver coinage of the dissolved Italian States, holding in particular large amounts of Neapolitan silver. For this reason and because of its structurally insufficient stock of coins Italy resisted the reduction of the yearly quotas of écus and the adoption of limping bimetallism (*bimétallisme boiteux*). The progressive banishment of silver was facilitated by the collapse of its price. There was also an unofficial punishment, threatened on misbehaving members (Belgium and Italy), the request of redemption in gold of their silver coins held in France. It was unofficial because article 8 of the Convention granted that right only for silver subsidiary coins and not for silver écus. Italy and Belgium would have to redeem their coinage at the legal price, in gold, while the market price had fallen and several million francs of loss would be incurred.

It must be stressed that the initial intention of the Italian and French governments was not to progressively cancel and abolish the production of silver coins, as in the case of the Belgian and Swiss governments. France did not want to introduce a gold standard but to protect bimetallism from the excess of speculation and restore the freedom to mint silver as soon as the transitory disturbances on the silver market had passed (the diplomatic definition of the German attempt to adopt gold standard dumping German silver on France and Belgium). The instructions given by Magne to the

[97] Parieu (1876).

Money and Politics

Table 4.3. *LMU limits to silver mintage (1865–97)*
(millions of francs, lire, and drachmae)

	Years	France	Italy	Belgium	Switzerland	Greece	Total
Silver	1865	239	141	32	17	—	429
divisionary	1867	239	156	32	17	—	444
coinage	1870	239	156	32	17	9	453
(total	1878	240	170	33	18	10.5	471.5
limit to	1885	256 + 8	182.4 + 20	35.8 + 5	19 + 6	15	551.2
issue)	1897	394	234.4	46.8	28	15	718.2
	1908	628.8	540.8	116.8	57.6	42.4	1386.4
Silver écus	1874	60	40 + 20	12	8	0	140
(yearly	1875	75	50	15	10	5	155
limit to	1876	54	36	10.8	7.2	3.6 + 8.4	120
issue)	1877	27	18	5.4	3.6	0	54
	1878	0	10	0	0	0	10
	1879	0	20	0	0	0	20
	From 1880	0	0	0	0	0	0
Total écus	1874–80	216	194	43.2	28.8	17	499

Sources: Data from the AMAE, AMdP, and reports attached to the *Minutes of Evidence of the Gold and Silver Commission* (London, 1879).

French delegates for the 1874 LMU Conference, confirmed by the General Director of the Ministry of Finance, Dutilleul, during the LMU Conference of 1875, supported by the Bank of France in 1874 and 1875, are very clear. Only in 1876 did the supporters of the gold standard succeed. Thanks to the continuing fall of the price of silver, the quotas adopted to protect silver coinage became quotas to extinguish it.

Graph 4.5 shows the yearly coinage of silver écus by France, Belgium, and Italy. It shows the beginning of the rush to coin silver in the late 1860s, halted by the Franco-Prussian War and the introduction of *cours forcé* in France between 1870 and 1873. As soon as the war indemnity had been paid to Germany, the rush started again with the impetus accumulated in the years of restricted issue, just to be restricted again by the introduction of LMU quotas. The peak of 308 million silver coins issued in the Union in 1873 was due to France and Belgium for 86.3 per cent. The two countries were the key to international bimetallic arbitrage until 1873 supplying the bimetallic block and serving as intermediaries between the gold block formed around England and the silver block formed around Germany.[98] Most of the silver minted in Belgium was minted by foreign financial interests.

The cost of membership in the LMU was unequally shared. The stronger economic system of the Union, France, served as a stabilizing factor during the first wave (1866–74), absorbing the migrating Italian and Pontifical coinage, through a reduced use of its large contingent. In the 1870s France was not ready to play such a role again.

---

[98] Flandreau (1995b).

The political reasons for supporting the Pope did not subsist, and the tolerance created by the desire to complete European monetary unification under a French hegemony had vanished together with Parieu's project and the role of Paris as the main financial centre of Continental Europe.

After the Franco-Prussian War the survival of the Union was continuously threatened by the attacks of monometallists and bimetallists locked in a bitter dispute worldwide. In 1875 Parieu was ready to kill his own creature in order to banish silver from the French mints despite the Italian resistance.[99] Once Parieu had succeeded and the LMU stopped coining silver écus, it was the turn of the bimetallists to ask for the termination of the Union, to permit a return of silver. In 1884 Cernuschi mounted a

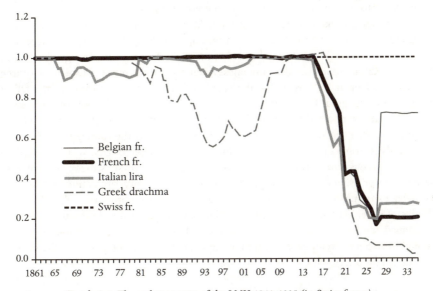

Graph 4.6 *The exchange rates of the LMU 1864–1935 (in Swiss francs)*

Sources: For the French, Italian, and Swiss rates between 1861 and 1890 see Ciocca and Ulizzi (1990–5: i. 341–68). For the Greek rate between 1880 and 1913, see Flandreau, Le Cacheux, and Zumer, (1998: 49). For the period 1890–1918 see Ministère du travail *Annuaire statistique*, (1919: XXXV, 291). For 1914–40 see Board of Governors of the Federal Reserve System (1943: 663–73). Rates are calculated in Swiss francs because Switzerland did not change gold parity for the whole period examined.

[99] 'Quoique j'aie eu plus de part à l'établissement du pacte monétaire de 1865 qu'à la formation de la doctrine de l'étalon or, recommandée fort avant moi par lord Liverpool en Angleterre et par Hofmann en Allemagne, je ne craindrais pas en ce qui me touche, de préférer pour mon pays une rupture temporaire, ou, pour mieux dire, suivant toute probabilité, une suspension de l'union de 1865 à une union qui devrait avoir pour résultat de vicier probablement à tout jamais, la circulation métallique de notre pays.' Parieu also indicated 'la France peut contenir les aspirations de fabrication illimitée pour l'Italie, supposée par forme comminatoire en état de rentrer sous la convention pure et simple de 1865, en laissant refuser à l'Italie la réception de ses écus d'argent à la Banque de France, comme elle est intervenue en 1874 pour convier la Banque à les recevoir' (Parieu 1875a: 156–72, esp. 167–8).

'great trial which must be ended by the dissolution of the Latin Union ... All should get ready, the days left to the Latin Union are counted.'[100] The Union survived but, as Graph 4.6 shows, it fulfilled only partially the role for which it had been conceived, to stabilize the currency market and to eliminate transaction costs. During repeated periods of inconvertibility the exchange rate of the lira and of the drachma continued to fluctuate substantially, while moderate fluctuations persisted even for the other currencies of the Union. The First World War knocked down all the LMU currencies, with the exception of the Swiss franc, *de facto* killing the Union. The LMU was formally dissolved only when the various currencies were stabilized and returned to a gold exchange standard at different levels of exchange rate in 1926. It is interesting to notice that exchange rate stability did not increase when the LMU countries passed from bimetallism to limping bimetallism or to the gold standard.

The question remains whether the Latin Monetary Union succeeded too well in checking silver issue and inflationist temptations, blocking for a time the necessary increase in the quantity of money needed to maintain the economy on a growing path. Milton Friedman, following the bimetallist tradition, claims that the suspension of free coinage of silver in 1873, reducing the supply of money, was the cause of the fall in prices and of the great Depression that started at the same time.[101] In recent research, Flandreau also supported the idea of a deflationist effect of the LMU policy.[102] Graph 4.4 suggests that, in the LMU countries, the limitations to the mintage of silver prevented silver from compensating the reduction in the supply of gold which took place in the late 1860s and in the late 1870s. According to Wolowski's theory of compensation, a larger silver component in the European monetary circulation would have allowed a smooth path of growth of the supply of money, without instability.[103] The figures of silver actually minted appear small, but, had the path of growth of 1868–73 continued without restrictions, silver would not have been able to displace gold. It would have been a relevant and useful complement to it, in the period of Depression and declining prices which started in 1874.[104]

4.2. THE FRENCH INTERNAL DILEMMA: CONFLICTING GROUPS PARALYSING POLICY

The success of the 1867 International Conference had been possible because the central nation of the Continental monetary system (France) had conceded to the secondary States and to the USA what they requested: the gold standard and the common

---

[100] Cernuschi, (1884: 3 and 69). He attacked Italy which was trying to introduce the gold standard, accusing it of ingratitude, irresponsibility, and of appropriation of 15 million francs every year from the rest of the Union, keeping 300 millions of its silver écus abroad and issuing internally paper money saving interest it would have had to pay on equivalent amount of national debt. Luzzati described Cernuschi as 'scintillante, volubilmente artistico, il quale nascondeva una tesi teorica errata sotto il fascino di una parola arguta, nella quale lo spirito parigino si temperava colla finezza italiana' (Luzzati 1883: 535).

[101] Friedman (1992).

[102] Flandreau (1995c: 40). See also his larger study rehabilitating bimetallism as a long lasting, stable and efficient international monetary system (Flandreau 1995b).

[103] Wolowski (1870a).   [104] See Einaudi (1997: 327–61).

25-franc piece. Immediately after the Conference was disbanded, a polemic on these two aspects of monetary unification began in France. Parieu deployed his rhetorical powers: 'In the history of mankind, the generous utopia of yesterday can become the practical and manageable achievement of tomorrow, because the world has moved. Well! Now Gentlemen, the world has moved.'[105] Europe had indeed moved towards monetary unification much more than many contemporaries wanted to acknowledge and certainly more deeply than modern scholars realize. But France, Germany, and England had not yet moved to a point where they were prepared to accept a unification of their currencies.

This chapter explores how the institutional debate took place in France. The efforts of the Ministry of Foreign Affairs and of the Council of State in favour of unification and of the gold standard will be described. The attitude of the Finance Ministry in favour of bimetallism and against further monetary unification will then be studied in connection with that of the Bank of France. Observers have always been puzzled about the French behaviour, inviting all European nations to join France in a monetary union and then refusing to act accordingly, once the goal was almost reached. The whole responsibility was usually attributed to the opposition of the Bank of France and the private bankers. It will be shown that this was not the case. Each of the four institutions (the Ministry of Finance, the Ministry of Foreign Affairs, the Council of State, and the Bank of France) had a separate agenda on monetary policy and the conflict between them could only generate a chaotic result, incomprehensible to outsiders.

The archives of the Quai d'Orsay about the Latin Monetary Union (LMU) and monetary unification have survived intact and complete in over ninety-five boxes of handwritten and annotated letters. All the letters received from Parieu and from the Finance Ministers are there, with the reports from every European city, and with comments on the margin by the Foreign Affairs Ministry. They are completed by corrected and annotated drafts of all the replies addressed by the French diplomatic administration, so that the evolution of the text of the letter is always clear. The material is of exceptional interest and offers a rich insight into the entire development of monetary unification in the nineteenth century. The archives of the Bank of France complement those of the Quai d'Orsay with an equally abundant and neglected collection of material, which has been sampled but has not been studied thoroughly yet. An important but smaller collection is also preserved at the Monnaie de Paris. These abundant archives compensate for the absence of archives from the Finance Ministry and from the Conseil d'État, which were burned by the Commune in June 1871, while the Bank of France organized its employees in a special fire brigade battalion and buried its deposits and part of its archives in tons of sand.

The introduction of a gold standard in France was the main requirement of the International Conference. A strong opposition to the establishment of the gold standard emerged in the administration. Progressively the apparent academic domination of

---

[105] 'Débat au Sénat sur les modifications au système monétaire francais' (*Annales du Sénat et du Corps législatif*, session of 1870, I, 25 Jan. (1870), 302).

the gold monometallists was also shaken by the bimetallists Wolowski and Cernuschi in extensive debates and articles on the subject. The bimetallists insisted on the relationship between the quantity of money and the level of prices, concluding that demonetization of silver would lead to deflation, producing a redistribution in favour of creditors (*rentiers*) and damaging debtors (States, taxpayers, and companies). They assumed that the contemporary use of two metals would serve as a parachute: when one of the metals became scarce the other one would compensate for the lack of the first and vice versa, protecting the stability of prices, both from inflation and from deflation. The partisans of gold claimed that the reduction in the world supply of money caused by the demonetization of silver would not affect the market for goods, insisting on the neutrality of money and the superior right that the law offered to creditors. To keep the heavy and cumbersome silver, which was starting to depreciate, was to ignore the course of history, to get back to the coach after the invention of trains and to expose France to becoming the dumping ground for silver demonetized by the rest of the world. This lively debate in 'civil society' provided a forum for conflicts between institutions and cabinet ministers, with the creation of a long succession of official commissions and enquiries at every level between 1867 and 1870. The Finance Ministry used these enquiries as a deliberate delaying tactic, because it felt unable to defeat openly the supporters of the gold standard.

The second measure that the French government was expected to implement to obtain monetary unification was the issue of the 25-franc gold coin. Chevalier and the 'metric fanatics' obstructed its path because they wanted any international coin to have a rounded weight in grams. Opponents of monetary unification also attacked the 25-franc piece as its appearance in the French circulation would have indicated a victory for the pro-unification movement, and would have been expected to exert a powerful influence in the USA, Spain, Austria, and perhaps even in England. The governor of the Bank of France, Gustave Rouland, resented the coin as a Trojan horse for monetary unification: 'It is obvious to everyone, Gentlemen, for all men of good sense and of good faith that a great question should not be addressed through a small aspect of it and thereby ensuring that the question escapes attention.'[106] In many cases the refusal of the 25-franc coin was hidden behind arguments of mathematical purity similar to those advanced by the metric fanatics.[107]

4.2.1. The negotiations with Austria and the persistence of a deadlock

The first sign of the incapacity of the French government to take a firm decision came just two weeks after the closure of the International Monetary Conference.

---

[106] Ibid., 28 Jan. (1870), 313.

[107] The French system of monetary units was constructed around the series 1, 2, 5, and its decimal multiples (10, 20, 50, 100). Some thought that the 25 francs was breaking that series or that it was too similar to the 20-franc piece which would complicate the system and confuse the users, generating mistakes. Other feared that the current 20-franc coin would be displaced by the 25 francs and a complete recoinage would have to take place. The fallacy of these considerations was proved by the introduction in France, some decades later, of 25-franc and 25-centime coins without any problem or complaint.

The French and the Austrian delegates met in July 1867 to discuss a monetary convention between the two countries. The French delegation was led by Parieu,
seconded by Herbet for the Foreign Affairs Ministry and by Dutilleul for the Treasury.
It was the same team which had been running the International Conference, but
Parieu's aide, Lavenay, had been replaced by the bimetallist Dumas, President of the
Commission des Monnaies, appointed by the Treasury. The Austrian government
accepted the LMU Treaty as a general framework for discussion. In addition it
expected to implement the conclusions of the International Conference with the
creation of a 25-franc–10-Austrian florin coin and the adoption of a gold standard,
limiting the Monetary Union to gold coins.[108] The behaviour of the French delegates
at the International Conference had implied that these points were accepted. The
Austrian negotiator, de Hock was therefore extremely surprised to hear from Parieu
that public opinion in France was not yet ready and the question of the standard was
not settled in France. The French delegation had voted for gold only because a
transitory period of undefined length was allowed before the final adoption of the
gold standard.

Mr Dutilleul declares that this morning His Excellency M. Rouher has discussed with him the
negotiations with Austria. The Minister of State and of Finances told him that his personal views
were favourable to the projected agreement, but that for the same reasons precisely indicated
just now by M. Parieu and M. Herbet, it is necessary to debate the question before the Emperor
in the Council of Ministers ... The project prepared [by de Hock] will be examined by the
government with the most sincere desire to accept it.[109]

Napoleon was called to arbitrate between bimetallists and monometallists in the
administration, but apparently the Emperor chose not to choose. A political decision at
that level was not possible because Napoleon had no personal opinion on the subject
and conflicting suggestions reached him from his ministers and advisers. A few days
later Rouher sent word that he was 'favourable to the project of agreement as long as
the French government kept an entire freedom of action in what concerns the abolition or the preservation of the silver standard.'[110]

Only the strong personal determination of Parieu and de Hock prevented the
suspension of the talks. A preliminary treaty was drafted, along the lines requested by
Austria, including therefore a commitment of both countries to a gold standard, but
awaited ratification. The Interior Minister, holding the interim of the Finance Minister
during the summer vacation, approved the draft of the treaty. But such an accident was
certainly not sufficient to break the opposition of the Treasury and the draft was never

---

[108] In 1867 the mint of Paris had prepared some specimens of the 25 franc-10 florin and 25 franc-5 dollar
coins. The coins bore the effigy of Napoleon III, without a national legend identifying them with France.
The value of the coins was expressed both in national units (dollars or florins) and international unit (francs
of the LMU). They were used when approaching foreign representatives, insisting on the importance of the
double value. Austrian, German, and US representatives received one or more specimens. 'Au sujet de la
pièce de 25 francs, Mr de Parieu offre à Mr le Baron de Hock un spécimen que Mr Marcotte de Quivière a
eu l'obligeance de faire préparer à la Monnaie de Paris' (Ministère des Affaires Étrangères, 1867b). The
specimens of both coins reproduced in the Appendix come from the Bank of France.
[109] Ibid. 34–5.   [110] Ibid. 59.

ratified. However, Austria decided to implement part of the treaty anyway, issuing gold coins in florins and francs.[111] It delayed the issue of the 25-franc–10-florin piece, waiting for France to issue it first. The proof minted in Paris for the negotiations of 1867 never materialized.

4.2.2. The Foreign Affairs Ministry and the Council of State for unification and gold standard

The intense exposure of the Ministry of Foreign Affairs to prevailing opinions in favour of gold in Europe and America convinced it many years before the Finance Ministry or the French Parliament that any form of international monetary cooperation required the adoption of the gold standard. The Quai d'Orsay could rely on high-quality reports from its network of Ambassadors and Consuls. Virtually every decision, every discussion and every publication on monetary issues in Europe and the USA was immediately reported to Paris. The Ministry and Parieu were as close as it was possible to be to perfect information on the subject. Parieu interacted constantly with the Ministry, in a symbiotic union, independently of who was the Minister.

It is difficult to distinguish between the position of the Council of State and the individual position of its Vice-President Parieu. On all official occasions Parieu represented the Council. When he needed backing and votes in favour of gold and unification in the various monetary commissions, he enrolled the support of the President of the Financial Section of the Council of State, de Lavenay, or of other councillors at the top of the French Civil Service, like Herbet, Ozenne, or De Franqueville.[112] All of them always voted according to Parieu's views, differing only in rare points of detail. The Council of State may have developed under Parieu's impulse a homogeneous position in favour of gold through the periodical discussions which took place in the general assembly of the Council. The destruction of the archives of the Council of State in 1871 prevent us from making anything more than a hypothesis.

Parieu's continuing concern was to conclude the work of the existing monetary commission and commit the government to its results, regularly favourable to the establishment of the gold standard after 1867. The Finance Minister Magne on the other hand always managed to convince the Emperor that further enquiries were necessary before such a dramatic decision could be taken. Parieu complained 'against these repeated procrastinations' through the Foreign Affairs Ministry and through his articles in the *Journal des économistes*, but he could not outweigh Magne.[113]

The persistence of Parieu's influence made him a sort of shadow Foreign Minister on monetary matters. In 1869, for example, the Quai d'Orsay would not communicate

---

[111] Austria and Hungary issued separately two types, 4 florins-10 francs and 8 florins-20 francs, between 1870 and 1892 (Leconte 1995: 302–8).

[112] Ozenne was Foreign Trade director and then General Secretary of the Ministry of Agriculture and Trade. De Franqueville was General Director 'des ponts et chaussées' and of railways at the Ministry of Public Works. The director of the consulates and commercial affairs at the Ministry of Foreign Affairs, Herbet, himself a frequent participant in the monetary negotiations, was another Councillor of State.

[113] Parieu (1872: 379–81).

to the Finance Ministry despatches unfavourable to monetary unification, withholding them until Parieu had examined them and provided a reply to all objections. Typically the Minister would then issue an order to 'Communicate the annexes to the [Ministry of] finances and use with discretion some of M. de Parieu's remarks'.[114] Parieu's strategy was meant to lead in time to a new international conference, aimed at improved conditions of implementation:

The idea of monetary uniformity has progressed notably in people's minds since 1867 and the subject sparks off new publications all over Europe. The more the idea grows, the more it is essential to strengthen the principles used for implementation. Either the rigid use of the basis fixed in 1867. Or critique and deep revision in a new conference.[115]

The French government had to defend the progress of unification from the speculators' attacks and the tyranny of routine. The Minister replied 'It is premature, let us try to convey the Conference with Austria first.'

In the course of 1869 and 1870 the strength of the proposal for unification increased. Several States had modified their monetary legislation either entirely in favour of the LMU model (Greece, the Pontifical State, Spain, and Romania) or just in relation to gold coinage (Sweden and Austria-Hungary). By 1870 most of them had already started to mint the new coinage, so that a total of 13 European States employed the LMU coinage.[116] In southern Germany the agitation in favour of the franc had brought about a favourable vote of the chambers of commerce in 1867 and of the trade Parliament in 1868. A proposal to equalize the US dollar to 5 francs was under examination by the Finance Committee of the Senate of the USA, proposed by the chairman of that Committee. In the United Kingdom the Chancellor of the Exchequer, informed by France of these successes, was convinced that unification would ultimately succeed and offered to negotiate with France the modification of the pound to 25 francs, revising the previously negative stance of the British government, as will be seen in Chapter 6.

Parieu's position was particularly strong at the beginning of 1870, when he became Minister presiding over the Council of State while his opponents Magne and Rouher had been excluded from the government and Fould was dead, leaving less experienced and committed men in charge of the Treasury and of the direction of the government. Parieu was then able to coordinate with the Ministry of Foreign Affairs a new offensive on a double front, internal and external.

Internally the new Finance Ministers (first Buffet then Ségris) would be pressed to ratify the agreement with Austria-Hungary, accept the gold standard and the 25-franc piece. The 25-franc piece was approved by the Senate in February and even Magne

---

[114] The Vice-President of the Council of State Parieu to the Foreign Affairs Minister, prince la Tour d'Auvergne, 2 Nov. 1869 (AMAE, ADC 604–2, fol. 258).

[115] The response of the Minister was negative: 'C'est prématuré, essayons d'abord de réunir la Conférence avec l'Autriche' (Parieu to la Tour d'Auvergne, 2 Nov. 1869 AMAE, ADC 604–2, fol. 258).

[116] The thirteen States were France, Belgium, Italy, Switzerland, Greece, Austria-Hungary, Spain, Sweden, Romania, the Pontifical States, Luxembourg, the Republic of San Marino and the Principality of Monaco. Some minted all types of LMU coinage, others only silver and bronze, others only bronze.

accepted it in principle in June. The Monetary Commission concluded again in favour of the gold standard at the beginning of July.

Externally a meeting of the Latin Monetary Union would have to be called as soon as possible to ratify further enlargements on the basis of gold. Southern Germany should be induced to join: 'emphasize to the cabinets of Munich, Stuttgart, and Karlsruhe the advantage for southern Germany to draw its monetary system closer to that of the neighbouring populations of France and Switzerland.'[117] When in May 1870 the Prussian government, with the help of Ludwig Bamberger, attempted to attract southern Germany into the monetary commission discussing monetary unification of the whole of Germany, Parieu and the French government became immediately alarmed.[118] Prussia had already attempted in 1868 to introduce monetary issues in the Parliament of the *Zollverein*, which included both the Prussian-dominated North German Confederation and the south German States. The southern States had successfully opposed the Prussian move denying to the *Zollparlament* any power on monetary questions. They had understood that Bismarck intended to use national monetary unification as an instrument for national political unification. The Prussian thaler was resisted by Bavaria and Württemberg as a forerunner of a Prussian-dominated German unity. Political unification had to precede a complete monetary unification.

Parieu called for renewed efforts and vigilance from French diplomats:

Why would the Prussians have involved the southern States in their inquiry, despite the resistance of an MP from Württemberg speaking in favour of the French system, if it was not to paralyse annexationist tendencies towards us ... All of this seems suspect to me and I beg you to keep the situation in Germany under surveillance with as many agents as you believe able to do so. We would be mocked at if we had not done all that was possible to prevent the dualism which is in preparation.[119]

Parieu then added instructions to

show to the States of southern Germany the interest they have in (1) not being carried away from the ideas they have accepted in 1867 and in preserving their freedom of action in the interest of their populations close to France and Switzerland, and (2) help them appreciate the chances of an agreement with Austria, preliminary in 1867 (31 July) and partly facilitated by the mintage of Hungarian and Austrian coins of 10 fr. and 20 fr.[120]

This appealed to French governmental officials, since the Ministry of Foreign Affairs was politically interested in isolating Prussia and building alliances for a war which seemed more and more likely. The administration worked for a long time to prepare an eighteen-page dispatch, according to Parieu's instructions, directed to Württemberg

---

[117] Parieu to the head of the government and interim Minister of Foreign Affairs Ollivier, 5 May 1870 (AMAE, ADC 616–1, fol. 124).

[118] French Ambassador to Prussia Benedetti to Ollivier, 6 May 1870 (AMAE, ADC 616–1, fols. 125–26).

[119] Parieu to Meurand, directeur des Consulats et des affaires étrangères, 10 May 1870 (AMAE, ADC 616–1, fol. 127). [120] Ibid., fol. 128.

and Bavaria. These two States themselves resisted the Prussian attempt and counted on some support from France:

The Minister of Foreign Affairs of Bavaria [de Bray] is very keen to see the southern States participating in the enquiry, since the presence of their delegates would increase in the commission the number of opponents to the thaler [,] which Prussia would like to impose on Germany as a monetary unit, and this would strengthen their resistance. This question is of great importance for [to] Bavaria and the southern states ... Concerning this [de Bray] asked me to receive from the imperial government the results of the last monetary enquiry which has taken place in France.[121]

The new French Foreign Minister Gramont[122] replied 'The reluctance of the Munich cabinet conforms with the views of the French government.' The French dispatch to Württemberg and Bavaria was sent on 29 June 1870, four days before the announcement of the candidature to the throne of Spain by the cousin of the King of Prussia. It was less than three weeks before the beginning of the Franco-Prussian War, in which the Bavarian troops distinguished themselves in fighting against the French on the Prussian side.

The Prussian victory meant the fall of the second Empire and the end of the French political and monetary influence which had permitted the construction of a sort of 'Eurofranc'. Parieu lost all executive power, being out of the cabinet, of the Council of State, and out of Parliament until 1876. His influence persisted on a much smaller scale thanks to his personal contacts with some of the new political leaders and with the higher levels of the public administration which remained unaltered regardless of which regime held office.[123] German political unification became a reality in 1871 and was followed by a national monetary unification which made an international agreement impossible.

4.2.3. The Finance Ministry and Parliament against change

For a long time the Finance Ministry did not seem to be able to state explicitly its opposition to the moves of Parieu and the Quai d'Orsay but used the delaying tactic of inquiries of increasing complexity and length, which also happened to turn more and

---

[121] Gramont noted in the margin: 'Cette réserve du cabinet de Munich est conforme aux vues du gouvernement français' (French Ambassador in Bavaria to French Foreign Affairs Minister Gramont, 24 June 1870, AMAE, ADC 616–1, fol. 152).

[122] The Duke of Gramont was considered by Bismarck as 'the most stupid man in Europe' (Herre 1992: 308). Gramont was a former Ambassador to Vienna. He represented the French desire to prevent German unification by military means. When the Hohenzollern candidacy to the throne of Spain in July 1870 offered the opportunity of a war against Prussia, a camarilla conducted by the Empress tried to seize it. She wanted to consolidate the dynasty and secure the throne for her son. The old guard of the authoritarian empire (Rouher, Baroche, Fourcade, David, and Cassagnac) wanted to regain power from the liberals and called for war as well, stirring nationalist passions through the Parisian press. Under the pressure of the right wing, Napoleon III and Gramont contributed to push France into war, despite the peaceful leaning of the Ollivier government. Parieu was one of the Ministers who resisted war.

[123] Dutilleul remained general director of the Treasury. The governor and deputy governors of the Bank of France preserved their seats. Dumas was confirmed president of the Commission des Monnaies.

more in favour of gold. A list of these commissions suggests the extent of the phenomenon:

- 1858 Commission for the study of the Monetary Question. Concluded in favour of measures to protect bimetallism.
- 1861 Commission to study the question of silver divisionary coinage. Concluded in favour of preserving bimetallism but demonetizing divisionary silver.
- 1867 Commission to examine the question of the monetary standard. Voted in favour of bimetallism.
- 1868 Enquiry on the monetary question with the directors of the local branches of the Bank of France, with a formal opinion of the Bank of France in favour of bimetallism.
- 1868 Enquiry on the monetary question with the Chambers of Commerce and the 'trésoriers payeurs généraux' (local state treasurers). The majority of both groups supported gold, but the ambiguity of the questions permitted the bimetallists to say that the majority of the replies were in favour of the double standard.
- 1868 Monetary commission to continue the examination of the monetary standard, established 'considering that the enquiry conducted on the subject of the monetary standard appear [*appears*] to make it desirable that the examination of the question should be continued.' Reported in favour of gold.
- 1869–70 Enquiry of the Superior Council of Trade, Agriculture, and Commerce on the Monetary Question. Concluded in favour of gold and unification.
- 1870 Debate in the Senate from 18 to 28 of January, on the modifications to be introduced in the French monetary system. Supported the 25-franc coin but rejected the gold standard.

In November 1867 Magne replaced Rouher at the Finance Ministry, while the latter retained the direction of the government. The relations with England illustrate very accurately the use made by Magne of these commissions. In May 1868, the Royal Commission on International Coinage, appointed by Disraeli, transmitted to France an official request to know what its position was in relation to the adoption of the gold standard.

The commissioners require information ... whether the French government has in its contemplation to take any steps for carrying out that portion of the recommendations of the International Monetary Conference of Paris which relates to the adoption of a single gold standard ... It is of importance that the intentions of the French government which has taken the initiative in the movement for promoting an international system of coinage should be ascertained with reference to this vital point, unanimity upon which is essential to the success of the proposed object.[124]

The French Foreign Minister Moustier transmitted the request to Magne, asking for an acceleration of the work of the commission to be able to reply to England.[125] Magne refused to commit himself to anything because 'the elements of the enquiry

---

[124] British Treasury to Moustier, 28 May 1868 (AMAE, ADC 604–1, fol. 140).
[125] Moustier to Magne, 6 June 1868 (AMAE, ADC 604–1, fol. 141).

have not been completed yet' and no reply was possible before the end of its work.[126] The British Commission did not receive a clear reply and then submitted a report against any changes in the pound to permit monetary unification.

The year after the new British Chancellor of the Exchequer offered to open negotiations with France on the subject and made a resounding speech in Parliament to that effect, as will be seen in Chapter 5. Like his predecessors, Lowe wished France to adopt a gold standard. The new French Minister of Foreign Affairs, la Tour d'Auvergne, described the communication as 'very important'. Magne wrote to his colleague six days after Lowe's speech, explaining that he had always supported monetary unification but considered the quarrel on standards an internal affair unconnected to unification. But in consideration of the persistence of those associating monetary unification with the establishment of the gold standard Magne conceded 'I would attach great importance ... to the opinion of Your Excellency and to an indication of the arguments which contributed to its adoption.'[127] La Tour d'Auvergne noted in the margin of a further despatch that

In this question there are technical considerations beyond the competence of the Ministry of Foreign Affairs. But apart from that, contrary to the Ministry of Finance's opinion, there is a link, an intimate correlation between the solution of the question of the standard and the question of unification. The reasons have already been transmitted on several occasions to the Finances. They are drawn from the various dispatches received from foreign governments, particularly by Belgium, Switzerland, Austria, and lastly by England.[128]

During this exchange of letters Magne asked in the Council of Ministers for a new inquiry and a further report on the relation between the gold standard and monetary unification, as the previous commission had discussed the issues separately and not in their intimate connection. The delaying tactic of Magne worked again. La Tour d'Auvergne fumed, writing on the margin of the letter sent by Magne that the new commission was only 'intended to cover the responsibility of M. Magne'. Lowe was attacked by the Bank of England and the British financial establishment for his plan for unification. He was forced to withdraw his proposal in February 1870, without receiving any support from the French government which had provoked his initial announcement.

It is difficult to accept that all Finance Ministers were captives of the Haute Banque and its financial interests, as sometimes claimed by Parieu and Feer-Herzog. For Droulers the Emperor needed the Bank of France for his policy of prestige and foreign intervention, and therefore ordered his Finance Ministers to follow the Bank's bimetallist opinion.[129] Of the various Ministers of the time, Fould was indeed a banker and Léon Say was closely connected to the Rothschilds, but Magne, Rouher or Poyer Quertier had no such background. It is difficult to see how the government or the

---

[126] Magne to Moustier, 15 June 1868 (AMAE, ADC 604–1, fol. 142).
[127] French Minister of Finance Magne to French Minister of Foreign Affairs de la Tour d'Auvergne, 12 Aug. 1869 (AMAE, ADC 616, dossier 1 (1869–71), fol. 5).
[128] Ibid. 19 Aug. 1869 (AMAE, ADC 616, dossier 1 (1869–71), fol. 6).
[129] Droulers (1990: 64–5). See also Willis (1901).

Ministry of Finance could actually depend on the Bank of France to the point of letting it decide its policy. Governmental loans were certainly facilitated by the Bank and anticipation of substantial amounts was granted to the Treasury account, but there was dependency on both sides. The Bank could not afford open warfare with the government. It was a private institution, but its governor and deputy-governors were appointed by the government, its monopoly of banknote issue had to be periodically renewed by the State, the freedom to increase exchange rates had to be negotiated with the government in 1857, and public accounts represented an essential share of its business. Between 1857 and 1864 the government repeatedly intervened to delay or block an increase in interest rates to prevent an excessively restrictive monetary policy.[130] Until 1864 the government had the upper hand in relations with the Bank, after the appointment of Rouland in 1864 less so, but the Bank certainly could not impose its views. The Finance Ministry had an independent policy which should not be understood only as the adoption of the views of the Bank of France.

It seems that the reasons for the reluctance of the government and Parliament to abandon bimetallism had more of an internal origin. The existing monetary system in France, as in England, was held in high esteem by public opinion and the fear of alterations by the government, who had debased the coinage so often in the past centuries, created a conservative attitude. Magne considered that the duties of a Finance Minister included the realization of reforms dictated by common sense and experience but also and especially to 'build up an energetic and steady opposition to the utopias abounding in such matters and attempting to impose themselves. *Here relentless war against wrong ideas*: such words should be inscribed on the entrance of the Finance Ministry.'[131] Parliament was also a devoted defender of existing monetary arrangements, fearing any change brought in by an executive hungry for new sources of income. The vice-president of the Corps législatif and member of the Budget Commission, Gouin, expressed this attitude: 'the law has responded to all needs, why change it? The needs of the circulation progress faster than production: therefore the suppression of a metal would create a great scarcity. The advantages of the two metals are very substantial for merchants.'[132] The Corps législatif had reiterated its support for bimetallism in 1864 and 1866 and the Senate in 1870. It is difficult to believe that Magne feared that Parliament would approve a measure in favour of the gold standard in the 1860s.[133]

Furthermore the second Empire was an authoritarian regime based on universal male suffrage which relied on the rural population to provide the mass of electoral support for the regime. A strong reaction in the provinces to demonetization of silver and the loss of value of the 5-franc piece would threaten the political support vital

---

[130] Plessis (1985*b*).

[131] Ibid. 27–8. Parieu's comment on yesterday's utopias quoted earlier can be considered as an indirect reply. 'Dans l'histoire de l'humanité, l'utopie généreuse de la veille peut devenir l'oeuvre pratique et abordable du lendemain, parce que le monde a marché.'

[132] Procès verbal de la commission de 1867, in Ministère des Finances, (1868: 41).

[133] Willis (1901: 105). Gallarotti (1995) shares Willis's erroneous belief in a French Parliament supporter of monometallism.

for the existence of the second Empire.[134] The enquiries revealed that the peasants, unlike the bourgeois, were attached to silver and to their écus, while they disliked the tiny gold coins. They would perceive the reduction of the fineness of écus as an attack on their purchasing power, but had a somehow contradictory and confused fear of the inflationist or deflationist effects of the gold standard. 'In the countryside the establishment of gold is already identified with the imperial government; the suppression of the silver standard coinciding with a general increase in prices would be interpreted very negatively. Only time, the absence of any appearance of pressure and the gradual disappearance of silver coins can overcome such prejudices.'[135] Another report stated that

The agencies of the Bank of France in La Rochelle and Strasbourg agree that important merchants, banks and the inhabitants of the cities would probably not be disturbed in any way by a change of standard, but that it would not be the same case with the public in the countryside and in manufacturing centres. There, the 5-franc gold piece is perceived negatively, and considering the relative weight of rural and industrial population in relation to the middle class, if the preferences of the masses were to be taken into consideration, then the silver standard must be preserved, together with the 5-franc écu, which is the really popular coin.[136]

In May 1870 Napoleon received an 83 per cent consensus in a referendum about his policy, but his majority was entirely rural as he had lost in all the major cities.

The weight of the past also meant that the cost of withdrawing the existing circulation of silver écus, estimated at between 1 and 2 billion francs, would be high for the government. The withdrawal and demonetization of silver would have modified completely the conditions of the market for silver, producing a fall in prices, as it effectively did in the 1870s when access to the mint for silver bullion holders was restricted. The government would lose the difference between the legal price and the market price. At the 1869 price of silver, demonetization would have cost 3.7 million francs, but this figure does not include the fall in market prices caused by demonetization. The costs in 1874 or in 1878 would give a better idea of the real impact of the decision. In 1874 the operation would have cost 45.4 million and in 1878 227.8 million.[137] Indeed, in the late 1870s, Bismarck was forced to suspend a similar operation of demonetization of the silver circulation of Germany because of its prohibitive cost. It was to respond to these objections that Lavenay, supported by Parieu, proposed to stop the issue of new écus without withdrawing the existing circulation. But to force the depreciation of silver and then to keep it as part of the currency was not really an exciting prospect, although that was the solution imposed by events after 1873.

---

[134] Flandreau (1995b: 273).

[135] Ministère des Finances (1868: 76–7): 'Enquête de 1868 auprès des trésorier payeur généraux. Avis du trésorier payeur général of the Dordogne.'

[136] Résumé des réponses à l'Enquete Monétaire données par les directeurs de succursales de la Banque de France, May 1868 (ABdF, 'Question Monétaire', IV, 22).

[137] The figures are obtained multiplying Flandreau's yearly estimates of the French silver circulation by the percentage of depreciation of silver in relation to the 15.5 ratio. Flandreau's estimates of the circulation are at the low end of the range, so that the total figure might be up to 80 per cent higher for each year (Flandreau 1995b: 337 and 340).

Furthermore, the Finance Ministry had experienced the risks and disturbances induced by monetary unification, dealing with Italian, Pontifical, and Greek problems. The more States belonged to the monetary union, the more difficult it was to monitor their policies and be sure they would not export their financial difficulties to France. If the Treasury and the Quai d'Orsay agreed in discouraging States like Romania, Serbia or Bulgaria from joining the Union, the situation was different with Austria-Hungary and Spain. These two large States were important for French foreign policy, but both faced considerable financial difficulties and a dominant circulation of paper money. They were useful political allies but dangerous monetary partners, a potential repetition of the Italian problems. At a different level, even the USA could be considered a threat, because of the forced circulation of depreciated greenbacks, the financial heritage of the Civil War. To introduce the gold standard was to favour monetary unification and therefore to favour the loss of control over internal monetary circulation. International speculative flows of divisionary silver, full écus, gold, and paper money could not possibly be welcomed by the French Treasury. They could mean higher prices and disruption of ordinary trade. They also implied a reduction of seignorage profits caused by a growing share of the French circulation having been issued by foreign States. These phenomena already existed, independently from further economic integration, but the French interventionist tradition from Colbert onwards did not accommodate itself to the impotence of the State. For the Treasury the LMU itself was an unsuccessful attempt to prevent such monetary migrations.

4.2.4. *The Bank of France's Resistance to all Changes*

The Bank of France consistently opposed all the steps leading to monetary unification and to the introduction of the gold standard because it had specific objections to both policies. The manifestation of the Bank's opposition to monetary unification and to the common 25-franc coin will be examined through the internal debates of the Bank, through various monetary commissions and parliamentary debates. Then the Bank's support for bimetallism will be discussed, considering the attention it attracted at the time and in later literature.

The Bank on Monetary Unification. The opinion of the Bank of France and specifically of some of its *régents* (directors), on the LMU and its effects can be traced in its archives. The Bank was called on to play a role not of 'lender of last resort' but of 'receiver of last resort', accepting the largest flows of coins from the whole Monetary Union. It was not a role assigned deliberately to the Bank by any international agreement. It was a role the Bank had not asked for, and it did not welcome it. Excessive issues of silver divisionary coins from peripheral members of the LMU would make their way to France and from there to the coffers of the Bank. Silver écus and gold coins of countries having the *cours forcé* would follow the same path. The LMU convention had not assigned a legal-tender status to the coins of the allied States, it only made them acceptable by the state cashiers. The state cashiers would deposit these foreign silver

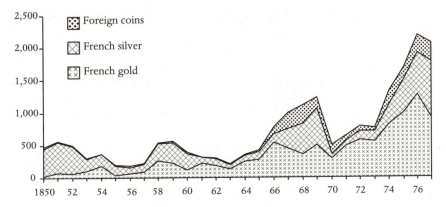

Graph 4.7 *Composition of the metallic reserves of the Bank of France, 1850–77 (million francs)*
Source: Willis (1901: 90).

coins at the Bank of France. The Bank by accepting or refusing them became therefore the arbiter of their market value in France. Following the governmental request, the Bank had initially accepted these coins without restriction, but soon its vaults were flooded (or at least it claimed so). The Bank's holdings of foreign coins progressed from 15 million in 1864 to an unprecedented 280 million in 1868, more than the total reserves it held in 1863 (Graph 4.7).

The *régent* Alphonse de Rothschild complained repeatedly in the Conseil Général (executive board of the Bank) about the limited legal tender enjoyed by the new silver divisionary coinage of the LMU. No individual was forced to accept more than 50 francs of it per transaction. This article of the Monetary Convention

subjects all public establishments that receive many coins because of their activities to a considerable accumulation of subsidiary coins, which they cannot get rid of and which cause serious inconveniences ... The Company of the Northern Railways is encumbered by coins it can dispose of neither through the banks nor circulation, both refusing the coins.[138]

Another regent, the private banker De Waru, insisted on the responsibility of foreign coins in the accumulation of an excessive amount of divisionary money, notably of 'a country which has adopted inconvertible paper money' (meaning Italy), which, in his opinion, had violated the limit of issue of 6 francs per inhabitant. The multiplication of foreign coins unknown to the public was also simplifying forgery. 'From such a point of view, the International Convention of 1865 could not be blamed excessively.'[139] The Bank was in a similar situation, resisting attempts of the commercial community to dump divisionary silver on the Bank. The governor Rouland

[138] Conseil Général de la Banque de France, 3 Dec. 1868 (ABdF, 'Question Monétaire', I, 577). Rothschild repeated his request for interventions towards the minister on 11 Feb. 1869 (ibid. 599).
[139] Ibid., I. 600.

complained to Magne in several occasions, insisting that the Bank had to defend itself.[140]

[T]he bulk of such coins, French as well as foreign, exceeds by far the need, since in order to get rid of them, merchants make full use of the right offered by the law to include 50 francs of subsidiary coins in every payment. The Bank is therefore obliged by [the course of] events to accumulate in its coffers the excess of subsidiary coinage. This accumulation, against which the Bank is struggling, would rapidly increase if certain payments on behalf of the Treasury continued to take place in subsidiary coinage.[141]

On April 1870 the veiled threat of refusing governmental deposits in divisionary silver became a reality, when the Bank's offices in Nancy and Amiens refused French and Italian divisionary coins presented by the *trésoriers généraux*. The Director of the Treasury, Dutilleul protested to Rouland, who annotated his reply on the margin of Dutilleul's letter.[142] If the Bank did not limit the deposit of silver divisionary coins in its coffers, it would collect involuntarily all the surplus existing in the French circulation. In such a case, the Bank would suffer a disastrous depletion of its reserves of gold and of silver écus, which possessed an unlimited purchasing power, unlike divisionary silver. The Bank would accept deposits of divisionary silver coins from the Treasury only separately from the ordinary accounts, leaving to the government the responsibility to get rid of them. In fact the divisionary coinage of the Union was not weakening the reserves of the Bank, which were unexpectedly booming at that time. On the contrary, they increased unwanted excessive reserves. In the 1870s the Bank would exert the same pressure towards the Finance Ministry and develop the same attitude towards silver écus. The Treasury would need to negotiate yearly with the Bank its toleration of new silver issues.

When called in 1868 to express its opinion, the Bank of France opposed without restriction monetary union. The Bank of France considered monetary unification useless for travellers because other forms of banking facilities than coins were employed by them. The regent De Waru declared: 'It is said that monetary unification is in the interest of travellers; but those travellers already have bills, letters of credit, cheques, all of them more comfortable than gold, and the 20-franc coin is already favourably received everywhere. Therefore it appears that nothing really useful is left to do.'[143]

The idea that transaction costs would be reduced by monetary unification was considered as having little weight by Rouland. The difficulty of calculations was already superseded by the existence of all sorts of exchange manuals. He quoted Feer Herzog on the effect of monetary unification:

With a universal money . . . , the price charged by the banker for his bills corresponds perfectly to the cost of transportation of the coinage between two centres, a cost not increased any longer

---

[140] Rouland to Magne, 4 Feb. 1869 (ABdF, 'Question Monétaire', I, 595).

[141] Ibid., 20 Feb. 1869 (ABdF, 'Question Monétaire', I, 603–5).

[142] Le directeur général du mouvement des fonds au Ministère des Finances, Dutilleul, to Rouland (ABdF, 'Question monétaire', I, 612–13).

[143] *Procès-verbaux et rapport de la commission monétaire de 1868* (1869: 41).

by the expenditure for melting and reminting; the largest differences of exchange between two centres with an identical circulation will never be higher than the sum of transportation costs of the metal, the insurance premium and the interest rate differentials.[144]

Rouland stressed how the differences between national coins were only a very small part of the exchange cost; transportation and insurance costs would remain, together with the cost of banking facilities (discount to transfer commercial paper or interest to obtain bank drafts). The influence of divergent foreign interest rates would also contribute to oscillating exchange rates even after monetary unification. The only element which would disappear would be the cost of melting and reminting coins. 'Let us acknowledge that most of the costs of exchange remain despite monetary unification.'[145] Rouland added that the cost of reminting was not worth the limited benefits of union. When Rouland talked of exchange rates, he assumed an exchange operation carried out through the use of commercial paper or bankers' drafts, bearing interest, not of mere coins or banknotes. The banker, the merchant, and the tourist did not understand the term 'exchange rate in the same way'. Rouland also stressed that monetary unions created a dangerous monetary solidarity between nations. How could France be sure of the quality and authenticity of all the foreign coinage arriving into its territory? If a member of the Union did not respect for its coinage the required weight, fineness or limit to issue, how would the delegates of the various nations act to repress violations without risking war?[146]

The 25-franc gold coin was victim of the Bank's policy. As the Governor of the Bank declared to the Senate during the debate in January 1870, the 25-franc coin was the beginning of the execution of the project of monetary unification, as nobody in France would dream of introducing such a coin otherwise. The 25-franc piece was useless for internal circulation because of its similarity to the 20-franc piece and would only create confusion. Rouland attacked the coin as a Trojan horse for monetary unification.[147]

The Senate in 1870 had finally decided against the adoption of the gold standard, against Chevalier's decagram, but in favour of the creation of a 25-franc gold coin to favour international monetary unification. This decision was neither a great victory for the supporters of international coinage nor for the bimetallists. Following the constitutional practice of the second Empire the vote of the Senate was not binding for the government and furthermore the liberalization of the regime was increasing the role of an elected Corps législatif, not of the Senate, whose members were appointed by the Emperor. However, the former Finance Minister Magne, who initially delayed decisions about the 25 francs, had finally accepted the necessity of issuing it on trial, as he declared to the Monetary Commission sitting in June 1870. In August 1870, after the first French defeat in the Franco-Prussian War, Magne was called back to the Ministry of Finance by the Empress in the last cabinet of the Empire. The first measure taken

---

[144] Conseil Supérieur du Commerce (1872: 52–3).   [145] Ibid. 54.   [146] Ibid. 60.
[147] 'Débat au Sénat sur les modifications au système monétaire francais' *Annales du Sénat et du Corps législatif*, session of 1870, I, 28 January (1870), 313.

was the introduction of forced paper currency, accompanied by the issue of a smaller denomination banknote of 25 francs, to replace the vanishing gold coins.[148] The Bank had lowered the minimal value of its banknotes to 50 francs only after the renewal of its privilege of issuing banknotes in the mid-1850s and had very little interest in issuing smaller denomination banknotes. The 25-franc note was created on 16 August but had a very short existence because of the Bank's hostility. It was replaced on 12 December 1870 by a 20-franc note.[149]

The Bank complained loudly about the introduction of the *cours forcé* and the loan imposed on it by the government. Some *régents* resigned in sign of protest. The 25-franc note was officially opposed because it did not correspond to any coin existing in circulation and because being issued in a hurry in the midst of war it was not properly protected from forgery by filigrane or other devices.[150] The minutes of the Conseil Général of the Bank of France give a clearer picture of what really happened. The councillors immediately opposed the 25-franc coin, asking it to be replaced by a 20 francs banknote. Rouland accepted without objections the Council's desires and echoed them forcefully to the various governments.[151] 'Several members of the Council express their disappointment that the law did not indicate a 20-franc note instead of the 25-franc note. Such disappointment is also expressed, apparently, by the public and by trade.'[152] Magne resisted the request to change the law as of very minor importance. After the fall of the Empire and the arrival of a new Finance Minister, less committed to previous decisions, the regent Alphonse de Rothschild pushed the governor Rouland to renew the request to replace the 25-franc coin, declaring on 24 November that the existence of the 25-franc banknote threatened to prepare the creation of a 25-franc coin.

The feelings of the Council about the preference which should be given to this note [20 fr.] over that of the 25 francs have not changed since the month of August, when M. Darblay [Censor of the Bank and MP] tentatively approached some members of the Corps législatif in order to substitute, by way of a modification of the law of 12 August 1870, a 20-franc note for that of 25 francs—an attempt which failed due to the resistance of M. Magne, then Finance Minister.

Trade keeps regretting not to have the 20-franc note and we have no reason to suppose that the government of national defence has anything against this note. The moment would be excellent to modify art. 5 of the law of 12 August 1870. In addition to the fact that this modification would respond to a more or less general wish ... it would also eliminate the grave inconvenience of the 25-franc banknote, namely that it prepares the decision to create of a 25-franc gold coin.[153]

---

[148] The law introducing the cours forcé from 12 August 1870 made the banknotes of the Bank of France the forced legal currency of the nation, suspending the obligation to redeem the banknotes in gold or silver. The maximum amount of paper the Bank could issued was raised to 1,800 millions. See J. Vincent (1953).

[149] Eleven million banknotes of 25 francs for a total value of 275 million francs were issued and then withdrawn from 1873 and destroyed. The issue of the 20-franc note was also stopped in 1874.

[150] Banque de France (1994: 68–70).

[151] Régistre manuscrit des *Délibérations du Conseil Général*, XLV, Archives de la Banque de France.

[152] Ibid., 16 Aug. 1870, XLV: 123.   [153] Ibid., 24 Nov. 1870, XLV: 215.

A committee for the creation of a new 20-franc banknote was set and its direction was taken by Rothschild, who insisted on the urgency of effecting the change before the 25-franc note became customary and difficult to eradicate.

The Bank is not able to anticipate when the last note will cease to be employed, such moment could be delayed by circumstances and we must not expose ourselves to see the 25-franc note take a foothold and become customary thanks to a prolonged use. The committee has therefore considered that the substitution of the 20 francs note for the 25 francs one should take place as soon as possible, provided that the government agrees to this substitution and authorizes it.[154]

Rothschild's position was supported in the council by the private banker Mallet and by the Governor Rouland. The committee decided to use for the 20-franc note the same design as the 25-franc note, with a different colour. The Comptroller of the Bank and two régents opposed the move in the council, because the new note would be easy to confuse and just as falsifiable as the old one which was withdrawn partly for the same reason. The bankers Rothschild and Mallet wanted to act as soon as possible to withdraw the 25-franc note, the manufacturer Davillier and Polles preferred to proceed more cautiously. The Conseil Général decided in favour of the bankers.[155] On 15 December 1870, Rouland informed the council that the Minister had approved the change but asked not to publish it on the *Moniteur* until the Bank had a sufficient reserve of 20-franc banknotes to face the requests of the public. This way difficulties would be avoided which would doubtless appear if an excessive demand arose immediately after the publication of the decree and the Bank were not able to satisfy it fully.'[156] Mallet again opposed any delay arguing that the Bank could not feel secure as long as the 25-franc banknote existed. As long as Paris was besieged by the Prussian troops there would not be a large demand for banknotes.

[M]ilitary events could precipitate and complicate circumstances, with the possible result of creating obstacles to the publication of the decree; [Mallet] believes it would not be wise to wait ... As long as the blockade on Paris will last, the public will not have a great need of 20-franc banknotes, especially with the presence of a certain number of 25 francs notes still being in circulation.[157]

Rouland and Rothschild seconded Mallet and the council approved. Rouland then announced he would go immediately to see the Minister to accelerate the publication of the decree. He could announce a week later his total success; he had personally written the note accompanying the decree in the *Journal Officiel*.[158] The abolition of the 25-franc banknote was secured on 22 December 1870. It was the final blow to the hopes that it would become the international coin of 1 pound, 5 dollars, and 10 florins. The Bank of France was not against the 25-franc coin because it was inconvenient for circulation or technically unsound, but because of its role as an international gold coin. The Bank attributed great importance to the survival of bimetallism against the establishment of gold standard.

---

[154] Ibid. 1 Dec. 1870, XLV, 219.   [155] Ibid. 222.   [156] Ibid. 15 Dec 1870, XLV, 231.
[157] Ibid. 232.   [158] Ibid. 236.

The Bank for bimetallism. The commitment of the Bank of France in favour of bimetallism was systematically recalled in all French discussions, usually to question the real motives behind the official façade. The Bank reminded its critics that the 'the monetary regime, established sixty-five years ago, has worked during this long period not only without great defects, but on the contrary to the great advantage of the country, during the most threatening crisis as well as under ordinary circumstances.'[159] The arrival of gold from America after 1848 had been absorbed without instability thanks to bimetallism. 'France has drawn from it those productive resources which contributed to developing its industry, its trade and its prosperity within a few years and to an unprecedented degree.' During the American Civil War, France had been able to finance cotton imports in silver, without problems, paying each nation in the metal it preferred. Rouland presented the practical merits of the double standard and the dangers of its demise before the Monetary Commission of 1868:

In principle I do not deny the superiority of the single standard, the gold standard, over bimetallism ... But we are not operating on an empty ground; the two types of money coexist since the origins of society, without any damage but, to the contrary, until now to a real advantage for the countries they serve ... Is it proved that the present and future quantity of gold is sufficient to give up silver today with the certainty of a transition without shock and disasters? ... The universal monetary unit, through the adoption of the single gold standard, is an idea which until now has existed exclusively in the scholarly world; it is not yet in the public; it does not impose itself as a necessity expressed by commercial and industrial interests. Nobody complains in the business world. On the contrary, in the recent past commercial relations have considerably expanded without any major difficulty caused by the diversity of coinage. Science seems to proceed faster than facts and interests ... The opinion of the Bank of France can be summarized in three statements: the public is not asking the demonetization of silver, the advantages of the measure are doubtful, the disadvantages certain. In such a situation the Bank is entitled to ask for the *status quo*, and shows a prudent and conservative attitude serving as a counterweight to those who are too daring or too much in a hurry.[160]

The most popular interpretation of the strenuous defence of bimetallism by the Bank of France is grounded on the influence of the private bankers. The institutional structure of the Bank of France was dominated by the interests of the Haute Banque. Therefore, its defence of bimetallism was a consequence of the private interests of the bankers. The existence of two metals permitted a continuous arbitrage between the two metals as well as between different currencies, providing a steady income for the banking profession.

The Bank of France was a private institution with private shareholders electing the members (*régents*) of its board (Conseil Général). The Governor and his two deputies were appointed by the government to represent the public interest in the decisions of the Bank. Three '*trésoriers payeurs généraux*' were also part of the board. Out of eighteen members of the Conseil Général six could be considered to depend on the

---

[159] Avis émis par la Banque de France, extrait du régistre des délibérations du Conseil, séance du 22 juillet 1868, (Ministère des Finances 142–3).

[160] *Procès-verbaux et rapport de la commission monétaire de 1868* (1868: 54 and 62).

government. This governmental influence became more theoretical than practical in the late 1860s. Once appointed to the Bank, the Governors tended to respond more to the interests of the organization they presided over than to external orders. This was particularly true of Rouland, who tended to accommodate governmental decisions but not on issues on which the Bank held a strong opinion such as the importance of bimetallism and the dangers of monetary unification. In 1864 the government had appointed Gustave Rouland to the position of Governor while he had no knowledge of financial questions, making him dependent on the other members of the board.[161] Rouland's position in the Bank seems to have been to defend loyally but not strenuously the government's point of view in the Conseil Général, accepting the decisions of the latter, independently of whether they were in favour of or against the government's will. Rouland would then defend strongly the Bank views before the public, Parliament and the government. In this decision-making process the influential members of the Conseil Général would have the key role in establishing the policy of the Bank. For Plessis Rouland 'appears more and more as the speaker [of the *régents*], if not their pupil, rather than the representative of a government, called to express, or even enforce, the will of the political power.'[162] The same was true for the deputy Governor Fréderic Cuvier. The second deputy Governor, Alexandre de Ploèc, a former president of the Imperial Ottoman Bank (1863–7), was also an associate of the Haute Banque (Mallet and Pillet Will) and of the Crédit Mobilier, which controlled his bank.[163] On the battle of the standards and on monetary unification there was not always a conflict between the Bank and the Finance Ministry, but when contrasts became apparent, the point of view of the most influential *régents* was determining. In the late 1860s these *régents* were mainly bankers. Eight members of the Conseil Général came from the Haute Banque, while only three or four were merchants and the three *receveurs généraux* did not play a major role in the Bank's decisions.[164]

The Bank was represented on the outside (in the Senate and in the monetary commissions) by Rouland and by the bankers de Waru, Rothschild, Mallet, and Pillet Will. This left the Bank of France open to criticism for the conflict between its role in the defence of public interest and the interests of the private bankers on its board. The Swiss Feer-Herzog attacked the Haute Banque explaining its opposition to the gold standard:

It appears undeniable to me that trade in precious metals in the financial centre of Paris has a direct interest in the continuation of the legal ratio between the two metals, because the legal

---

[161] Gustave Rouland (1806–78), lawyer and politician, was Minister of Education (1856–63) and then Minister President of the Council of State until he was appointed to the Bank in 1864. He arrived to the Bank without economic knowledge but learned fast and served the Bank well. When the President of the Republic Thiers replaced Rouland with Former Finance Minister Picard in 1871, the resistance of the Bank forced Picard out in a few days. Rouland remained governor until his death in 1878.

[162] Plessis (1864: 335).   [163] Ibid. 340–9.

[164] The most influential were Alphonse de Rothschild (Bank 'de Rothschild frères'), Alphonse de Waru (Bank 'A. de Waru et C.ie'), Alphonse Mallet ('Mallet frères et C.ie', the oldest Parisian bank), Alexis Pillet-Will ('Banque Pillet-Will et C.ie'), and Rodolphe Hottinguer (Bank 'Hottinguer et C.ie') (Plessis 1864: 335).

value always represents a centre of attraction for the metal whose commercial value (in comparison to the other metal) falls below the level guaranteed by the official ratio ... it is therefore a free insurance against a fall in price below a certain level.[165]

The future Italian Finance Minister, Magliani, confirmed Feer-Herzog's views.

There is only one branch of trade which would be damaged by the suppression of bimetallism; there is only one trade which benefits in a privileged way from the protective action of the Latin Union system: precious metals trade ... [This] is sufficient to explain why the most pugnacious supporters of bimetallism can be found within the ranks of the great bankers and the great merchants of precious metals.[166]

The Bank of England avoided this form of conflict of interest, recruiting its directors exclusively from the commercial world. Still, the Bank of England was a private enterprise which at times was tempted to compete with the banking system it was supposed to oversee and guide.[167] The conflict between a coordinating role and the necessity to compete on the financial market was another form of conflict between public functions and the interests of the private shareholders of the Bank of England. The unresolved nature of national banks of issue, which refused to be considered as central banks but were progressively acquiring such a role, bears considerable responsibility for the failure of monetary unification in the 1860s. The single gold standard and/or unification were opposed in some form by the Bank of France, but also by the Bank of England (see Chapter 5), by the Bank of Prussia,[168] and by the Bank of the Netherlands.[169] The Bank of Italy was initially neutral on the subject because of the inconvertibility of its banknotes, but in the 1870s, with low silver prices, it attempted to delay the reduction of silver issue. Fortamps, director of the Bank of Belgium, repeatedly expressed in an official way his government's policy in favour of the gold standard, but the independent opinion of his bank was not stated. The Swedish banker Wallenberg was the only banker strongly committed in

---

[165] Feer-Herzog (1870: 62).   [166] Magliani (1874: 201–2).   [167] De Cecco (1984).

[168] 'La remarquable insistance avec laquelle les grands établissements financiers et la haute banque prennent le parti du double étalon ne saurait être mieux rendue que dans les trois articles de la *Gazette d'Augsbourg*, du 3, 10 et 20 mars [1870], ayant pour but de demander pour l'Allemagne l'établissement—non pas transitoire—mais définitif du double étalon. L'auteur de ces articles commence par dire que le double étalon se recommande par la qualité de répondre à l'intérêt des grandes institutions financières et surtout à l'intérêt de la Banque de Prusse. Dans le troisième il explique à quelle somme considérable, le rapport légal a fait monter en France le bénéfice des opérateurs en métaux précieux pendant l'invasion de l'or, et il promet le double de ce bénéfice pour la période prochaine où l'argent viendra de nouveau chasser l'or. Il ajoute il est vrai que ces bénéfices appartiennent presque exclusivement aux grands établissements de banque, mais qu'il n'en était pas moins un bénéfice national et très réel—Un pareil degré de franchise ne laisse plus rien à désirer' (Feer-Herzog (1870: 61).

[169] Mees wrote in support of the Dutch opposition to the conclusions of the Paris Conference of 1867. Parieu replied: 'Certaines influences du monde banquier, aussi contraire que l'État Néerlandais aux principes de la conférence de 1867, ont été difficiles à éviter complètement dans le travail du savant et honorable directeur de la Banque d'Amsterdam [Mees]' (Parieu to la Tour d'Auvergne, 2 Nov. 1869, AMAE, ADC 604–2, fol. 258).

favour of monetary unification.[170] The Bank of England expressed dogmatically its opinion when consulted by the Chancellor of the Exchequer in 1873 about a minor change to the pound: 'It is always an evil to make a change in the monetary system of a country.'[171] It was the British version of Rouland's 'esprit de prudence et de conservation'.

Few contemporaries took at face value either the Bank's statements or Wolowski's claim that bimetallism was a self-regulating and stable monetary system. In Chapters 1 and 3, it has been argued that the gold standard's superiority was not as clear as the majority of the economists claimed. The introduction of the gold standard and monetary unification was understood by the Bank of France as an attempt to impose rules destroying its discretionary power to stabilize the money market. Paying in silver discouraged runs on the currency because of the cumbersome weight of such metal and left greater room for manoeuvre to defend the convertibility of the banknotes into specie. 'It is easear to build up strong reserves with silver than with gold: gold is a portable metal, it does not create the need to get rid of it; holders of silver instead ... have a tendency to exchange it at the Bank for more comfortable values or metals.'[172] In 1858 the Governor de Germiny stated that silver reserves were easier to constitute and defend, they constituted an alternative measure to the much disliked increase of the discount rate as used in England. The Bank officially reaffirmed this line of defence ten years later: alternate use of silver and gold to satisfy the requests for specie by the public reduces the drainage of its metallic reserves 'without aggravating too abruptly the conditions of its discount, working to provide reimbursement of its banknotes with the other metal ... The services offered by our monetary regime ... could not be underestimated; that is why it is important that this regime survives and coexists with universal money.'[173]

Flandreau, who studied in detail the policy of the Bank, believes the argument to be artificial and stresses the growing interdependence between the Paris and the London markets, which did not permit the isolation of one market for precious metals from a crisis in the other. For Flandreau, the bank, notwithstanding its official ideology, did not benefit from the bimetallic system either in terms of monetary policy or in terms of arbitrage profits.[174] Flandreau rightly points to the impossibility for the Bank of using its reserves held in the appreciated metal, because it would be immediately deprived of

---

[170] The tendency to denounce the opposition of the banking system to monetary unification is a real 'phénomène de longue durée', persistent in historical terms. In January 1996, Valéry Giscard d'Estaing (former French President and Finance Minister) reproached the banks in general and Marc Viennot, president of the Société Générale in particular, for opposing European monetary unification because of their financial interests. Giscard asked the European Commission to investigate the profits made by the large European companies thanks to intra-European monetary fluctuations (P. A. Delhommais, 'Les banques auront plus à gagner qu'à perdre avec la monnaie unique', *Le Monde*, 11–12 Feb. 1996: 13).

[171] The Governor of the Bank G. Lyall and the deputy Governor B. B. Greene, to the Chancellor of the Exchequer R. Lowe, 19 July 1872 (ABoE, Secretary Letter Book, 17: 44).

[172] ABdF, 'Question Monétaire', i, 155.

[173] Avis émis par la Banque de France, in Ministère des Finances (1868: 143).

[174] Flandreau (1995*b*): see 'Les banques et les banquiers: le double étalon comme moyen de collusion', 186–91.

those reserves by the arbitragists. Bullion dealers would present banknotes to be changed into specie until they had acquired all of the most valuable reserves.[175] Flandreau then shows the swaps of silver reserves carried in the 1850s and 1860s by the Bank of France with its homologues of England, Russia, and Italy and with some private bankers, in exchange for gold reserves. He deduces from these swaps that the Bank of France was getting rid of the appreciated metal (silver) in exchange for the depreciated metal (gold), because only the depreciated metal could be introduced into circulation without creating a run on its reserves. The difficulty of these operations and their partial failure led the Bank to increase the use of the discount rate as an alternative instrument for maintaining an appropriate level of reserves, the ultimate goal being to guarantee the stability of the value of the franc through the convertibility of banknotes into gold and silver. According to Flandreau the Bank did not need bimetallism, but the imposition of the gold standard implied a series of legal obligations which would break its cooperation with the private bankers, forcing it into an unknown territory.

Flandreau's conclusions can be accepted generally but with an important exception for the years 1864–70, when low interest rates and increasing reserves were obtained by the bimetallic Bank of France, while the monometallic Bank of England failed to achieve the same result. Graph 4.8 shows how the increase in the discount rate raised the level of reserves, by reducing the Bank's resources employed in commercial advances.

The actual figures between 1844 and 1873 show a French discount rate more stable than the British one, with its fluctuations less frequent and contained within a smaller range (Graph 2.1). The price paid by the Bank of France for this achievement was a greater instability of its metallic reserves (Graph 4.9). The national banks seemed to

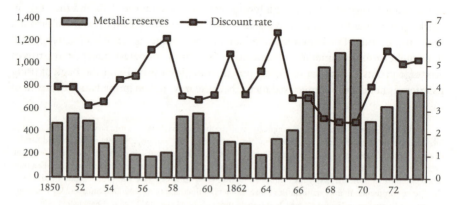

Graph 4.8 *The discount rate and the metallic reserves of the Bank of France*

Sources: Reserves are expressed in million francs, see Willis (1901: 90). The discount rate is a yearly average percentage, calculated from Seyd (1874).

[175] Flandreau (1995b: 858).

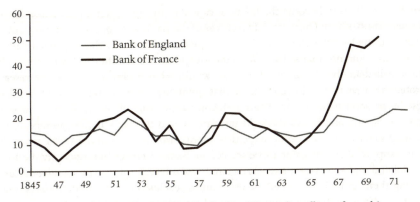

Graph 4.9 *The metallic reserves in England and France (in millions of pounds)*
Source: Seyd (1874: 10–11 and 15).

have the choice between a stable discount rate, which favoured economic activity or a stable level of reserves, which secured better the convertibility of banknotes in specie. This situation is quite clear until 1863–4, when the French discount rate begins to decline to lower levels than the British rate and the French reserves climb to an unprecedented high level of over a billion francs (the contemporary press defined it the strike of the billion, 'la grève du milliard').[176] This later phase of French bimetallism was much more in accordance with the views of the Bank of France, with plenty of gold *and* silver reserves, and a low interest rate, while Britain struggled alone with a further monetary crisis and three months of 10 per cent interest rate in 1866. The solidarity with the unstable British market had vanished. The worrying signs for the future were the declining French growth rate, unmodified by low interest rates. As the reluctance to modify interest rates was due to the pressure from the government and the commercial world, in favour of cheap money for economic growth, it is difficult to find a systemic advantage for France from such a situation. In Keynesian terms the French situation could be seen as a liquidity trap. Economic activity stagnated and monetary policy was unable to accelerate a return to growth however low the interest rate was set.

The situation of 1864–7, with a relative advantage for France in relation to British monetary difficulties, was short-lived. The British position was re-established rapidly and further improved with the French military defeat in 1870, which destroyed the

---

[176] This sudden increase in reserves puzzled contemporaries. Some explained it with the cours forcé in Italy, USA, Austria, Russia, and Turkey, and the free flow of species enhanced by the LMU had its influence. France also benefited during that period from a large and prolonged trade surplus, ultimately paid in specie. Finally, the growing confidence in banknotes increased their circulation, confining a growing share of the gold and silver circulation in the vaults of the Bank of France. These reasons combined with the reduced opportunities for the Bank of France to employ its resources for discount, because of lower economic activity and increased competition from the new commercial banks (Plessis 1985b: 310–17); Flandreau (1996: 854–5).

ambition of Paris to become the financial capital of Europe. After a brief pause due to the war of 1870–1, the massive gold reserves of the Bank of France became permanent, making it the largest holder of gold in Europe (Graph 4.7). But this happened despite bimetallism and not thanks to it. With the low price of silver after 1872, the bimetallic rules, called for by the Bank of France, would have meant a larger silver reserve protecting a smaller gold reserve. At that point the Bank did not wish a prevalent reserve of depreciated silver. The restriction to the issue of silver, 'limping bimetallism', an approximation to the gold standard, suited the Bank better, preserving the existing silver reserves without increasing them. From the end of the 1870s, when the world supply of gold became more scarce, the Bank of France but especially the Bank of Holland and the Bank of Belgium employed silver for domestic circulation, protecting their limited gold reserves, used almost exclusively for international transactions.[177] Without the opportunities offered by limping bimetallism, these countries could not have maintained a gold standard system for their international transactions.

   Ultimately the Bank opposed monetary unification because it would radically change the existing monetary arrangements. The first years of the LMU had shown how the Bank of France had to play the role of the central bank of the Monetary Union, with all the burdens and the costs connected to such a role. Both the French and the English national banks showed a persistent reluctance to accept responsibility for the international monetary system over the remaining years of the century, giving priority to the interest of the institution or to its national system.[178] It is not surprising therefore that the Bank of France refused to enlarge its geographical area of responsibility in the 1860s, having a limited confidence in the financial rectitude of some monetary allies. Furthermore the introduction of the gold standard had possible destabilizing effects and the conservative instinct of national bankers did not welcome monetary reforms with unknown effects. The interest of the private bankers on the board of the Bank corresponded to a 'natural' resistance to reform and certainly reinforced it, but the Haute Banque was not the exclusive cause of the Bank's opposition to the gold standard and to monetary unification.

----

[177] Luzzati (1883).   [178] Gallarotti (1995).

Enthusiasm and Resistance to Union in Britain and Germany

5.1. UNITED KINGDOM: THE POUND DEBASED TO ADAPT TO THE FRANC?

The international debate on a common European coinage initiated by the formation of the Latin Monetary Union reached the United Kingdom as well as the Continent. The British attitude towards the French and Continental proposals for monetary unification was ambivalent, reflecting the desire to compete on equal terms without being excluded from a Continental monetary union but also the attempt to strengthen the pound as the key international currency. Although some early discussion on international coinage took place in England between 1853 and 1868, attention focused only with the Royal Commission of 1868, followed by the economist W. S. Jevons's intervention. An important debate developed in 1869 when the Chancellor of the Exchequer Lowe decided to change governmental policy and look for an agreement with France.

5.1.1. Decimalization and Internationalization of the Pound

The growing commercial intercourse of England with the Continent and the international exhibitions of London (1851) and Paris (1855) called for an effort towards the rationalization and the internationalization of the units of measure. The metric system was legalized in the UK in 1862 but did not replace the British units, and reform of the coinage proved even harder. From 1853 to 1859 the pressure for the decimalization of the British currency was very strong, endorsed even by a select committee of the House of Commons, but nothing came of the agitation. The supporters of decimalization presented conflicting proposals. All wanted to reduce the number of monetary units by establishing simple decimal relations between them, in order to simplify calculations and accounting. The 'Pound and Mil' scheme preserved the pound but introduced new decimal division into 100 new pence and 1,000 new farthings. It was the most popular proposal in the 1850s and was eventually implemented in the 1960s. Other schemes based decimalization on the preservation of the pence or of the farthing but introduced new multiples. Thanks to the lack of unity of the reformers, the British government could delay its reply to the request advanced by the House of Commons in 1855 to adopt the 'Pound and Mil' scheme. Instead a Commission on Decimal Coinage was appointed to enquire into the matter.[1]

The Commission produced a report opposing any change, four years after it had been formed, when the campaign for decimalization had lost momentum. It was argued that the poor would not understand the difficult exchange rates between old and new coins. The existing binary system of coinage was better adapted to the British system of measures and weights, based on 12 or 20 units, than a decimal one would be. The 'Pound and Mil' appeared to be the only acceptable scheme, but it could not 'be looked upon as a well-assured or demonstrated improvement on our present coinage; but must rather be considered as an experiment of very doubtful result, accompanied, beyond all question, by many serious transitional difficulties.'[2] The report on decimalization was written by the only two surviving commissioners, Lord Overstone, a banker, leader of the Currency School and financial adviser to the Liberal governments, and John Hubbard, Governor of the Bank of England and Conservative MP. Both Overstone and Hubbard would play a key role in opposing any monetary change in the following fifteen years. O'Brien described Overstone's role as 'such an effective piece of destruction that what the supporters of decimalism had expected to be a mere completion of their task of achieving official and popular recognition of the rectitude of their case, proved to be the end of decimalism for more than fifty years.'[3] The conclusion of the 1859 report on decimalization anticipated very precisely both the intellectual approach and the final decision of the 1868 Royal Commission on International Coinage.

During the debate on decimalization frequent references were made to the advantages offered to foreign countries by a decimal system, but few to a common international unit of money. G. Oliphant produced the only scheme that decimalized the British currency by equalizing the pound (also known as the sovereign) to 25 French francs, reducing its gold content by 0.88 per cent from the current par of the exchange at 25.22 francs. After a period of transition, Oliphant wished to create a piece of 20 French francs called a 'Queen' as the largest unit of the system, replacing both the old sovereign and the new pound of 25 francs.[4] This Franco-British coin would impose itself as the standard of all international transactions. The proposal was mocked by the Chancellor of the Exchequer, Cornewall Lewis, and ridiculed by the Commons in 1855. 'He [Oliphant] says we ought to adopt the principle of coinage of foreign countries, and he starts on the French system. He proposes that one farthing shall be equal to 2 centimes, 1 lion to 10 farthings, 1 florin to 10 lions, and 1 queen to 10 florins (A laugh).'[5]

Oliphant's proposal of 1855 became a part of the larger scheme for monetary unification advanced in 1863 by the International Statistical Congress of Berlin. After 1865 it was considered the most appropriate way of transforming the Latin Monetary Union into a European monetary union, and of linking the British coinage to the Latin

---

[1] *Debate on the Decimal Coinage Question in the House of Commons* (1855).

[2] Decimal Coinage Commissioners (1859: 3).   [3] O'Brien (1871: i. 52).   [4] Oliphant (1855).

[5] *Debate on the Decimal Coinage Question* (1855: 30).

one. The discussion produced a scheme for the equalization of international coins with 1 new pound = 5 US dollars = 10 Austrian florins = 25 French francs. This scheme far exceeded Oliphant's original idea. It involved more countries and pointed to the advantages of a gold standard with subsidiary silver and bronze coinage.[6]

The main theoretical proponents of monetary unification in England were F. Hendriks, W. S. Jevons, E. Seyd, and L. Levi. The British actuary F. Hendriks launched the debate in England in 1866 with a detailed pamphlet, praised by Parieu, Jevons, and Seyd, and offering a more carefully researched version of Oliphant's plan.[7] Hendriks announced the birth of the Latin Monetary Union, speculated on the French hopes of enlarging the Union with flexible and adaptable arrangements, and proposed a change in the pound (reduction of its weight, through the introduction of a mint fee) which would equalize it to 25 francs. The pound would be decimalized and made equal to ten florins of 2.5 francs each and 1,000 mils of 2.5 centimes each. This proposal was taken as part of the scheme worked out by the International Monetary Conference in Paris in 1867.

A second version of the same idea was elaborated by Prof. Leone Levi, of King's College London, a leading member of the Metric Committee and of the International Association for obtaining a Decimal System of Measures, Weights and Coins. Levi wished to base the new British and international coinage on the 10-franc piece, called a Ducat of 100 pence.[8] He differed from Hendriks only in choosing 10 francs instead of 25 francs as a unit of reference. This version was personally favoured by Parieu, Jevons, Wallenberg, and the Master of the British Mint, Graham. The difference between the '10-franc scheme' and the '25-franc scheme' was small. The latter was more popular because it accommodated the British wish to retain the pound, as well as the requests of delegates from the USA, Austria, and Spain.

The British response to the creation of the LMU was lukewarm, though it was generally acknowledged that monetary union was a positive sign of progress. For the *Edinburgh Review* 'these changes are one of the progressive signs of the age',[9] for *The Times* 'a most important step in the process of European Civilization'[10] and for the *Economist* 'one of the most characteristic treaties of the nineteenth century'.[11] However, most newspapers questioned the possibility of extending the union further. For *The Times* 'we may reasonably expect to see a complete uniformity in weights measures, and currency throughout the whole of what, after the Emperor Napoleon, we may call "the Latin races", of the Continent.' *The Times* expected only Spain to join the monetary union of the Latins, and the rest of Europe to be organized into large but separate monetary areas. The 'German races' should adopt the thaler throughout the new North German Confederation, while southern Germany should join Austria in a

[6] Jevons (1875: 173).
[7] Royal Commission, (1868: 14–26 and 142–8); Parieu (1866*a*). Hendriks had been in contact with Parieu at least since 1858, when he translated Parieu's book on John de Witt.
[8] Levi testified in front of the Commission, Royal Commission (1868: 26–33).
[9] 'International Coinage' (1866: 399).
[10] A column without title nor signature on, *The Times*, 8 Sept. 1866, 8.
[11] 'Monetary convention between France, Belgium, Italy, and Switzerland' (1866: 1077).

separate monetary union. In this way

the European system would be as simple as we can reasonably expect. A universal adoption of the same system is neither to be expected nor, perhaps, desired. The assimilation, for example, of our own coinage, weights, and measures to the French system would not bring us advantages sufficient to compensate for the immense inconvenience of the change. So long as there are a few and well adjusted systems, we shall have all that we can desire . . . We congratulate the four governments who have signed this convention upon having furnished so good a precedent and we trust the example may be speedily imitated.[12]

The *Edinburgh Review,* which supported both unification and decimalization without reservations, had already used the insular nature of Britain as a metaphor for its monetary position: 'Our own country has hitherto stood aloof from any of these combinations, and we are separated from the rest of Europe and America by the duo-decimal system of numeration, and by the high value of the unit, the pound, almost as much as by the sea which surrounds these islands.'[13] The *Economist* joined the debate, rejecting union because of the heretic nature of French bimetallism:

[W]e see no reason why each State should have a separate money . . . This [LMU] gold coinage in practice is superior to ours . . . If we adopted it, we might hope that it would become first the sole European money and then the sole money of the civilized world . . . [But the convention] falls into the heresy of the double standard. The English, therefore, though they should regret that they are by inevitable causes excluded from the benefits of this convenient and uniform continental coinage, may yet congratulate themselves that their old standard of value was fixed on principles both wiser and more scientific than this new one.[14]

The official position of the British government at the beginning of 1867, as described in Chapter 2, was close to the positions developed by the *Economist* and *The Times*. Britain had no wish to modify the existing monetary system. The British delegates refused to consider the Conference as anything more than a debating society. Rivers Wilson, representative of the British Treasury, was very dismissive of the whole project:[15]

[T]he English Government, while acknowledging the great and general value of the question, and consenting therefore to take part in the examination of it, instructed its representatives to refrain from any act or opinion which might appear to pledge it to the adoption of any particular course of action. Similar instructions, indeed, seem to have been given by all the other countries to their representatives; the proceedings, therefore, although valuable as ventilating the merits of what might become a measure of far-reaching importance, had merely an academic interest.'[16]

Unanimity in favour of the gold standard was a 'singular feature in the deliber-ations', due exclusively to Parieu's very strong views, as far as France was concerned.

---

[12] *The Times*, 8 Sept. 1866, 8.   [13] 'International Coinage' (1866: 392–3).

[14] 'Monetary convention between France, Belgium, Italy, and Switzerland' (1866: 1077–9).

[15] Rivers Wilson was a Treasury official, British delegate to the International Monetary Conferences of 1867 and 1892, secretary of the Royal Commission on International Coinage in 1868, and private secretary to the Chancellor of the Exchequer Lowe from 1868 to 1873. He also became Finance Minister of Egypt in the 1870s on behalf of the British bondholders who had lent massively to the Egyptian government.

[16] McAlister (1916: 49).

Rivers Wilson rejected the 25-franc scheme and the two pence reduction of the pound: 'As might have been expected we did not support such an expedient, which would certainly be inadmissible in England, and could only be carried out at the cost of a recoinage of our whole gold currency, estimated at from £80,000,000 to £120,000,000.'[17]

5.1.2. The Royal Commission on International Coinage

The unanimous conclusions of the International Monetary Conference of 1867, in favour of an international coinage based on the gold standard reopened the debate and required a more articulate response. A Royal Commission was set up by Disraeli to provide an official response to the proposed 'inadmissible expedient' of reducing the weight of the pound to 25 francs. Rivers Wilson was secretary of the Commission and again described it without second thoughts: 'the Commission was appointed really out of compliment to the French government, who had first started the idea of the Conference; and although nothing came and was likely to come out of it, it was of very great interest, owing chiefly to the many able men who took part in it.'[18] The Commission worked fast and after a few months, in July 1868, was able to report that 'we found among the witnesses . . . a general concurrence of opinion in favour of the great advantage, which they anticipate from such a measure [the introduction of an international currency].'[19] Because of the extensive recoinage costs for a temporary reform and the damage it would cause to creditors, the Commission recommended, however, not to adopt the 25-franc coin but 'felt it [their] duty to state the grounds on which, with a view to the general interest of the commerce of the world, the English sovereign and pound might form a convenient basis for an international currency.'[20]

Many witnesses testified to the Commission that a common currency would intensify international competition, to Britain's advantage, by expressing all prices in the same units, and by simplifying accounts and comparisons between different goods. International trade would be enhanced, through the fact that even those not conversant with foreign units would be able to judge the true price of commodities. Smaller firms would be able to compete with larger enterprises without bearing the high fixed cost of clerks specialized in foreign exchange. Various types of transaction cost would be reduced, as would the risk of exchange fluctuations. The chambers of commerce were almost unanimously in favour of monetary unification.[21]

The Commissioners were not impressed and considered that the advantages of monetary union were overrated. They would bear full fruit only after a common system of weights, measures, and coins had been attained. Implicitly the commissioners considered such an event as an impossibility. They stressed the prominent role of uncoined bars of gold as the principal means of discharging international payments, means not affected by monetary unification.[22] The Commission followed Goschen's

---

[17] McAlister (1916: 50–1).   [18] Ibid.
[19] Royal Commission (1868, p. vii). The Commission was presided over by Viscount Halifax, and included the Governor of the Bank of England, the two most important private bankers (Rothschild and Baring), the two former British delegates to the Conference of Paris and several Members of Parliament.
[20] Ibid., p. xviii.   [21] Ibid., p. vii.   [22] Ibid., p. viii.

argument that some exchange costs would remain even after unification. George Goschen was a liberal MP for the City, a former director of the Bank of England and a financier of high reputation. In a speech delivered shortly after he had addressed the Royal Commission, he expressed the feelings of the Commission:

Admitting all the advantages of a uniform system of coinage, I cannot but feel that it is a doubtful matter, seeing how the question affects the National creditor, and, indeed all contracts, whether the immense disadvantage of depreciating the value of the sovereign, as is proposed, be it by ever so little, does not outweigh the benefit of a community of coins. If we could get rid of all fluctuations of Exchange, that would, indeed, be a very agreeable result. But even if the piece of 25 francs were made equal to the Sovereign, and the two coins were absolutely identical—were two Sovereigns in fact—the Sovereign in France would not necessarily be equal to the Sovereign in England. It would still depend upon the balance of trade, upon the demand for Gold for remittance to England, or for remittance to France; you would never get rid of the fractions.[23]

Goschen suggested that unification of the law on Bills of Exchange was far more important for payments to foreign countries than the system of coinage.

One of the members of the Commission was the master of the Mint, the eminent chemist Thomas Graham. He was the second British commissioner in Paris in 1867 and had prepared a report favourable to the ducat, a 10-franc—4-florin gold token coin to be minted for trade with France or, as an alternative proposal, in favour of the adoption of a 25-franc pound.[24] Graham associated internationalization with decimalization and prepared some proof international coins.[25]

The president of the Commission, Lord Halifax, was mainly concerned with the evaluation of the proposal advanced by Hendriks and endorsed by many supporters of union.[26] To avoid compensation and redenomination for all existing contracts for the reduction in weight of the pound, Hendriks had suggested levying a charge for the mintage of coins equal to the reduction of weight in the pound. An individual owning gold bars would bring 25.22 francs of uncoined gold to the mint (equivalent to an old pound) and would receive in exchange a new pound-25-franc gold coin, while the 22 centimes would be held as a tax. The technical name of the tax on coinage was seignorage. It had to be distinguished from *brassage,* which was a mere fee to cover the cost of mintage, also called mint fee (see the Glossary for more details). Hendriks suggested that, so long as France agreed to impose the same tax, at the same level, then the new sovereign of 25 francs + tax of 22 centimes would have the same value as

[23] Seyd (1868: 684–5). Goschen spoke in Liverpool on 7 Feb. 1868.

[24] The report of the English Delegates is in Royal Commission (1868: 190–3).

[25] The mint prepared in 1867–8 several proof coins in gold and silver, according to the specification of the 1867 International Monetary Conference. These coins were (1) the gold unit recommended by the conference, the 'double florin-five francs International', (2) the 10-franc coin supported by Graham and Levi, the 'ducat-100 pence' in gold, (3) a silver coin of '1 franc-10 pence'. In 1857, during the debate on decimalization, Graham had minted some proofs of bronze decimal coins: '5 farthing-10 centimes', 'decimal halfpenny-5 centimes', and 'farthing-2 centimes'. These patterns are preserved in the Coin Department of the British Museum in London. Some of them are reproduced in Josset (1962: 118), and in an Appendix to this work.

[26] Charles Wood, a former Liberal Chancellor of the Exchequer, was created Lord Halifax in 1866.

the old pound of 25.22 francs minted for free. Therefore old and new coins could circulate together without any adjustment, leaving previous prices and contracts unchanged, making the transition from the old national pound to the new international pound of 25 francs completely imperceptible, at no cost to anyone and with a profit for the Treasury.[27]

Hendriks advanced his proposal with the best of intentions in order to smooth the path of transition to the new monetary system. This proved however a serious mistake. Opponents of monetary unification used the proposal skillfully to show that creditors would be defrauded and to demonstrate the logical flaws of the scheme. No coin on earth could be worth at the same time and in the same place both 25 francs and 25.22 francs. Discussion started with the Commission of 1868 but acquired a greater importance in 1869, as will be seen further on.[28]

Halifax seemed initially favourable to the international proposal. After a long exchange of letters with Lord Overstone, he came round to the latter's view that it would not be right to defraud creditors of 1 per cent of their property. Overstone did not believe that, after the introduction of a 1 per cent seignorage, the British people would accept the reduction of intrinsic gold in sovereigns. He expected some people to prefer bars and refuse sovereigns at their legal value.[29]

After the report of the Commission, which requested a new international monetary conference based on sounder principles, Walter Bagehot, editor of the *Economist*, offered a different plan.[30] Bagehot accepted the necessity of monetary unification, 'Commerce is anywhere identical: buying and selling, lending and borrowing, are alike all the world over, and all matters concerning them ought universally to be alike too.' The existence of different price languages reduced international trade because only expert merchants understood the prices published in foreign gazettes. A single currency would facilitate immensely international transactions, reducing asymmetric information, the cost of exchange, and its uncertainty. Bagehot was worried that 'If things remain as now, [Germany] is sure to adopt the French currency; already there is a proposal in the federal parliament that she should take it. Before long all Europe, save England, will have one money, and England will be left outstanding with another money.'[31] Bagehot refused the franc because of its bimetallic nature. As a counterbalance to the franc zone formed around the Latin Monetary Union, Bagehot planned an Anglo-American currency enlarged to Germany. The pound would be decimalized and divided into 1,000 farthings, increasing its weight by 4.17 per cent, and equalizing it to approximately five dollars.

---

[27] The seignorage proposed was 0.88%, compared to the French seignorage of 0.21% and 0.5% in the USA. Until then the coinage of gold had been theoretically free in the UK, but in fact holders of gold bullion had to deal with the Bank of England which charged 0.16% as, since the 1840s, the mint had accepted bullion only from the Bank of England.

[28] The discussion was confused by the uncertain definition of the difference between what was the simple cost of coining (mint fee or brassage) and the additional profit imposed by the State for the benefit of the Treasury (called seignorage). Seignorage was the difference between the legal value attributed to the coin and the market value of its metallic content together with brassage.

[29] O'Brien (1971: iii. 1138–47).   [30] Bagehot (1869).   [31] St John-Stevas (1965–86: xi. 65).

No doubt it would not be long before the French and the other nations which have adopted their money would change and adopt the Anglo-Saxon money. But still the mercantile transactions of the English-speaking race are so much greater than those of any other race ... that in the course of years the Anglo-Saxon money would become the one money ... Looking to the commercial activity of the teutonic races and the comparative torpor of the Latin races, no doubt the teutonic money would be most frequently preferred.[32]

The modification to the pound proposed by Bagehot was substantially larger than the one suggested by Hendriks which had been turned down for its allegedly ambitious scope. But this time it was England not France which would be at the centre of the new international monetary system. This reflected both Britain's economic import-ance and a certain prejudice against southern Europe ('the comparative torpor of the Latin races'). Bagehot's plan received no support.

5.1.3. Jevons's Intervention, the Gladstone Government, and the Arrival of Lowe to the Exchequer

Jevons explored the condition of the metallic currency of the United Kingdom, and introduced a new point of view on the question of international coinage.[33] He called the report of the Royal Commission 'ambiguous', the difficulties it advanced 'imaginary', due to 'misapprehension of theory' and to 'prejudice'.[34] The boasted perfection of the British coinage hid a substantial alteration of the standard of value. Thanks to an extensive statistical enquiry conducted with the help of several banks, Jevons demonstrated that 31.5 per cent of the British gold sovereigns were 'light', worn down over the limit tolerated by the law to remain legal currency. Forty-six per cent of the gold half-sovereigns were in the same situation. A general recoinage of the British gold circulation on the basis of a new pound of 25 francs was nothing less than a necessity, 'placing the realization of a world wide money beyond doubt ... A con-currence of circumstances truly remarkable renders it almost indispensable that we should make the change required ... Instead of occasioning cost and difficulty the trifling alteration of the sovereign is the only mode by which we can impart practical as well as theoretical perfection to our metallic currency.'[35] Jevons added that

The most formidable of these prejudices [of the Royal Commission] arises from our national pride in the fact that the sovereign is known and respected in nearly all parts of the world ... If we are not misled by foolish pride, we shall take, while we can do it with good grace, the step of adopting our sovereign to become the new gold currency of the world. I may add that if we place any opposition or obstruction in the way of the International Monetary Convention, they have a most justifiable and powerful weapon ready to ensure our defeat. It is only necessary for the continental nations and the United States to issue, as is already proposed, a piece of 25 frs. in order to supplant the sovereign.[36]

---

[32] St John-Stevas (xi. 92–3).

[33] Jevons (1868: 426–64). William Stanley Jevons was an English economist, one of the founders of marginalism and of modern mathematical economics. His opinions on currency and finance and on the coal question were highly considered by the Liberal governments.

[34] Jevons (1868: 427).   [35] Ibid.   [36] Ibid. 428–9.

Jevons confided to his brother that 'I have some hope that when Mr Gladstone is Premier, with a great majority on his back, he may give some attention to the subject.'[37] A few weeks later the large majority indeed materialized and Gladstone occupied 10 Downing Street, appointing Robert Lowe to 11 Downing Street. Gladstone's first government replaced the Disraeli government in December 1868, a few months after the Royal Commission presided over by Lord Halifax had rejected the conclusions of the International Monetary Conference of 1867. Gladstone had already corresponded with Parieu in 1866, explaining that 'undoubtedly as far as England is concerned, the first and most indispensable consideration, in treating of any proposed measures, would be the maintenance of its exclusive gold standard.'[38] No other part of the letter has survived, but Parieu had received the impression that once France had adopted a gold standard an agreement with Gladstone and the Liberals could be possible. The Conservatives seem to have opposed such an agreement outright, judging from Lord Stanley's statements quoted in Chapter 2 and from Hubbard and Disraeli's opinions quoted further in this chapter. In the event it turned out that all the Conservatives who took part in the debate were against the LMU, but not all Liberals favoured it either.

Gladstone did not intervene personally although he was aware of the issue. At the beginning of February 1869, he participated in a debate on seignorage, presided over by Bagehot, at the Political Economy Club, and six days later he read Bagehot's book advocating an Anglo-America coinage.[39]

The initiative was taken by the Chancellor of the Exchequer. Robert Lowe was one of the leaders of the Liberal Party. In 1866 he had sent his own party into opposition, by leading the revolt of the 'Adullamite' faction against an extension of voting rights (the Reform Bill) supported by Gladstone and Russell. After the Conservatives had carried reform even further, Lowe returned to the Liberal fold. Once in the Cabinet, he took to heart his role as the government's watchdog on spending,

---

[37] 'I have just been in one of my journeys to London, to read a paper to the Statistical Society on the Gold Currency. It is the result of a rather elaborate enquiry during the past nine months, which has proved rather successful, and is likely to prove useful, I think.' Jevons to his brother Herbert, 20 Nov. 1868, (Jevons, 1886: 245).

[38] The Gladstone Diaries indicate that Gladstone wrote to Parieu on 2 March 1866, but the letter is not in Gladstone's letterbook (Matthew 1968–94: vi. 422). We know part of the content from Parieu who quoted a sentence of the letter in 1870. 'M. Gladstone m'a fait l'honneur de m'écrire en 1866' (Conseil Supérieur 1872: i. 109). Parieu had been introduced to Gladstone by Chevalier in 1860. 'Notre confrère de l'Institut, M. de Parieu, Vice Président du Conseil d'État, Ancien Ministre de l'instruction Publique, va passer quelques jours à Londres. Il s'est adonné particulièrement aux finances depuis qu'il a quitté le ministère. Il a composé sur ces délicates matières un ouvrage considérable qui est une mine de renseignements bien digérés. Comme vous êtes notre maître à tous dans cette branche importante de l'administration des États, M. de Parieu s'estimerait heureux de s'en entretenir avec vous.' Chevalier to Gladstone, 14 July 1860, (GPBL, *Correspondence Gladstone–Michel Chevalier*, coll. 44127, fol. 8).

[39] Matthew (1964–94: vii. 22): 24, 11 February 1869 and 5 March 1869: 'Read Bagehot on Univ. Money.' The question debated by the Club at Bagehot's request was 'Ought a government to impose seignorage on coins which are legal tender for an unlimited amount and if it ought, how much should that seignorage be?' Gladstone, Lowe, Bagehot, and Rivers Wilson participated in the debate (Political Economy Club 1921: vi. 89).

aiming at retrenchment and the reduction of the national debt. He did not possess specialist financial experience, but was strongly determined to reduce spending.

Lowe began to enquire into the subject of international coinage and to formulate policy from the beginning of his tenure at the Exchequer, asking the master of the British Mint, Graham, and the former master of the Calcutta Mint, J. B. Smith, to prepare a report on the cost of British coinage. Lowe needed to know the level of seignorage appropriate to cover that cost and to justify the change in the weight of the pound that would equalize the pound to 25 francs. The terms used by Lowe were misleading because he called seignorage (the arbitrary profit by the State on the issue of money) what was in fact brassage or mint fee (the payment by the user of the cost of mintage).[40] This difficulty in distinguishing between the two contributed greatly to obscure the discussion that followed. The report of the Masters was presented on 6 April and stated that, in order to pay the full cost of mintage and of keeping all the coinage at its standard weight through time, a 1.5 per cent charge would be needed if the State bore the cost of recoining and the loss of gold by wear and tear.[41] On 2 June Lowe prepared a confidential memorandum printed for the Cabinet. All of his arguments were derived from Jevons's paper on the British coinage and from Graham's report on the 1867 International Monetary Conference. Three reasons were advanced for his intervention in favour of reducing the intrinsic gold content of the pound and the introduction of a 1 per cent Mint fee. The first reason was the necessity to stop the drainage of gold coins from England, freely used abroad. The second was the necessity to save on the total recoinage of British gold coins that had lost weight by wear and tear. Jevons had proved this point and the Treasury and the Royal Mint accepted the figures he had advanced. His third reason for modifying the pound was international:

The question of international coinage cannot be disregarded by this country, and it is highly probable from the rapid progress that it is making all over the world, that one system of coinage will within no distant period be almost universally adopted, from which it will be impossible for Great Britain to stand aloof. As a necessary condition to our joining in such a scheme we should be forced to abandon our system of free mintage.[42]

The French government wrote to the British government on 20 June, transmitting the report of the French Commission on the monetary standard, which favoured the

---

[40] In a memorandum to the Cabinet Lowe talked about 'the imposition of a mint charge', explaining that it was only to cover the cost of minting, 'the charge required to defray all expenses of manufacturing the gold coinage, and maintaining it in a state of constant integrity, would amount to about 1 & 1 : 2 per cent (more or less) on all gold bullion brought to the mint.' Confidential report for the Cabinet, Necessity for imposing a Charge upon the Coinage of Gold Bullion at the Royal Mint, 2 June 1869 (Gladstone Papers, Apr.–July 1869, coll. 44610, fol. 83). In the House of Commons instead Lowe chose to use the threatening term of seignorage: 'A seignorage of one per cent would be sufficient to meet the expense of coinage, and of keeping the coin up to the value.' McLaren (1869: 4).

[41] Memorandum on the mintage necessary to cover the expenses of Establishing and Maintaining the Gold Currency (Gladstone Papers, Apr.–July 1869, coll. 44610, fol. 85).

[42] Confidential report for the Cabinet, Necessity for imposing a Charge upon the Coinage of Gold Bullion at the Royal Mint, 2 June 1869 (Gladstone Papers, Apr.–July 1869, coll. 44610, fol. 83).

adoption of a gold standard.[43] It was one of the periodical circular letters in favour of monetary unification sent to twenty different governments by the French Ministry of Foreign Affairs, following the mandate received in 1867 by the International Monetary Conference. On 29 July Lowe replied expressing his satisfaction and praising the soundness of the arguments, but recalling that

until however these principles have been formally adopted by the French government and sanctioned by legal enactment, no common ground for the negotiation of a system of international coinage between Great Britain and France can exist ... [the adoption of a single gold standard] will afford to Her Majesty's government the opportunity of considering the question of a common coinage with a fair expectation of a successful result.[44]

Following conventional views Lowe argued that French bimetallism was an alternative standard, not a double standard. Therefore if silver was to displace gold again in France, England would be left with nothing to compare to, not having a fixed relationship between its gold and the French silver. The negotiations would require an agreement for a coinage with a common weight, fineness, brassage and mintage conditions. In a word, Lowe was laying down the basis for a serious negotiation with France.[45]

It does not seem that Lowe discussed the question with Gladstone or any other of his colleagues in the Cabinet before his speech to the Commons.[46] Neither his correspondence with Gladstone nor the Cabinet minutes record any trace of it. Apparently Lowe decided to face the Commons on his own responsibility. Gladstone, busy fighting the Lords on the Irish Church Bill, only read Lowe's speech two weeks after it had been delivered.[47]

---

[43] AMAE, ADC 616–1 (1869–71), 20 June 1869, fol. 3.

[44] AMAE, ADC 604–2, Convention de 1865 et de 1867 (1869), fol. 208–9.

[45] At the beginning of July 1869 Jevons could savour the excitement of success: 'My sovereign research has been more successful than I expected. The Chancellor of the Exchequer has adopted the notion, and quoted some of my figures in the House of Commons lately; and he has had a report prepared partly based on my figures. I do not know whether he will succeed in carrying any change through, but I shall not wonder if he makes some attempt next session. At present the Irish Church [Bill] stops the way.' Jevons to his brother Herbert (Jevons 1886: 248): 7 June 1869: 248.

[46] On the day of his speech to the Commons, Lowe sent a 3-page note to Gladstone without a reference to coinage. Lowe only advanced the urgent request to change the Secretary of the Treasury and expressed his surprise at the low salaries paid to Irish schoolmasters, 'No wonder they teach Fenianism and Socialism.' Lowe to Gladstone, 6 August 1869 (GPBL, Correspondence Gladstone–Robert Lowe, coll. 44301, fol. 63–4). Lowe had apparently forgotten the good advice offered by Gladstone a few month before about the presentation of measures to the Commons on his own responsibility: 'I believe you will find it very useful to fortify yourself beforehand by calling in the common responsibility of your colleagues in the Cabinet generally. No man wants so much sympathy as the Chancellor of the Exchequer, and—unless human nature has much altered in the last 2 or 3 years—no man gets so little. Nor is any position so lamentable for him as to be defeated in proposing some new charge on the public[,] conceived or adopted by himself. It is like an ancient soldier wounded in the back. Whereas even defeat in resisting the raids of the House of Commons on the public purse is honourable, it always turns out well in the End.' Gladstone to Lowe on the duties and on the risks attached to the position of Chancellor of the Exchequer, 26 Dec. 1868 (GPBL, Correspondence Gladstone–Lowe, coll. 44301, fols. 35–6).

[47] Matthew (1964–94: vii. 118): 21 August 1869. Gladstone read 'Ch. of Exrs Speech on Coinage', fifteen days after the speech. Gladstone was recovering from illness and exhaustion from the Irish Church Bill negotiations, which hit him on 22 July 1869.

5.1.4. *Lowe's Speech in the Commons and the Ensuing Public Debate*

On 6 August 1869, the liberal MP and free trader J. B. Smith questioned Lowe in the House of Commons about the English coinage and the possibility of joining the countries of the Latin Monetary Union.[48] Lowe, who probably had discussed the question with Smith beforehand, agreed with him about the opportunity of such a move and explained Jevons' findings about the poor state of the gold coinage of the United Kingdom. 'After all our expenses and trouble, 31.5 per cent of our sovereigns and 47 per cent of our half-sovereigns are not a legal tender, because they are light weight; and that, for a country which prides itself above all things upon keeping up its gold standard, and upon having a circulation above all doubt and suspicion, is not only a very great and serious evil but a great reproach and discredit.'[49] In order to pay for complete recoinage of the British gold currency, Lowe proposed to reduce the quantity of gold in the sovereign and to create a mintage fee, which would fund a first recoinage and guarantee in the future the integrity of the coin. *En passant*, this measure would also permit the equalization between pound and 25 francs, provided that France introduced the same mintage fee as well. 'The blessing of one coinage throughout Europe, [is] a great step in civilization.'[50]

With regard to the question of international coinage. If we impose a seignorage of one per cent, and take it from the coin, our sovereign would be identical with the 25-franc piece, which the French government propose to coin. The sovereign would still remain a current coin in this country at exactly the same value as now and it would have the additional advantage of being identical in value with the 25-franc piece.[51]

The speech attempted to present the equalization of the pound with the 25-franc coin as if it was completely incidental, and as if it was not the motive that was pushing the British government towards action. The emphasis Lowe placed on the obligation for Great Britain to join a successful single currency, as shown by the Cabinet memo of 2 June, seems to indicate that savings were not the main motive of the proposed reform. Still Lowe's move to stress the objective of achieving some savings on the currency in order to avoid arousing fears of subservience to French monetary imperialism, ended up revitalizing the old and powerful fear of currency debasement.

Debasing the currency had been a highly profitable activity for most States, which had repeatedly reduced either the weight or the fineness of the coins they issued, imposing each time a legal value superior to the market value of the metallic content. The operation would produce an increase of prices expressed in the new coins, generating what amounted to an inflation tax in favour of the monarch.[52] In England the practice reached its peak under Henry VIII but had been progressively discredited and substituted with a more organized and effective tax system. After the great recoinage

---

[48] J. B. Smith (–1879) was a veteran of the free trade movement and was associated to the British chambers of commerce. A merchant by profession, he had presided over the Manchester chamber of commerce (1839–41) and was the first Chairman of the Anti-Corn Law League. He was MP for Stockport from 1847 to 1874.   [49] ABoE (1870: 3–4).

[50] Hansard Parliamentary Papers, 3rd series, 198, 6 Aug. 1869, col. 1421.

[51] McLaren (1869: 6).   [52] Kindleberger (1993: 27–30).

of 1696–9, when Newton fixed the value of the English currency, the United Kingdom had no longer experienced this form of abuse.[53] The only event comparable to debasement present in the memory of Lowe's contemporaries, could have been the suspension of specie payments during the Napoleonic Wars.[54] The fear of debasement in 1869 can be explained only by the heterodox financial opinions of Lowe and by a certain prejudice against change.

Lowe had not defined accurately the difference between *brassage* (mint charge) and seignorage in his speech, but the quotations from Adam Smith, Ricardo, Mill, and McCulloch used by him reflected the absence of such a distinction in the minds of most British economists. Lowe claimed that the seignorage levied would increase proportionately with the value of the coin.

Lowe inherited the mistakes made by Hendriks and echoed by Col. Smith, former master of the Calcutta Mint. He tried to show that the change had only positive consequences and refused to face the readjustments and the costs required. The simplicity of the change could have been enhanced if, instead of claiming that the value of debts and credits was unchanged, Lowe had accepted the readjustment of all values in the proportion indicated by Jevons, by 113/112. This would have permitted him to ask for a mint charge that was not exactly equal to the change in the weight of the pound (0.88 per cent). A lower mint charge would have calmed down the opponents of seignorage and those worried by currency debasement. Nevertheless the accusation of altering the standard of value would have remained, and those opposed to any sort of change because they believed in the intrinsic superiority of the British currency would have maintained their pressure.

Although Lowe's speech contained technical and tactical mistakes of some consequence, he had indicated two serious problems: the unsatisfactory state of the British coinage and the need to join an international decimal currency, together with the general lines of a solution. His speech was not meant as a formal proposal to the Commons but as a 'wish to ventilate the subject and give the Honourable Gentlemen and the public at large the means of thinking over this matter'.[55]

Reactions to Lowe's speech. The reactions to this speech were mixed, but a strongly hostile mood soon prevailed. Lowe was supported by the academic world, by economists, statisticians, and mint masters, together with the mercantile community which faced international competition in foreign markets. The financial world, the Bank of England, most newspapers, and a degree of popular public opinion opposed Lowe. In part this represented a repetition in the open of the positions expressed in the sessions of the Royal Commission one year earlier, but Lowe's mistake about the introduction of a high mintage fee shifted the debate. Attention was diverted from the general discussion of advantages and disadvantages of a common currency, on which supporters of unification tended to prevail, to technical discussions of Mint regulations, seignorage, brassage, and other minutiae, where bullion dealers and bankers excelled, while academics got confused and merchants declined to intervene.

---

[53] Davies (1994: 244–7).   [54] Feavearyear (1963).
[55] Hansard Parliamentary Papers, 3rd series, 198, 6 Aug. 1869, col. 1419.

Many people were outraged both by the insult to the pound produced by its debasement, and by the impoverishment of creditors which would follow. The articles and pamphlets which flourished on the subject rarely referred to the international aspects of the question, except to stress the international role of the pound. Debasing the coinage, even if only by 0.88 per cent, would open the way to future larger introductions of seignorage by the State.

Within fifteen days of Lowe's speech the discussion of minutiae had clouded the question beyond recovery. Every new letter or article was discussed and dissected up to its most irrelevant detail, and controversy sometimes turned into personal insult against Lowe, Jevons, and the two Smiths. *The Times* warned in vain: 'If we might venture to offer a word of advice ... beware of being lost in a multiplicity of detail.'[56] The *Economist* complained about the scheme's lack of intelligibility, and concluded that 'a plan in England can only be adopted either because everybody understands the reason of it, or because the most respected persons say it is right. But here nobody understands the reason, and the most respected persons do not agree.'[57]

Popular feeling was immediately aroused to defend the sanctity of the pound. According to an anonymous 'bullionist', 'the maintenance of our standard of money is a sacred obligation'.[58] For *Punch*, 'Mr Lowe wants to debase the sovereign ... to please the French.'[59] In summarizing the controversy, the barrister MacLaren commented on Lowe's proposal: 'These speeches, coming from a Chancellor of the Exchequer, will appear very ominous to all those who are at all familiar with the history of our currency, and they immediately called forth a great amount of criticism.'[60] An anonymous pamphlet violently attacked Lowe's 'irrelevant nonsense', adding that 'These frivolous and most inappropriate and ignorant remarks on our currency are unworthy of a schoolboy' ... 'Mr Lowe does not understand the currency question ... every creditor of the nation would be defrauded of one per cent.'[61] J. Aytoun of the *Morning Advertiser* distinguished himself with several attacks of particular violence: Lowe was a 'chartered libertine', falling into 'gross blunders', and issuing 'great absurdity'. 'It is really too bad that the whole trade and commerce of the country should be exposed to injury by the freaks and vanity of a man who, on account of the mere interest of party, has been placed in a situation for which he is totally

---

[56] *The Times*, 20 Aug. 1869, in Bank of England (1870: 67).

[57] *Economist*, 21 Aug. 1869, in Bank of England (1870: 71).

[58] *The Bullionist*, 14 Aug. 1869, in Bank of England (1870: 42).

[59] *Punch or the London Charivari*, 57, 14 Aug. 1869, 57. *Punch* later added in its usual satirical vein: 'Lowe Jokes. The Conservatives appear to be stunned. They raise little or no outcry against Mr Lowe's proposal to lower the Standard. To be sure your gold is not your paper. But the Chancellor of the Exchequer proposes bringing down the Sovereign. It is however true that he contemplates doing this without prejudice to the Crown' (*Punch*, 57, 21 Aug. 1869, 67). In a full page cartoon, entitled 'Bob and the Bobby, or only his fun', a suspicious John Bull, dressed as a policeman, threatenend Lowe: 'Hullo, young feller! If you're a goin' in for "sweatin'" the gold, you'll be gettin' yourself into difficulties.' Exchequer Bob, busy handling a box of gold coins and a bag of the Royal Mint replied 'Lor' bless yer, Mister Bull, why I'm only a makin' the income-tax lighter!' (*Punch*, 57, 16 Oct. 1869, 148).

[60] McLaren (1869: 7).

[61] *A Defence of the British Currency; Showing its Necessity and Utility* (1870: 2–3).

unfitted.'[62] *The Bullionist* stated that 'The proposal is one which deserves to be dismissed simply with a laugh.'[63] To the *Morning Advertiser* Lowe's plan was a 'financial crotchet',[64] to the Liberal MP, Alderman Lawrence, it was a 'conundrum', and to the bullion dealer Seyd a 'hocus pocus.'[65] Aytoun and Hubbard wondered why Lowe did not 'put himself under the tuition of his colleague Mr Goschen, who was once a Bank director', to learn something about the currency.[66] To counter the idea of a worn-down British coinage, Hubbard attempted to demolish Jevons's statistics in *The Times*, and losing his temper on the way, 'I must distinctly declare that Mr Jevons's method of calculation in connection with the subject is fallacious, and the conclusions derived from it utterly worthless.'[67] Jevons replied that 'with a curious propensity to error, which I know not how to characterize, Mr Hubbard has falsified at once the Rule of Three and the facts of the case.'[68] *The Echo*, who supported unification, sarcastically summarized the feelings of the 'anti-Lowe league':

It is well known by this time that a conspiracy has been laid to tamper with the beautiful Sovereign—to reduce the shining gold which it contains, and to alter its purity by increasing its alloy. The plot was concocted at Paris at the International Monetary Conference in 1867, but the scene of action has since been transferred to London, and the Chancellor of the Exchequer has placed itself at the head of the conspirators.[69]

A more articulate expression of opposition came from the City. The resistance to the reform was headed by the former Governor of the Bank of England, John G. Hubbard, and by the former president of the decimal coinage commission and main inspirer of the Bank Act of 1844, Lord Overstone. The Bank of England did not offer any official reaction during the debate, but in addition to Hubbard the former Governor Hunt took a decided stance against Lowe. Another experienced director, Norman, expressed his horror in his letters to Overstone, confirming that the Bank was against Lowe's project. The current Governor of the Bank of England, Crawford, decided to collect all the contributions to the debate in a book.[70] Crawford, who was also a Liberal MP, replied to Lowe's announcement of the withdrawal of his plan in 1870 that 'the statement of the right hon. Gentleman had relieved his mind of a great

[62] J. Aytoun, 'The Chancellor of the Exchequer must be taught political economy', *Morning Advertiser*, 14 Aug. 1869 (Bank of England 1870: 36).

[63] *The Bullionist*, 25 Sept. 1869 (Bank of England 1870: 224).

[64] Aytoun, 'Lowe's Seignorage Scheme', *Morning Advertiser*, 23 Aug. 1869 (Bank of England 1870: 77).

[65] Seyd, 'Gold coinage', *The Times*, 20 Aug. 1869 (Bank of England 1870: 60).

[66] Aytoun, 'The Chancellor of the Exchequer ... ' (Bank of England 1870: 36).

[67] J. G. Hubbard, 'The Gold Coinage', *The Times*, 20 Aug. 1869 (Bank of England 1870: 59).

[68] Jevons, 'Gold Coinage', *The Times*, 24 Aug. 1869 (Bank of England 1870: 84).

[69] 'The Sovereign', *The Echo*, 30 Sept. 1869 (Bank of England 1870: 239). This paragraph could be usefully compared with the title of *The Express's* on 30 Apr. 1997: 'Major's rage at Euro plot. Premier attacks arrogant bid to expel UK from world elite.'

[70] Overstone gloated: 'Of course I am pleased to learn from you that my ideas on the mintage question receive the approval of the Patres Conscripti of Treadneedle Street—nor can I make any objection if the Pontifex Maximus [the governor] really wishes to mingle them with the mass of nonsense which, it appears, he is accumulating for some mysterious process in the dark recess of his temple of Mammon. By this strange chemistry he will produce probably the most powerful soporific yet known to the intellectual world' (O' Brien 1971: iii. 1189). The collection of articles is in Bank of England (1870).

weight, and he was sure that many other persons would be gratified to learn that it was not his intention to carry out his proposals.'[71] In Overstone's words 'I think there is a danger that Bobby Lowe will get himself and the Country in a serious mess with his rash theories.'[72]

The opposition included Bagehot and the *Economist*, the *Daily Telegraph*, and *The Observer*. The columns of *The Times* were the principal battleground, where forty-one letters and four leading articles in less than three months dissected the issue. *The Times* was torn between loyalty to Lowe, who had been its main contributor until a few months earlier, and its readers, which were generally opposed to any change.

Three main arguments were used:

1. Lowe's claim that seignorage added to the value of the coin was considered erroneous. The old pound of 113 grains of pure gold and 25.22 francs would be replaced by a lighter new pound of 112 grains and 25 francs. If the new and the old pound had a different value in francs abroad, the two could not possibly have the same value in the UK. The standard of value was therefore altered by 0.88 per cent and all debts should be revalued by the same amount so as not to defraud the creditors. The argument was correct, but it was not used to ask for the readjustment of values, rather to portray Lowe's proposal as a theft damaging creditors and an unacceptable alteration of the pound of Newton and Peel. An implicit equation was established in the mind of the reader: alteration = depreciation = debasement = abuse; therefore any alteration must be resisted. In Hubbard's words: 'the prevailing impression in this country [is] that the wisest course to pursue with our own coinage is *to leave it alone*.'[73] Lord Overstone's highly regarded intervention in *The Times* came to an identical conclusion: 'It is for the interest of justice and the well-being of the community that the value of the pound sterling should continue as nearly as possible invariable, and with this end in view it is our duty to leave it alone.'[74] The *Observer* on 26 September 1869 declared that, in its view, Overstone's intervention against Lowe's plan had solved the dispute.[75]

The opposition of the *Economist* was not merely an example of the frequent low-key conservative idolatry of the pound.[76] The review understood Lowe's concerns for a

---

[71] Hansard's Parliamentary Papers, 3rd series, 190, 10 Feb. 1870, col. 155. R. W. Crawford (1813–89) was a merchant connected with East India trade and railways, a director of the Bank and its governor in 1869. He was a liberal MP for the City of London from 1857 to 1874.

[72] Overstone to Norman, 18 Aug. 1869 (O' Brian 1971: iii. 1178).

[73] Hubbard, *The Times*, 7 Oct. 1869 (Bank of England 1870: 261).   [74] McLaren (1869: 13).

[75] *The Observer*, 26 Sept. 1869 (Bank of England 1870: 226).

[76] *The Economist* concluded its review of McLaren's book, supporting his views against unification: 'Though the cost of production regulates the price of gold coins as everything else, and to charge a seignorage would add to its value, in the first instance, yet the demand for coin is very variable, and intervals would be of frequent occurrence when the oversupply would cause depreciation, until the cessation of production brought things round again. On this account he [Mc Laren] maintains, a coin on which no seignorage is charged, is more useful, as the oversupply of coin is at once checked by its conversion into bullion, and the consequent depreciation prevented ... A very little risk of depreciation, it should be remembered, will be a strong argument against any change, as it can not be said that the present system, which secures us against the risk, costs us anything to speak of in comparison.' Review of McLaren's 'A Brief Review', *Economist*, 27, 25 Dec. (1869), 1531. *The Economist* published on the subject other articles on 14 and 21 Aug. and 11 Sept. 1869.

more flexible form of money, more paper and less bullion, reserving gold to inter-national trade and for the reserves of the Bank of England. Bagehot's 'Lombard Street' would come only four years later, identifying in the Bank of England the supplier of credit of last resort, protecting its stability against crises of liquidity through its gold reserves that should not ordinarily be dispersed in the circulation.[77] Bagehot was not against any modification of the pound; he had indeed proposed to equalize it to 5 dollars, but he opposed a currency area dominated by the franc.

2. Much discussion took place over seignorage. Hubbard and Seyd would concede a mint charge between 0.15 per cent and 0.30 per cent, but declared that anything higher was theft. For Hubbard the charge should be levied by fixing a special amount in addition to the weight of bullion brought to the mint, without a deduction from the weight of the sovereign. 'The pound sterling, our measure of value, is a definite portion of fine gold in the shape of a coin; not a bag of golddust or a piece of a bar: and we ought not and must not alter this, and take in its place a coin having artificial value.'[78] If a seignorage as high as 0.88 per cent was levied, the pound would become

a metallic monster—a coin which would be neither a token nor a standard of value. It would not be a token, for a token is a domestic coin, and it is limited in its legal exchangeability; nor would it be a standard of value, for a standard coin, while unlimited as a legal tender, is, at the same time, exchangeable within the area of civilized commerce at its professed value. The pound sterling has been hitherto a truth; let it not become a sham.[79]

Overstone stressed that the stability of the weight of the pound was the current rule: 'To introduce any other rule is to introduce endless confusion, conflict and injustice, and to afford facility and encouragement to that most dangerous tendency, from which a community is never altogether free, to seek immediate ease, and a state of hollow, factitious prosperity, by the gradual debasement of the standard of value.'[80] In a secret memorandum to Norman, Overstone revealed his true fears: 'if the principal countries of the world can by acting in common accord deduct, say one per cent, from their coins, without injustice to the creditor interest, on account of the asserted undiminished purchasing power of the coins, what limit is there to this process? Why not deduct 10 per cent or 50 per cent of the gold in their coins?'[81]

The bullion trader Ernest Seyd, a German living in Great Britain and author of one of the best manuals of the time on foreign exchange, added that a small mint charge of no more than a third per cent was 'a fair and legitimate charge which can be borne, but

[77] Just a month before Lowe's speech on the pound, *The Economist* praised him for his proposal to introduce a £1 note because it would lead to the concentration of gold coinage in the Bank of England. The Bank could use the gold reserve to pay international balances when need came, without having to collect it from the general circulation and wasting time and credit. The common complaint was that the banknotes took the place of the sovereign, driving it out of circulation 'but all banknotes take the place of coin, and are only valuable because they do so. If £1 banknotes are more successful than other banknotes in replacing the Sovereign, then it means they are better than other banknotes, not worse' ('Mr Lowe on £1 notes', *Economist* 27, 3 July (1869), 772).

[78] Attributed to Hubbard by McLaren (1869: 9).
[79] Hubbard, 'The Gold coinage', *The Times*, 17 Aug. 1869, in Bank of England (1870).
[80] McLaren (1869: 15).   [81] O'Brien (1971: iii. 1180).

anything above this charge takes the character of seignorage, and in that character it is nothing but a sham, against which logic, commerce and the common sense of the people will rebel, and this rebellion, in spite of political authority, will be successful in the end.'[82]

What makes this harsh statement so interesting is that Seyd was a supporter of unification before Lowe's speech and again after Lowe's proposal was withdrawn. He had warmly endorsed the reduction of the pound to the weight of 25 francs in his manual of foreign exchange published one year earlier. 'Even we in England, however strongly we may be attached to our pound sterling system, if we desire to share in the benefits sure to result from the general introduction of uniform currency, must make up our minds to assimilate our coinage to that of France.'[83] Seyd was in favour of universal coinage based on a bimetallist system, a rare case in the United Kingdom. But he was also a dealer in precious metals, a business which flourished thanks to currency arbitrage, remelting and exporting–importing metal in coins or bars.[84] This trade would have been severely affected by the introduction of a tax. This tax however, would have had more important general consequences for foreign exchange. Trade of gold and silver, between the UK and France, implied transportation costs, handling, bags, and insurance costs. The total reached approximately 0.4–0.5 per cent of the value of a large shipment. Shipment of metals from one country to the other took place when the exchange rate had moved up or down from the gold or silver parity (relation between the pure content of metal of the coins of two countries in question) by more than the transportation costs. These upper and lower limits constituted the gold points, or effective margin of currency fluctuation in a gold standard. With the introduction of a 1 per cent Mint charge, the fluctuation of exchange rates that made arbitration profitable would have to increase by 1 per cent to keep the same opportunities of profitable arbitrage. It is likely that this would have been a source of increased fluctuations of exchange rate and of the relative price of silver and gold.[85]

---

[82] Letters to *The Times* by E. Seyd on Aug. 13, 20, 28, and Sept. 13 (*A Defence of the British Currency* (1870: 34)). [83] Seyd (1868: 682).

[84] Once the ground was cleared from the defective details of Lowe's proposal, Seyd reintroduced the question of unification under a different light. He described Britain as having lost ground to France in international banking operation in the last twenty years because 'we neglect to hold bill claims (a form of disposable capital) on foreign nations, and in the event of a crisis, we are pushed back upon our own discounts and investments, which, by themselves, cannot bring bullion to us, whilst we are driven to squeeze them to the utmost for gold. At other times, when money is abundant, we are induced to encourage local discounts beyond what is strictly prudent. We foster local speculation' (Seyd 1870: 48). France instead has created a large protective portfolio of claims over England that could be mobilized in case of need (as it happened after the Franco-Prussian War) and thus stabilize its financial situation. 'The London market for foreign exchanges, in spite of its productiveness in continental bills, instead of leading the rates, has become a passive one, operated upon principally by French bankers to their profit. Paris rules the exchanges, instead of London' (ibid. 49). To accept monetary unification would make British bankers more readily available to deal with foreign bills and exchanges and not just endorse them as they currently did, while the French perform exchange arbitration (ibid).

[85] Hubbard had perceived this, when he declared that a large seignorage would 'obstruct the free circulation of gold acting as the adjuster of international balances of trade, enlarge the scale of variation of exchange, and, by increasing the uncertainties of commerce, enhance the price of commodities' (Hubbard, *The Times*, 16 Aug. 1869, in Bank of England 1870).

3. The status of the pound in international payments was another important argument against change. The pound was the main international currency for the Empire and China and was legal tender in such countries as Portugal and Brazil. For Sir J. Herschel, former master of the London Mint, the pound was a real and tangible thing, namely a coin with a fixed weight of fine gold. 'All our public acts and arrangements from Sir R. Peel's Act of 1819 downward ... have been based on this definition.'[86] Public faith in the value of the pound both internally and internationally required its stability.

Much less attention was devoted to the discussion of the effects of a common currency on trade, but the usual argument was that international coinage was not worth the effort of change. A few stressed that exchange rates and transaction costs would remain even after unification, as Robert Lowe himself had declared when he was opposing Samuel Brown and the Decimal Association in 1855. Even 'if different countries should adopt the same coins, the variation in the rate of exchange would render them of different value.'[87] Therefore unification was pointless. The balance of trade, the interest rates, and the general conditions of the economy would continue to fluctuate and determine the exchange rate of banknotes and bills. It was added that 'no exporter, unless for some peculiar operation, would ship sovereigns if he could purchase bar gold'.[88] The different perception of the relative importance of bars, coins, banknotes, and bank drafts between the United Kingdom and Continental Europe depended in part on the different financial structure of the pound zone and the franc zone.

The supporters of a European monetary unification had already exposed their arguments between 1866 and 1869. Lowe having laid down the arguments for unification in a very peculiar and indirect way, the initiative rested with his opponents and the debate was not on the issues of free trade, growing international transactions and comparative costs favoured by the internationalists. The former master of the Calcutta Mint, Col. J. T. Smith, the Liberal MP J. B. Smith, the economists W. S. Jevons and Leone Levi, the statisticians Hendriks and Farr, and many merchants and chambers of commerce supported Lowe.[89]

The two Smiths were the most ardent defenders of every detail of Lowe's plan, while Levi in the *Daily Telegraph* and Jevons in *The Times* attempted to familiarize the public with the wider debate taking place on the Continent about the opportunity to achieve monetary unification, explaining the larger context. Hendriks campaigned from the columns of the *Economist*. An anonymous merchant B[90] stated the commercial point of view:

A universal measure of value would remove an artificial difficulty from international transactions, be they great or small, and would direct trade to that country which offers the greatest

---

[86] McLaren (1869: 11).   [87] *Debate on the Decimal Coinage Question* (1855: 24).

[88] T. Hankey, *The Times*, 10 Aug. 1869 (Bank of England 1870: 27).

[89] Farr (1870); Hendriks (1869: 1191–3).

[90] Mr B. was probably J. Behrens, an international merchant established in Manchester and Bradford, who had testified in front of the Royal Commission, using the same words employed in the letter to the *Economist*, Royal Commission (1868: 6).

natural advantages. There can not be a doubt that, all things being equal, *England is that country*; but we must not forget that steam, telegraphs and the accumulation of wealth abroad, have deprived England of the most exclusive monopoly of the world's trade which she once possessed, and that she can not afford to stand still while all the world is moving and moving in concert. Already now English merchants and manufacturers have to struggle hard to maintain their positions against a competition which is daily getting more formidable, and they therefore hail with satisfaction the prospects of obtaining by means of Mr Lowe's scheme a chance of meeting their foreign competitors on equal terms in neutral markets.[91]

5.1.5. *Governmental Discussion and International Reactions*

The deluge of criticism that followed Lowe's speech was also echoed inside the Cabinet. The War Secretary E. Cardwell accused Lowe of debasing the currency and altering the standard of value. The Prime Minister Gladstone was 'astonished' at Lowe's proposal, the President of the Poor Law Board, G. Goschen considered the whole attempt useless. Goschen is likely to have objected to Lowe's plan, judging from his speech already quoted and from his statement to the Royal Commission of the previous year.

Lowe tried to explain his reasons in a detailed letter to Cardwell on 7 September, printed confidentially for the Cabinet a few days later, insisting on the importance of the change and fighting back against the accusations. Lowe excused his previous silence 'I did not like to trouble you with my coinage questions, but as you have started the subject, I will put the case to you.' Lowe explained the real state of the worn-down British currency, specifying that light coins, theoretically illegal:

circulate without depreciation; and nobody, except the Bank of England, troubles itself about sovereigns below legal tender, because they will circulate as well as the legal tender sovereign. If the value of the sovereign did depend upon its weight, the nuisance of our present system would be utterly unbearable, and no one could give or receive change without a pair of scales to determine the amount of depreciation ... I think it follows from this that there is no necessary connection between the diminution in the weight of a sovereign and its depreciation.'[92] [underlined by Gladstone]

Lowe then discussed what was the standard of value in England;

It is not the quantity of gold actually contained in the sovereign ... Those who think as I do that a banknote discharges the office of money, and is not a mere instrument of credit, will be disposed to hold that the value of money does not depend at all primarily on the material of which it is made ... Sir Robert Peel defined a pound to be 'a certain definite quantity of gold with a mark upon it to determine its weight and fineness', from which it follows that the only standard we have is a new sovereign of full weight—a definition which would condemn every

---

[91] Letter by B. on Mr Lowe and the coinage, *Economist*, 27, 21 Aug. (1869), 1074–5.

[92] Report printed for the Cabinet, 'Mr Lowe to Mr Cardwell', dated 7 Sept. 1869, printed 13 Sept. 1869 (GPBL, coll. 44611, fol. 54, p. 1). It was customary in the Gladstone government that letters exchanged between two ministers, of some importance for the discussion of policy, would be confidentially printed for the whole Cabinet, to enlarge the discussion.

metallic currency, unless it were made of indestructible materials ... The truth is that the value of a currency depends far more on its quantity than on its quality.[93]

Lowe emphasized the archaic character of the conception of money displayed by his opponents, who refused to acknowledge banknotes as a form of money, and denied pursuing any alteration of the standard or debasement of the currency. Lowe was defending a conception of money as a public good managed by the State with a deliberate policy against the conception of money as a private good, 'a commodity like everything else' for Goschen.[94] Cardwell reacted, calling Gladstone's attention to the matter:

I was very sorry to see that Lowe had given way to what seems to me a mischievous fallacy about the sovereign and I thought it only a friendly act to give him a hint of it. This brought a printed indication of his views, which, in case you had not seen it, I enclose. It was far from my intentions to occupy the opposite side to his in a controversy.

If I were residing in Paris, deriving an income of £1,000 a year from the English Funds, and I suddenly found that the payment was made in sovereigns, not equal as now to 25 francs 4 sous, but to 25 francs 0 sous, it seems to me that, non-obstante the enclosure, I should consider the English currency to have been depreciated—and the standard of value altered, quo ad the National Debt.[95]

Gladstone's reply is partially illegible, 'Many thanks for your advice. I am also in favour of a Mint charge, but am no f.a to Lowe and I am astonished.'[96]

Lowe later wrote to Gladstone proposing new reforms at the Mint, abolishing the position of Master, reducing the degree of error tolerance in the weight of coins and delays in minting.[97] Gladstone sent to Lowe an unusually imperious note, ordering him to suspend action on the Mint. 'Be quite understood about the Mint that I do nothing until the question of the [unreadable: sovereign's weight?] has been disposed of.'[98] The note could be interpreted as an order to stop any further discussion on the alteration of the weight of the sovereign, but could also have referred to the appointment of a new master after the death of Graham or to the conflict between Lowe and the Commissioner of Public Works, Ayrton, about the construction of the new Mint building.

In November 1869 Lowe printed for the Cabinet a confidential memorandum by J. B. Smith, suggesting that he wanted to go ahead with the project despite all the criticism. Col. Smith explained that the pound had several defects, which would be solved by the introduction of seignorage.[99] In the final page of the memorandum, Smith suggested what would amount to a gold exchange standard; a circulation of banknotes backed by gold reserves, held mainly in the form of bullion bars by the

[93] 'Mr Lowe to Mr Cardwell.', 1   [94] Royal Commission (1868: 125).

[95] Cardwell to Gladstone, 19 Sept. 1869 (GPBL, Correspondence Gladstone–Cardwell, coll. 44119, fol. 66).

[96] Gladstone to Cardwell, 20 Sept. 1869 (GPBL, Letter Book, coll. 44537, fol. 66).

[97] Lowe to Gladstone, 11 Oct. 1869 (GPBL, Correspondence Gladstone–Lowe, coll. 44301, fol. 85 bis).

[98] Gladstone to Lowe, 12 Oct. 1869 (GPBL, Letter Book, coll. 44537, fol. 92).

[99] J. T. Smith, *Remarks on the Currency*, dated 12 Nov. 1869, printed 26 Nov. 1869, (GPBL, Official Papers, Aug.–Nov. 1869, coll. 44611, fol. 146, p. 7).

Central Bank.[100] A managed currency with a larger proportion of banknotes now became Lowe's objective and in 1870 and 1872 he proposed the demonetization of the gold half-sovereign and the concentration of gold sovereigns in the vaults of the Bank of England, replaced by new £1 banknotes.

Seen from Continental Europe Lowe's proposal was appreciated by the supporters of the programme like Parieu and Feer-Herzog, because it indicated some degree of willingness by Great Britain to participate in the creation of an international money. Nevertheless Lowe's mistake about the seignorage was well understood.[101] Feer-Herzog, Swiss representative at all monetary conferences of the period, commented on Lowe's plan:

From an international point of view, it presents a difficulty consisting in the fact that monetary unification supposes that participating States agree on the Mint fee, or as the English say *seignorage*, and that the latter can not be calculated by some governments *inside* and by others *outside* the coin. Even if Mr Lowe is right to say that the costs of production and maintenance of the coin can fully be considered as part of its value, he should not forget that a seignorage of 1 per cent paid today in France in addition to a 25-franc coin is not the same thing as 25 francs of a future system from which 1 per cent of mint fee has been deducted.[102]

Feer-Herzog proposed instead three steps; (i) reduce the pound to 25 francs, transform all debts by 113/112, in order not to defraud any creditor, (ii) Mint all coins according to the 1867 convention and (iii) accept for a transitional period the old pound in the Monetary Union for eight years, at the fixed value of 25 francs, provided that the single coin is not excessively worn.

Lowe was not willing to accept such suggestions as his speech to the Commons had shown. He anticipated that any complication would make the plan enormously unpopular.[103]

The reaction of the French government to Lowe's offer was disappointing: the Minister of Foreign Affairs, la Tour d'Auvergne, defined the communication 'très importante' and pressed his colleague at the Finance Ministry for the introduction in France of the gold standard, as requested by Lowe and the International Conference. Magne temporized and his delaying tactic prevented the Quai d'Orsay from accepting Lowe's proposals.

---

[100] 'If we were to reverse the "currency system", and instead of the great bulk of our currency consisting of gold coins, and an exceptional part of notes, the greater part of it were composed of notes and the smaller of gold bullion and coin, it might be possible to arrange a system equally convenient and safe with the present one, and a considerable saving to the public. One method of effecting this would be to adopt Mr Ricardo's proposal as to the redemption of notes; and to issue notes of the lower denominations, 3£ and 2£ only ... The number of sovereigns left in circulation might be, in great measure, regulated by orders from time to time to the Bank authorities requiring them to issue, on average, certain proportions of notes and coins' (Smith, *Remarks on the Currency*, 8–9).   [101] Bonnet (1869b: 628–49).
[102] Feer-Herzog (1870: 18–20).
[103] 'Nobody is more opposed than I to any attempt to tamper with the current value of the sovereign. Anything which would alter the current value of the sovereign—that is the value of the sovereign wherever it is legal tender—and oblige a man to make calculations how much more he should pay or receive for the sovereign than he is accustomed to pay or receive, would be impossible to enforce in this country' (Hansard's Parliamentary Papers, 3rd ser., 198, 6 Aug. 1869, col. 1417).

When the House of Commons reassembled after the recess, Lowe moved on 10 February 1870 a new Coinage Bill to abolish the office of Master of the Mint and to consolidate all the mint regulations and laws in a single text. In the meantime, he announced that the question of international coinage could not be brought with any profit before the House for a time, because France had further delayed any decision on the adoption of the gold standard and the Emperor had appointed a new commission to enquire into the question. 'Consequently, as a single gold standard is indispensable for the advancement of a scheme of international coinage, the matter must stand over until the French government shall have arrived to a conclusion on that all important subject.'[104] That was the last word heard in the Commons about the French project of monetary unification in the nineteenth century. Lowe, however had not yet given up his idea and the British chambers of commerce were still lobbying him on the subject. The Chancellor of the Exchequer had simply decided to wait for further developments in France before resuming the matter.[105]

Lowe was not interested in international money for its own sake. He was not a keen francophile and did not favour in any way French expansionism, nor England coming to the rescue of France against Prussia, as is clear from his reaction to the French defeat at Sedan in September 1870. He wrote to Gladstone to discourage him from attempting any intervention in the war: 'I don't think the stupendous catastrophe of France imposes a new duty on us. It is quite clear that Germans would bitterly resent and be slow to forgive and certain to disregard any advice from us and France[,] if we [secure] concessions sufficient to ensure peace[,] would always look upon us [as] having been parties to their humiliation.'[106] With Lady Derby, Lowe was even more explicit than with Gladstone: 'I always hated the Emperor [Napoleon III] who seemed

---

[104] Hansard's Parliamentary Papers, 3rd ser., 199, 10 Feb. 1870, col. 153.

[105] On 22 Feb. 1870 the Assembly of the British chambers of commerce had decided not to endorse the 25-franc scheme, despite a favourable report by a committee presided by Lloyd and composed of Behrens, and two liberal MPs, Akroyd and Whitwell. The opposition of the Bristol chamber of commerce led to a compromise, endorsing the report of the Royal Commission of 1868 but appointing a 'deputation to wait upon the Chancellor of the Exchequer, urging him . . . in order that an agreement might be arrived at for an international system of coinage' (*The Times*, 23 Feb. 1870, 12). On 25 Feb. 1869, the delegation, led by the president of the English chambers of commerce, the supporter of the 25-franc pound, Samuel Lloyd, paid a visit to the Chancellor of the Exchequer. Lowe's response was sent by Lloyd to Parieu, who transmitted it to the French Monetary Commission. 'M. Lowe n'est pas personnellement favorable à l'idée d'une conférence internationale. On a déjà beaucoup parlementé sur ce sujet, et les choses n'ont pas marché. Le rapport des Commissaires royaux conclut à la conservation du souverain anglais actuel, et la seule chose qu'ils semblent recommander c'est une conférence. Mais comment se présenter à une conférence avec l'idée bien arrêtée de ne pas changer le souverain. Les autres nations peuvent aussi très justement faire de semblables réserves. La France parait vouloir conserver son étalon et il semble qu'il est inutile d'ouvrir des négociations avec elle si on n'est pas prête a s'entendre sur quelque point. Le mieux serait donc de déterminer les concessions qu'on peut faire et de négocier avec chaque pays séparément; tant qu'on n'aura pas fait cela, cette conférence serait condamnée à l'avortement. Les journaux ont prétendu qu'il (M. Lowe) a changé d'opinion sur la question, mais il n'en est rien. Il pense donc que le meilleur parti à suivre est d'attendre le moment d'entrer en arrangement avec la France, qui semble près de mettre en circulation une pièce de 25 francs, ce qui ferait faire un pas à la question.' Conseil Supérieur du Commerce (1872 : i. 178).

[106] Lowe to Gladstone, 3 Sept. 1870 (GPBL, Correspondence Gladstone–Lowe, coll. 44301, fol. 152).

to me the incarnation of the worst ends sought by the worst means, and shall regard his fall as a clearing of the moral atmosphere.'[107]

It was clear that Lowe saw international coinage as an external imposition, inescapable if the rest of the world adopted it but of no particular need otherwise, just as many countries regard EMU today. As soon as the Prussian victory ended French hegemony on the Continent and defeat blocked the process of monetary unification, Lowe dropped from his currency plans any reference to international coinage. In 1873 Bagehot described the change: 'Since the Franco-German War, we [the British] may be said to keep the European reserve [of gold] ... Formerly for many purposes Paris was a European settling-house, but now it has ceased to be so.'[108] The bitter view on the other side of the channel was: 'before the fatal date of July 1870, France was seriously competing with England for the pre-eminence in great financial operations ... now there is only one cosmopolitan clearing house left, it is in London.'[109]

Lowe, who was still convinced of the necessity of reforming the coinage and of restricting the use of gold coins, turned to the idea of a larger issue of paper money, with new notes of small denomination. He wanted the State to acquire a monopoly of issue in the UK, by discontinuing the banknote issue of the Bank of England and of the Scottish, Irish and English provincial banks. This new struggle with the Bank of England was even less successful than the previous one, and Lowe was not even able to inform Parliament or the press about his plans before they were blocked by the Cabinet at the end of 1872. In 1873 Gladstone even decided to remove Lowe from the Treasury, and took it over himself. Scottish and Irish banknotes have survived to this day, but Lowe's project of a centralized public control over the issue of paper money in England was achieved in 1946 with the nationalization of the Bank of England.

The Gladstone government was defeated in the elections at the beginning of 1874 and replaced by a Conservative government headed by Disraeli. Disraeli considered the International Monetary Conference of 1867 as the 'fons et origo malorum' of the 'great disturbance and immense fluctuation' deriving from the French and Belgian desire to move to the gold standard, cause of the depreciation of silver, despite the 'very beautiful idea of cosmopolitan philantropy'.[110] For Disraeli, England was not a European power but an international power turned towards its Empire, which should not focus on European questions. Something of this approach still survives in today's perception of Europe. Realizing that the race towards the gold standard by all European powers was exacerbating the competition to hoard the limited quantities of gold available and threatening the stability of the British reserves, Britain under Disraeli became a supporter of bimetallism outside its own frontiers. In 1878 the British position was 'We considered that, while a universal double standard was a utopian impossibility, a single gold standard throughout the world would be a false utopia, and

---

[107] Burghclere (1933: 275): 13 Aug. 1870.   [108] St John-Stevas (1965–86: ix, 63).
[109] 'Avant la date funeste de juillet 1870, la France commençait à disputer sérieusement à l'Angleterre la prééminence des grandes opérations de crédit ... [désormais] Il n'y a plus qu'une *clearing house* cosmopolite, elle est à Londres' (Menier 1873: 3–4).   [110] Quoted from Hendriks, (1874: 129–131).

that further steps in that direction might tend to produce incalculable disasters to the commerce of the world.'[111]

In the 1850s and 1860s, the pound survived all proposals for decimalization, internationalization, and reform, to become the major international currency of the age of the classical gold standard. Universal money could come to life only with British participation. Canada was willing to participate provided that the USA would participate; the USA and Portugal wanted to participate provided that Britain would participate as well. Therefore Great Britain held the key to North American participation, as well as that of India and the other British colonies. Universal money without the English-speaking world could have been a Continental European money. This hypothesis came close to realization but required the agreement of some of the German States. The persistent Franco-Prussian tensions in 1866–70 ensured that no real progress could be expected in that direction and that the threat of a monetary and financial domination of Europe by France could be effectively countered by an undeclared Anglo-Prussian alliance, dictated by converging interests.

The British financial establishment opposed monetary unification by defending the national standard and its own monetary practices as much as its French counterpart did. In one country bimetallism was the focus of resistance, in the other it was the sacred nature of the pound. In both countries all changes were intensely resented, making general reforms impossible. Change was left to the natural evolution of the monetary system, determined by exogenous shocks (wars and forced paper currencies) and endogenous transformation (the diversification of the forms of money permitted by a growing banking system).

5.2. THE GERMAN INFLUENCE

5.2.1. *The Impact of the Paris Conference of 1867 in Germany*

The need for unification. The proponents of monetary unification understood the central role of the attitude of the German-speaking countries for the final success or failure of their initiative. This section analyses how the French proposals were received in Germany, emphasizing the distinction between Prussia and south Germany and between some particular pressure groups (financial and commercial interests). The evolution of the monetary discussion reflected very closely the political path to national unification. The archival resources used here are predominantly French; they report carefully all developments and translate parliamentary discussions but they also reflect French hopes and prejudices, later shattered by defeat at Sedan. The selection of the authors to be translated was biased in favour of the supporters of unification, but opponent's views were also presented and they have been integrated here with other German pamphlets and speeches.

The monetary fragmentation of Germany had already attracted the attention of the commercial interests and of the governments before the creation of the Latin

---

[111] *Report of the Commissioners appointed to represent Her Majesty's Government at the Monetary Conference* (1878: 6). Goschen was the British Chief Commissioner at the International Monetary Conference of 1878.

Monetary Union. The *Münzverein* (monetary union of the thirty-five German States and of Austria) of 1857 had simplified the situation but not achieved unification. With the annexation of Hanover, Nassau, Frankfurt, and other small States by Prussia in 1866 and the creation of the North German Confederation, the Prussian thaler had expanded its circulation. Its partial adoption by the south German States since 1857 had already marked its prominence, but all forms of resistance to its becoming the German national currency had not been vanquished. The three main German currencies persisted: the north German (Prussian) thaler, the south German gulden, and the Austrian florin. These currencies were linked by a simple fixed exchange rate implicit in their silver content, 1 to 1.5 and 1.75.[112] Separate currencies were employed by the free mercantile cities of Hamburg and Bremen. The thaler itself was not a homogeneous currency throughout the North German Confederation. It had a variety of different divisions: it was worth 360 pfennig in Prussia, 480 in Hamburg, and 300 in Saxony.[113] Elsewhere it was divided in a variable number of groschen, schellings or kreuzers, adding to the general confusion. A variety of older and foreign currencies circulated. In Frankfurt for example fourteen different types of currencies still circulated in the late 1860s.[114]

Economic transformation and international trade had particularly modified the circulation of the small southern States, exposed to French, Swiss, and Austrian coinage. Particularly important was the circulation of foreign gold coins, mainly 20-franc French coins. The influx of gold into Europe and the growing scale of business transactions had spread the commercial use of this metal, regardless of the official silver monometallism. An example of the situation is the estimate of the composition of the monetary circulation employed by large companies in Württemberg in 1868: 38.3 per cent of it was composed of paper money, 31 per cent of gold coins, and 30.7 per cent of silver coins. The gold coinage was mainly French, while the silver coinage was composed of south German guldens for 42 per cent, north German and south German thalers for 37 per cent, Austrian florins for 17 per cent, and foreign coins for 4 per cent.[115] When Bismarck himself ventured on the battlefield of Königgrätz-Sadowa in 1866, he carried with him a hoard of coins to be used in case of emergency, composed of more Austrian and French coins than Prussian.[116]

The growing use of gold coins, deprived of a fixed relation with German silver coins, was a substantial burden in ordinary transactions. This was exacerbated by exchange costs and by the risk associated with the depreciation of the silver currency in relation to

---

[112] Holtfrerich (1989: 224).   [113] Hellferich (1969: 147).

[114] French Consulate in Frankfurt to French Minister of Foreign Affairs Moustier, 2 Feb. 1867 (AMAE, ADC 600, fol. 28).

[115] French Consulate in Frankfurt to French Minister of Foreign Affairs, 5 Dec. 1868 (AMAE, ADC 604–1 bis, fol. 203). The divisionary silver coins (Scheide münze) have not been considered. Many of the thalers of the north German valuation circulating in the south had been issued by the south German States themselves. More than a third of the monetary issue in the south between 1837 and 1867 was in thalers (Soetbeer 1869: 79). Holtfrerich believes that after 1857 90% of the monetary issue in Germany was in thalers, but he did not consider the particular situation of the southern States.

[116] The banker Bleichröder had given him 1,000 thalers composed of German silver for 29%, of French gold for 27%, of Austrian gold for 16%, and of old Prussian gold for 28% (Stern 1977: 88).

gold, even if the depreciation of silver was more imagined than real in the 1860s. Furthermore it was impossible to use silver coins for the kind of large payments frequently needed for merchants. 20,000 francs required 100 kilos of silver coins and would pay two months of the salary of the British Chancellor of the Exchequer (or eight months of a French senator). The alternative was a growing use of banknotes which in turn was intensely disliked by economists and publicists (but apparently not by the public) because of the untrustworthiness of paper money in times of crisis. Runs on the banking system to convert banknotes into species generated financial crisis. The argument was not just economic; the German tradition of national economics placed at the centre of its attention the interest of the State in having a solid currency during periods of war. Economists willingly accepted that the mobilization of the Prussian army should not be hampered by a rush of the population to exchange its paper money into specie.[117]

Economists and chambers of commerce shift towards a gold franc. The result of such a situation was a unanimous call by business circles and by economists for a single German currency as a relief from this untenable backwardness in the payment system. The German chambers of commerce had already discussed the issue of national monetary unification before the International Conference of 1867. The Handelstag (German Commercial Diet or Congress) had recognized the need for a reform of German currency based on the adoption of a single type, the thaler, decimalized in its subdivisions, and for the introduction of the gold standard. These recommendations to the various German governments had been advanced in 1861 and repeated in 1865. Decimalization and the introduction of the gold standard retained the favour of the large majority of chambers of commerce and of economists throughout the debate. Their opinion wavered only on which type of currency was more suited to accomplish unification, decimalization, and abolition of silver. The unanimous votes of the International Monetary Conference of Paris, French diplomatic initiatives, and Parieu's publications succeeded in 1867–70 in promoting in Germany the franc side by side with gold. Through the efforts of Prof. Adolf Soetbeer, a highly reputed economist and statistician, specialized in currency matters and a leading supporter of the gold standard, the chambers of commerce came to advocate in 1868 a German system organically integrated into an international system based on the franc.[118] Soetbeer had

---

[117] Prof. Tellkampf declared in 1868 to the German society of political economists in Berlin that gold helped the defence of the State, while paper damaged it: 'Cela peut paraître un paradoxe, mais il est certain que le retrait du papier monnaie et son remplacement par l'or et l'argent auraient pour conséquence une augmentation de la puissance du pays. En effet le papier monnaie de 1, de 5 et de 10 thalers, dominant dans les relations journalières écartent l'or et l'argent. Ce papier monnaie se trouve habituellement entre les mains de gens peu aisés qui, dans les moments de dangers, se hâtent de l'échanger contre des monnaies sonnantes.' Therefore in times of war paper money flows back in the coffers of the State which is unable to employ it. Prof. Soetbeer shared this view (French Embassy in Prussia to Moustier, Berlin, 13 Nov. 1868, AMAE, ADC 604–1 bis, fol. 151).

[118] The Belgian economist Merterns argued that 'Soetbeer s'attacha avec toute sa compétence et son infatigable activité à ce problème et devint le champion de l'étalon-or. Son influence sul l'évolution monétaire de l'Allemagne fut décisive' (Mertens 1994: 117). The fourth congress of the Handelstag (association of German Chambers of Commerce) voted on 20 Oct. 1868 (French Consulate in Cologne, 22 Oct. 1868, AMAE, ADC 604–1 bis, fol. 89).

already succeeded in August 1867 in convincing the German Congress of economists in Hamburg to declare its support for German monetary unification based on the French gold currency with a subsidiary silver divisionary coinage in marks, derived from the Prussian thaler. These deliberations, aimed at convincing the politicians, were not without effect and were followed by similar resolutions adopted in 1868 by the Reichstag (Parliament of the North German Confederation) and in 1869 by the *Zollparlament* (the customs parliament of the *Zollverein*, which included the south German States as well).[119] The official motion stated that 'the *Zollparlament* invites the governments of the States represented in this assembly to agree as soon as possible on the adoption of a purely decimal monetary system presenting as much as possible all the conditions needed to be accepted by all civilized nations as the universal system.'[120]

Two main schemes for a joint national and international unification were competing for the favour of the public. Both were taken into consideration by the Reichstag when it launched its monetary enquiry in 1869.[121] Soetbeer's proposal was a more orthodox interpretation of the conclusions of the Conference of Paris of 1867. He wanted the introduction of a German gold thaler of 5 francs, with the 25-franc pound as its multiple.[122] A second scheme was proposed by the secretary of the chamber of commerce of Cologne, Weibezahn. He introduced a gold gulden of 2.5 francs, identical to the new Austrian florin and more in touch with German traditions. Ten gulden would form a 25-franc piece.[123]

Some chambers of commerce of the Rhineland and Württemberg, more closely connected to France, Belgium, and Switzerland, had expressed the desire for even closer monetary integration by the adoption of the entire French system. The Cologne chamber of commerce had stated in 1865 'We are keen to maintain that the straightforward and simple accession to the French monetary system seems to us to be dictated by logic and common sense, and we will be the first to defend this point of view before the government.'[124] The chambers of commerce of Stuttgart, Ulm, Frankfurt, and Mainz advanced the same request. The publicist Carl Schultz defended the option of adopting the franc, wished northern and southern Germany to join the LMU, and attacked nationalist critics: 'Does Mr Grote feel disturbed by the fact that the franc originates from our political rivals, the French, and that our national honour might thereby be threatened! I think we have been above such concerns since 1866.'[125]

---

[119] See also Mertens (1944: 113–35); Hellferich (1969: 152).

[120] The Handelstag had petitioned the *Zollparlament* to introduce a common currency, decimalized, universal, and based on the gold standard (French Consulate in Frankfurt to French Minister of Foreign Affairs La Valette, 25 June 1869, AMAE, ADC 604–2, fol. 64).

[121] French Consul in Cologne Tolhausen to French Minister of Foreign Affairs la Tour d'Auvergne, 24 Dec. 1869 (AMAE, ADC 604–2, fols. 284–90).

[122] The ninth congress of political economy met in Hamburg and deliberated on Soetbeer's impulse on 28 Aug. 1867 (French Embassy in Prussia to Moustier, Berlin 31 Aug. 1867, AMAE, ADC 600 bis-3, fol. 111).

[123] A summary of a pamphlet on monetary reform by Weibezahn is sent by the French Consulate in Cologne to the French Minister of Foreign Affairs, 1 Oct. 1868 (AMAE, ADC 604–1 bis, fol. 13). For a later statement of Weibezahn's persistent support for the 25-franc scheme see Weibezahn (1871).

[124] French Consulate in Cologne to Moustier, 8 May 1867 (AMAE, ADC 600, fol. 173).

[125] Schultz (1869: 14).

Most economists did support gold, discussing exclusively the means to obtain reform and the speed of transition.[126] Tolhausen, French Consul in Cologne, reported 'high commerce vigorously demands gold coinage as an intermediary instrument for an immense development of business. This is a truth which has become an axiom even in Germany.'[127] Gold had become a status symbol, identified closely to wealth through Britain: 'gold is the currency of rich nations'[128] and 'the choice of modernity and progress'.[129] Furthermore 'gold coinage ... has the advantage of creating a barrier against excessive issue of paper money.'[130] J. S. Mill and M. Chevalier were the most popular authorities quoted in favour of gold monometallism. The great concern was how to acquire and keep a sufficient stock of gold for the German circulation without having to pay a disproportionate price. If France adopted the gold standard before Germany or did it in reaction to the latter's decision, then the price of silver would fall and the transformation would become excessively expensive.[131] The refusal to drop depreciating silver would however mean a net impoverishment of Germany in comparison to Britain and France. According to the leading German monetary economist Soetbeer, if gold proved to be insufficient for an adequate monetary supply, then banking developments would increase the velocity of circulation of money avoiding deflation.

However, some economists did support bimetallism, including Prince Smith, president of the German Political Economy Society as well as Wiss and Mohl.[132] Their concern was the fall in the price of silver caused by its general demise as a monetary instrument. Price instability would be the outcome of the demise of bimetallism. The attempt to sell German silver to France was recognized as an impossibility, as France would close its mints in response. It was much better to collaborate with the Latin Monetary Union for an international bimetallism which would guarantee the stability of prices by the sheer extension of the use of the two metals, while permitting the introduction of gold where it was not already circulating.[133] When in need of a theoretical framework, German economists referred to the French publications of Wolowski, who had been developing his scientific defence of bimetallism in the heat of the Parisian discussions of 1866–70. For Michaelis, financial counsellor of Bismarck, 'considering all these difficulties, we must thank Mr Wolowski to have been courageous enough to oppose the doctrine of the single gold standard, so common

---

[126] Lefèbvre de Bécarine compiled a report with large translations of the discussions of the Society of Political Economy (French Embassy in Prussia to Moustier, Berlin, 13 Nov. 1868, AMAE, ADC 604–1 bis, fol. 143).

[127] French Consul in Cologne Tolhausen to la Tour d'Auvergne, 24 Dec. 1869 (AMAE, ADC 604–2, fol. 288).

[128] Ibid.   [129] James (1997: 8).

[130] Chamber of commerce of Frankfurt in French Consulate in Frankfurt to Moustier, 2 Feb. 1867 (AMAE, ADC 600, fol. 34).

[131] French Consulate in Frankfurt to la Tour d'Auvergne, 13 July 1869 (AMAE, ADC 604–2, fol. 108).

[132] French Consulate in Stettin (Prussia) to la Tour d'Auvergne, 21 July 1869 (AMAE, ADC 604–2, fols. 180–3).

[133] Prince Smith published an article in the *Correspondence of Political Economy*, a German review published by Dr Wiss. The text is translated in the letter sent by the French Embassy in Prussia to la Valette, 5 Jan. 1869 (AMAE, ADC 604–2, fol. 2).

today.'[134] Michaelis recognized the need for gold but warned the public about the difficulty of selling several hundred million silver thalers (450 million in Soetbeer's estimate). His ambiguous conclusion was that 'the continuation of the silver standard however will isolate our financial market and might provoke serious embarrassment. It is therefore necessary to accept some sacrifices.'[135] No one defended openly the single silver standard after 1867. The question was whether gold should be added to silver as a legal standard or whether it should replace silver altogether. In contrast with bimetallist bankers, politician or civil servants, bimetallist economists were usually not against unification, as in the case of Prince Smith who proposed the 5-franc gold thaler as national and international currency, or the economist from Württemberg Moritz Mohl or the bullion dealer Ernest Seyd. Nevertheless many of the complaints against the difficulty of transition to gold were aimed simply at discouraging the introduction of the French monetary system in Germany under the cover of international currency.

The shift of part of the German public opinion towards the French–LMU monetary system was not dictated by a belief in its intrinsic superiority or by an unfailing support for international money. It was simply perceived to be the most likely solution to the problem of national monetary unity, which was otherwise prevented by persistent domestic political divisions. The southern States were defending actively their monetary independence from northern German encroachments, just as they defended their political independence from Prussia. In 1868–70 German unification was not advancing anymore. The opportunistic support for international money was not deeply rooted, reversible as soon as other roads to national monetary unification appeared to guarantee a faster success.

The resistance of the financial world to monetary integration. Two different types of opposition to the introduction of the gold standard and to monetary unification came from the world of finance. One was originated by the Bank of Prussia, which feared the end of its local privileged position and the 'globalization' of banking operations brought by new international capital flows. The Bank of Prussia anticipated the destabilization of the domestic market brought by fluctuating interest rates introduced by the need to compete with London for capital denominated in gold. As the French consul in Cologne wrote:

The discount rate [of the Bank of Prussia] never falls below 4 per cent. What the Bank seems to fear above anything else is that once Germany will have the same standard as the other States, capital will flow from Paris and London, where it is less well remunerated, to Berlin, in order to take advantage of the higher rate offered in Prussia ... The Bank of Berlin also fears that under the influence of a universal monetary standard Germany would be involved more than in the past in the great commercial crises which periodically disrupt the old and the new world. Attracted by the appeal of the high discount rates offered in France and England, German capital ... will look to these countries for higher returns than they can find domestically, causing an equivalent increase in the Prussian discount rate. This is the cause of its secret opposition to monetary innovations.[136]

---

[134] French Embassy in Prussia to Moustier, Berlin, 13 Nov. 1868 (AMAE, ADC 604–1 bis, fol. 157).
[135] Ibid.
[136] French Consul in Cologne Tolhausen to Moustier, 30 Oct. 1868 (AMAE, ADC 604–1 bis, fols. 98–9).

The Bank of France and the Bank of Holland shared the Prussian worries about the destabilizing influence of the British money market.[137] Private bankers like Bleichröder, personal adviser of Bismarck, also expressed their reservations about the gold standard.[138] He claimed that diversity in monetary units but especially in metallic standards had permitted until then a higher degree of independence of the domestic monetary conditions of Prussia, isolated from what was perceived to be foreign financial instability. Bleichröder feared that a gold standard in comparison to bimetallism would increase the cyclical tendencies in the money supply. It would increase interest rates during periods of recession when the Reichsbank would have to defend its monometallic reserves from excessive withdrawal and from increases in the Bank of England interest rate. German companies, Bleichröder claimed, in contrast to their British counterparts, did not have access to a great amount of capital but were dependent on bank credit and would suffer from a fluctuating interest rate, which increased the difficulty in purchasing credit in difficult times.

It is likely however that the banks were attributing to the monetary system an excessive share of the responsibility for an instability largely due to industrialization and stronger economic growth. The Bank was mounting a defence of old and rigid practices, which lead to dear credit in ordinary periods and only partially lower discount rates in periods of crisis.[139] Furthermore, the emphasis on the independence of domestic markets was overstated, as Parieu claimed (see Chapter 3). A certain degree of interdependence existed even without unity in monetary standards and there was no explicit monetary policy to reduce the effects of instability.[140] From the 1840s to the

[137] The use of discount rate in a gold standard regime to raid each other's gold reserves was highlighted by the President of the Bank of Netherlands Mees, who confirmed in 1883 his views of 1867, to the Italian economist Luigi Luzzati. 'Sull'Olanda come e più che sul Belgio si abbattono alla ricerca dell'oro Tedeschi e Inglesi, sottraendolo coi cambi e cogli arbitraggi. Da ciò la necessità dei frequenti rialzi della ragione dello sconto che tanto dispiacciono al commercio e che pure sono indispensabili per non lasciar scendere le riserve dell'oro oltre certi limiti. Il Mees ... dolevasi meco che in tal guisa si riscuotesse troppo spesso una imposta a favore degli azionisti della Banca e a carico dei commercianti' (Luzzati 1883: 540–1).

[138] 'By making money dearer, the gold standard would threaten industry.' In his opinion a broader bullion basis, consistent with bimetallism, was therefore desirable, and until 1876 Bleichröder warned Bismarck against demonetization of silver (Stern 1977: 179–81).

[139] The same conclusions are reached if one uses the German private discount rate instead of the official rate of the Bank. Nevertheless the phenomena of relatively dear credit during periods of calm (4%) is weakened. The market rate shadowed the official discount rate when it was over 4%, in troubled times, but declined further than 4% otherwise, remaining usually higher than the London rate but only slightly. Data given by Marc Flandreau and used for Flandreau (1994).

[140] In the 1860s, when the private national banks (not yet transformed into public central banks) used their discount rate to influence the economy, they did not do so to influence the price level or the level of economic growth. They acted exclusively to protect their gold or silver reserves, increasing the discount rate to call back loans and discourage new applications for credit, in order to preserve the convertibility of their banknotes in coins and prevent suspension of cash payments (see Plessis 1985b). Only indirectly could they be said to aim at a stable price level, considering that inconvertibility implied a fall in confidence and the depreciation of the value of paper money, therefore increasing prices. The British policy of frequent manipulation of the discount rate followed this rule. In times of financial and commercial distress or even panic, the Bank of England increased the discount rate to prevent the complete withdrawal of its gold reserves in exchange for credit or of banknotes (see Andreades 1909). Today most economists would argue that increasing interest rates in periods of economic recession or of financial crisis would deepen the

1870s the 'normal' level of the official discount rate in good times was around 3 per cent in England, between 3 and 4 per cent in France, and 4 per cent in Prussia. In 1866 the Bank of England kept its rate at 10 per cent for three months during the Overend–Gurney crisis. The Bank of Prussia was partially forced to follow, even more so than during the previous financial crises of 1857 and 1864 (see Graph 5.1).

The Bank of Prussia was of course concerned about its private interests as well, foreseeing losses of profits and reductions in dividends caused by the change to the gold standard and an increase in international competition. The French consul Tolhausen had gathered from private conversations and from the debates of the Handelstag that 'the Bank of Prussia feels attacked in its vital interests. It is well known that the organization of the Bank of Berlin is entirely based on the silver standard and that the metallic reserve of this institution is exclusively composed of silver bars.' The Bank anticipated a reduction of the dividends for its shareholders in case of intro-duction of the gold standard and demonetization of its stocks of silver. 'Finally the bankers of Berlin see a threat to the monopoly they currently share with Hamburg and Amsterdam to serve as financial intermediaries between Northern Germany and the gold standard countries connected with the *Zollverein* by commercial relations.'[141] Another reason for the defence of the silver standard by the Bank of Prussia was the profits accruing from the issue of paper money. An economist from Bremen, Boehmert, could contrast the moderate increase in the issue of paper money by the Bank of England, restrained by the gold standard, to the multiplication of paper of the Bank of Prussia, fuelled by the need to replace silver with a more portable form of currency. The British paper circulation had increased by a mere 12 per cent between

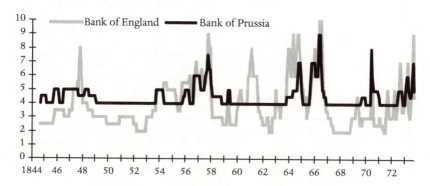

Graph 5.1. *Discount rate in London and Berlin between 1844 and 1873*
Source: Seyd (1874).

recession or the financial crisis. High interest rates discourage investment and deprive sound companies going through a liquidity crisis of the support they need to overcome a temporary liquidity crisis. The advice of the nineteenth-century continental bankers seems from that point of view more in line with twentieth-century practice, in opposition to the policy of the Bank of England (Gallarotti 1995).

[141] French Consul in Cologne Tolhausen to Moustier, 30 Oct. 1868 (AMAE, ADC 604–1 bis, fols. 98–100).

1848 and 1862 while the paper issue of the Bank of Prussia had increased by 220 per cent between 1856 and 1863.[142] Gold was seen as a disciplinary factor in the monetary circulation, preventing a paper inflation which was in turn facilitated by the bulky nature of a silver currency. The diffusion of gold would also reduce excessive issue of paper money by small States and by unregulated private banks.[143]

Financial interests in Frankfurt expressed the opposite type of concern, when they were incorporated in the North German Confederation. They expected their integration in the thaler zone to separate them from their natural markets of southern Germany and Austria.[144] They had already suffered in 1848 from being cut off from the Swiss financial market, largely financed by Frankfurt until then, by the decision of the Helvetic Confederation to adopt the franc as national currency. A report of the Chancellor of the French consulate, Petit-Pierre, explained the position of Frankfurt. The Senate and the Chamber of Commerce of the city opposed the introduction of the Prussian thaler in the old free city recently annexed by the North German Confederation. Berlin was decided to 'assimilate in financial terms the territories annexed to the other parts of the kingdom'. The city resisted because the bulk of its trade and of its financial dealings was with southern Germany, in south German currency, 'bills of exchange are drawn via Frankfurt in florins and the same unit is used to denominate foreign deposits in the banks of the city. Prussian coins circulate with difficulty, while Prussian banknotes and subsidiary coins do not circulate at all. The southern States, the railroad companies, industrial and commercial businesses have borrowed in florins.' Coupons and dividends were in florins (*gulden*), making the reduction in thalers difficult. The change of currency would break the commercial relations with southern Germany according to the chamber of commerce. The stock exchange would lose its role. Frankfurt used to be the banker of the Swiss industrialists because

---

[142] French Embassy in Prussia to Moustier, 12 Nov. 1866 (AMAE, ADC 603–2, fol. 19).

[143] In fact the increase of the paper money issue in Germany reflected largely the increase in output and exchanges caused by industrialization. The growing need for instruments of exchange had been met in France by the large flows of Australian and American gold discoveries, in Great Britain by improvements in the banking system, and in Germany by banknotes, due to an insufficient output of silver. The controversy did not die out in the 1870s. In 1879, when Bismarck suspended the demonetization of silver in Germany (required by the law of 1873 introducing the gold standard in the German Reich), the president of the Reichsbank, Von Deckend, defended Bismarck's decision against the gold monometallists Delbrück and Bamberger. Soetbeer 'avvertì tra il brusco ed il dolce Bismarck di non prendere le sue ispirazioni dal presidente della Banca Imperiale, e sostenendo che l'oro caccia i biglietti di banca, mentre l'argento ne estende e provoca la circolazione, mette in sospetto il patriottismo disinteressato del Von Deckend, il quale suggerirebbe al Gran Cancelliere la riabilitazione funzionale dell'argento per accrescere la circolazione dei biglietti della Banca a beneficio dei suoi azionisti e a danno della nazione tedesca' (Luzzati 1881: 257).

[144] 'Les chefs des principales maisons de banque de Francfort ne semblent pas partager la satisfaction que le vote du Handelstag cause au commerce de la ville et dans les États du midi de l'Allemagne. Ils affectent de ne pas attacher d'importance à cette motion et laissent entendre qu'une assemblée comptant dans son sein plus de théoriciens que d'hommes d'affaires, n'est pas apte à résoudre des questions de cette gravité.' Frankfurt's financial world 'son intérêt particulier lui fait désirer le maintien de l'état de choses actuel qui lui assure dans les opérations de banque des bénéfices certains. Il pense du reste que le gouvernement Prussien remontrera de sérieuses difficultés le jour où il voudra changer sons système monétaire et passer sans transition de l'étalon d'argent à l'étalon d'or' (French Consulate in Frankfurt to Moustier, 15 Nov. 1868, AMAE, ADC 604–1 bis, fol. 166–67).

the south German gulden was commonly accepted for 1.5 old Swiss francs, but after the adoption by Switzerland of the French franc, with the reform of 1848 everything had changed:

[S]ince the adoption of the French monetary system by Switzerland, the situation has completely changed: Paris has replaced Frankfurt, Swiss commercial movements have been concentrated towards France, the florin circulates in Switzerland only at a heavy loss and all efforts attempted by Frankfurt bankers to preserve their relations with Swiss merchants have remained fruitless. In Frankfurt these facts are considered as a lesson for the future and when the time will come to establish monetary uniformity in Germany, commerce will declare itself in favour of a radical reform and all its efforts will aim at the adoption of the franc as monetary unit. A reform in this direction, it is hoped, will re-establish Frankfurt on an equal footing with Paris, permitting the regaining of the ancient positions towards Switzerland.[145]

5.2.2. The Attitude of the German Governments

France had already regrouped a dozen European countries around its currency by 1868–9, including Italy, Belgium, Switzerland, Greece, Spain, Austria-Hungary, Romania, the Pontifical State, Sweden, Luxembourg, San Marino, and Monaco. It needed only British or German support to achieve the critical mass necessary to ensure the success of its European currency programme. The German position was therefore essential and would ultimately be decided by the governments. German economic conditions of the time required monetary unification, but was such a need stronger in the late 1860s than in the previous decades? The main change was the take-off of industrialization and economic growth, together with the multiplication of international exchanges favoured by the new free trade of the 1860s. Such a need could be fulfilled either through a national or through an international solution. The international solution would have been more welcomed by commercial and industrial interests, but not by banking interests. The national solution still suited everyone. The conflicting aims of commerce and finance meant that there was no obvious solution to the monetary question in Germany. It was political leadership which would turn the balance towards a gold standard without a supranational system of coinage. Bismarck decided the course of events even if he let a banker politician like Bamberger influence the detail of the new German legislation between 1871 and 1875.

The Prussian policy towards international money had been cautiously negative since 1866. Prussia hoped to realize a single German currency on its own terms, imposing the thaler. The Bismarckian declaration of non-committed favour for monetary unification, expressed to the French at the end of 1866, can be compared to analogous declarations on the compensations France hoped to receive for the Prussian annexations after Sadowa. It was all part of Bismarck's strategy to 'leave the French statesmen in their peculiar illusions as long as that is possible without expressing any consent, even a verbal one'.[146] The diplomatic despatches on the matter were

---

[145] Ibid. 12 Feb. 1868 (AMAE, ADC 604–1, fols. 77–81).

[146] Bismarck in Herre (1992: 265). Another letter written in October 1866 reiterated the concept: 'The French must retain hope and especially faith in our goodwill without our giving them definite commitments,' wrote Bismarck on 22 Oct. 1866 (Pflanze 1990: i. 374).

deliberately misleading.[147] The Prussian delegate at the Conference of Paris, the Privy Councillor for finances Meinecke, had declared 'in Prussia we are satisfied of the silver standard; the monetary circulation on which it is based is excellent, and we have no urgent reason to introduce any change.'[148] But he declared that the question would be carefully studied if the conference agreed on gold. He personally voted for gold and considered sufficient the unity of metal, allied with easily convertible national gold coins of the Union. No complete identity of coinage for silver, bronze, or paper was necessary in his view.[149]

The Prussian government was internally divided about the relative merits of silver, gold, and bimetallism. The Prussian Finance Minister, Ludolf Camphausen, and the Councillor for Financial Affairs in the Federal Chancellor's Office, Michaelis, opposed the gold standard while Rudolf von Delbrück, President of the Federal Chancellor's office of the North German Confederation, supported it.[150] Furthermore the Prussians were restrained by the resistance of other German governments.

The thaler was not as dominant in the *Münzverein* after 1857 as some authors claimed, nor is it possible to say that monetary unification preceded political unification as Holtfrerich argues.[151] After ten years of intense issue, the *vereinsthaler* (thaler of the union) represented only a fraction of the silver coinage of the south. The thaler's role was growing but it was an open situation which could evolve in any direction. In politics not to go forward is to go backwards, and with the stalling of political unity new alternatives acquired credibility. Not only some commercial interests in the regions bordering France asked to adopt purely and simply the French franc and gold, but the influence of Austria in the decisions of the Germans after 1866 was more important on currency matters than could be expected. Austria had not been expelled from the *Münzverein* as a result of its military defeat in 1866, but it had acquired the right to negotiate an eventual withdrawal from it. Austria decided to make use of this right in 1867, as a consequence of the French offer to join the Latin Monetary Union. Austria decided to reform its currency equalizing its florins to 2.5 francs, inscribing both national and international value on its coins, and adopting a gold standard. Such

---

[147] Bismarck's deputy reassured the French diplomats about Prussian favour: 'Mr de Philipsborn, que j'ai vu récemment, m'a dit que dans son opinion la question recevrait la solution que nous proposons et qui répond à l'intérêt général. Toutefois il pense qu'il sera nécessaire au préalable de travailler l'opinion et, en tous cas, il ne prévoit pas qu'il soit possible au gouvernement Prussien, surchargé en ce moment d'une tache très lourde, de préparer pour ce qui concerne la Confédération du Nord l'arrangement spécial dont il s'agit avant le printemps de l'année prochaine' (French Embassy in Prussia to Moustier, 2 Sept. 1867, AMAE, ADC 600 bis-3, fols. 115–6). The official newspaper of Bismarck, the *North German Gazette*, of Berlin had informally presented the Prussian position as recognizing the chances of success of the French manoeuvre but warning against excessive ambition: 'la création d'une grande monnaie universelle (*Weltmünze*) suffit pour satisfaire aux besoins des échanges internationaux, mais que l'unification des monnaies destinées à la circulation intérieure est une question à part qui doit rester étrangère au grand problème, puisque ces monnaies, toutes locales, sont sujettes à la loi des échanges journaliers et des transactions du marché. Il serait à regretter qu'en élargissant outre mesure le cercle de la réforme, on la fît avorter' (French Consulate in Cologne to Moustier, 8 May 1867, AMAE, ADC 600, fol. 172).

[148] Royal Commission on International Coinage (1868: 166).   [149] Ibid. 176–7.
[150] Zucker (1975: 64).   [151] Holtfrerich (1989: 224).

an international gold currency, based on the south German tradition of the gulden, became an attractive model for some Germans, particularly in the south, an alternative to the thaler, favourably viewed by France. A banker from Stuttgart, Mr Dreyfuss, summarized the monetary debate in Württemberg and a translation of his text was transmitted to Paris.

Thanks to the Austrian accession to the Monetary Convention, the French system has achieved a victory with incalculable consequences ... If southern Germany's participation was still not possible, held back exclusively by Prussia, it will be inevitable once the effects produced by the convention with Austria will become tangible and southern and northern Germany will be encircled by the States which have adopted the universal system.[152]

An international florin of 2.5 francs was attractive because, as the Master of the Stuttgart Mint, Friederich Xeller, put it, 'our own monetary system is untenable since Austria has left the *Münzverein* area, so that we are even weaker ... while the thaler foot like a conqueror keeps penetrating further into southern Germany.'[153]

The southern German States defended actively their monetary sovereignty. Bavaria, Württemberg, Baden, and Hesse were not included in the North German Confederation and struggled to maintain their political independence, especially Bavaria and Württemberg. South Germany had a certain degree of commercial and monetary integration through the *Zollverein* and the *Münzverein*, it had pledged to adopt the Prussian military organization and to surrender the command of its armies to the Prussian General Staff in case of war. These commitments were strong but the governments of Bavaria, Württemberg, and Hesse wished to preserve their full sovereignty and to keep the Prussians at arm's length. They had agreed to the military alliance only to avoid annexation of territory or the payment of heavy indemnities after losing the war against Prussia in 1866. The south German populations had fought the military reforms imposed by Prussia, particularly the three years' military service, the increase in military spending (and therefore of taxation), and the Prussian military discipline. Refusing to see South Germany transformed in a Prussian barrack, ruled by a Protestant regime, socially aristocratic and politically authoritarian, the opponents of German unification had recovered the upper hand after the disaster of 1866. Catholics, progressives, and particularists joined forces and won the elections for the *Zollparlament* and the local Parliaments in Bavaria and Württemberg in 1868 and in 1869, and achieved the majority of votes but not of seats in Baden, where the ducal government had chosen to apply for membership of the North German Confederation.[154] The French government, busy organizing an alliance with Austria and possibly with Italy, against Prussia, offered political support to the south. France had weakened its position by asking for the Bavarian Palatinate in 1866 as a compensation for the Prussian expansion in North Germany. The south German States at times evoked the

---

[152] Annexe to the despatch of the French Legation in Württemberg to Moustier, 11 Sept. 1867 (AMAE, ADC 600 bis-3, fols. 149–50).   [153] Xeller (1869: 150).
[154] Pflanze (1990: i. 367–409).

possibility of asking for a French intervention in case of a Bismarckian attack, but never entirely trusted Napoleon III either.[155]

The diplomatic postures of the south German governments on monetary unification reflected this political situation. They declined to join the LMU in 1866 because they were already tied to the German coinage union (*Münzverein*) of 1857, but agreed to the principles of the Paris Conference of 1867 even if they repeatedly stressed that they could not act alone, without a common decision of the *Zollverein*. A substantial literature in favour of monetary unification on the basis of the outcome of the Conference flourished between 1867 and 1870, supported by the Handelstag.[156] The head of the government and Foreign Affairs Minister of Württemberg, Varnbühler, was extremely francophile in tone, entertaining French hopes in order to maintain a useful ally, but without taking any practical action or committing himself to anything. His words could never be taken entirely at face value. The French Prime Minister of 1870, Emile Ollivier, later referred to him as the 'the weathercock of Württemberg', directing his policy following the direction of the strongest wind.[157] The historian Pflanze described him as a pragmatic politician, accepting Prussian leadership as unavoidable but attempting to preserve as much freedom of action as possible. In 1867 Varnbühler declared to the French diplomats his personal support for the French project of monetary union.[158] In 1868 he confirmed his favour and explained his refusal to accept to discuss the matter in the *Zollparlament* by the necessity of preventing Prussia from taking over all economic and monetary powers in Germany through the illegitimate extension of the attribution of the trade Parliament.[159] He resisted

---

[155] 'On August 10 [1866] Edouard Lefebvre de Béhaine [later author of many diplomatic dispatches on the German debate on monetary unification] was told by Dalwigk [Chief Minister of Hesse-Darmstadt] that in the event of war with Prussia French troops would be welcome in southern Germany' (Pflanze 1990: i. 370).

[156] The Swiss politician and economist Feer Herzog listed the works on monetary union which had appeared in Germany between 1867 and 1870. He counted eleven publications in favour of a system connected to the franc (Soetbeer, Lammers, Weibezahn, Augspurg, Xeller, Prince-Smith, Schultz, and others), one favourable to a unit close to the US dollar (Augspurg changed his mind seeing that France was not dropping bimetallism) and two supporting the old German crown of the *Münzverein* (Nothomb and Mosle) (Feer-Herzog 1870: 40–2).

[157] Ollivier summarized the attitude of the southern German States during the summer of 1870 and the crisis which led to the Franco-Prussian War: 'Les États allemands ne nous accordèrent pas l'assistance que Gramont attendait d'eux. Il démontrèrent une fois de plus combien était aveugle la politique qui faisait un dogme de leur défense et ils commencèrent dès lors à nous tourner le dos. La girouette du Wurtemberg, Varnbühler, dont Saint Vallier [French diplomat posted in Stuttgart] partageait trop docilement les impressions, commença à tourner' Ollivier, (1917: 99).

[158] Announcing in 1867 the participation of Württemberg in the International Monetary Conference of Paris, Varnbühler flattered the French: 'il ne m'a pas caché que son opinion personelle était parfaitement arrêtée en faveur de notre système décimal, dont la supériorité était incontestable et qui devrait, selon lui, être adopté dans toute ses branches. Mr de Varnbühler est en conséquence décidé à faire tout ce qui dépendra de lui pour seconder les intentions du gouvernement de l'Empereur' (French Legation in Württenberg to Moustier, 3 June 1867, AMAE, ADC 600 bis-2, fol. 47).

[159] The French despatches indicated how favourably the conclusions of the conference of Paris had been received in Stuttgart by 'le Gouvernement, les hommes éclairés, le commerce et l'industrie secondaire du Württemberg'. Nevertheless 'Mr Varnbühler n'avait aucunement l'intention de soulever la question [de l'unification monétaire] à Berlin: non seulement le ministre Wurtembergeois se gardera de prendre l'initiative à ce sujet, mais encore si elle est prise *vis-à-vis* de lui, il déclinera l'ouverture et s'efforcera

monetary unification with the north to resist political unification. In 1869 Varnbühler announced to the French diplomats (described as excessively credulous by Ollivier himself)[160] that the whole government of Württemberg wished for the adoption of the franc system in Germany and would act in favour of such solution. Varnbühler argued that

[I]f Württemberg was not linked to the German States by the treaties forming the *Zollverein*, [Varnbühler] would not hesitate to adopt immediately the decimal system and the monetary unit of the franc; he would foresee considerable advantages for commercial transactions; he would be following the wishes expressed repeatedly by the intelligent class of the country and would advance in the direction of progress.[161]

The Bavarian government did not open its heart to the French ambassadors as ostensibly as Varnbühler did, but it expressed its dislike of seeing silver disappear, resisted Prussian ouvertures, and called for French support in 1870 when a new attempt was made to involve the south in a Prussian-led German monetary unification.[162]

An economic basis for the southern German desire to participate in a monetary union with France, Switzerland, and Austria-Hungary existed because of a large frontier trade. But once diplomatic thrills and decorations were set aside, political reality revealed a circular game: after 1867 France wanted to use the south German States to weaken Prussia's hold on the *Zollverein*. In the meantime the southern German States attempted to use France as a shield from Prussian pressures for unification, just as much as they wanted to use Prussia's military might to be protected from French expansionism. Finally Bismarck provoked France to declare war, using the French aggression to force the southern governments to join the German Empire, 'kicking and screaming'. The Franco-Prussian War was the tragic result of this perilous diplomatic acrobatic feat.

---

d'obtenir que les pourparlers sur cette matière soient renvoyés à plus tard, tout au moins après la session du parlement douanier. Mr de Taube ne m'a point caché que la crainte seule de donner un prétexte à de nouvelles tentatives pour entraîner l'assemblée douanière au delà de la sphère de ses attributions, motivait la résolution de Mr de Varnbühler' (French Legation in Württemberg (Chateaurenard) to Moustier, Stuttgart, 11 May 1868, AMAE, ADC 604–1, fols. 130–1).

[160] Ollivier (1917: 99).

[161] Varnbühler declined to express his opinion about which metallic standard should be employed but 'il a tenu à me dire de vive voix, en son nom et au nom de tout le ministère, qu'il souhaitait vivement voir établir en Allemagne le système décimal et métrique; qu'il savait que tel était le voeu de toutes les personnes instruites et intelligentes qui s'occupent d'affaires, soit dans la banque, soit dans l'industrie ou le commerce.' He was unable to progress without the consent of the rest of Germany but he attempted to push it in the direction desired by the French. Varnbühler was 'radicalement opposé à la pièce de 25 francs qui ne lui parait pas conséquente avec le système décimal.' The Quai d'Orsay passed this last piece of information to Parieu, but not to the Ministry of Finance (marginal notes fol. 71) (French Legation in Württemberg to the French Minister of Foreign Affairs La Valette, Stuttgart, 1 July 1869, AMAE, ADC 604–2, fols. 69–71).

[162] Bavaria expressed its willingness to be represented at the Paris Conference but confirmed it was linked to the *Munzverein* until 1878 and 'verrait le plus grave inconvénient à l'adoption de l'étalon d'or, qui aurait pour conséquence de faire disparaître la monnaie d'argent' (French Embassy in Bavaria to Moustier, Munich, 2 June 1867, AMAE, ADC 600 bis-2, fol. 2). See also the evidence presented in the chapter about the French dilemma.

5.2.3. *National Unification Against International Unification*

The development of cosmopolitan ideas of money had produced a strong enthusiasm and such enthusiasm had carried away many economists, merchants, industrialists, and intellectuals. But the enthusiasm for ideas which did not produce rapid tangible results declined rapidly. The resistance of the southern States to the extension of the powers of the *Zollparlament* to monetary questions, coupled with the Prussian refusal to accept a franc-based currency had paralysed all institutional opportunities for the reform movement. Furthermore, French uncertainties about the adoption of the gold standard made that country less likely to satisfy the longing for gold of German commercial circles. The British refusal to participate in a common currency showed that universal money was not likely to extend further than Continental Europe, reducing its appeal. Support for a franc-based international money began to weaken in Germany in 1869, at a speed perceived by the French diplomatic corps. In July 1869 the French Embassy in Prussia reported to Paris the adoption of the French metric system by the North German Confederation together with some reassuring declarations by Delbrück concerning coinage. The French diplomat added a warning: 'I would like to emphasize that the special monetary unification of Germany is at the moment much closer to the heart of German publicists than the solution of the problem of international or universal monetary unification.'[163] The French consul in Bremen signalled that: 'the unanimous opinion which had some time ago still prevailed among German economists in what concerns international monetary union, has unfortunately lost some of its strength.' Those who had enthusiastically supported the franc at the congress of economists had cooled down since,

reflecting on the real difficulties appearing from all sides, they have, even if they did not modify completely their opinion, at least acquired the conviction that for the moment it would be better to be content with partial reforms and wait until a not too distant future, when a wider knowledge of economic science in the public and the administration will permit a resumption of this task with more success and carry it to a positive conclusion.[164]

The nationalist position was also expressed in some pamphlets: for Mosle 'coinage unification would be an excellent way to subject these so-called justified idiosyncrasies of the different branches and random partitions of our great tribe to a melting process.' An international coin based on the franc was an illusion but furthermore 'our flourishing national consciousness would have to suffer from … continued frenchification'.[165] The French Consulate in Frankfurt indicated in December that despite the unanimity of the economists in support of the international coinage and their invitation to the southern States to seize the initiative, the lack of action by the latter was modifying the position of the former. 'They wish the task of elaborating a project of monetary reform would now be entrusted to the Prussian Finance Minister, and then

---

[163] The French Embassy in Prussia (Lefebvre de Béhaigne) to la Tour d'Auvergne, 19 July 1869 (AMAE, ADC 604–2, fols. 176–7).

[164] French Consulate in Bremen to la Tour d'Auvergne, 1 Sept. 1869 (AMAE, ADC 604–2, fol. 245–6).

[165] Mosle (1870: 8).

presented to the Bundesrat [Federal Council] which in turn would be called to start negotiations with the southern States, and they express at the same time the opinion that an international agreement might produce the most desirable solution.'[166]

Many started to think that the most important advantages of an international currency union would be achieved through the generalized adoption of the gold standard, regardless of the actual diversity in the single coins. Complete unification required a recalculation of all prices, wages, and debts and a modification of the habits of the people. Furthermore, an unwanted solidarity would be established with foreign currencies of uncertain trustworthiness, introducing in Germany coins of unwarranted weight, fineness, and quantity. Some alarming reports about the exactness of the French coinage were deliberately circulated to spread suspicion.[167]

All those dissatisfied with the slow pace of international reform promoted by the French turned to Prussia for the leadership of internal unification. The national liberal politician Bamberger reflected and channelled with his initiatives the changing mood. Ludwig Bamberger's prominent role in Germany's political and monetary history calls for a short biographical notice. He was a Hessian citizen from a family of Jewish bankers of Mainz. As a leader of the local democratic movement during the revolution of 1848–9 he had been forced into exile, spending fifteen years in Paris as a banker. When he returned in his native country in 1866, after the Prussian victory over Austria and the rest of Germany, he became one of the leading south German politicians to advocate national unification under Prussian leadership, subordinating to it his democratic preference. He was elected to the *Zollverein* Parliament as a National Liberal in 1868, for the southern State of Hesse, on an annexionist and pro-Bismarck platform. Mainz had been French for twenty years, during the French Revolution and the Napoleonic period and some pro-French feelings had remained. Bamberger himself continued to live for most of his time in Paris between 1866 and 1870 and 'saw himself as an agent of Franco-German understanding'.[168] Nevertheless he became a close ally of the Chancellor Bismarck and a proponent of a purely national monetary unification, as a consequence of his wider political preference, without conceding anything to his French friends, whom he warned against their illusions about German feelings on unity.[169] In 1869–70 the drive towards political unity seemed stalled. Bamberger loathed south German particularists: 'the Jesuits and democratic phrase-mongers have the upper hand. With this pack in the rear how can one uphold German autonomy *vis à vis* France, as long as one is not actually determined to make war.'[170]

The North German Confederation decided at the beginning of 1870 to form a commission to investigate monetary reform.[171] In May 1870 Bamberger called in the *Zollparlament* for the inclusion of the southern States in the enquiry for monetary

---

[166] The despatch estimated the total amount of silver to be demonetized in Germany to between 1.5 and 1.9 billion francs (French Consulate in Frankfurt to la Tour d'Auvergne, 18 Dec. 1869, AMAE, ADC 604–2, fol. 282).   [167] Hellferich (1969: 152–3).   [168] Zucker (1975: 49).

[169] Bamberger (1868: 8–49, 256–83).   [170] Zucker (1975: 56).

[171] Delbruck announced on 5 March 1870 that the inquiry would concern unification and the selection of a standard. (French Ambassador in Prussia, Benedetti to French Foreign Affairs Minister, Daru, 9 March 1870, AMAE, ADC 616–1, fols. 52–4).

reform. The move was designed to extend the powers of the customs Parliament to currency and force the resistance of the south. The motion was opposed without success by the progressives of Württemberg.[172] Delbrück announced Bismarck's willingness to proceed on these lines, while the National Liberals took the opportunity to warn the south about any attempt to break free from the Prussian hegemony: 'a decision by the *Zollparlament* would not fail to become obligatory for the southern States, that are not any freer to form a monetary union of their own than a political union.'[173]

The French government reacted, but the economic and peaceful approach of the Minister President of the Council of State, Parieu, was overwhelmed by the political hostility to Prussia of the new Foreign Affairs Minister, the long-time French ambassador to Austria, the Duke de Gramont. The French pressure on Bavaria and Württemberg was not entirely deprived of chances of success. Only the government of Baden was committed to closer union with northern Germany, while Varnbühler in Württemberg and Bray in Bavaria intended to defend all the national prerogatives left to their governments. The desire of the Bavarian Foreign Affairs Minister Bray to participate in the Commission to increase the chances of the anti-thaler party and the silence of most other southern States led in June to a further adjournment of the German Monetary Commission.[174]

A few weeks later Bismarck had found the final opportunity to overcome the resistance of south German States to complete unification thanks to the Hohenzollern–Singmaringen candidature to the throne of Spain. Bray advised the French he would not be able to come to their side 'despite the pro-French feelings of the Bavarian population' because the candidature was the wrong issue for war, with Napoleon III posing as the aggressor.[175] After some hesitation Bavaria and Württemberg followed Prussia after France had declared war. Varnbühler was dismissed the same day that news of the French defeat at Sedan broke in Stuttgart and Bray survived a little longer to be voted down by the Bavarian Parliament for having negotiated the incorporation of the Kingdom of Bavaria into the German Reich.

In the end of 1869–70 France had come to be seen as the solution to German internal problems. A war against France or French threats would help to create the political union indispensable to achieve national monetary unification. In the meantime the decision by the French Finance Minister Magne to delay the decision about the gold

[172] French Ambassador in Prussia Benedetti to French Chief Minister Ollivier, interim Foreign Affairs Minister, 6 May 1870 (AMAE, ADC 616–1, fols. 125–6).

[173] Benedetti to Ollivier, 6 May 1870 (AMAE, ADC 616–1, fols. 126).

[174] The inquiry was suspended for the summer, in order to receive the final decision of France on the 25-franc coin and to negotiate the participation of the south to the inquiry (French Consulate in Cologne to Gramont, 22 June 1870, AMAE, ADC 616–1, fol. 149).

[175] Bray declared to the French during the crisis of July 1870 'Vous rendez notre situation fort difficile. J'ai toujours soutenu que les traités d'alliance avaient un caractère défensif; si la Prusse pouvait, avec quelques apparences de raison, vous accuser d'être les agresseurs et que vos armées pénétrassent les premières sur le sol allemand, nous serions obligés de marcher contre vous, ce que je regretterais vivement, car la Bavière n'a jamais eu qu'à se louer de la France, et, de tous les États allemands, c'est celui où le sentiment public vous est le plus favorable' (Ollivier 1917: 99).

standard was seen as an excellent opportunity for Germany to adopt the gold standard and dump all its silver on France, which would be forced to pay for it at a fixed price because of its bimetallic law.[176] Old German silver thalers and florins could be melted, coined into francs in every French mint, and then exchanged for banknotes, which would be used to withdraw gold francs from the Bank of France.

5.2.4. German Monetary Unification and a Confrontational Gold Standard

After the Franco-Prussian War and the creation of the Reich, Bismarck set aside any pretence of being interested in a European currency. German monetary unification did not succeed in the 1860s because it was seen by the south German governments as a step towards political unification. Only when the political unification of Germany had taken place could monetary unification follow without major obstacles. The war removed the political capacity of the southern States to resist Prussia, although they retained individual governments inside the Reich. It also made a mockery of the French pretension to offer its own system to the world. In Bamberger's words 'France, according to its fancy, was imposing on the world one time war, another time brotherly love, and also threw into the world the beautiful ideal of a coinage system common to all civilized nations ... The French simply said: we want to make an international coinage system, would Europe kindly accept *our* system. They make it very easy for themselves.'[177] The ambiguous policy of Napoleon and German triumphant nationalism cancelled the last hopes. The German victory at Sedan in 1870, the invasion of France, and the long siege of Paris alienated permanently many financial operations located in France during the second Empire, in favour of London, safer from invasions and political instability. The dream of Paris as the major financial centre of Europe vanished together with French prestige and political influence, which helped to create the coalition of States supporting monetary unification. France recovered surprisingly fast a substantial part of its financial power, but proved unable to follow the demographic and industrial growth of a united Germany.

---

[176] When Magne announced his intention to call for a new monetary enquiry in France before any decision could be taken regarding the introduction of the gold standard, Tolhausen informed Paris of the favourable reception of this decision by the Gazette of Cologne. French indecision would give to Germany the opportunity to sell silver to France at a fixed price and to adopt the gold standard. Germany had already lost an opportunity in 1857–63, when the price of silver was high, if it did not take this second opportunity to get rid of its silver there would not be a third one. 'La décision que vient de prendre la France de surseoir jusqu'à plus ample informé à l'abolition du double étalon et à la démonétisation de l'argent, nous offre de nouveau l'occasion, pourvu que les gouvernements allemands y mettent de l'intelligence et de l'énergie, de mener la réforme monétaire à bonne fin, ou du moins lui frayer des voies, sans nous imposer de sacrifices trop onéreux per rapport au placement de l'argent. Si par incurie ou par indifférence, l'Allemagne laissait encore échapper cette fois-ci l'occasion, qui sait si elle la retrouvera si belle une troisième fois?' The Gazette expected the price of silver to collapse when France would reject it. After a fall in the price of silver it would be difficult to establish an equation to convert in gold contracts denominated in silver and the opposition of debtors and creditors to the adoption of gold would become a major obstacle (French Consulate in Cologne (Tolhausen) to la Tour d'Auvergne, 29 Nov. 1868, AMAE, ADC 604–2, fols. 263–7).

[177] Bamberger (1872: 22–4).

The 5 billion francs indemnity imposed on France also seemed to offer Germany a free ride to the gold standard. The message of Bismarck to the Reichstag in October 1871 when the question came to a final proposal was explicit:

The most important and favourable change in our situation [due to our victory in the last war] derives from the war indemnity which France is paying us. In fact since these payments are carried out mainly in gold, this brings about options on which we could not have relied before to overcome the most difficult obstacle towards a monetary reform, the replacement of the silver standard with the gold standard.[178]

Despite that, France paid in gold only 250 million francs, adding 250 million of silver, employing commercial paper payable in England, Belgium, Holland, and Germany for the rest, a large part of which was paid in silver.[179] Furthermore in the following years the reversal of the exchange ignited a flow of gold returning to France from Germany.[180] The price of silver collapsed in 1873, following the formal adoption of the gold standard by Germany and the retaliation by France and Belgium, which suspended silver mintage in order not to be invaded by demonetized silver thalers. These factors made the adoption of gold much more difficult and expensive than expected in the euphoria of 1871 and some silver thalers continued to circulate in Germany until the beginning of the twentieth century.

Bismarck added to the Reichstag that 'due to serious obstacles the imperial government is obliged to drop for the moment one of the goals it had pursued, and to abandon the idea of preparing an agreement [on monetary union] with foreign countries and especially with France.'[181] A monetary inquiry was declared superfluous on the grounds of unanimity of opinion in favour of gold and of the mark system, confirmed by the Reichstag in June and by an Economic Congress in August 1871.[182] The mark system proposed by Bismarck, Delbrück, and Camphausen was a thinly disguised thaler system, associated with bimetallism.[183] The mark was a third of a thaler and some coins were planned to keep the thaler in circulation, the 15- and 30-gold mark pieces were none other than 5- and 10-thaler coins. The Bavarian economist Prof. Adolf Wagner even suggested calling the 2-mark coin a 'Bismarck'.[184] Bamberger's strong speeches in the Reichstag cleared many of the Prussian hopes.[185]

---

[178] Message of the Federal Chancellor of the German Empire, translation annexed to the despatch of the French Embassy in Berlin to French Minister of Foreign Affairs, 7 Oct. 1871 (AMAE, ADC 616–1, fol. 204).

[179] Hellferich (1969: 155).

[180] Kindleberger (1993: 237) also records the French minting in Hamburg, in a German valuation, silver bars bought on the market.

[181] French Embassy in Berlin to French Minister of Foreign Affairs, 7 Oct. 1871 (AMAE, ADC 616–1, fol. 206). [182] Hellferich (1969: 154).

[183] The government had not yet been forced by the Reichstag to accept the gold standard (Mertens 1944: 126–30).

[184] *Stenographische Berichte über die Verhandlungen des Deutschen Reichtages*, Berlin, I Legislatur, II Session (1871), 317.

[185] The 'opportunism' of the supporters of international money was showed by their easy conversion to the mark. Soetbeer for example was quite content to see national unification with the gold standard even without 25-franc units and wrote to Bamberger in 1871 that 'my entire hope rests on your effectiveness in the Reichstag' (Zucker 1975: 84).

The 15 and 30 marks were refused in favour of a more decimal 10 and 20 marks, the provisional bimetallism requested by the government was replaced by an explicit gold standard, and the separate rights of the component States of the Reich were minimized. The cruelly disappointed *Economist* protested: 'That is nothing more nor less than a new international vexation. At present, the principal coinages of Europe contain several coins all but equal to the English sovereign, and yet not equal to it ... It is simply a new difficulty in international coinage; an unhappy addition to the semi-equivalents which for years have baffled and beaten us.'[186] While the pound was worth 25.22 francs, the 20 marks were worth 24.69 francs and the American half-eagle was worth 25.96 francs.

The French option was not dead for the south of Germany even after the establishment of the Reich and the introduction of the gold coinage bill in the Reichstag. Over 800 petitions were sent to legislators from all over Germany to influence their views. The summary produced by a Parliamentary Committee shows that the chambers of commerce of Frankfurt, Württemberg, and Bavaria still insisted that the German gold coinage had to be based on the international 25-franc coin. The chambers of commerce of Baden even asked to adapt to the French franc–Austrian florin system all gold, silver, and bronze coins.[187] A progressive member of the Reichstag, the economist Moritz Mohl, introduced an amendment in favour of the 25 francs international coinage, supported by other progressives. Mohl insisted on the interest of southern Germany, of trade and travellers in an international currency, and refuted the international claims of the supporters of the mark which he defined 'a great step backwards' giving inconvenience to the south without international unification.

[The] 20-mark piece would be 24.691358 francs. I could continue this decimal fraction for longer. Hence this gold coin will never be current in the French countries and we are isolated from these countries by this gold piece. Now I ask you gentlemen, what kind of international compatibility is this? ... Two or three years ago, when you were discussing the metrical system, had the government proposed to introduce the French system ... I believe you would have accepted it, but now gentlemen, we now have had a bloody war ... Had we lost I would understand such a hate.[188]

Again he insisted 'The most important chambers of commerce ... like Frankfurt, Strasbourg, Mulhouse, and a whole range of partly southern and partly northern chambers of commerce have asked to have at least the gold coins minted according to the franc system' to facilitate trade and avoid isolation from the monetary systems of the rest of the world.[189]

Bamberger fought and defeated Mohl's proposal. He 'denied that international commerce required an international coin. Rather it was necessary that all currencies were based on the same metal.'[190] Small trade did not need international currencies and large trade was forced anyway to employ the services of the banking system to

---

[186] 'The grave demerits of the proposed new coinage for Germany' (*Economist* 29: 21 Oct. (1871), 2. Anonymous article probably by Bagehot).   [187] *Stenographische Berichte*, 317–18.
[188] Ibid. 245–6.   [189] Ibid. 318–9.   [190] Zucker (1975: 66).

send payments abroad, with bank drafts or bills of exchange, as transportation of coins was too expensive on an individual basis.[191] The argument was the same as that of the banker-politicians of France and England, particularly Rouland and Goschen, but to purely economic arguments Bamberger added the new brand of German nationalism:

Mohl ... has told us what happens in border traffic. Another representative, Prof. Zeelig, I believe, has talked about other borders. Well gentlemen, it is an unavoidable phenomenon that at each border you come in contact with the coin of the neighbouring country, but you would not draw the conclusion from that that we should accept the coins of all bordering countries and have none of our own. This was perhaps to be recommended in a time when we accepted the policy of all foreign countries and had none of our own and that is of course why we were so praised in all countries, as we would also be praised now if we accepted a foreign monetary system.[192]

Bamberger was concerned with an efficient, centralized, and secure gold standard, without loopholes permitting the smuggling of silver by southern States or any sort of peripheral abuses. Nevertheless when his nationalist pressures threatened all concessions either to internationalist or to particularist requests, Bismarck himself had to intervene in defence of some concessions to the south, acknowledging its separate identity.

Is there any stronger pledge of alliance of the German sovereigns to the Reich than the coinage as it has been suggested? If his majesty the King of Bavaria has minted on one side his portrait and on the other side the Imperial crest of the Reich, is there any more obvious and substantial way of confessing 'I adhere to the Reich', 'I want to be a member of the Reich'? What do we gain if we alienate a justified sense of identity of the South, sacred by centuries of traditions and if we nourish the insinuations and persuasions of those who tend to appeal to centrifugal instincts?[193]

Bismarck carried this point against Bamberger. The obverse of each coin was unified with the common denomination and the symbol of the empire, but the reverse would recall the prime issuer, the individual principality, duchy, grand Duchy, kingdom or free city.[194] In a similar compromise between the old and the new, the division of responsibility for the imperial coinage among the mints of individual States reflected the political arrangements of a federal State. Legislation ensured that central control by the Imperial Chancellor was effective on the amount of gold to be coined, the division of these amounts between the various coins and the mints of the different States, supplying centrally the mints with gold. The final text of the legislation did not allow for the minting of gold coins for private account but that provision was introduced with the 1873 monetary law that completed the previous one. A Reichsbank was also created in 1875 to regulate the unified currency and Bamberger convinced the Reichstag to concentrate financial authority in it.[195] The Reichsbank incorporated the Prussian State Bank, but left thirty-two other local note-issuing banks. However, these *Zettelbanken* were limited in their operations to the area of their state territory and

---

[191] *Stenographische Berichte*, 324–5.   [192] Ibid. 325.   [193] Ibid. 337.
[194] Art. 5 of the 1871 coinage law of the Reich.   [195] Zucker (1975: 67–70).

fifteen of those stopped immediately to issue notes, while sixteen others gave up by 1905, leaving only progressively the monopoly to the Reichsbank.[196]

Supporters of international monetary unification were quick to condemn the German decision. For Jevons the action was 'retrograde',[197] Bagehot and Hendricks were baffled, and Parieu bitter.[198] Some German economists were more optimistic but they were looking at a much more distant future than they thought: 'after the shattering experience of 1870, the result was that people were no longer discussing a direct incorporation [*Anschluss*] of the German system into the French system, they were no longer pursuing the Paris ideas for unification ... As soon as these crises are over, nations will compete peacefully and the question of international monetary unification will be on the agenda again.'[199] When the proposal for the German gold currency was passed into law at the beginning of December 1871, the idea of a European monetary unification was dead and buried for a long time. It would take two more 'bloody wars' between France and Germany to see Parieu's and Mohl's ideas resurfacing in Europe.

---

[196] Kindleberger (1993: 127).   [197] Jevons (1875: 166).

[198] Parieu quoted the Moniteur universel of 24 Oct. 1872 on the introduction of the mark in Germany 'Les journaux anglais blâment cette décision. Ils font observer qu'elle créera des embarras multiples dans les rapports de peuple à peuple. Mais le journal officieux du cabinet de Berlin se soucie médiocrement de ces difficultés et ne se préoccupe que de l'intérêt national, entendu dans le sens le plus égoïste du mot, de l'empire allemand: "le capital mobilier, dit-il, n'a déjà que trop de propensions internationales: le dénationaliser encore davantage serait, à notre avis, une grande faute politique." L'Allemagne est assez forte désormais pour ne pas craindre l'isolement commercial et industriel; c'est à elle au contraire de faire la loi au reste du monde' (Parieu 1872: 383).   [199] Weibezahn (1871: 6 and 17).

Epilogue

What remained of the programme of monetary unification after 1871? The programme was apparently dead, Parieu was marginalized and the growing wave of nationalism was destroying all that had been achieved. Parieu realized that his campaign had profited Germany which adopted the gold standard but refused monetary unification. In his own bitter words: 'for me, who has struggled since 1858 for the principles which Germany is appropriating today and who has presided uselessly over so many commissions and written so many articles for an idea I would have liked to see work for the glory of my country, at times I only see in it the ornament of the triumph of our opponents.'[1] Unification and coordination could not survive the poisoned atmosphere between France and Germany. Europe was fragmented again in various zones of monetary influences. Admittedly, these zones were fewer and larger than before the 1860s. Southern Europe was covered by the LMU and its monetary satellites (Spain and the Balkans). Northern Europe was divided between the influence of the pound and of the mark, with an independent Scandinavian Monetary Union and Holland squeezed between England, Germany, and the LMU.

Contemporary actors immediately understood the new situation provoked by the creation of an Imperial mark of Germany, hostile to the franc of the LMU. In 1872 Sweden decided to abandon the franc zone and to unite with Norway and Denmark in what would become the Scandinavian Monetary Union. With the German conversion to gold, the two main trading partners of the Scandinavian countries (England and Germany) were now on a gold standard. The needs of international trade and the fear of becoming the victims of the demonetization of silver, decided by Germany, dictated the policy of the small countries, which were forced to imitate their larger neighbours in order not to remain stuck with a depreciated silver currency.

The reactions of the French governments to later Swedish and Austrian overtures reveal the change of atmosphere. In 1872 Oscar Wallenberg proposed the franc as the common currency of the Scandinavian Union (SMU), in opposition to the proposal of the Norwegian Broch to adopt the mark. Both were excluded from the Scandinavian Commission formed to draft the proposed common currency. The Commission concluded in favour of the adoption of an independent Scandinavian unit, very close to the ones already existing in the three countries. The Scandinavian Commission had started its work considering the possible adoption of the franc because of its recent status as candidate for universal unification or at least for European unification, confirmed by

---

[1] Parieu (1872: 381).

the previous Swedish monetary commission of 1869, as stated in the report, 'with the idea of adopting the French system as universal system being abandoned for now or at least for the nearest future, given the well-known position of England and the USA, and Germany's recent introduction of a system of its own, the commission had to decline joining the [French–LMU] system.'[2] The pound was then rejected because it was not decimal and because Great Britain did not accept its old and worn coins at par when they were returned from abroad. The mark failed the political test, since Denmark feared further links with Germany would threaten its independence.

Wallenberg tried to influence the choice of the Commission in favour of the franc, asking France to award free circulation on its territory to the Swedish carolin-10-franc coin. He acted with the support of the French Ambassador in Sweden, J. A. Gobineau, and travelled to Paris, where he was introduced by Parieu to the French Foreign Affairs Minister Rémusat.[3] Wallenberg's arguments were successful, and the carolin was admitted to circulate side by side with the other LMU coins. Nevertheless this proved to be a futile victory, since attitudes had changed in France. The French Foreign Ministry could not capitalize any more on the favourable momentum towards European monetary unification. Parieu was no longer a close adviser in shaping its policies. The Finance Ministry was determined more than ever to reject further encroachments on its control of internal monetary circulation. The campaign for monetary unification was reduced to one of the aspects of the French financial war launched to isolate Germany and provide capital to all possible allies of France in a future war of 'revanche'. From the 1880s Russia would be the prime beneficiary of this new French policy. The carolin was accepted by France in 1872 exclusively with a ministerial decision, revocable unilaterally by France whenever any 'inconvenience' should appear. By 'inconvenience' the French authorities meant any real impact of the circulation of carolins in France:

[I]f these inconveniences appeared, they could not acquire threatening proportions, given that the measure to be adopted by M. le Ministre has only a theoretical and moral character, given that Swedish carolins should not appear in France except in isolated and exceptional cases. But, as M. Wallenberg explains, from a different point of view there might be a real interest to facilitate his task to keep the Scandinavian States in the monetary direction which they have chosen and which the German influence would want them to leave.[4]

---

[2] French Legation in Denmark to French Minister of Foreign Affairs, 6 Oct. 1872 (AMAE, ADC 616–2, fol. 59).

[3] Gobineau warned Paris that 'la difficulté du double étalon peut amener ce résultat de faire entrer, quoi qu'ils en crient, les trois royaumes du Nord dans la sphère financière de l'Allemagne' (French Ambassador in Sweden Conte de Gobineau to French Foreign Affairs Minister Rémusat, 10 Sept. 1872, AMAE, ADC 616–2, fol. 46). See also Gobineau to Rémusat, 14 Sept. 1872 (AMAE, ADC 616–2, fol. 47). Gobineau demanded the admission of the Carolin in the French public circulation to keep the struggle between franc and mark alive for the future. He expected the SMU to be transitory. 'Dans une sorte d'ardeur générale à se porter en tout lieu, les capitaux allemands commencent plus que par le passé à dériver vers cette région. On a pu déjà constater, avec vérité, que la majeure partie de la dette hypothécaire de la Suède était désormais entre des mains allemandes' and that the Germans attempted to acquire the control of the railway concessions in Scandinavia (ibid., 20 Oct. 1872, AMAE, ADC 616–2, fol. 103).

[4] Director of the Treasury Dutilleul to Secrétariat Général of the Finance Ministry, 2 Dec. 1872 (AMdP, K2 23, 1).

The Minister added that the decision was aimed exclusively at exercising 'a favourable influence on the Danish and Swedish-Norwegian governments.'[5] The same considerations dictated the reaction to further requests by Austria-Hungary to have its coins accepted at par in the French circulation. The first measure was accepted by France exclusively to 'link to our monetary system, even if imperfectly, a country which would otherwise risk to be attracted soon towards the new German monetary system'.[6] Had the measure been substantial and not theoretical, the Finance Ministry would have blocked the admission of the Austro-Hungarian coinage into public coffers, requiring guarantees about the quality and quantity of the coinage and about the procedures of exchange of migrated coins. Dutilleul concluded:

[T]he monetary administration should be consulted on the intrinsic qualities of the coins in question; it would be advisable to conclude an agreement with the Austro-Hungarian government on the exchange of these coins, which would encumber the Treasury if the public refused to accept them, as it would be entitled to; I would wish to receive information about issues having already taken place and those planned.

But, considering the required admission as a measure without practical consequences in the current circumstances, and considering the monetary situation of the two countries, I do not object, acknowledging the urgent and important interest attached to this matter by the Ministry of Foreign Affairs. At the same time I expressly maintain the right to reconsider at a later moment such authorization.[7]

The Austro-Hungarian candidacy for full membership of the LMU was then blocked the following year. The Minister explained 'I see perhaps more problems than advantages proceeding any further, since once again we would have to lose our freedom of action.'[8] In the following years political relations between France and Italy began to turn sour. In 1889 a French newspaper encouraged the dissolution of the Union in order to gain political advantage.

If we denounce the Convention, Italy will be forced to reimburse us an amount in gold estimated by some persons at 100 million, not lower than 60 million according to the most prudent calculation ... Sixty million! But this would mean that [the Italian Prime Minister] Crispi would be overthrown from one day to the other; it would break the triple alliance into pieces, France would be freed of its enemy [Crispi] cultivated by Bismarck from the other side of the Alps.[9]

The negative experience with large speculative migrations of coinage and with inconvertible paper currency in Italy and Greece, together with the fear of a repetition of the Pontifical speculation of 1866–70, had already shaped the final opinion of the

---

[5] French Finance Minister M. de Goulard to French Minister of Foreign Affairs Rémusat, 6 December 1872 (AMdP, K2 35, 1).

[6] Dutilleul to the Secrétaire Général, 2 July 1873 (AMdP, K2 23, 1).   [7] Ibid. K2 23, 2–3.

[8] Finance Minister Mathieu Bodet to Minister of Foreign Affairs Decazes, 14 Nov. 1874 (AMdP, K2 23, 1–2).

[9] 'Crispi c'est l'ennemi ... c'est l'âme damnée de M. de Bismarck: traiter avec lui c'est traiter avec le chancelier prussien.' 'Question Urgente—La Convention Monétaire—Dénonciation nécéssaire, dépréciation de l'argent, pressant délais, l'avis du Parlement, défendons nous' (*La Lanterne*, 12 Oct. 1889, AMdP, K2 20).

French Treasury. From that point of view the Franco-Prussian War did not change anything. Monetary unification failed because the States whose public finances were heavily unbalanced used monetary issues (paper in Italy and Greece, divisionary silver in the Pontifical States) as a source of income. Excessive money supply spilled through the Union, making France and Switzerland partially liable for Belgian private speculation on silver and for Italian, Pontifical, and Greek budgetary difficulties. It must be said that the additional inflationary pressure and the reduced state income generated by these phenomena was usually overstated. The incompleteness of the rules of the Union implied a painful process of learning by doing, where previous mistakes were corrected and new rules introduced.

Monetary union was not necessarily incompatible with a disciplined issue of money, as the experience of the LMU in the 1860s and 1870s showed. The price to pay for such an outcome was however a centralized control, a reduced membership, and a tendency towards over-restrictive rules of monetary issue. The Union was useful enough for intraregional trade to subsist until 1926, but its impact was progressively weakened (the issue of new silver écus was prohibited, for long periods the Italian and Greek divisionary coinage were renationalized and excluded from the convention). The influence of the LMU over monetary circulation progressively decreased when alternative forms of money, not included in the Union, developed at a much faster pace (banknotes and cheque-bank deposits). Monetary unification was limited in fact to gold which already circulated freely before the formation of the Union and would have circulated anyway later on thanks to the international gold standard.

The failure of the programme of European monetary union should not be ascribed entirely to the shortcomings of the LMU. An agreement limited to gold coinage did not present the threats of bimetallic unions, on condition that the number of nations on forced paper currency did not become overwhelming. Such an agreement required the participation of France, Great Britain, and the USA, followed by the German States. This turned out to be impossible because of a deeply rooted conservatism about existing monetary arrangements, more pronounced in England than elsewhere, but determinant everywhere. The causes of this conservatism were the cost of changing the price system, of disturbing people's habits, and the threat to the recent acquisition of parliamentary control over the stability of national monetary systems against predatory monarchs. The financial community echoed and developed these considerations to oppose a process which threatened banking commissions on foreign currencies and speculative profits on metallic arbitrage. Nevertheless the argument that these profits would reappear in a different form even after monetary unification was essentially right and was never really disputed. Transaction fees for the use of banking facilities would replace the crude commission of the money changers.

The nationalistic appeal of currencies seems to have been weak in the 1860s in the smaller States, thanks to the skilful preservation of diversity in unity (preservation of national currency name and symbols in the coinage of the Union).

The four nations [of the LMU] ... decided that from Antwerp to Brindisi ... a traveller carrying coins from one of the four countries should not be exposed to any exchange fee, regardless of whether gold or silver pieces represented the effigy of free Helvetia, the cross of Savoy, the laureate head of the victor of Solferino or the image of one of the two Leopolds, successively kings of Belgium ... They wanted silver and gold coins of the four countries to be manufactured in identical condition ... but with the distinct effigy of each State, accepting also, thanks to the silent consent of the Convention, the ancient right of Italy to keep on calling *lira* what the other three States call *franc*. In a word, they have realized Napoleon's desire in St Helena, 'one money under different dies'.[10]

The major States, particularly England and Prussia-Germany, wanted more; they aimed at the status acquired by France after 1865 as the nation setting the standard of the Union. The international coin of 25 francs–10 florins–5 dollars–1 pound was supposed to heal those divisions, but it was only the 'petit coté de notre plan de réforme'[11] and did not take off. Great Britain considered the golden pound the symbol of its economic success. It had no wish to see it overshadowed and partially replaced in the UK itself by a larger circulation of 25 francs, mainly originating from its neighbour and competitor on the other side of the Channel.

The flexibility of a Monetary Union formed by combining several compatible national systems permitted its relative popularity, because it avoided creating a single central system imposing itself on various countries. At the same time, the survival of the national currencies in the Union facilitated the dissolution of the recently established links making the Union reversible with almost no cost except the redemption of its own coins abroad. In fact, members of the Union could informally leave it unilaterally by declaring their paper money inconvertible. Inconvertible paper money would automatically depreciate, becoming a fiduciary money and the depreciation would become a devaluation of the currency. The preservation of national systems in the Union also secured the dominant role of the franc at a time when monetary union had no stronger enemy than monetary nationalism.

In the late 1860s the large majority of European governments were favourable to monetary unification as a matter of principle, but refused to act unless others preceded them. Obviously it was a self-defeating decision, leading to a standstill where each actor sticking to his initial statement watched his neighbour's immobility. Having established this, the logical conclusion for the supporters of monetary unification was to create the expectation that the majority of nations were moving towards monetary unification. In Parieu's and Feer-Herzog's articles and in the French diplomatic dispatches for foreign consumption, the reader always felt that substantial progress had been achieved and the whole process was on the verge of a final breakthrough. No individual writer or foreign government had complete access to information the French had, hence they could not assess entirely the weight of the French claims. Few would know that the Swedish and Austrian gold coins in francs were only trade coins, without any extended internal circulation, or that the Greek and Romanian LMU issues were initially limited to bronze, or more generally that most statements in favour of monetary unification were counterbalanced by opposed statements.

---

[10] Parieu (1867: 327).   [11] Parieu (1872: 380–1).

The French campaign generated the feeling that refusing to take action would mean to risk isolation, as Lowe thought in 1869. A self-reinforcing process had been built up where the decision of one country to move towards monetary unification put pressure on its neighbour to imitate it. The Franco-Prussian War and the creation of the Imperial mark broke this process, but a similar tendency was still at work in relation to the adoption of the gold standard. There was a mainstream consensus on its necessity in the commercial world, supported by the majority of economists and by many politicians (outside France). The French negotiations on monetary unification highlighted and reinforced the preference for gold expressed with conviction by Belgium, Switzerland, Austria, Great Britain, the USA, and initially more weakly by Italy, Prussia, and the German States. These national preferences were combined in the most spectacular way in Paris in 1867, revealing the consensus and convincing the nations which had expressed more doubts about gold, such as the German States. The political desire to act upon it was strengthened, with the same multilateral imitation effect as for unification. It was not excessively useful to move to gold alone if other commercial partners remained on silver or on bimetallism, since trade would be made more difficult and exchange rate volatility would increase, following the fluctuation of the gold/silver ratio. Once it was clear that all the nations wished to adopt gold, it was impossible not to follow the trend and a strong incentive to act first appeared. The latecomers to gold would have to buy gold and sell their silver stock when previous demonetization of silver had already depressed its price. Nobody expected the dimension of the silver price plunge which took place after 1873, but all countries knew it would eventually take place.[12] The French campaign for monetary unification must therefore be ranked among one of the main causes of the establishment of the gold standard as the international standard. It was not a deliberate policy, but hardly any historical transformation is the result of a linear implementation of carefully prepared plans.

Were Parieu's ideas ultimately vindicated by the progressive switch to gold of most European countries? A positive reply would stress the triumph of the gold standard. With the reduction of transportation costs, the increased mobility of capital, and the growing integration of markets for goods, the cohabitation between several types of standard (gold, silver, and bimetallism) had become more difficult. This cohabitation was subjected to too much international arbitrage, with huge alternate inflows and outflows of silver and gold, which was becoming too destabilizing for national monetary systems. If a common monetary system had to be found, it required that all the members adopted the same type of standard although not necessarily a 'single standard'. The gold standard was internationally chosen but 'international bimetallism' could also have worked, on condition that all the major States adopted it with the same gold/silver mint ratio. The large preference for gold made a consensus for bimetallism impossible. At that point it was inevitable in the medium term that the gold standard should become the international standard. It was not a casual scramble for gold that

---

[12] Parieu repeatedly indicated in the late 1860s that France needed to act fast for this reason. Rouland replied 'M. de Parieu a peur que l'Allemagne, en passant avant nous de l'étalon argent à l'étalon or, ne nous inonde de son argent; mais je réponds, d'abord, que c'est vous qui la provoquez à ce changement qu'elle ne peut faire et qu'elle ne fera sans vous' (*Procès-verbaux et rapport de la commission monétaire de 1868:* 55).

brought about this situation, but the outcome of an animated debate on international monetary unification.

Nevertheless the efforts of Parieu, de Hock, Wallenberg, Feer-Herzog, Hendriks, Ruggles, and many others were directed towards a more complete international arrangement, whose only missing element in the end appeared to be the 25-franc gold coin and simple connections between national coins. As long as the common gold standard fixed exchange rates, within very reduced fluctuation bands the essence of monetary unification was achieved. Many economists believe that the rules of the international gold standard 'in effect created an international monetary union by either solving automatically or making it easier to solve several problems normally associated with the establishment of a viable international financial system.'[13] The present work has suggested a far more sceptical view of this supposedly automatic and smooth monetary system, especially in comparison to a well organized bimetallic or a managed currency. Throughout the nineteenth century, French bimetallism was at least as successful as the gold standard in terms of price stability associated with a very moderate fluctuation of the exchange rate.

The International Gold Standard was supposed to work automatically without the political collaboration between countries sought by Parieu, but it crashed every time the lack of collaboration became open warfare (1914) or economic warfare (the 1930s). Parieu personally felt that his ideas had been defeated because of political antagonism. The 'peaceful federations of the future' and his 'European union' had to wait a further century. The age of the gold standard was the age of hostile protectionism, of competitive imperialism, and of irreconcilable enmity between France and Germany. The International Gold Standard was established through the demise of free trade.[14] For political reasons Prussia excluded Austria from the *Zollverein* in 1866, and Franco-German relations prevented any free trade between these two countries after 1870. The protectionist party in France weakened the Commercial Treaty with Great Britain in 1872–4 until it was repealed in 1882. Even Italy adopted a protectionist tariff against French goods in 1887, after the former had joined Germany and Austria in the Triple Alliance. France replied by waging a financial war, selling enormous amounts of Italian public debt in the European markets, denying credit, and reducing imports from Italy by more than 70 per cent.[15] The European free trade zone, established in the 1860s, was shattered by the rise of nationalism with the creation of an uneasy armed peace.[16] Protectionist interests were strengthened by the need of governments for the income produced by high commercial duties. The programme of monetary union could instead have contributed to the extension of peace and cooperation through intense economic relations, as Parieu and Lavelaye wanted.

[13] Panic. In line with Bloomfield, Panic denies that the traditional view of the classical gold standard is confirmed by historical research. To him the real pillars of the gold standard were very intense international movements of capital, an unparalleled level of international migration, and a differentiation of trade policies according to the level of economic development achieved.

[14] Cunningham (1904: 85–92).   [15] Poidevin (1970: 82–94).

[16] 'Changing economic conditions in the 1870s and the successive waves of protectionism finally drove industry over to advocating the use of money as a protectionist device through the instrument of devaluation' (Hefeker 1995: 523).

Postscript

The elements of similarity between the projects of monetary unification in the 1860s and in the 1990s are not the least interesting aspect of this study. Historians never stop reminding their readers that history does not repeat itself with identical conditions and does not provide a recipe for future policies. But history does sometime describe similar episodes whose distinctive characters and differences can be fruitfully studied.

Even if it is often true that the only thing we learn from history is that we have forgotten its lessons, in this specific case past experiences do not seem to have been wasted. The institutional structure of today's European Monetary Union (EMU) closes many of the gaps left by the LMU. A repetition of the problems of excessive monetary issue encountered with Italy, the Pontifical States, Greece or Belgium is not possible anymore. A European Central Bank has been created to prevent the monetization of national budget deficits and free-riding behaviour. Rules have been carefully discussed and specific goals and related powers have been decided upon. There seems to be no source of monetary creation left to national governments outside the control of monetary authorities. A much more substantial threat to monetary stability is now represented by the capacity of financial systems to create alternative monetary instruments. Furthermore, the convergence process associated with the Maastricht criteria has contributed decisively to the restoration of fiscal balances in many countries, eliminating one of the main reasons to manipulate common monetary rules in order to obtain seignorage. Today, the amount of information available, together with continuous multilateral monitoring, eliminates any possible chance of tricks similar to those performed by the Pontifical State between 1866 and 1870.

It is clear that no monetary union can last for long if a member country is able to unload a consistent part of its internal imbalances on its neighbours through the monetary channel, as was the case at the beginning of the LMU. At the same time it is also clear that the different economic conditions of the participants require some form of transfers and implicit cross-subsidies, either through monetary creation or through the effects of the common interest rate. If such transfers are measured with excessive zeal and the strongest members complain of all advantages obtained by the weakest, union becomes even more difficult. A delicate equilibrium has to be achieved between economic and financial convergence and a necessary solidarity between monetary allies. This kind of balance, however, is the typical outcome of political mediation and it is difficult to imagine how central bankers could avoid dealing with political authorities on those matters.

Since the 1860s the monetary system has moved from a commodity-based system to a fiduciary one, increasing the variability of exchange rates, inflation, and the margins of discretionality of monetary policy. These changes make comparisons between the technical aspects of money in these two periods very difficult and often not relevant.[1] Through these changes, however, money remains one of the most political of all economic variables. Today, political instability can sink a good currency, just as inconvertibility could create a foreign exchange crisis in the nineteenth century. Foreign and domestic policies are still conducted with the support of monetary instruments and monetary unification is one of those instruments. It is incorrect to refer to the era of metallic money as an example of separation between money and politics, since politics always intervened to mediate the conflicts of interests which necessarily arise when choices of monetary policy take place. It is therefore misleading to ask politics to step aside completely from monetary policy, as is implied by some of the twentieth-century literature on monetary unification.

The creation of the European single currency in the 1990s is not the victory of the concept of depolitization of money. It is in fact the victory of Parieu's political project, after more than a century. It reflects the constant French preoccupation about its loss of hegemony over Continental Europe and the necessity to find a permanent settlement of its old conflict with Germany. German political unification, its demographic and economic growth were shifting the balance of power against France in 1870 as well as in 1990. In the 1990s, as in the 1860s, the French government has been the strongest supporter of monetary unification in Europe, despite the existence of internal dissent. France was faced by a historical choice: to associate with Germany on an equal footing, accept either political and economic subordination, or to face recurrent wars of containment. In the 1860s only few politicians like Parieu perceived clearly the alternative between war and federalism. Parieu rushed forward the project of monetary unification, trying to combine it with the tendency of Napoleon III to accept the completion of the process of German unification. Napoleon, however, did not follow a firm course of action and, under pressure from the right wing of Bonapartism, ended up accepting the war prepared by Bismarck and by French imperialists. After three Franco-German 'bloody wars' in seventy-five years, the project of a united Europe took off in the 1950s, but without placing monetary union at the centre of the construction of Europe. In 1990, faced by the second German unification, Mitterrand reacted as Parieu would have wanted Napoleon to react in 1870, accepting a stronger Germany but attempting to neutralize further sources of conflict within a European federation, trying to disarm nationalism in its economic basis. Initially worried by German unification, Mitterrand announced in 1990 to the French Council of Ministers 'the return of Bismack's Germany' but rapidly moved together with the Italian government to

---

[1] To give just one example, today's fear that becoming a member of EMU with the wrong exchange rate could damage the long-term competitivity of a member State could not exist at the time of the LMU. In 1865 it would have made no sense to enquire into the appropriate level of the exchange rate between France and Italy, since both countries had a currency whose value depended on the gold or silver weight of its national coins. As long as banknotes were freely convertible into coins, the par of the exchange rate between franc and lira depended exclusively on relative metallic weight.

convince Kohl to begin immediately a process of monetary union.[2] After some initial resistance Kohl accepted and finally adopted the French point of view, even declaring in 1995 to the Bundestag that 'we need the Union, it is a question of war or peace for Europe.'[3]

Superimposing the map of the countries participating in these two episodes of European monetary unification, it is impossible to avoid noticing how persistent national policies are, especially in what concerns the countries of the LMU and Great Britain. Three of the founders of the LMU, France, Italy, and Belgium, are part of the Euro, while Greece is, as in 1867, a later participant. Only Switzerland has radically altered its policy, having established since the nineteenth century the most stable European currency. Most of the other participants in the Euro were either members or candidates to enter the LMU (the candidates were Austria in 1867, Spain in 1868, Luxembourg in 1869, and Finland in 1878). Even the candidacy of eastern European countries follows the patterns of the LMU, from the Romanian application of 1868 to the adoption of the LMU standard in Poland in 1926. On the northern borders of Europe, Britain, Norway, and Denmark have confirmed in 1998 their decision to reject monetary union as in the previous century. Germany, the Netherlands, Portugal, and Ireland are countries which decided to modify their position in favour of union, while Sweden has temporarily decided to remain out, contrary to its decision of 1868. The evolution of the German position is of the highest importance. Just as Bismarck's decision in favour of monetary unification would have permitted a European common currency in 1870, in the 1990s it was Kohl's choice in favour of Europe which created the political consensus needed to achieve EMU. While the second German unification could have boosted German nationalism, Kohl opted to proceed towards a European federation. He recognized the complete destruction of the political credibility of nationalism in Germany, sanctioned by the history of the twentieth century.

Britain is still characterized by a schizophrenic split between a form of popular conservatism opposed to Europe in all its manifestations, including monetary unification, and a more cautious and realistic support for Europe, often dictated by the fear of isolation and the need to be integrated in larger currents of trade and ideas. The words used by Lowe in 1869, 'the question of international coinage cannot be disregarded by this country . . . it will be impossible for Great Britain to stand aloof'[4] are strikingly similar to those of Kenneth Clarke, Gordon Brown or Robin Cook in the 1990s. In the words of the Labour Foreign Secretary 'if monetary union proved to be successful it could be difficult and unwise to stay out of it for long.'[5] As in 1869 however, part of the British popular press rises up in arms against any manifestation of sympathy for the common currency. The tabloids continuously denounce a federalist conspiracy, as if the process of European unification, of which EMU is an important

---

[2] Valance (1996: 384–91).   [3] Ibid. 410.

[4] Confidential report for the Cabinet, 'Necessity for imposing a Charge upon the Coinage of Gold Bullion at the Royal Mint', 2 June 1869 (Gladstone Papers, Official Papers, Apr.–July 1869, coll. 44610, fol. 83).

[5] *The Times*, 30 March 1998, 1, 'Britain cannot ignore thriving Euro, says Cook', by P. Webster.

part, was not the official goal of European policy at least since the Schuman declaration in 1950.[6]

The position of European national bankers today has some common features with that of their predecessors of the nineteenth century. The old conflict between the public duties of the national banks and the interests of their private shareholders has progressively been solved with the withdrawal of the latter and the development of central banking theory and practice. Nevertheless many important public central banks have resisted EMU as their predecessors did with LMU. In Germany the Governors of the Bundesbank, Karl Otto Pöhl, Helmut Schlesinger, and Hans Tietmeyer, have all tried throughout to prevent, delay or restrict participation to the EMU to a smaller number of countries. Pöhl declared in 1991 'Why create a common currency? There is already one: it is the Deutschmark.'[7] In Great Britain 'the most detailed economic case against joining the single currency has been made, perhaps surprisingly, by Eddie George, Governor of the Bank of England ... His growing concern about EMU centres on the loss of exchange rate adjustments as a mean of economic adjustment.'[8] The former Italian Prime Minister Romano Prodi declared in November 1998 that if it had been for the Governor of the Bank of Italy, Antonio Fazio, Italy would not have participated to the single currency. This position was not shared by all central bankers as was the case with the self-declared Euro-enthusiast Carlo Azeglio Ciampi in Italy or the Governor of the Bank of France, Jean-Claude Trichet. A cynical explanation of the less than enthusiastic opinion of many national central bankers would emphasize that the institutions they lead have lost a large part of their role and of their influence with the creation of a European central bank. However, this would not be sufficient to explain their objections. Their worries centre on the loss of control over internal monetary policy, the fear of less disciplined neighbours but also depend on the impact of a centralized single interest rate on desynchronised local economic cycles. Political advantages deriving from monetary union could be seen to be stronger than economic ones and the point of view of central banker is necessarily focused on the economic aspect of the issue. Discussing about the advantages and the drawbacks of the Euro, Eddie George stated that 'I recognize at the outset that the EU is, fundamentally, about politics, inspired by the need to ensure that Europe is never again devastated by war', but added 'My interest is in the economic dimension of Europe.'[9] The intrinsic nature

---

[6] By defending an inflated and outdated notion of national sovereignty, the British popular press has achieved in the last decades the very opposite result. It has contributed to establish the policy of the British government which, in the last fifty years, has resisted every major European innovation. The British opposition has usually been unsuccessful, overestimating British influence over Continental Europe. The UK has then decided to stand aside for a time, hoping that the whole initiative would fail on its own. At a later date, once the other Europeans had decided the new policies and set the rules without and despite the UK, then Britain would be forced to join by economic and political realities. (Olivi, 1998: 66–71 for the earliest manifestation of this policy). See also H. Young, *This Blessed Plot, Britain and Europe from Churchill to Blair*, 1998, London: MacMillan.   [7] Milesi (1998: 23).

[8] 'Should Britain join the single currency?', *Independent*, 21 Oct. (1996), 8.

[9] E. George, *Speech at the Financial Times Euro-Mediterranean Capital Markets Conference*, 26 March 1998, http://www.bankofengland.co.uk/speech17.htm, p. 1

of money as a combination of political and technical issues will never permit to attribute an exclusive competence either to central bankers or to politicians.

On European monetary unification as in any other area of policy, geographic position, economic situation, and political realities continue to pose similar dilemmas in ever-changing forms. The radically different policy adopted by Germany in 1991 as opposed to 1870 is a sign that, after several centuries of wars, different answers have finally been given.

Appendix: The Effect of Monetary Unification and the Metallic Standards on Exchange Rate Fluctuation

When the exchange is higher than the gold parity (upper part of Graph A.1) then the exchange is 'favourable to England', the pound is at premium, and the franc is at a discount. When the exchange is lower than the par, then it is 'favourable to France' and the franc is at a premium (lower part of Graph A.2). Until the early 1850s the exchange fluctuated moderately (2–3 per cent away from the par), but was always favourable to Britain. After 1850 the margin of fluctuation was reduced to around 1 per cent and the exchange was rather more favourable to France. Feer-Herzog expected the margin to narrow further with the fall of transportation costs. It is possible to evaluate the pure benefits of a monetary union in terms of exchange rate fluctuation separated from the effects of a common metallic standard looking at the Paris exchange rates in the age of the classical standards (Graph A.2). The two countries of the sample which were still part of the LMU between 1890 and 1914, Belgium and Switzerland, displayed a very stable exchange rate (yearly averages varied less than 0.65 per cent around the parity, over a quarter of a century). The German mark and the Dutch gulder exhibited a slightly higher variability, but the pound, not in the LMU, proved slightly steadier than the Belgian and Swiss francs. At the same time, in periods of inconvertibility, the Italian lira lost up to 10 per cent of its value on the par with the franc and the Greek drachma up to 80 per cent despite their membership of the LMU. In order to achieve stable exchange rates, participation in a monetary union was less important than geo-

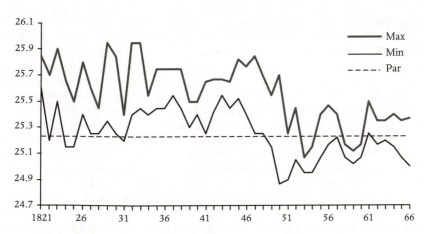

Graph A.1 *Margins of fluctuation of the Franco-British exchange rate (1821–66). Maximal and minima of three days' bills of exchange over Paris acquired in London*

Source: Ministère des Finances, *Procès verbaux et rapport de la commission monétaire, suivis d'annexes ralatifs à la question monétaire*, 148. Figures compiled by Clément Juglar. The par is the gold parity of the exchange, 25.22 francs per £.

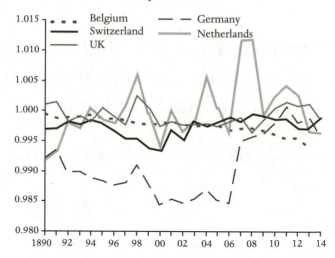

Graph A.2 *Variability of the exchange rates with France during the classical gold standard in Paris*

Sources: Ministère du Travail, *Annuaire statistique* (1919: XXXV, 291). Yearly averages of rates in Paris, normalized according to the gold par with the French franc, on three months' bills until 1907 and on bills at sight after 1907.

graphical proximity and strict respect of banknote convertibility in gold or in a bimetallic coinage.

To show how much of the reduction in exchange rate volatility depended on the harmonization of the metallic types adopted by Britain and France, Graph A.3 has been traced to compare it to the evolution of the gold/silver market ratio over the long term. The fluctuation of the exchange rate was contained within the boundaries of the fluctuation of the gold/silver market ratio. Two cases were possible. The first was when the market ratio of silver was higher than the official French Mint price (1 to 15.5, indicated by 'par' in the graph). Then silver was depreciated and, because of Gresham's law, the French monetary circulation was mainly composed of silver. French depreciated silver would therefore be at a discount compared to the British gold currency and the exchange would be favourable to Britain. This was the situation between the resumption of convertibility in gold of the banknotes of the Bank of England in 1821 and the great inflow of gold of 1848 which depressed the price of gold. When the market ratio of silver was lower than 15.5, gold was the depreciated metal which gradually came to represent the bulk of French monetary circulation. The two countries would then have the same metallic currency and the exchange would fluctuate around the par, according to the balance of trade and the movements of capital influenced by interest rates, but within the gold points (less than 1 per cent). The fluctuation of the exchange would not depend any more on the gold/silver ratio; as long as the latter was under 15.5, it would operate as if it was under a gold standard. The situation of the French exchange rate with silver monometallist countries like the German States, Austria, the Netherlands, and Scandinavia was the symmetrical opposite of that with gold monometallist Britain. When French transactions were conducted in gold, the exchange with silver currencies would tend to fluctuate more. Consequently the most consistent supporters of monetary union advocated a formal introduction of the gold standard in France and in the rest of Europe because it was the only way to have steady rates with all the other European countries at

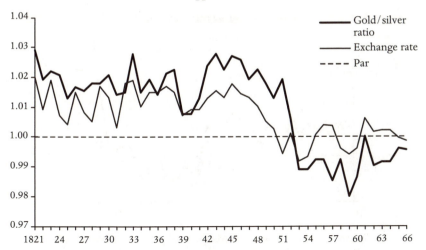

Graph A.3 *The influence of bimetallism on Franco-British exchange rates*

Note: Fluctuation of the gold/silver market ratio around the mint parity of 1/15.5, and of the exchange rate around the gold parity of 25.22 francs, in Paris, both expressed in per cent.

Source: The series of yearly exchange rates is an average of min and max of the year. Ministère des Finances, *Procès verbaux et rapport de la commission monétaire, suivis d'annèxe relatifs à la question monétaire*, 148; Flandreau (1995b: 31).

the same time. If France maintained a strict bimetallism, the Franco-British exchange rate would return to much higher fluctuations as soon as the price of gold returned over 15.5 and silver returned in France, effectively cancelling most of the advantages of monetary unification. The reduction in exchange fluctuation due to the adoption of the gold standard in France was much higher than the reduction due to monetary union. Adopting a modern point of view one could say that bimetallists insisted on internal price stability but accepted a higher exchange rate instability while gold monometallists were more interested in exchange rate stability, expecting internal price flexibility to adjust foreign trade imbalances.[1]

Graph A.4 gives the *ex-post* view of what happened after bimetallism was destabilized in 1873 by the limitation of silver issues by France and Belgium and by the adoption of the gold standard in Germany and the USA.[2]

[1] A counterfactual proof of the bimetallist theory was that between 1848 and 1866, when gold coinage flowed in large quantities in Europe, its effect on prices was moderate, being partially compensated by the contemporary disappearance of silver coinage, thanks to the bimetallic mechanism (and by higher economic growth). The fluctuation of prices of the following period was much more substantial and price deflation accompanied the formal introduction of the gold standard in most European countries after 1873, when silver was demonetised and gold supply proved inadequate (see De Cecco 1984: 41).

[2] The victory of gold over silver after several millenniums of effective bimetallism was in part due also to governments tired of shifting from one metal to the other. This frequent shift had happened often in European history, but each time it had been accompanied by some debasement which made the recoinage highly profitable for governments. In the nineteenth century such profit had become impossible to reap, because elective Parliaments watched aggressively the stability of the currency. Some form of political assembly existed in every major European State and the representatives of the commercial and industrial classes always possessed enough strength to prevent an inflation tax. Governments were then forced to bear the full cost of the each change of metal, while the benefits accrued to the private sector (bankers and bullion dealers).

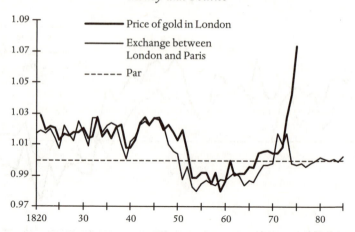

Graph A.4 *The exchange rate with France in relation to the price of gold in terms of silver (London prices, normalized per cent variation, 1820 – 85)*

Sources: The price of gold in terms of silver, in London, is in Flandreau (1995b: 34); Conférence monétaire internationale (1892: 147). The graph was traced by the delegate of British India to the International Monetary Conference of 1892, Sir Guilford L. Molesworth.

The relation between the exchange rate and the gold/silver market price was broken, stabilizing the former, as the monometallists wished, and destabilizing the latter, as the bimetallists feared. Both were somehow right but the impact of a lower exchange instability between gold monometallist countries was much smaller than the instability created between those countries and the rest of the world. The reduction of the former from less than 3 per cent to 0.5–1.5 per cent has to be compared with the much larger fall in the value of silver which still regulated the exchange with Latin America, India, Austria-Hungary, and other countries on silver or bimetallic standards. By 1874 silver was losing 4 per cent of its value compared to 1867, by 1878 13.5 per cent, by 1885 20 per cent, and by 1900 53.5 per cent. Furthermore the downwards pressure on prices proved very substantial in the following years, with a reduction of a composite index of prices up to 40 per cent by 1894. However, the monetary factor was certainly not the only element causing the fall in prices; the second Industrial Revolution taking place in the last quarter of the century and growing competition were important factors as well.[3]

[3] De Cecco (1984: 40–1).

List of Maps

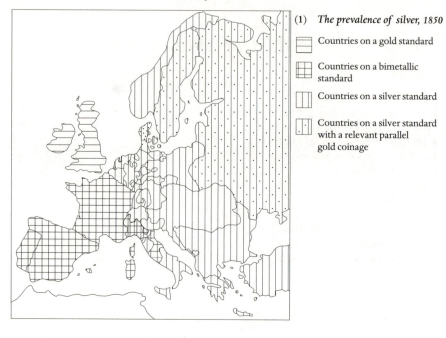

(1) *The prevalence of silver, 1850*

Countries on a gold standard

Countries on a bimetallic standard

Countries on a silver standard

Countries on a silver standard with a relevant parallel gold coinage

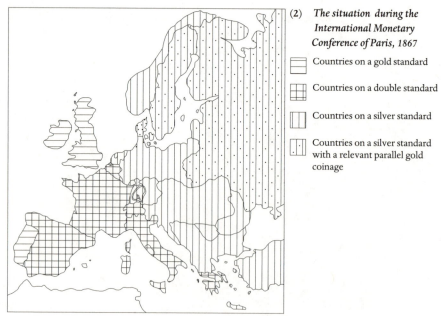

(2) *The situation during the International Monetary Conference of Paris, 1867*

Countries on a gold standard

Countries on a double standard

Countries on a silver standard

Countries on a silver standard with a relevant parallel gold coinage

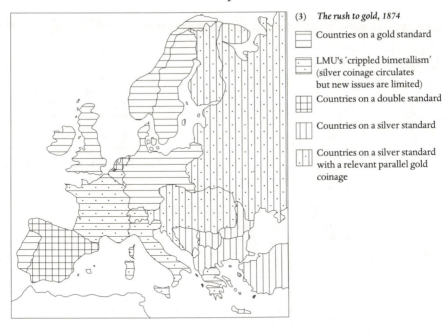

(3) *The rush to gold, 1874*

Countries on a gold standard

LMU's 'crippled bimetallism' (silver coinage circulates but new issues are limited)

Countries on a double standard

Countries on a silver standard

Countries on a silver standard with a relevant parallel gold coinage

(4) *The imperial franc of Napoleon I, 1812*

Territories of the French Empire using the franc

Territories of allied States where the franc-lira had been introduced (effective in Kingdom of Italy, limited in the Kingdom of Naples and in Westphalia, only symbolic in Baden and in Switzerland)

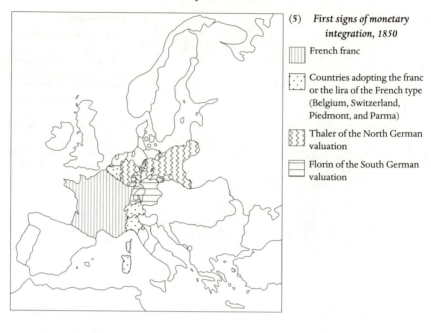

(5) *First signs of monetary*
     integration, 1850

☐ French franc

☐ Countries adopting the franc
  or the lira of the French type
  (Belgium, Switzerland,
  Piedmont, and Parma)

☐ Thaler of the North German
  valuation

☐ Florin of the South German
  valuation

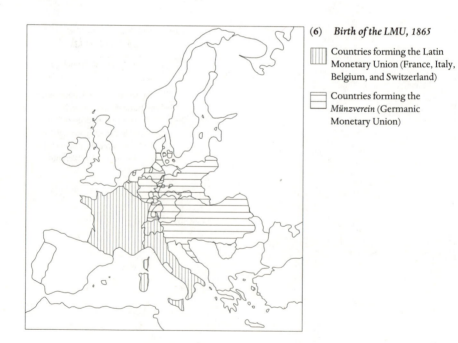

(6) *Birth of the LMU, 1865*

☐ Countries forming the Latin
  Monetary Union (France, Italy,
  Belgium, and Switzerland)

☐ Countries forming the
  Münzverein (Germanic
  Monetary Union)

(7) *Monetary unions as seen by* The Times *in 1866*

⬚ Latin Monetary Union + Spain

⬚ North German Monetary Union

⬚ Monetary union of Austria and south Germans

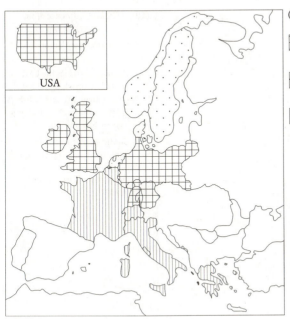

(8) *Bagehot's proposal in 1869*

⬚ Anglo-American (Teutonic) Monetary Union

⬚ States likely to adopt soon Teutonic coinage

⬚ Latin Monetary Union

(9) *Feer-Herzog's expectations in 1869*

▥ Continental European Monetary Union

▦ Likely members of the Continental European Union

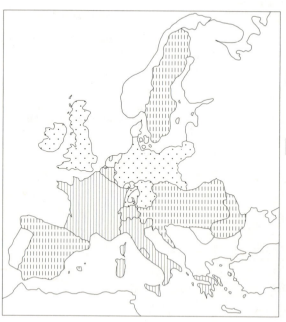

(10) *Highest influence of the LMU, 1869*

▥ Latin Monetary Union (LMU)

▦ Candidates to join the LMU or States having adopted LMU gold coinage (Austria-Hungary, Spain, Romania, Sweden, and Rep. of San Marino)

▦ Countries discussing the opportunity of implementing the monetary system of the international conference of 1867

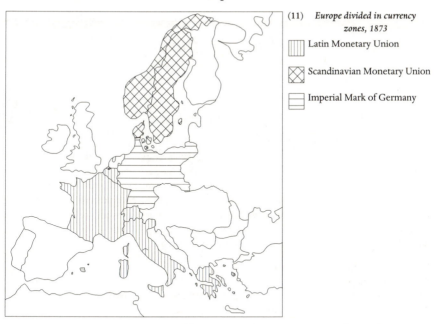

(11)   *Europe divided in currency zones, 1873*

Latin Monetary Union

Scandinavian Monetary Union

Imperial Mark of Germany

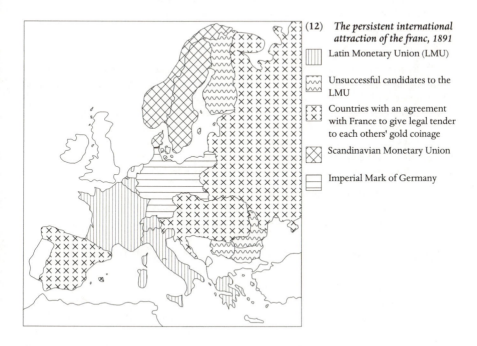

(12)   *The persistent international attraction of the franc, 1891*

Latin Monetary Union (LMU)

Unsuccessful candidates to the LMU

Countries with an agreement with France to give legal tender to each others' gold coinage

Scandinavian Monetary Union

Imperial Mark of Germany

Bibliography

Archival Resources

Archives du Ministère des Affaires Étrangères (AMAE), Paris

These archives contain ninety-five boxes regrouping the correspondence with all the Ministries, embassies, consular offices, foreign governments, and individuals concerning the LMU and the 'Universal' coinage. The original drafts of the outgoing letters are kept together with the replies, with comments by the Quai d'Orsay. The series is 'Sous-direction commerciale, affaires diverses antérieures à 1902'. Each box contains several *dossiers*. The most interesting boxes are ADC 600 to 624, but ADC 530 to 599 contain some additional material, at times mixed with other subjects. The most important boxes used for this research are:

ADC 530 'Monetary negotiations with Austria'
ADC 582 'Relations of Romania and Serbia with the LMU'
ADC 600 'Monetary conference establishing the LMU, Nov.–Dec. 1865'
ADC 600 bis 'Correspondence on mon. unif. 1 July 1867 to 31 Dec. 1867'
ADC 601 'Accession to the LMU of Greece and the Pontifical State. Italian role'
ADC 602 'Demands of accession to the LMU by Venezuela, Spain, Colombia, and St Marino'
ADC 603 and 604 'Correspondence on mon. unif. 1865–9'
ADC 616 'Correspondence on mon. unif. 1869–74'

Archives de la Banque de France (ABdF), Paris

The collection 'La Question Monétaire' is composed of sixteen volumes for a total of approximately 12,000 pages. It covers the process of monetary unification between 1865 and 1885. It includes all official reports, minutes of international conferences, bilateral or multilateral, handwritten copies and originals of correspondence between the Bank, the Treasury, the Foreign Affairs Ministry, and foreign States, internal correspondence and enquiries of the Bank of France, and systematic newspapers clippings. In comparison with the archives of the Ministry of Foreign Affairs this collection is more complete on the economic and journalistic side of the question, but does not include most of the diplomatic correspondence.

ABdF: *Question Monétaire* 1: coll. 6112 DC 98, to 16: coll. 6127 DC 113.
ABdF: Banque de France, *Délibérations du Conseil Général de la Banque de France*, 43–7, *Procès verbaux et index des procès verbaux* 1865–71.
ABdF: Dossier of Governor Rouland (not classified)
ABdF: numismatic collections, including LMU coins and proofs of the 'universal' 25-franc coins.

Archives Nationales de France (AN), Paris

The AN preserve the papers of Napoleon III and of his chief minister Rouher. The 'papiers secrets du second Empire' are the papers of the cabinet of Napoleon III, seized by the crowd which invaded the Tuileries on 4 September 1870, when the Empire fell after Sedan. The papers were classified and partially published by a special commission set up by the Government of National Defence. They clarify aspects of Napoleonic foreign policy. The papers of Rouher were seized in 1870 by the Prussians and were returned to France thanks to a specific clause of the treaty of Versailles (1919).

AN, Archives privées Rouher, 45AP, carton 20, Dossier finances et impôts: 'Emprunts d'État'. 'Constitution et organisation financière des États Allemands Hanovre, Saxe-Weimar, Brême, etc.' 45 AP, carton 20, dossier 2, 'Conférence monétaire'.

AN Gouvernement de la Défense Nationale, Commission des papiers, AB XIX, Cartons 173 à 176. Dossiers with correspondence on and from German States.

Archives de la Monnaie de Paris, Paris (AMdP), Paris

The series K regroups two boxes (K2 and K3) divided into several fascicles of correspondence between the mint and the Treasury and copies of many letters between various Ministries, governments, and individuals including Parieu, Wallenberg, and Magne. Each fascicle is organized on a chronological basis and has no specific title. The fascicles used are: K2.15 to 17, K2.19 to 23, K2.27, K2.29, K2.31, K2.35 to 36, K3.38, K3.40 and K3.43.

A detailed listing of the contents of each fascicle is included in the article published by the archivist of the Monnaie, Jean Marie Darnis, 'L'Union Monétaire Latine (1865–1925)', *Histoire économique et financière, Etudes et documents*, vi, 1994.

Archives du Conseil d'État (ACdE), Paris

Most of the archives of the Council of State and of the Ministry of Finance were burned during the last days of the Commune of Paris in 1871. The only useful documents left are the personal 'dossiers de fonction' for the Councillors of State F. E. de Parieu, M. Chevalier, and V. de Lavenay (the files are ordered alphabetically and need no specific reference).

Gladstone Papers in the British Library (GPBL), London

The Gladstone papers include the correspondence with R. Lowe, M. Chevalier, and G. Cardwell on the alteration of the pound. They also include the reports on the pound prepared for Lowe by his various advisers and Lowe's plans to nationalize and extend the British paper currency after 1870.

Correspondence Gladstone–Michel Chevalier, coll. 44127, (1) fol. 1. Chevalier to Gladstone, 1859, (2) fol. 8, Chevalier to Gladstone, 14 July 1860.

Correspondence Gladstone–Robert Lowe, coll. 44301, (1) fol. 35–6, Gladstone to Lowe, 26 Dec. 1868, (2) fol. 63–4, Lowe to Gladstone, 6 Aug. 1869. (3) fol. 85 bis, Lowe to Gladstone, 11 Oct. 1869, (4) fol. 152, Lowe to Gladstone, 3 Sept. 1870.

Correspondence Gladstone–Cardwell, vol. 44119, fol. 66, Cardwell to Gladstone, 19 Sept. 1869

Letter Book, coll. 44537, (1) fol. 66, Gladstone to Cardwell, 20 Sept. 1869 (2) fol. 92, Gladstone to Lowe, 12 Oct. 1869.

Official papers, Apr.–July 1869, coll. 44610, (1) fol. 83. Confidential report for the Cabinet, 2 June 1869, 'Necessity for imposing a Charge upon the Coinage of Gold Bullion at the Royal Mint' (2) fol. 85, 'Memorandum on the Mintage necessary to cover the expenses of Establishing and Maintaining the Gold Currency.'

Official Papers, Aug.–Nov. 1869, coll. 44611, (1) fol. 54, Report printed for the Cabinet, 'Mr Lowe to Mr Cardwell', dated 7 Sept. 1869, printed 13 Sept. 1869. (2) fol. 146, J. T. Smith, *Remarks on the Currency*, signed 12 Nov. 1869, printed 26 Nov. 1869,

Archives of the Bank of England (ABoE), London

The archives contain some references to Lowe's plans on currency but mainly on the paper currency reform. The minutes of the Court of Directors are not very detailed. The privately printed collection of letters and tracts on the debate about unification in 1869 is in the Library of the Bank. Some information is in the Minutes of the Committee of Treasury, G8-40 to B8-42. The opinion of the Bank on monetary reforms is in:

Secretary Letter Book, G3-64, vol. 17, p. 44, 19 July 1872, 'The Governor of the Bank G. Lyall and deputy Governor B. B. Greene, to the Chancellor of the Exchequer R. Lowe.'

Bank of England, *Speeches, Letters, Articles, etc. on the Gold Coinage Controversy of 1869*, London, 1870.

Archivio Storico Diplomatico (ASD), Italian Ministry of Foreign Affairs, Rome

The Italian archives are not comparable to the French ones for quantity or interest of the material. Some correspondence with the Italian Ministry of Finance is useful, but largely occasional.

Political section, outgoing letters, Moscati VI–1143.

Political section, notes of the Italian Finance Ministry to the Foreign Affairs Ministry, Moscati VI–644 to 646

Archivio Storico della Banca d'Italia (ASBI), Rome

The Bank of Italy has inherited few archives from the National Bank in the Kingdom of Italy. The papers of its general director Bombrini were privately held and perished by fire in Genoa during the Second World War. An inquiry into the opportunity for Italy of adopting the gold stardard has been preserved, together with the bimetallist statements of Bombrini in 1881. A larger amount of documentation exists on the dissolution of the LMU in the 1920s.

Segretariato, Pratiche, n. 467, fasc. 3: contains a substantial correspondence on the dissolution of the LMU in the 1920s.

Segretariato, Pratiche, n. 612, fasc. 2: Enquiry done by the National Bank in the Kingdom of Italy into the monetary question. Various documents on the LMU and bilateral monetary agreements.

Direttorio, Stringher, pratiche, n. 33, fasc. 4 and 12: Dissolution of the LMU.

Direttorio, Grillo, pratiche, n. 3, fasc. 1. Agreement between the Italian government and the National Bank for the mintage of silver ecus.

French Official Publications

Annales du Sénat et du Corps Législatif (1862–70) (Paris).

Commission chargée d'examiner la question des monnaies divisionnaires d'argent, *Rapport à S.E. M. le Ministre des Finances* (Paris, 1862).

Conseil Supérieur du commerce, de l'agriculture et de l'industrie (1872), *Enquête sur la question monétaire*, 2 vols. (Paris).

Exposition Universelle de 1867 (1867), Comité des poids et mesures et des monnaie, *Rapport concernant l'uniformité des poids* (Paris).

Ministère des Affaires Étrangères (1865), *Conférence monétaire entre la Belgique, la France, l'Italie et la Suisse, Procès verbaux, Novembre et Décembre 1865* (Paris).

—— (1867*a*), *Documents diplomatiques*, VIII (Paris).

—— (1867*b*), *Conférence monétaire internationale. Procès-verbaux* (Paris).

—— (1867*c*), *Négociations monétaires entre la France et l'Autriche, commencée le 23 juillet 1867* (Paris).

Ministère des Finances (1858), *Rapport de la Commission chargée d'étudier la question monétaire* (Paris).

—— (1867), *Rapport de la commission chargée d'examiner la question de l'étalon monétaire* (Paris).

—— (1868), *Documents relatifs à la question monétaire* (Paris).

Procès-verbaux et rapport de la commission monétaire de 1867, relatifs à la question de l'étalon, 2 vols. (Paris, 1868).

Procès-verbaux et rapport de la commission monétaire de 1868, suivis d'annexes relatives à la question monétaire, 2 vols. (Paris, 1869).

British Official Publications

Decimal Coinage Commission (1859) *Final Report of the Decimal Coinage Commissioners* (London).

Minutes of Evidence of the Gold and Silver Commission (1879), (London).

Report of the Commissioners appointed to Represent Her Majesty's Government at the Monetary Conference held in Paris in August 1878 (London, 1878).

Report of the International Conference on Weights, Measures and Coins, held in Paris, June 1867; Communicated to Lord Stanley by Professor Leone Levi; and Report of the Master of the Mint and Mr River Wilson on the International Monetary Conference held in Paris June 1867 (London, 1868).

Royal Commission on International Coinage (1868), *Report, Minutes of Evidence and Appendix* (London).

Other Official Publications

Commission Nationale pour la publication de Documents Diplomatiques Suisses (1979–92), *Documents Diplomatiques Suisses, 1848–1945,* 15 vols. (Bern: Benteli Verlag).

Camera dei deputati (1874), 'Illustrazime del proyetto dilegge 93, Conveenzione monetaria addizimale a quella del 23 dicembre 1865, tra l'Italia, la Francia, il Belgio e la Suizzera, sottosoritta a Parigi il 31 gennaio 1874', *Atti Parlamentari,* 21 Feb., 2.

Conférence monétaire internationale (1892), *Procès verbaux* (Bruxelles).

International Monetary Conference (1879) (Washington).

Ministère du travail et de la prévoyance sociale (1919), *Annuaire statistique, résumé rétrospectif, pays divers,* XXXV (Paris).

Ministero degli Affari Esteri (1952–90), *I documenti diplomatici italiani 1861–70,* 1st ser., 13 vols. (Rome: Istituto poligrafico e zecca dello Stato)

Stenographische Berichte über die Verhandlungen des Deutschen Reichtages, Berlin, I Legislatur, II Session (1871).

Contemporary Literature

A Defence of the British Currency; Showing its Necessity and Utility ... By a Bath Brick. In reply to a speech made by the Chancellor of the Exchequer in the House of Commons, 6 Aug. 1869 (London, 1870).

Augspurg, M. (1868), *Zur Deutschen Münzfrage,* 4 vols. (Bremen).

Bagehot, W. (1868a), 'The alleged and the real advantages of an international coinage', *Economist* 26, 31 Oct.: 1241–2.

—— (1868b), 'The real advantage of an international measure of account', *Economist* 26, 7 Nov.: 1271–2.

Bagehot, W. (1869), *A Practical Plan to Assimilate British and American Money, as a Step towards a Universal Money* (London).

—— (1871), 'The grave demerits of the proposed new coinage for Germany', *Economist* 29, 21 Oct.: 1265–6.

Bamberger, L. (1868), 'Monsieur de Bismarck', *Revue Moderne*, 25 Feb. and 10 Mar.: 8–49 and 256–83.

—— (1872), *Zur Deutschen Münzgesetzgebung* (Berlin).

Bank of England (1870), *Speeches, Letters, Articles, etc. on the Gold Coinage Controversy of 1869* (London).

Behrens, J. (1869), Letter by B[ehrens] on Mr Lowe and the coinage, *Economist* 27, 21 Aug.: 1074–5.

Bonnet, V. (1869a) La question de l'or', *Revue des Deux-Mondes*, 80, fasc.2, 15 Mar.: 373–96.

—— (1869b), 'Le Chancelier de l'échiquier et son projet de monnaie internationale', *La Revue des Deux Mondes* 80, fasc.6, 1 Dec.: 628–49.

Cantù, C. (1867), 'Dell'unificazione monetaria', *Reale istituto lombardo di scienze e lettere*, Rendiconti delle classe di scienze matematiche e naturali, IV, fasc.3, March.

Cernuschi, H. (1866), *Contre le billet de banque* (Paris).

—— (1884), *Le grand procès de l'union latine* (Paris).

Chevalier, M. (1859), *On the Probable Fall in the Value of Gold*, 3rd edn. (Manchester).

—— (1866a), *Cours d'économie politique, iii, La monnaie*, 2nd edn., 3 vols. (Paris).

—— (1866b), 'La guerre et la crise Européenne', *Revue des Deux Mondes*, 63, 1 June: 758–85.

Chevalier, M. (1868), 'De l'établissement d'une monnaie universelle', *Journal des économistes*, 3rd ser., 12, Oct.: 178–210.

—— (1871), 'Comment une nation rétablit sa prospérité, erreurs qu'elle doit éviter', *Journal des économistes*, 3rd ser., 23, July: 5–18.

—— (1933), 'Journal', *Revue Historique*, 171, Jan.: 115–42.

Courcelle-Seneuil (1866), 'Le billet de banque n'est pas fausse monnaie', *Journal des économistes*, 3rd ser., 3, Sept.: 342–9.

—— (1868), 'Projet d'une monnaie internationale', *Journal des économistes*, 3rd ser., 10, Apr.: 76–81.

Debate on the Decimal Coinage Question in the House of Commons (1855), with Remarks [by Augustus de Morgan] *on the speech of the Hon. Member for Kidderminster* [Robert Lowe] (London).

Durif, H. M. (1868), *Félix Esquirou de Parieu, essai sur sa vie et ses ouvrages, extrait du Moniteur du Cantal* (Aurillac).

Economist, The (1866), 'On Monetary Unification Advantages', 24 (Sept.), 1078.

Fabbri, G. (1893), *Storia della Banca Nazionale* (Teramo).

Farr, W. (1870), *Report [on coinage] to the international Statistical Congress held at the Hague in 1869* (London).

Feer-Herzog, C. (1869), *L'unification monétaire internationale, ses conditions et ses perspectives* (Geneva).

—— (1870), *La France et ses alliés monétaires en présence de l'unification universelle des monnaies* (Paris).

—— (1873), *Or ou argent?* (Aarau).

Frère-Orban, H. (1874), *La question monétaire, examen du système et des effets du double étalon suivant les idées de M. Émile de Lavelaye, et réfutation des doctrines monétaires de M. Malou, ministre des finances* (Bruxelles).

Hansard Parliamentary Papers (1869–73), 3rd ser., vols. 198–215, London.

Hendriks, F. (1869): 'Four Letters on Mr Lowe and the Coinage', *Economist* 27, 9 Oct.: 1191–3, 13 Nov.: 1339, 20 Nov.: 1373, 25 Dec.: 1529.

Hendriks, F. (1874), 'France, Her Monetary Allies and the Single Gold Standard', *Economist* 32, 31 Jan.: 129–131.

'International Coinage' (1866), *Edinburgh Review*, 124, Oct.: 383–99.

Jevons, W. S. (1868), 'On the Condition of the Metallic Currency of the United Kingdom, with Reference to the Question of International Coinage', *Journal of the Statistical Society of London*, 31, Nov.: 426–64.

——(1875), *Money and the Mechanism of Exchange* (London).

——(1886), *Letters and Journal of W. S. Jevons, edited by his wife* (London).

Journal des économistes (1870), 'Chronique économique', 3rd ser., 19 (September).

Las Casas, E. (1823–4), *Mémorial de Sainte Hélène, ou Journal où se trouvent consignés, jour par jour, ce qu'a dit et fait Napoléon durant dix-huit mois*, 10 vols. (Bruxelles).

Lavelaye, E. de (1867), 'La monnaie internationale, projet de confédération monétaire', *Revue des Deux Mondes* 68, fasc.3, Apr.: 614–36.

Léon, A. (1862), *De l'uniformité des poids et mesures, et de l'établissement possible d'une monnaie universelle* (Toulouse).

Le Touzé, C. (1868a), 'De l'uniformité monétaire et de l'unité de l'étalon', *Journal des économistes*, 3rd ser., IX, Mar.: 404–20.

——(1868b), *Traité théorique et pratique du change, des arbitrages et des matières d'or et d'argent*, 2nd. edn. (Paris).

Levi, L. (1851), *International Code of Commerce in connection with the Law of Nature and Nations* (London).

Luzzati, L. (1881), 'Le controversie monetarie e l'Italia', *Nuova Antologia*, 2nd ser., LVI, fasc.6, 15 Mar.: 250–81.

——(1883), 'Delle attinenze dei biglietti di banca col bimetallismo', *Nuova Antologia*, 2nd ser., LXXII, fasc.23, 1 Dec.: 524–45.

McLaren, J. (1869), *A Brief Review of Some of the Principal Arguments for and against the Chancellor of the Exchequer's Proposal to Reduce the Quantity of Gold in the Sovereign. With Observations* (London).

Magliani, A. (1874), 'La quistione monetaria', *Nuova Antologia*, 2nd ser., XXVI, May: 190–224.

Marbeau, M. (1866), *Proposition d'une monnaie internationale* (Paris).

Menier (1873), *L'unité de l'étalon monétaire* (Paris).

Minghetti, M., and Finali, N. (1875), 'Relazione sulla circolazione cartacea, presentata dal Presidente del Consiglio, Ministro delle finanze Minghetti e dal Ministro di agricoltura, industria e commercio Finali', *Camera dei Deputati, atti parlamentari*, no. 94, Rome, 15 Mar.

Mirabeau, H. G. R. (1825), *Œuvres*, 7 vols. (Paris).

'Monetary convention between France, Belgium, Italy and Switzerland' (1866), *Economist* 24, 15 Sept.: 1077–9.

Morley, J. (1896), *The Life of Richard Cobden*, 2 vols. (London).

Mosle, N. G. (1870), *Das teutonische Münzsystem, ein Beitrag zur Lösung der deutschen Münzfrage, zunächst geschrieben für die Mitglieder des deutschen Handelstags* (Bremen, January).

'Mr Lowe on £1 notes' (1869), *Economist* 27, 3 July: 772.

Nahuys, M. (1865), *De l'établissement d'une monnaie universelle* (Utrecht).

Oliphant, G. H. H. (1855), *A Proposed System of International Decimal Coinage* (London).

Parieu, F. E. de (1856), *Histoire de impots généraux sur la propriété et le revenu*, 3 vols. (Paris).

——(1865), 'La question monétaire en France et à l'étranger', extracted from *Revue contemporaine*, 31 Dec.

——(1866a), 'Compte rendu à l'Académie des sciences morales et politiques de la brochure de M. Hendriks, sur le monnayage décimal', *Journal des économistes*, 3rd ser., II, May: 304–7.

——(1866b), 'L'union monétaire de la France, de l'Italie, de la Belgique et de la Suisse: le Münzverein latin', extracted from *Revue contemporaine*, 31 Oct.

——(1867), 'De l'uniformité monétaire', *Journal des économistes*, 3rd ser., VI, June: 321–56.

——(1868a), 'Situation de la question monétaire internationale', *Journal des économistes*, 3rd ser., X, April: 38–76.

——(1868b), 'Lettre à Mr Ruggles', *Journal des économistes*, 3rd ser., XI, Sept.: 420–3.

——(1869a), 'Les conférences monétaires internationales de 1865 et 1867 et leur résultats', *Journal des économistes*, 3rd ser., XIII, Feb.: 243–66.

——(1869b), 'Progrès récents et avenir de l'unification monétaire', *Journal des économistes*, 3rd ser., XVI, Dec.: 372–92.

——(1871), 'La question de l'unification monétaire en 1870', *Journal des économistes*, 3rd ser., XVIII, May: 147–57.

——(1872), 'La question monétaire internationale', *Journal des économistes*, 3rd ser., XXVIII, Dec.: 377–88.

——(1875a), 'La révolution monétaire par la dépréciation de l'argent', *Journal des économistes*, 3rd ser., XXXIX, Aug.: 156–72.

——(1875b), *Principes de la science politique*, 2nd edn. (Paris).

——(1876), *Discours au Sénat et interpellation adressée au Ministre des Finances* (Paris).

Poulet-Malassis, A. (ed.) (1873), *Papiers secrets et correspondance du second Empire*, 2nd edn. (Paris).

Rapet, J. (1869), 'Facilité du changement du système monétaire, ses rapports avec la consommation et avantages de la pièce de 10 francs', *Journal des économistes*, 3rd ser., XV, July: 42–57.

'Rapport de la commission sur l'étalon monétaire au ministre des finances' (1869), *Journal des économistes*, 3rd ser., XIV, Apr.: 100–29.

Review of McLaren (1869), '*A Brief Review*', *Economist*, 27: 25 Dec.: 1531.

Rossi, G. (1867), *Sulla Unità Monetaria Europea, lettera al cavalier Cesare Cantù per commento sopra gli opuscoli 'La question Monétaire en France et à l'étranger' e 'L'Union monétaire ou Münzverein Latin'* (Milan).

Russell, H. B. (1898), *International Monetary Conferences* (New York).

Sacerdoti, A. (1869), *Sulla unificazione internazionale del sistema monetario* (Padua).

Scaruffi, G. (1582), *L'Alitinonfo, per fare ragione et concordanza d'oro et d'argento, che servirà in universale, tanto per provvedere agli infiniti abusi del tosare, et guastare le monete; quanto per regolare ogni sorta di pagamenti, et ridurre anco tutto il mondo ad una sola moneta* (Reggio [Emilia]).

Schultz, C. (1869), *Die Deutsche Münzreform und der Anschluss an das Frankensystem unter Berücksichtigung der gekröntenPreisschrift von H. Grote* (Berlin).

Seyd, E. (1868a), *Bullion and Foreign Exchange Theoretically and Practically Considered; followed by a Defence of the Double Valuation, with Special Reference to the Proposed Universal System of Coinage* (London).

——(1868b), *The Question of Seignorage and Charge for Coining, and the Report of the Royal Commission on International Coinage* (London).

——(1870), On international coinage and the variations of foreign exchange during recent years', *Journal of the Statistical Society of London*, 33: Mar., 42–73.

——1874, *The Bank of England Note Issue and Its Error* (London).

Sismondi, S. de (1827), *Nouveaux principes d'economie politique*, 2nd edn. (Geneva).

Slater, R. (1868), *International Coinage Critically Considered* (London).

Società di economia politica italiana (1868), 'Se la circolazione di una moneta fittizia a corso forzato possa giovare alle industrie nazionali', *Nuova Antologia*, 2nd ser., IX, fasc.12, Dec.: 807–17.

——(1869), 'Dibattito sulla moneta internazionale', *Nuova Antologia*, 2nd ser., XI, fasc.6, June: 418–27.

Société d'économie politique (1867), 'La question monétaire, première discussion', *Journal des économistes*, 3rd ser., VI, June: 430–54.

——(1868), 'Discussion sur la question monétaire, historique du mouvement actuel, le franc d'or, 2ème discussion', *Journal des économistes*, 3rd ser., XII, Nov.: 305–19.

——(1869), 'La question monétaire, 3ème discussion', *Journal des économistes*, 3rd ser., XIII, Jan.: 142–68.

——(1870), 'Réunion du 5 septembre 1870: nature et fonction du billet de banque et du papier monnaie', *Journal des économistes*, 3rd ser., XX, Sept.: 441–50.

——(1871), 'Réunion de décembre 1871, Sur une nouvelle émission de billets de la Banque de France', *Journal des économistes*, 3rd ser., XXIV, Dec.: 470–87.

Soetbeer, A. (1869), *Denkschrift betreffend Deutsche Münzeinigung* (Berlin).

Stoney, O. J. (1871), *The Natural System of Coinage. An Appeal to the Intelligence of Germany* (Berlin).

Vaporeau, G. (1893), *Dictionnaire universel des contemporains*, 6th edn. (Paris).

Vasquez Queipo (1867), *La Cuadrupla Convencion monetaria considerate en su origen* (Madrid).

Weibezahn, H. (1871), *Mark oder Goldgulden, so wie Die Internationale Seite der Deutschen Münzreform* (Leipzig).

Wolowski, L. (1870a), *l'Or et l'Argent* (Paris).

——(1870b), 'Lettre sur l'erreur et danger du cours forcé des billets de banque', *Journal des économistes*, 3rd ser., XIX, Aug.: 281–90.

Xeller, F. (1869), *Die Frage des Internationalen Münzeinigung und der Reform des deutschen Münzwesens mit besonderer Rücksicht auf Süddeutschland. Kritish und geschlichtlich beleuchtet* (Stuttgart).

Modern Secondary Literature

Andreades, A. (1909), *History of the Bank of England, 1640–1903*, 2 vols. in one (London: King & Son).

Arnold, P., Küthmann, H., and Steinhilber, D. (1970), *Grosser Deutscher Münz Katalog von 1800 bis heute* (Munich: Ernst Battenberg Verlag).

Banque de France (1994), *Les billets de la Banque de France* (Paris: Banque de France).

Bayoumi, T., Eichengreen, B., and Taylor, M. (1996), *Modern Perspectives on the Gold Standard* (Cambridge: Cambridge University Press).

Beales, D. (1969), *From Castlereagh to Gladstone, 1815–1885* (London: Nelson).

Bloomfield, A. (1959), *Monetary Policy under the International Gold Standard* (New York: Federal Reserve Bank of New York).

Board of Governors of the Federal Reserve System (1943), *Banking and Monetary Statistics* (Washington, DC: Federal Reserve Board).

Bordo M., and Capie F. (eds.) (1993), *Monetary Regimes in Transition* (Cambridge: Cambridge University Press).

—— and Rockoff, H. (1996), 'The Gold Standard as a Good Housekeeping Seal of Approval', *Journal of Economic History*, 56: June, 389–428.

——and Schwartz, A. (eds.) (1984), *A Retrospective on the Classical Gold Standard, 1821–1931* (Chicago: University of Chicago Press).

Bourne, K. (1970), *The Foreign Policy of Victorian England* (Oxford: Clarendon Press).

Braga de Macedo, J., Eichengreen, B., and Reis, J. (eds.) (1996), *Currency Convertibility. The Gold Standard and beyond* (London: Routledge).

Brugmans, H. (1970), *L'idée Européenne, 1920–70,* 3rd edn. (Bruges: Collège d'Europe).

Burghclere, L. (1933), *A Great Lady's Friendships, Letters to Mary Marchioness of Salisbury, Countess of Derby* (London: Macmillan).

Cameron, R. (1981), *France and the Economic Development of Europe* (Princeton, NJ: Princeton University Press).

——(1967), *Banking in the Early Stages of Industrialization* (Oxford: Oxford University Press).

——(1970), (ed.) *Essays in French Economic History* (Homewood, Ill.: Irwin).

Capie, F., and Webber, A. (1985), *A Monetary History of the United Kingdom, 1870–1982,* 2 vols. (London: Allen & Unwin).

Ciocca, P., and Ulizzi, A. (1990–5), 'I tassi di cambio nominali e reali dell'Italia (1861–1979)', in *Ricerche per la storia della Banca d'Italia,* 6 vols. (Rome: Laterza), I, 341–68.

Clapham, J. (1944), *The Bank of England, a History,* 2 vols. (Cambridge: Cambridge University Press).

Crocella, C. (1983), *Augusta Miseria, Aspetti delle finanze pontificie nell'età del capitalismo* (Milan: Nuovo Istituto Editoriale Italiano).

Cunningham, W. (1904), *The Rise and Decline of the Free Trade Movement* (London: Clay).

Darnis, J. M. (1994), 'L'Union Monétaire Latine (1865–1925)', *Centre d'Histoire économique et financière, Etudes et documents,* VI: 329–59.

Davies, G. (1994), *A History of Money* (Cardiff: University of Wales Press).

De Cecco, M. (1984), *The International Gold Standard, Money and Empire,* 2nd. edn. (London: Pinter).

——(1991), *L'Italia ed il sistema finanziario internazionale 1861–1914* (Rome: Laterza).

——(1992), 'European Monetary and Financial Cooperation before the First World War', *Rivista di Storia Economica,* 3rd ser., IX, fasc-2, June: 55–76.

——and Giovannini, A. (eds.) (1989), *A European Central Bank?* (Cambridge: Cambridge University Press).

De Mattia, R. (1959), *L'unificazione monetaria italiana* (Turin: ILTE).

——(1982), 'Moneta, credito e finanza', in A.A.V.V. *1861–1887: il processo di unificazione nella realtà del paese, atti del L Congresso di Storia del Risorgimento Italiano* (Rome: Istituto di Storia del Risorgimento Italiano).

Droulers, F. (1990), *Histoire de l'Ecu européen du moyen-age à nos jours et des précédentes unions monétaires* (Lagny sur Marne: Éditions du Donjon).

Duroselle, J. B. (1965), *L'idée d'Europe dans l'histoire* (Paris: Denoel).

Edelstein, M. (1994), 'Foreign Investment and Accumulation, 1860–1914', in R. Floud and D. McCloskey (eds.), *The Economic History of Britain since 1700, 1860–1939,* 2nd edn., 3 vols. (Cambridge: Cambridge University Press).

Eichengreen, B., and Flandreau, M. (eds.) (1997), *The Gold Standard in Theory and History,* 2nd edn. (London: Routledge).

Einaudi, L. (1997), 'Monetary Unions and Free Riders: the Case of the Latin Monetary Union (1865–78)', *Rivista di Storia Economica,* new ser., fasc.3, Dec.: 327–61.

——(2000a), 'From the Franc to the "Europe": Great Britain, Germany and the attempted transformation of the Latin Monetary Union into a European Monetary Union (1865–73)', *Economic History Review,* May.

Einaudi, L. (2000*b*), '1000 years of Monetary Unions', *National Institute Economic Review*, 172: April 90–104.

Etienne, R., and Etienne, F. (1992), *The Search for Ancient Greece* (London: Gallimard).

Feavearyear, A. (1963), *The Pound Sterling, a History of English Money*, 2nd edn. (Oxford: Clarendon Press).

Felisini, D. (1990), *Le finanze pontificie e i Rothschild 1830–70* (Naples: Edizioni Scientifiche Italiane).

Flandreau, M. (1994), 'Was the Latin Monetary Union a Franc Zone?', in J. Reis (ed.), *International Monetary Systems in Historical Perspective* (London: Macmillan), 71–90.

—— (1995*a*), 'Coin memories: Estimates of the French Metallic Currency 1840–78', *Journal of European Economic History*, 24(2): fall 271–310.

—— (1995*b*), *L'or du monde, la France et la stabilité du système monétaire international 1848–73* (Paris).

—— (1995*c*), 'Monnaie commune, décentralisation et inflation; *Hujus regio, cujus pecunia*', *Revue de l'Observatoire Français des Conjonctures Économiques*, 52 (Jan).

—— (1996), 'Les règles de la pratique, la Banque de France, le marché des métaux précieux et la naissance de l'étalon or 1848–76', *Annales*, 4, (July–Aug): 849–72.

—— Le Cacheux, J., and Zumer, F. (1998), 'Stability without a Pact? Lessons from the European Gold Standard 1880–1914', *Centre for Economic Policy Research*, London, Discussion paper 1872.

Fourtens, B. (1930), *La fin de l'Union Latine* (Paris: Recueil Sirey).

Frattiani, M., and Spinelli, F. (1984), 'Italy in the Gold Standard Period, 1861–1914', in M. Bordo, and A. Schwartz (eds.), *A Retrospective on the Classical Gold Standard, 1821–1931* (Chicago: Chicago University Press), 405–51.

Friedman, M. (1990), 'Bimetallism revisited', *Journal of Economic Perspectives*, IV: 85–104.

—— (1992), *Money Mischief, Episodes in Monetary History* (New York: Harcourt Brace Jovanovich).

Gallarotti, G. (1995), *The Anatomy of a International Monetary Regime* (Oxford: Oxford University Press).

Garelli, F. (1946), *La coopération monétaire internationale depuis un siècle* (Geneva: Imprimerie populaire).

Girard, L. (1986), *Napoléon III* (Paris: Fayard).

Goodhart, C. (1988), *The Evolution of Central Banks* (Cambridge, Mass.: Massachusetts Institute of Technology).

Gorman, M. (1989), *The Unification of Germany* (Cambridge: Cambridge University Press).

Hefeker, C. (1995), 'Interest Groups, Coalitions and Monetary Integration in the XIXth Century', *Journal of European Economic History*, 24(3): winter 489–537.

Helfferich, K. (1969), *Money* (New York: Augustus M. Kelley Publishers).

Henderson, W. O. (1939), *The Zollverein* (Cambridge: Cambridge University Press).

Herre, F. (1992), *Napoleone III* (Milan: Mondadori).

Holtfrerich, C. L. (1989), 'The Monetary Unification Process in Nineteenth-Century Germany: Relevance and Lessons for Europe Today', in M. De Cecco and A. Giovannini (eds.), *A European Central Bank?* (Cambridge), 216–40.

Housman, L. (1937), *The Golden Sovereign* (London: Johnathan Cape).

James, H. (1997), 'Monetary and Fiscal Unification in Nineteenth-Century Germany: What can Kohl Learn from Bismarck?', *Essays in International Finance*, Princeton University, 202 (Mar.).

Janssen, A. E. (1911), *Les conventions monétaires* (Paris: V.ve F.Larcier).

Josset, C. R. (1962), *Money in Britain, a History of the Currency of the British Isles* (London: Frederick Warne & Co.).

Kindleberger, C. (1993), *A Financial History of Western Europe*, 2nd edn. (Oxford: Oxford University Press).

Krämer, H. (1970), 'Experience with Historical Monetary Unions', *Kieler Diskussionsbeiträge zu aktuellen wirtschaftspolitischen Fragen*, Institut für Weltwirtschaft, Kiel, June.

Krause, C., Mishler, C., and Bruce, C. (1994), *Standard Catalogue of World Coins, Nineteenth and Twentieth Century*, (Iola, Wis.: Krause Publications).

Landes, D. (1956), Vieille banque et nouvelle banque: la révolution financière du XIXe siècle', *Revue d'histoire moderne et contemporaine*, 3: 204–22.

Lazaretou, S. (1995), 'The Drachma in the Gold Standard Period', *Explorations in Economic History*, 32(1): 28–50.

Leconte, J. M. (1995), *Le bréviaire des monnaies de l'Union Latine* (Paris: Cressida).

Levy Leboyer, M. (1977), *La position internationale de la France, au XIXe et XXe siècle, aspects économiques et financiers* (Paris: Éditions de l'École des hautes études en sciences sociales).

——and Bourguignon, F. (1990), *The French Economy in the Nineteenth Century* (Cambridge: Cambridge University Press).

MacAlister, E. (ed.) (1916), *Chapters from My Official Life, by Sir C. Rivers Wilson* (London: Edward Arnold).

Marconcini, F. (1929), *Vicende dell'oro e dell'argento. Dalle premesse storiche alla liquidazione dell'Unione monetaria latina (1803–1925)* (Milan: Vita e Pensiero).

Massoulié, F., Gantelet, G., and Genton, D. (1997), *La costruzione dell'Europa* (Florence: Giunti-Casterman).

Matthew, H. G. C., and Foot, M. R. D. (eds.) (1968–94), *The Gladstone Diaries*, 14 vols. (Oxford: Oxford University Press).

Mertens, J. (1944), *La naissance et le développement de l'étalon-or, 1696–1922* (Louvain: E.Warny).

Milesi, G. (1998), *Le Roman de l'Euro* (Paris: Hachette).

Mill, J. S. (1963–86), *Collected works of John Stuart Mill,* ed. by M. J. Robinson, 33 vols. (London: Routledge).

Minghetti, M. (1978), *Copialettere 1873–1876*, 2 vols. (Rome: Istituto per la Storia del Risorgimento Italiano).

Ministère du travail et de la prévoyance sociale (1919), *Annuaire statistique, statistique générale de la France, résumé rétrospectif* (Paris: Imprimerie Nationale), vol. 35.

O'Brien, D. P. (ed.) (1971), *The Correspondence of Lord Overstone*, 3 vols. (Cambridge: Cambridge University Press).

Olivi, B. (1998), *L'Europe difficile, Histoire politique de la Communauté européenne* (Paris: Gallimard).

Ollivier, E. (1917), *Philosophie d'une guerre* (Paris: Flammarion).

Oppers, S. (1945), 'Recent Developments in Bimetallic Theory', in J. Reis, (ed.) *International Monetary Systems in Historical Perspective* (London: Macmillan), 47–70.

Palmade, G. (1972), *French Capitalism in the Nineteenth Century* (Newton Abbot: David & Charles).

Panic, M. (1992), *European Monetary Union, Lessons from the Classical Gold Standard* (London: Macmillan).

Perlman, M. (1993), 'In Search of Monetary Union', *Journal of European Economic History*, 22(2): Fall, 313–32.

Pflanze, O. (1990), *Bismarck and the Development of Germany*, 3 vols. (Princeton: Princeton University Press).

Pinchera, S. (1957a), 'Monete e zecche dello Stato Pontificio dalla Restaurazione al 1870', *Archivio Economico dell'Unificazione Italiana*, I, fasc.5' Rome.

Pinchera, S. (1957b), 'Corso dei cambi sulla piazza di Romadal 1838 al 1870', *Archivio Economico dell' Unificazione Itàlianà*, VI, fasc.3, Rome.

Plessis, A. (1984), *Régents et gouverneurs de la Banque de France sous le second empire* (Geneva: Droz).

—— (1985a), *The Rise and Fall of the Second Empire, 1852–71* (Cambridge: Cambridge University Press).

—— (1985b), *La politique de la Banque de France de 1851 à 1870* (Geneva: Droz).

Poidevin, R. (1970), *Finances et relations internationales, 1887–1914* (Paris: Armand Colin).

Political Economy Club (1921), *Minutes, Proceedings, Roll of Members and Questions Discussed* (London: Political Economy Club).

Rastel, G. (1935), *Les controverses doctrinales sur le bimetallisme au 19ème siècle* (Paris: Imprimerie les presses modernes).

Redish, A. (1993), 'The Latin Monetary Union and the Emergence of the International Gold Standard', in M. Bordo and F. Capie (eds.) (1993), *Monetary Regimes in Transition* (Cambridge: Cambridge University Press), 68–85.

Reis, J. (ed.) (1995), *International Monetary Systems in Historical Perspective* (London: Macmillan).

—— (1996), 'First to join the Gold Standard [Portugal] 1854', in J. Braga de Macedo, B. Eichengreen and J. Reis, (eds.), *Currency Convertibility. The Gold Standard and Beyond* (London: Routledge), 159–81.

Renouvin, P. (1949), *L'idée de Fédération Européenne dans la Pensée Politique du XIXe Siècle* (Oxford: Oxford University Press)

Rist, M. (1970), 'A French Experiment with Free Trade: the Treaty of 1860', in R. Cameron (ed.), *Essays in French Economic History* (Homewood, Ill.: Irwin), 286–314.

Roccas, M. (1989), 'L'Italia ed il sistema monetario internazionale dagli anni 60 agli anni 90 del secolo scorso', *Temi di discussione del servizio studi della Banca d'Italia*, 92.

Romanelli, R. (1979), *L'Italia Liberale (1861–1900)* (Bologna: Il Mulino).

Sabbatucci, G., and Vidotto V. (eds.) (1994–7) *Storia d'Italia*, 5 vols. (Bari: Laterza).

St John-Stevas, N. (ed.) (1965–86), *The Collected Works of Walter Bagehot*, 15 vols. (London: Routledge).

Schnerb, R. (1949), *Rouher et le second Empire* (Paris: Armand Collin).

Schumpeter, J. A. (1934), *Business Cycles, A Theoretical, Historical and Statistical Analysis of the Capitalist Process* (Cambridge, Mass.: Harvard University Press).

Stern, F. (1977), *Gold and Iron* (London: Harmondsworth).

Swartz, M. (1985), *The Politics of British Foreign Politics in the Era of Disraeli and Gladstone* (London: Macmillan).

Thuillier, G. (1993), *La réforme monétaire de l'An XI, la création du franc germinal*, Comité pour l'histoire économique et financière de la France, Ministère de l'Economie et du Budget (Paris: Imprimerie Nationale).

Tilly, R. (1967), 'Germany 1815–1870', in R. Cameron, *Banking in the Early Stages of Industrialization* (Oxford: Oxford University Press), 151–82.

Toniolo, L. (1988), *Storia Economica dell'Italia Liberale, 1850–1918*, 2nd edn. (Bologna: Il Mulino).

Trebilcock, C. (1981), *The Industrialization of the Continental Powers, 1780–1914* (London: Longman).

Valance, J. (1996), *La légende du franc de 1360 à nos jours* (Paris: Flammarion).

Vanthoor, W. (1996), *European Monetary Union since 1848, a Political and Historical Analysis* (Cheltenham: Edward Elgar,).

Varesi, C. (1984), *Monete italiane contemporanee* (Pavia: C. Varesi).

Vincent, J. (1953), 'Les billets de la Banque de France et du Trésor (1800–1952)', *Bulletins de la Société d'Etude pour l'Histoire du Papier-Monnaie*, Auxerre, 8–9.

—— (ed.) (1994), *A Selection from the Diaries of Edward Henry Stanley, 15th Earl of Derby*, 2 vols. (London: Royal Historical Society).

Willis, H. P. (1901), *A History of the Latin Monetary Union* (Chicago: Chicago University Press).

Wright, V. (1972), *Le Conseil d'État sous le second Empire* (Paris: Armand Colin).

Young, H. (1998), *This Blessed Plot, Britain and Europe from Churchill to Blair* (London: MacMillan).

Zucker, S. (1975), *Ludwig Bamberger, German Liberal Politician, and Social Critic, 1823–1899* (Pittsburgh: University of Pittsburgh Press).

Unpublished Dissertations

Flandreau, M., 'L'Union Latine et la Monnaie Universelle (1865–1881)', unpublished Mémoire pour une Maîtrise d'histoire contemporaine, Université de Paris X, Nanterre, under the direction of Alain Plessis, 1989.

Oliveira, M. de, 'La question Monétaire et l'Union Latine (1865–1873)', unpublished dissertation for the Mission des travaux historiques de la Caisse des Dépôts et Consignations, Paris, 1991–2.

Glossary

Bimetallism or double standard: Monetary regime in which gold and silver coins represent equally the standard of value, without restriction in the issue, circulation or transformation into bars of both metals.

Brassage: French term for the fee levied by the Mint to cover the cost of transforming gold or silver bullion into coins. Does not include any profit for the State.

Limping or crippled bimetallism: A form of bimetallism which limits the freedom to issue one of the two metals constituting the legal metallic standard but preserves the freedom of circulation of both metals. Between 1874 and 1918 France, Italy, Belgium, and Switzerland restricted the issue of silver but maintained the circulation of existing silver coins.

Divisionary or subsidiary coinage: The term indicates small silver coins which do not enter in large transactions and international trade. These coins are frequently tokens, i.e. they do not contain an amount of silver corresponding to their facial value. Subsidiary coinage can only be used for small payments, up to £2 in the UK and 50 francs in the LMU. In the LMU divisionary coinage included 2, 1, 0.5, and 0.2 francs coins, in the UK it includes all silver coins.

Écu: The écu was the most important representative of the silver standard, being used in large transactions. It was a silver coin of 5 francs (in France, Belgium and Switzerland), 5 lire (in Italy and in the Pontifical State), 5 drachmae (in Greece), 5 pesetas (in Spain), 5 lei (in Romania), 1 peso (in Argentina). The silver content of the écu was equal to its face value (900/1000 of fineness).

Fineness: Proportion of precious metal in a coin. A certain percentage of alloy always needs to be added to make gold and silver hard enough to resist deformation, wear and tear. Coins' fineness was expressed in 1000 thousands in France and in the Continent (usually 900/1000 for full coins and 835/1000 for divisionary coins). In the UK gold coins' fineness was in 24 carats (23/24 or 0.917) and silver in thousands (925/1000).

Gold standard: Monometallic monetary system in which gold is the only standard of value, without restriction to its use, circulation or transformation into bars. Silver is minted only as subsidiary coinage, paper money circulates only because it is backed by gold reserves in the issuing bank.

Mint fee (brassage): Fee levied by the Mint to cover the cost of transforming gold or silver bullion into coins. Does not include any profit for the State.

Mint ratio: Price of gold in term of silver fixed by the Mints of bimetallic countries, following national legislation. The Mint ratio is the stabilizing factor for the markets for silver and gold in France and the other countries following bimetallism. Anyone can transform into coin any amount of silver or gold bullion he holds when the market price for such metal descends below the Mint price-ratio.

Seignorage: *Ad valorem* tax imposed by the State in addition to the simple payment of the costs of the mint. It is paid by all those deciding to mint the silver or gold bullion they hold. Alternatively the State can acquire seignorage profits reminting on its own responsibility all of the coinage, reducing the precious metal content of the coinage in comparison to its nominal value. The latter way of collecting seignorage is called debasement of the currency.

Single standard or monometallism: Monometallic monetary system in which only one metal is the standard of value (usually gold or silver), without restriction to its use, circulation or transformation into bars.

Biographical Notices

Antonelli, Giacomo (1806–76): Italian Cardinal, Secretary of State (Prime Minister and Foreign Affairs Minister) of the Pontifical government from 1848 to 1876.

Artom, Isacco (1829–1900): Italian diplomat, secretary to Cavour, Counsellor of the Italian Embassy in Paris (1864–7), Italian delegate at the Monetary Conferences of Paris in 1865 and 1867. Senator from 1876.

Bamberger, Ludwig (1823–99): German politician and economist, exiled in France from 1848, banker in Paris from 1853 to 1867, MP for Hesse for the National Liberal Party from 1868, main author of the legislation creating the mark, introducing the gold standard in Germany and forming the Reichsbank.

Bismarck, Otto von, Prince (1815–98): Prussian conservative politician and diplomat, Ambassador to Vienna, St Petersburg, and Paris, Prime Minister and Foreign Affairs Minister of Prussia (1862–90), Chancellor of the German Empire (1871–90).

Bonnet, Victor (1814–85): French economist and director of the *Revue des Deux Mondes*.

Buffet, Louis (1818–98): French politician, Trade and Agriculture Minister (1849), leader of the third party (liberal supporters of the Empire), Finance Minister (1870), President of the National Assembly (1873–5), Head of the government and Interior Minister (1875–6).

Camphausen, OttoVon (1812–96): German liberal politician, Prussian and German Finance Minister under Bismarck (1869–78).

Cardwell, Edward Viscount (1813–86): British politician, Conservative-Peelite-Liberal, War Secretary in the Liberal administration of Gladstone (1868–74).

Chevalier, Michel (1806–79): French economist and politician, Saint-Simonian in his youth, Professor of Economics at the Collège de France, occupying the chair of J. B. Say and Pellegrino Rossi, thanks to the support of Thiers. Became the most well-known French economist of the second Empire, adviser of Napoleon III, Councillor of State (1852–60), negotiator of the Franco-British Free Trade agreement of 1860, senator (1860–70).

Daru, Napoléon Conte de (1807–90): French politician, leader of the 'third party' (liberal supporters of the Empire), Vice-President of the Corps législatif (1869–70), Foreign Affairs Minister (1870).

Delyannis, Théodore (1826–1905): Greek Ambassador in Paris, and Greek representative at the 1867 Monetary Conference of Paris. Foreign Affairs Minister in the 1860s, several times Minister and Prime Minister until the beginning of the twentieth century.

Disraeli, Benjamin, Earl of Beaconsfield (1804–81): British Conservative politician and writer, Chancellor of the Exchequer (1852, 1858–9 and 1866–8) and Prime Minister (1868, 1874–80), Leader of the Conservative Party 1868–81.

Drouyn de Lhuys (1805–81): French politician and diplomat, bonapartist, Foreign Affairs Minister (1848–9, 1851, 1852–5, 1862–6). Defended the temporal power of the Pope.

Dumas, Jean Baptiste (1800–84): French chemist and politician, senator during the second Empire, President of the Commission des Monnaies from 1867. Delegate at the Franco-Austrian monetary negotiations of 1867 and at the LMU conferences in the 1870s.

Dutilleul, François Ernest (1827–1907): French civil servant, director of the general movement of funds (included monetary policy) at the Finance Ministry at the end of the second Empire and at the beginning of the third republic. Finance Minister in 1877, Conservative MP from 1876.

Feer-Herzog Carl (1820–80): Swiss politician and industrialist, member of the Swiss Assembly (Grand Conseil, 1852–80), president of the Bank of Argovia, of the Gothard Railways, owner of a silk factory. Negotiated for Switzerland free trade treaties with France, Italy, Austria, North Germany Confederation, and Spain, as well as LMU membership and renewals. Influential supporter of the gold standard.

Frère Orban, Hubert (1812–96): Belgian liberal politician, Finance Minister (1847, 1848–52, and 1861–70), Prime Minister (1868–70 and 1878–84) and Foreign Affairs Minister (1878–84). He was the Liberal and free-trader opponent of the Catholic Jules Malou. Formed the National Bank of Belgium and supported the gold standard.

Fould, Achille (1800–67) French politician and banker, bonapartist, Finance Minister (1849–52 and 1861–7), Minister of State (principal Minister) 1852–60. Close to the Rothschilds, his brother was a founder of the Crédit Mobilier, the Bank of the Pereire brothers, and of the Imperial expansion.

Garnier, Joseph (1813–81): French economist and politician, perpetual secretary of the Société d'Économie Politique and editor of the *Revue d'Économie politique*, Republican Senator from 1876.

Gladstone, William Ewart (1809–98): British politician, Conservative-Peelite-Liberal, leader of the Liberal Party, Chancellor of the Exchequer (1852–6, 1859–66, 1873–4, and 1880–2), Prime Minister (1868–74, 1880–5, 1886, 1892–94).

Gobineau, Joseph Arthur, Conte de (1816–82): French diplomat, secretary to the French Foreign Affairs Minister Aléxis de Toqueville in 1849. Involved in monetary negotiations while French Ambassador in Greece in the late 1860s and in Sweden in the early 1870s. Author of the 'Essai sur l'inégalité des races humaines' (1854), a racist essay popular with the extreme right wing.

Goschen, George, Viscount Hawkhurst (1831–1907): British banker and politician of German origins, briefly Director of the Bank of England, Liberal MP for the City, President of the Poor Law Board (1868–71) and First Lord of the Admiralty (1871–4 and 1895–1902), Liberal Unionist Chancellor of the Exchequer (1887–92).

Graham, Thomas (1805–69): British chemist, Master of the Royal Mint in London until his death in 1869, delegate at the 1867 Monetary Conference of Paris, member of the Royal Commission on International Coinage in 1868.

Gramont, Antoine Duc de (1819–80): French diplomat, Ambassador to several German States and to Austria (1861–70), Foreign Affairs Minister in 1870 at the outbreak of the Franco-Prussian War.

Granville, George Earl Granville (1815–91): British politician, Whig-Liberal, Colonial secretary (1868–70) and then Foreign Secretary (1870–4, 1880–5) in the Liberal administrations.

Halifax, Charles Wood Viscount Halifax (1800–85): Whig-Liberal MP (1832–66), member of the House of Lords (1866–85). Chancellor of the Exchequer (1846–52), Lord Privy Seal (1870–74). President of the Royal Commission on International Coinage in 1868.

Hendriks, Federick: British actuary and economist, wrote and testified in support of monetary unification and decimalization.

Herbet, Edouard (–1867): French civil servant, Councillor of State, Director of the consulates and commercial affairs at the Ministry of Foreign Affairs at the end of the second Empire. French representative at the Monetary Conferences of 1865 and 1867.

Hock, Karl von Baron (1808–69): Austrian economist, historian and politician, free trader, Privy Councillor and member of the Upper House. Presided over the Austrian monetary commission of 1867, Austrian representative at the Paris Conference of 1867, negotiated with Parieu the Franco-Austrian monetary agreement the same year.

Hubbard, John Gildebrand, First Lord Addington (1805–89): Merchant and Conservative politician, Director of the Bank of England from 1838, deputy Governor (1851–3), Governor (1853–5), Chairman of the Public Works Loan Commission (1853–89), member of House of Commons (1859–68 and 1874–87) and then of the House of Lords (1887–9). Authoritative spokesman for the Bank of England and the Conservatives in monetary issues.

Jevons, William Stanley (1835–82): British economist, professor at Owens College, initiator of marginalism and mathematical economics in England, together with Walras in France and Menger in Austria. Wrote in favour of monetary unification and testified in front of several commissions. Adviser to the Chancellor of the Exchequer Lowe.

La Tour d'Auvergne, Henri, Prince de (1823–71): diplomat and Minister of Foreign Affairs of France (1869–70), ambassador in Rome, London, Florence, Turin, and Vienna.

La Valette, Charles Marquis de (1806–81): diplomat, Minister of Interior (1865–7) and Foreign Affairs (1868–9), Ambassador in England (1869–70)

Lavenay, Victor de (1814-?): French civil servant. Councillor of State (1860–70), President of the Financial section of the Council of State (1867–70).

Levi, Leone (1821–88): Italian lawyer and economist, established and naturalized in England in 1844, professor of commerce at King's College London, member of societies for the decimalization of coinage, and unification of weights, measures, and coinage. Testified in front of French and British commissions and statistical congresses.

Louvet, Charles (1806–82): French politician, bonapartist, Vice-president of the Corps Législatif, Minister of Commerce in 1870, protectionist.

Lowe, Robert, Viscount Sherbrooke (1811–92): British Liberal politician, Chancellor of the Exchequer (1868–73) and Home Secretary (1873–4) under Gladstone.

Magne, Pierre (1805–79): French politician, bonapartist, Finance Minister under the second Empire (1855–60, 1867–70, 1870) and the third republic (1873–5), Minister of Public Works (1851–5).

Menabrea, Luigi: Piedmontese General and Italian Prime Minister and Foreign Affairs Minister (1867–9).

Minghetti, Marco (1818–86): Italian Liberal politician, Finance Minister (1862–4, 1873–6), Prime Minister (1863–4, 1873–6).

Mohl, Moritz (1802–88): German politician and economist, progressive MP for Württemberg at the Zollparlament 1868–71 and at the Reichsparlament 1871–3, opponent of German unification.

Moustier, Lionel Marquis de (1817–69): French diplomat, Ambassador to the Ottoman Empire, Foreign Affairs Minister (1866–8).

Napoleon III (1808–73): Louis Napoleon Bonaparte, nephew of Napoleon I, President of the French Republic (1848–52). After the *coup d'état* on 2 December 1851 re-established the Empire (1852–70). Defeated and captured at Sédan 2 Sept. 1870. The demise of the Empire was voted in Paris two days later. Died in exile in England in 1873.

Ollivier, Emile (1825–1913): French politician, originally a republican opponent of Napoleon, accepted the liberalized regime, Justice Minister and Chief Minister in the first liberal and parliamentarian government of the Empire (1870), swept away by the Franco-Prussian War which he tried to prevent ineffectively.

Overstone, Samuel Loyd Baron Overstone (1796–1883): British banker and monetary theorist, leader of the currency school, inspirer of Peel's Bank Charter Act of 1844. President of the Royal Commission on Decimal Coinage (1855–9), leading voice on monetary theories and adviser to the Liberal governments.

Parieu, Félix Esquirou de (1815–93): French lawyer, politician, and economist, liberal Catholic, Minister of Education (1849–51), President of the financial section of the Council of State, Vice-President (1855–70) and Minister President (1870) of the Council of State, Senator (1876–85). Responsible for the French plan of International Monetary Unification, President of most French monetary commissions, French representative at the Monetary Conferences of 1865, 1867, 1874, 1875, and 1876.

Pelouze, Jules: French chemist, senator, President of the Commission des Monnaies until 1867.

Pius IX (1792–1878): Giovanni Maria Mastai-Ferretti, Pope (1846–78), started as a liberal in 1846 but became a conservative. Introduced the dogma of the immaculate conception in 1854 and the doctrine of Papal infallibility in the Vatican Council of 1869–70.

Rivers, Wilson Charles: British civil servant, Treasury official, delegate at the International Monetary Conference of Paris in 1867, secretary of the Royal Commission on International Coinage in 1868, private secretary of the Chancellor of the Exchequer (1868–73). Finance Minister of Egypt in 1877–9, on behalf of British bondholders.

Rothschild, Alphonse de (1827–1905): French private banker, first son of James, became the head of the bank 'Rothschild frères et Cie' in 1868. Régent of the Bank of France from 1855.

Rouher, Eugène (1814–84): French politician, bonapartist, Minister of Justice (1849–51), of Commerce, Agriculture and Public Works (1855–63), of the Council of State (1863) and of Finances (1867), Minister of State (Chief Minister, 1863–9), President of the Senate (1869–70). After the fall of the Empire leader of the Bonapartist party 'L'Appel au Peuple' (1872–81).

Rouland, Gustave (1806–78): French politician, bonapartist, Councillor of State, Minister of Education (1856–63), Minister President of the Council of State (1863–4), Governor of the Bank of France (1864–78), Senator during the second Empire and the third republic, Thiers removed him from the Bank of France in 1871, but the Bank called him back refusing his republican successor.

Ruggles, Samuel Bulkley (1800–81): lawyer, US delegate at the International Monetary Conference of Paris in 1867.

Sacerdoti, Adolfo: Italian economist from Padova, wrote in support of monetary unification.

Say, Léon (1826–96): French economist, politician, and financier, liberal centre-left, Prefect de la Seine (1871–2) Finance Minister (1872–3, 1875–7, 1877–9, 1882), Ambassador in London, President of the Senate. Close to the Rothschilds, concluded the payment of the Prussian War indemnity, directed the LMU towards the extinction of silver coinage although he was a bimetallist.

Seyd, Ernest: German banker and bullion dealer, established in London, wrote extensively about banking, in favour of bimetallism and of monetary unification.

Stanley, Edward Henry (1826–93): 15th Earl of Derby from 1869, British politician, Conservative-Liberal-Liberal Unionist, Foreign Secretary in 1866–8, under his father [Edward George Stanley, 14th Earl of Derby (1799–1869)] and under Disraeli (1868, 1874–8). Colonial Secretary (1882–5) under Gladstone.

Thiers, Adolphe (1797–1877): French conservative politician, Minister (1832–40) and Prime Minister (1836–40) under Louis-Philippe, leading Orleanist opponent of the Empire from 1863 and president of the French Republic (1871–3).

Wallenberg, Oscar: Swedish banker, member of the Swedish Parliament, president and founder of the Bank of Stockholm and of the Wallenberg financial empire. Swedish delegate at the Monetary Conference of Paris in 1867 and active diplomatically in favour of monetary unification until the mid-1880s.

Wolowski, Louis (1810–76): Polish politician and economist, fled to France after the revolution of 1848 in which he had participated, naturalized French, founder and first director of the Crédit Foncier (1852–4), Professor of Economics at the Conservatoire des Arts et Métiers in Paris, close to the Bank of France, prolific writer in favour of bimetallism and of the unity of banknote issue. Participated or testified in most monetary commissions of the time. MP in 1848–51 and 1871–2, Senator from 1872 for the centre-left.

Index of Names

Index of Subjects

3 5282 00500 4083